INSIGHT GUIDES

CHILE
& Easter Island

Discovery CHANNEL

APA PUBLICATIONS
Part of the Langenscheidt Publishing Group

INSIGHT GUIDE
CHILE

ABOUT THIS BOOK

Editorial
Project Editor
Natalie Minnis
Managing Editor
Huw Hennessy
Editorial Director
Brian Bell

Distribution

UK & Ireland
GeoCenter International Ltd
The Viables Centre, Harrow Way
Basingstoke, Hants RG22 4BJ
Fax: (44) 1256 817988

United States
Langenscheidt Publishers, Inc.
46–35 54th Road, Maspeth, NY 11378
Fax: 1 (718) 784 0640

Canada
Thomas Allen & Son Ltd
390 Steelcase Road East
Markham, Ontario L3R 1G2
Fax: (1) 905 475 6747

Australia
Universal Publishers
1 Waterloo Road
Macquarie Park, NSW 2113
Fax: (61) 2 9888 9074

New Zealand
Hema Maps New Zealand Ltd (HNZ)
Unit D, 24 Ra ORA Drive
East Tamaki, Auckland
Fax: (64) 9 273 6479

Worldwide
**Apa Publications GmbH & Co.
Verlag KG (Singapore branch)**
38 Joo Koon Road, Singapore 628990
Tel: (65) 6865 1600. Fax: (65) 6861 6438

Printing

Insight Print Services (Pte) Ltd
38 Joo Koon Road, Singapore 628990
Tel: (65) 6865 1600. Fax: (65) 6861 6438

CONTACTING THE EDITORS
We would appreciate it if readers
would alert us to errors or out-
dated information by writing to:
**Insight Guides, P.O. Box 7910,
London SE1 1WE, England.
Fax: (44) 20 7403 0290.
insight@apaguide.co.uk**

www.insightguides.com

This guidebook combines the interests and enthusiasms of two of the world's best-known information providers: Insight Guides, whose titles have set the standard for visual travel guides since 1970, and Discovery Channel, the world's pre-mier source of non-fiction television programming.

The editors of Insight Guides provide both practical advice and general under-standing of a destination's history, culture, institutions and people. Discovery Channel and its website, www.discovery.com, help millions of viewers explore their world from the comfort of their own home and also encourage them to explore it first-hand.

How to use this book

The book is structured to convey an understanding of Chile and its culture and to guide readers through its sights and attractions:

◆ The **Features** section, with a yellow color bar, covers the country's history and culture in lively authoritative essays written by specialists.

◆ The **Places** section, with a blue bar, provides full

details of all the sights and areas worth seeing. The chief places of interest are coordinated by number with specially drawn maps.
♦ The **Travel Tips** listings section, at the back of the book, offers a convenient point of reference for information on travel, accommodation, restaurants and other practical aspects of the country. Information may be located quickly using the index on the back-cover flap, which also serves as a bookmark.

The contributors

This new edition, edited by **Natalie Minnis**, builds on the last version edited by **Tony Perrotet**, and written by **Tim Frasca, Lake Sagaris, Patricio Lanfranco, Imogen Mark, Malcolm Coad** and **Rebecca Gorman**. The principal updater of the 1999 edition was **Ruth Bradley**, a British journalist who lives and works in Santiago de Chile. The history section was revised and updated by **Mike Gonzalez**, senior lecturer in the Department of Hispanic Studies at Glasgow University. The Adventures and Wildlife chapters were updated by **Jane Letham** and **Mark Thurber**, who run Inti Travel (adventure sports) in Quito, Ecuador. Salsa expert **Shannon Shiell** and ethnomusicologist **Jan Fairley** updated the Cultural Renaissance chapter.

For the 2005 update, Ruth Bradley assembled a team of Santiago-based journalists with inside knowledge of Chilean life. **Claudio Alvarez**, information editor for the daily newspaper *PubliMEDIA*, revised the Cultural Renaissance chapter. **Mark Mulligan**, a *Financial Times* correspondent now working in Madrid, updated the chapters on Chilean wine and the Central Valley. Freelance journalist, **Patrick Nixon**, covered the Lake District. **Marta Infante**, editor of the Chilean magazine *Outdoors,* contributed new material for the Adventure Activities chapter.

Principal photographers were **Eduardo Gil, Helen Hughes, Daniel Bruhin, Gunther Wessel** and **Andreas Gross**.

This version was edited in the London office by **Alyse Dar** and proofread by **Sylvia Suddes**. Thanks also go to **Paula Soper**.

Map Legend

— - -	International Boundary
— — —	Regional Boundary
⊖	Border Crossing
—•—	National Park/Reserve
— — —	Ferry Route
Ⓜ	Metro
✈ ✈	Airport: International/ Regional
🚌	Bus Station
Ⓟ	Parking
❶	Tourist Information
✉	Post Office
† ⛪	Church/Ruins
†	Monastery
☾	Mosque
✡	Synagogue
🏰	Castle/Ruins
∴	Archeological Site
∩	Cave
🛈	Statue/Monument
★	Place of Interest

The main places of interest in the Places section are coordinated by number with a full-color map (e.g. ❶), and a symbol at the top of every right-hand page tells you where to find the map.

INSIGHT GUIDE
CHILE

CONTENTS

Maps

The magnificent Torres del Paine.

BIENVENIDOS

A long, thin country of astounding beauty and diversity,
Chile's well-developed infrastructure makes traveling a joy

Squeezed between the Andes and the Pacific, this spaghetti-like strip of land was affectionately tagged "the thin country" by the Nobel Prize-winning Chilean poet Pablo Neruda. It is never more than 355 km (221 miles) wide, and its coastline extends over 4,300 km (2,700 miles). Within its borders are the world's driest desert, lush expanses of forest and a spectacular array of glaciers and fiords. And, stretched directly along the Pacific "ring of fire," Chile has some 2,085 volcanoes, of which 55 are active. In some parts of the country, earth tremors occur almost weekly.

This wild geography hasn't stopped Chile from becoming one of the continent's most developed nations. In fact, you will soon tire of hearing it described as "the Latin American country that works." Travelers are often surprised by the efficiency of Chile's banking system, its transport and services – but behind the affluent surface are social and economic imbalances waiting to be redressed.

Chileans are predominantly *mestizos* – the descendants of mainly Spanish immigrants and indigenous peoples – although there are pockets of pure-blooded Mapuches, as well as direct descendants of German, Swiss and other immigrants. Indeed, the feeling of Chile's cities and the manners of Chileans are strongly European. They are an urbane and courteous people, who will go 10 blocks out of their way to show a stranger directions. Among Latin Americans, Chileans are renowned for their creative flair: Chilean folk musicians, poets and painters are followed in every country on the continent. And their reputation for legalizing and business acumen has earned them the somewhat facetious label as the "English of South America."

But it is the political history since 1970 that has done most to push the country into the world's view: in that year, Chile elected a socialist government, then, in 1973 it suffered a bloody military coup. For the next 16 years of dictatorial rule under Augusto Pinochet, Chile's freedom became an international *cause célèbre*, which was revived in 1998 when the ex-dictator was arrested in London on charges of crimes against humanity. However, since March 1990, three center-left democratic governments have presided over a period of political stability and, for the most part, high economic growth.

The traditional hospitality of Chileans, noted by travelers from the 18th century onward, is even more evident today. After years of dictatorship, Chileans have welcomed the influx of foreigners as a sign of support for their democracy. Prosperity is now increasing more slowly than in the boom 1990s, but Chile has one of Latin America's most robust economies to add to its already invigorating Andean atmosphere. ❏

PRECEDING PAGES: Grey Glacier, Torres del Paine National Park; Mapuche farmers in the Lake District; coastal village of Vichuquen; Castro, Isla Chiloé.
LEFT: Mapuche children.

EARTH, FIRE AND ICE

*From searing desert heat to sub-Antarctic chills, with volcanoes, lakes and geysers
along the way, the natural world makes its presence strongly felt in Chile*

Chile must be a top candidate for the world's strangest geographical layout. With a landmass smaller than any other South American republic except Ecuador, Chile's 4,300-km (2,700-mile) coastline makes it seem enormous. Though the country is never more than 355 km (221 miles) wide, a trip from Arica in the north to the port of Punta Arenas in the far south covers the same distance as New York to Los Angeles or Paris to Tehran. Parts of Chile are so narrow that in some areas the Andean peaks of its eastern border can be seen from the Pacific beaches.

Yet the Pan-American Highway, which runs down the country's spine, connects every imaginable climatic zone: it crosses vast expanses of total desert, an agricultural valley the size of California's, and a province of mountain lakes and volcanoes. Farther south, car ferries and the Carretera Austral highway – actually a dirt road – connect Chiloé, the continent's second-largest island, to hundreds of kilometers of scarcely inhabited fiords and islands. A spectacular glacier field then divides these from the sheep farms of Chilean Patagonia, which is only accessible by road from Argentina.

A land of extremes

Geographically, Chile has a sense of separateness and forbidding boundaries. Its northern desert, the Atacama, is one of the driest places on earth. The Andes, which form the 4,000-km (2,500-mile) frontier with Argentina, rise in sharp grades on the Chilean side, from sea level to as high as 7,000 meters (23,000 ft) in little more than 100 km (60 miles).

Chile's far southern tip points towards the polar ice of Antarctica. The country's western coastline faces the Pacific, the broadest ocean in the world. One of Chile's south-sea possessions, Easter Island, is the most isolated bit of inhabited land on earth, a thousand kilometers away from any other inhabited island. "Such a

country should be called an island," wrote the Chilean geographer Benjamín Subercaseaux, "even though its borders do not strictly fit the definition."

Perhaps it is this geographical isolation that causes Chileans to reflect so obsessively on themselves, to examine their national charac-

ter and their prized idiosyncrasies, to lay claim to myriad faults and virtues.

From lush valleys to dry desert

In the semi-arid Norte Chico (or "Little North"), irrigation has extended Chile's agricultural heartland north to the dusty valley town of Copiapó. Here, the many mountain rivers maintain a year-round flow, fed by seasonal rains and Andean snows. Despite the blistering sun, there is considerable humidity and minimal temperature change, making the region excellent for irrigated farming. Tropical fruit, especially papaya and *chirimoya* (custard apples) for which La Serena is especially known, is

LEFT: Araucaria trees, Parque Nacional Conguillío.
RIGHT: Puchuldiza Geyser, Parque Nacional Isluga.

commercially grown. The region's ideal atmospheric conditions for astronomical work have led to the construction of important observatories in the hills near La Serena.

The vegetation ends where the Norte Grande ("Great North,") begins. The extreme north of Chile, annexed from vanquished Peru and Bolivia after the 19th-century War of the Pacific *(see page 39)*, does not at first glance seem worth the trouble. Among the brown, barren hillsides and parched Atacama Desert are places where no rain has ever been recorded. But for the visitor, this barren region is fertile in geological spectacle and the fascinating remains of lost civilizations.

The tangible wealth of Chile's north lies beneath the ground, which yields ample mineral deposits, like nitrates, the fertilizer ingredient that was once the basis of Chile's economy, and copper, of which it is now the world's largest exporter. Silver and gold are also present in commercial quantities.

Chile's capital city, Santiago, is located at the country's latitudinal mid-point, next to the steep Andean foothills. The city, with a population of just over 5 million, is surrounded with a lovely but unfortunately placed set of smaller hills that trap its heavy air pollution. In this central region and along the coast, rains come sporadically from May to October while the intervening summer months of January to March are almost uniformly cloudless and hot.

The Central Valley has abundant agriculture with ample rivers, fed by the melting Andean snows, which cut across Chile at regular intervals. The famous wine grapes and other fruit such as peaches, nectarines, apples, pears, kiwis and cherries, flourish in the intense, dry heat.

Towards the chilly south

Further south in the Lake District, year-round precipitation keeps the landscape green, but limits farming to the cultivation of more traditional grains and the rearing of animals. An active volcano belt provides picturesque landscapes (most of Chile's 55 active volcanoes are in this area), but also can disrupt the lives of villagers with dangerous clouds of toxic particles. Twelve great lakes, including the continent's fourth largest, Lago Llanquihue, give the

LEFT: signs of life in the Atacama Desert, northern Chile, the driest place on earth.

area its dominant characteristic – even the high Andean plateaux in this region are strewn with large lakes.

Where the lakes meet the Pacific Ocean, the coastal mountain range becomes a 1,000-island archipelago headed by Isla Chiloé. The Chilote people's surviving folklore and the island's unique stilted buildings are renowned throughout Chile. Rainfall of over 4,000 mm (157 inches) annually is registered in Chiloé and its satellite islands, giving Chile both precipitation extremes.

On the mainland, the Carretera Austral begins at this point: an unpaved road from Puerto Montt allows access to one of the most remote zones on the continent. Foreign trout fishermen fly to the provincial capital of Coyhaique to fish in the pure streams and lakes of the region. The road sweeps past beautiful Lago General Carrera and basks in the micro-climate around Chile Chico, ending in the 500-inhabitant frontier town of Villa O'Higgins, where the only landmass is covered by impassable glaciers.

The furthest tip of Chile is accessible only by boat, plane, or via a long detour through Argentina if you prefer to travel overland. This inaccessibility seems to make Magallanes all the more exciting for many visitors, who come to explore the vast wilderness of Parque Nacional Torres del Paine, with its relatively tame wildlife, accessible glaciers and trademark mountain peaks. Punta Arenas, with just over 100,000 inhabitants, is the southernmost city of its size in the world. It is an oil production center as well as the gateway to the Chilean Antarctic. Temperatures rarely rise above 10°C (50°F) in this gusty port, which is almost perpetually shrouded in cloud.

Farther south lies Tierra del Fuego, the "land of fire" at the tip of South America, whose name was inspired by the smoke from the fires of its now-extinct Amerindian tribes. South America's largest island forms the main part of this forbidding archipelago, which Chile shares with Argentina. (Chile nearly went to war with Argentina here in the late 1970s, until the Vatican sponsored peace negotiations.)

Beyond Tierra del Fuego lies the considerably harsher territory of Antarctica, a large part of which Chile claims. ❑

LEFT: the lush, rain-drenched forests of Aisén, in Chile's deep south.

Decisive Dates

PREHISTORIC TIMES

13,000–10,000 BC A group of mastodon hunters settle in the area now known as Monte Verde, near modern Puerto Montt.

EUROPEAN CONQUEST AND SETTLEMENT

Around 1450 The Incas conquer northern Chile, but fail to subdue the southern tribes.

1520 The Portuguese explorer Ferdinand Magellan becomes the first European to glimpse Chile as he sails through the straits now named after him.

1533 Inca rule ends when they are defeated by Spanish *conquistador* Francisco Pizarro.

1536 Pizarro's comrade Diego de Almagro travels from Cuzco to Copiapó and then the Aconcagua Valley in search of gold.

1541 Pedro de Valdivia sets off to conquer Chile and founds Santiago.

1550–1 Valdivia establishes the settlements of Concepción, Valdivia, Villarrica and other cities.

1553 Valdivia is killed by the native Mapuches , led by Lautaro, near Concepción.

1557–61 A new governor, called García Hurtado de Mendoza, re-establishes Spanish rule in Concepción and founds Osorno and Cañete.

1599 A major uprising by the local Amerindians wipes out all Spanish settlements south of the Bíobío River in the Central Valley.

17th century Ranching becomes Chile's primary export trade, with large estates *(haciendas or latifundas)* employing bonded *mestizo* peasants to replace *encomiendas* as European diseases reduce the native population.

18th century Around 20,000 Spaniards emigrate to the new colony.

1740 Chile loosens its bonds with the Viceroyalty of Peru, seat of the Spanish American Empire, as direct trade is permitted with Spain and other colonies in the New World.

1750 Chile is permitted to mint its own coins.

INDEPENDENCE FROM SPAIN

1808 The French emperor Napoleon invades Spain, dethroning King Ferdinand VII.

1810 Leading Chilean citizens force the Spanish governor in Chile to resign and, following the example of Spanish cities, select a ruling *junta* in the name of King Ferdinand.

1811 The first Chilean National Congress gathers, swearing loyalty to the Spanish king.

1812 Following a *coup d'état*, the Carrera Government proposes that the Spanish king should recognize Chile's constitution and sovereignty and establishes democratic rule.

1813 Spain invades Chile.

1814 Chilean nationalists are beaten at Rancagua, and their leaders flee to Argentina.

1817 The nationalists defeat the Spanish forces with the help of Argentine hero General José de San Martín.

1818 Chilean independence is declared.

GROWTH AND STABILITY

1823 Slavery is abolished.

1829–30 A lengthy period of "Conservative Republic" is ushered in under Diego Portales.

1839 The first bank notes go into circulation.

1840s Prosperity grows as more silver is discovered in the north, Chilean farmers supply Californian gold-diggers and Magallanes (now Punta Arenas) is founded to take advantage of European trade routes.

1843 The University of Chile founded.

From 1848 German settlement is encouraged, as immigrants flee the revolutions in Europe, bringing European political and revolutionary ideas to Chile. Work begins on Chile's first railroad, from Copiapó to Caldera.

1850s Guano is discovered, putting the area north of Coquimbo into dispute with both Peru and Bolivia.

1860 Free primary education introduced.

1876–8 Flooding in the south and drought in the north

lead to famine. Agricultural problems combined with a fall in the demand for silver lead to economic crisis.

1879 Chile declares war on Bolivia and Peru.

1881 Last uprising of Chile's indigenous peoples. The rebellion is quashed by the army, and the territory of the Mapuches is declared state property.

1883 Peru cedes Tarapacá, Tacna and Arica to Chile.

1884 Bolivia cedes Antofagasta to Chile.

1891 Civil war breaks out over the issue of presidential powers. After defeat, President José Manuel Balmaceda commits suicide.

THE 20TH CENTURY

1907 Massacre of striking mine workers at Santa María de Iquique ends a period of intense union activity.

1912 Chilean Socialist Workers Party founded.

1918 The invention of synthetic nitrates makes Chile's "desert gold" obsolete.

1927 Economic and political crises bring army officer Carlos Ibáñez to power. He creates a powerful state system.

1929 The Wall Street Crash and world depression lead to political instability.

1931 Ibáñez resigns and goes into exile.

1932 Arturo Alessandri returns to power, ushering in a period of economic recovery and political stability.

1945 Chilean poet Gabriela Mistral wins the Nobel Prize for literature.

1949 Women win the right to vote.

1952 Carlos Ibáñez returns to power.

1964 Eduardo Frei leads the Christian Democrats to power with US support.

1970 The leftwing coalition Popular Unity, led by Salvador Allende, scrapes to victory, becoming Chile's first Socialist government.

1971 The Allende government nationalizes the copper mines as part of a sweeping reform program. Chilean poet Pablo Neruda wins the Nobel Prize for literature.

1973 The Allende government is overthrown in a violent military coup, ending in the alleged suicide of Allende in Santiago's Moneda Palace, which brings General Augusto Pinochet to power. Thousands are tortured and murdered during his regime.

1980 A new Constitution stipulates a referendum on continued military rule in 1988.

1982–3 Chile's economy nosedives sparking off strikes and protests.

1986 An attempt to assassinate Pinochet fails.

PRECEDING PAGES: *Presence of Latin America* by Jorge Gonzalez Camarena, in the Pinacoteca at Concepción.
LEFT: Diego de Almagro.
RIGHT: saying "No" to Augusto Pinochet.

1988 Fifty-four percent of voters reject Pinochet's regime in a referendum.

1989 Christian Democrat Patricio Aylwin elected President as the country returns to democracy. Pinochet stays on as Army commander in chief with his 1980 Constitution firmly in place.

1990s During a period of strong economic growth, prosperity increases rapidly, although income distribution remains extremely unequal.

1991 The National Commission on Truth and Reconciliation establishes military guilt in violating human rights, but few are punished.

1994 Eduardo Frei, son of 1960s President Frei, heads a Christian Democrat government.

1998 Pinochet retires as army commander in chief and takes up a life Senate seat, reserved for him under the 1980 Constitution. Later that year, he visits Britain. While in London, Spain requests the General's extradition for human rights abuses against Spanish citizens. He is held under house arrest pending a legal decision.

2000 Released by the British Home Secretary, Jack Straw, on grounds of ill health, Pinochet returns to Chile. Socialist and Christian Democrat coalition leader, Ricardo Lagos, elected president.

2002 Pinochet declared mentally unfit to stand trial; all charges are dropped. He retires from public life.

2004 Supreme Court ruling strips Pinochet of immunity from prosecution, with no right of appeal. ❑

THE WILD FRONTIER

Prehispanic Chilean society was as diverse as the latitudes it covered, which helped the southern tribes to repel invasions by the Incas as well as the Spanish

Chile was never a top priority for South America's explorers or colonizers. The Incas made their way down from Peru in the mid-15th century, less than 100 years before the Europeans arrived, when Tupac Yupanqui defeated the northern tribes and established Inca rule as far south as present-day Santiago.

The native Atacameño and Diaguita cultures, which had thrived in the northern deserts for centuries, were fairly organized societies compared with the Araucanians farther south. Both of the northern groups were farmers. They grew beans, maize, potatoes and coca, using irrigation techniques that suggest they had a central authority strong enough to impose rules on their small societies. They kept llamas, wove cloth and baskets, made and decorated pots, and traded with each other and with the peoples in Peru. The Atacameños mummified their dead in preparation for some kind of afterlife, while the Diaguitas took their wives to the grave with them. Little more is known about their civilizations, though their numbers were estimated to be about 80,000.

Unconquered tribes of the south

Beyond present-day Santiago, the Incas ran into serious opposition. The Araucanian tribes, who numbered around one million in total, lived from the River Aconcagua (just north of Valparaíso) down to Chiloé. There were three main groups, all speaking the same language, but they had significant cultural differences.

The Picunches ("men of the north"), lived in the fertile Central Valley between the rivers Aconcagua and Bíobío. They grew most of the same crops as the Diaguitas and Atacameños to the north, but with much less effort required in their temperate climate and well-watered soil. The Picunches lived in small, generally peaceful, self-sufficient family groups, and were no match for the Incas when they arrived.

LEFT: fine ancient tapestry of the Atacameño culture.
RIGHT: Atacameño mummy in the Museo Gustavo Le Paige, San Pedro de Atacama.

It was the less submissive Mapuches ("men of the land"), the Huilliches ("men of the South") and, to a lesser extent, the nomadic Pehuenches, Puelches and Tehuelches, whom the Incas called "the rebel peoples" and gave up trying to conquer. The Mapuches lived precariously, farming temporary clearings in the dense forests and moving on once the land was exhausted, in the area between the Itata and Toltén rivers. The Huilliches lived in the same way between the Toltén and the island of Chiloé. Both groups were full of warriors, not obeying a single leader except in wartime. The Incas gave up on these loosely grouped nomads, who did not recognize a central authority or understand any form of tribute. The new rulers set their frontier at the River Cachapoal, near Rancagua, and left the rest of the Araucanians to themselves.

The Incas interfered little with the customs and practices of the peoples that they colonized, as long as they paid tribute, in gold, and provided labor. Inca rule lasted less than 40 years. An internal power struggle developed, and the Inca garrisons were withdrawn from Chile back to Cuzco in present-day Peru. The quarrel ended with their defeat at the hands of the Spanish *conquistador* Francisco Pizarro and the end of their empire.

Their lasting contribution in Chile was "the trail of the Incas," a series of paths which went as far south as Talca. There were three routes, one along the coast, one through the desert, and one over the Altiplano (high plain) and along the Andes. They were used by the Spanish explorers later, to access their base in Peru.

A solitary captain and 80 men were sent down to the Magellan Straits, but they returned, having got no further than the Itata River, with terrifying tales of ferocious natives. Spirits sank, and Almagro's men resisted his proposal to stay and colonize the new territory. Returning empty-handed to Peru in 1537, Almagro tried to take on Francisco Pizarro for control of the Andes. He lost the civil war that followed and paid for the uprising with his life.

The reward for one of Pizarro's backers was Chile. Pedro de Valdivia set off to subdue the southern territory. He was to take for himself and his followers any land he found. But Alma-

The Spaniards' conquest begins

The first European to see Chile was the Portuguese explorer Ferdinand Magellan, who sailed through the straits which took his name on November 1 1520. He only glanced at the new territory as he sailed up its coast. Next to arrive was Pizarro's comrade, Diego de Almagro, who made his way over the cordillera from Cuzco in 1536 with a couple of hundred men and high hopes of treasure. They reached Copiapó, where the native people received them peacefully enough, and then they traveled on to the Aconcagua valley. All the time the Spaniards scouted about in vain for the fabulous gold mines of which the Incas had spoken.

gro's unfruitful trip had discouraged fortune-seekers, and Valdivia had a hard time finding recruits. Eventually he set off with only a dozen others, and his faithful mistress, Inés de Suárez.

As Valdivia had hoped, other marauder-explorers joined him on the way. There were 150 in the motley band when they reached the River Mapocho in the fertile Central Valley, and decided to make their first settlement. This was Santiago, founded on February 12 1541.

Pressganged into service by the newcomers, the local Mapuches waited for a few months and then rebelled. On September 11 a local chief, Michimalongo, attacked the settlement while Valdivia and most of his men were away.

Inés de Suárez, in a chainmail jacket, fought alongside the men in a day-long battle. By the end of it, the Spaniards stood, triumphant, on the burned-out site, but all of their belongings – food, seeds, even clothes – were destroyed.

Despite living in hunger and scarcity, Valdivia fell in love with the new land, and he wrote to the king with great enthusiasm: "This land is such that life here cannot be equaled. It has only four months of winter... and the summer is so temperate and has such delicious breezes that men can walk all day in the sun and not suffer for it. It is abundant in grass, and can support any kind of cattle or livestock and

to his followers, along with groups of Mapuches bonded to labor in *encomiendas*. Theoretically, that made the Spaniards trustees charged with the care and conversion of the local population. In fact they became feudal estates, with the native people simply enslaved labor to work the land or pan for gold

In 1550 Valdivia founded Concepción, and a year later, Imperial, Valdivia, Villarrica and Angol. In each settlement, Valdivia left 50 or 60 men to build the "city" with the help of the subdued Mapuches. But his troops were stretched thin. At the end of 1553 he left Concepción with only 50 men. The fort at Tucapel when

plants that you can imagine; there is plenty of very beautiful wood for building houses, great quantities of wood for fuel for heating and working the rich mines. Wherever you might dream of finding them, there is soil to sow, materials for building and water and grass for the animals, so that it seems as if God had created everything so that it would be at hand."

Death by gold

Gradually the Central Valley Mapuches were subdued. Valdivia handed out parcels of land

LEFT: one of the last Inca strongholds in Chile.
ABOVE: Inés de Suaréz defends Spanish battlements.

they reached it, on Christmas Day, was a smoking ruin. As they surveyed the wreckage, the Mapuches attacked. Valdivia and his men fought back, but by dusk most of them were dead, including Valdivia. He was tied to a tree by his conquerors, legend has it, and forced to swallow molten gold.

The victor was Lautaro, who had worked for the Spaniards before going off to fight against them. He was said to be the first Mapuche to realize that the Spaniard and his horse, which was a creature completely unknown to the native Chileans, were two separate animals. Lautaro advanced on Santiago, but was knifed by a traitor on the night before the planned attack. Morale fell, and smallpox decimated his men. Santiago was saved. With Valdivia's death, three rivals fought to succeed him as governor, until in 1557, Peru sent a new governor, García Hurtado de Mendoza. Mendoza re-established Spanish rule in the area around Concepción, restored the city and subdued the Mapuches in the region. Two new cities, Osorno and Cañete, were founded. His period as governor, up to 1561, marks the end of the period of conquest.

But the war with the native people of Araucania was far from over, and the Spaniards, fighting as a part-time citizens' army, were ill-

equipped to win it. At the end of the 16th century, another Governor, Martín García Oñez de Loyola, lost his life in a major native uprising. The settlements south of the Bíobío were wiped out, and the northern bank of the river became the frontier of the Spaniards' territory. By then, the colony numbered about 5,000 Europeans.

Life on the wild frontier

War with the Araucanians was a background noise for the whole of the next century, and most of the one that followed. There were periodic uprisings and massacres, and the governor of the territory was based permanently down on the frontier in Concepción. By this time the colonizers had recognized that there were no rivers of gold or fabled silver cities in Chile, and that wealth needed to be tilled from the land or dug from the mines. Native people, or mixed-race *mestizos* were put to work, and before long the new territory was exporting wheat, copper, leather and wine.

But the Spanish authorities sent from Madrid could not impose law and order. A sinister and unscrupulous figure, Doña Catalina de los Ríos y Lisperguer, known as *la Quintrala*, reflected the worst aspects of the colony in the 16th century. An upper-class lady, she is credited with poisoning her father, cutting off the ear of one of her lovers, arranging a tryst with another and then having him murdered while she watched. "Lower" beings such as servants and slaves were killed or mutilated according to her whims.

Many members of the Church set no better example for their congregations. Chroniclers recorded open fights between members of the Augustinian and the Franciscan orders. The clergy had to be banned by the bishop from going into public gambling houses, or from having packs of cards in their own homes. Gambling was a passion in the new colony, and the main entertainment for men. Clothes were of prime importance for society women, and for some men too – the richer and more ostentatiously embroidered, the better.

Cultural influences

By the late 17th century Chile was becoming more civilized. The influence of the French Bourbons (now rulers of Spain) brought French culture and manners to the distant colony. Governor Cano de Aponte arrived in his new domain in 1720 with "twenty-three boxes of furniture and dishes, a clavichord, four violins, a harp and various Andalusian tambourines, as well as fifteen mules loaded with fine clothes."

The Jesuits brought over craftsmen – architects, engineers, pharmacists, weavers, painters and sculptors. They also collected the best library in the colony – 20,000 volumes by the mid-18th century. Chile was already on the way to becoming the prosperous and highly Europeanized country that would later be seen as an example to the more turbulent emerging nations of Latin America. ❑

LEFT: Pedro de Valdivia.
RIGHT: the foundation of Santiago.

INDEPENDENCE AND PROSPERITY

Once independence had been won from Spain, there was no stopping the new republic, and Chile soon became one of the strongest economies in the Americas

Spain tried to keep its colonies free of foreign influences. It banned the entry of books printed outside Spain and prohibited printing presses within the colonies. But colonials still traveled to Europe, picking up "subversive" books, and new ideas.

The French Revolution and the revolt of the British colonies in North America in the late-18th century set conflicting examples. The excesses of the French rebels could be held up as an awful warning. But the sober, enterprising North Americans were rather an encouragement to their southern neighbors.

As it turned out, it was the ambitions of Napoleon that led to the independence of the Spanish colonies. When the French emperor invaded Spain, he forced the abdication of the king, Ferdinand VII, and placed his own brother, Joseph Bonaparte, on the Spanish throne. In Spain itself, there was immediate resistance. In each city the leading citizens set up a junta to govern in the name of the deposed king. Soon, the local bodies delegated power to a central junta in Seville.

A new Congress

According to the Spanish governor in the American colonies, the junta in Seville represented authority while the true king was absent. But many colonials felt they shared the same status as the Spanish cities, and that they should have the right to elect their own authority, subject only to the king.

In Chile that was what they did. The inept Spanish governor was persuaded to resign in favor of a native Chilean, Don Mateo de Toro Zambrano. The next step was to form a ruling junta, as the Argentines had done. In Chile the governor called a *cabildo abierto*, a formal meeting of the leading citizens. They gathered on September 18 1810 and chose a junta, which swore undying loyalty to the Spanish king.

LEFT: *La Visión de San Martín*, painting in the Instituto San Martiniano in Buenos Aires, Argentina.
RIGHT: footsoldier in Chile's revolutionary army.

Their first act was to secure the defense of their new nation. An infantry battalion was formed, along with two cavalry squadrons and more artillery. Envoys were sent to buy arms in England and Argentina. The junta also decreed free trade with all nations, hoping to boost the state's income from customs duties.

Finally, it convoked a National Congress, which was to be representative and also to guarantee that there were no abuses of power – two radical new notions that had infiltrated from Europe and the United States. The voters were people who "by their fortune, work, talent or qualities enjoy consideration in the parts where they reside, being older than 25 years." They elected deputies who "for their patriotic virtues, talents, and acknowledged prudence may have merited the esteem of their fellow citizens."

The selection of the deputies went ahead in early 1811. The first National Congress gathered on July 4 and, once again, its members swore loyalty to the Spanish king. A majority of its members were conservative landowners, who wanted only a minimum of reforms. But an energetic elite wanted radical change.

A radical *coup d'état*

The first to make a bid for the leadership of the nation were the Carreras. Three brothers – José Miguel, Juan José and Luis – and one sister, Javiera, came from a wealthy Santiago family. But their ideas were extreme for the day. On September 4 1811, Juan José and José Miguel stormed the Congress at the head of a mob and presented a list of "the people's demands." It was a *coup d'état*. A cowed Congress agreed

Spanish monarch. However, it proposed that the king should in turn recognize Chile's own Constitution and sovereignty. The new Constitution also established the rights of the individual, and set limits on the powers of the government, which was now to be elected by the people. This was a drastic change from being ruled by a monarch.

Most of José Miguel Carrera's compatriots, especially among the aristocracy, were not ready for such revolutionary gestures, and did not like either the man or his ideas. But before they could get together to do anything about him, the Spaniards took a hand.

to sack some of its most conservative members and set up an executive junta. After that, the reforms came faster, but still not fast enough for the Carreras. José Miguel forced Congress to set up a new junta, with himself at the head, and in December 1811, dissolved the Congress.

The Carreras had their sights set on Chile's independence, but they were in a minority. One of their first acts was to acquire a printing press and put a radical priest called Fray Camilo Henríquez in charge of it. He began publishing revolutionary ideas about popular sovereignty in a weekly paper, *La Aurora de Chile*.

In 1812, the government promulgated a new Constitution. Formally, this still recognized the

The wars of independence

On March 26 1813, Spain invaded the Chilean Central Valley, using officers from Peru and 2,000 men recruited among royalists in Valdivia and Chiloé. They took Talcahuano and Concepción, and started to move north. Carrera took command of the army and organized the defense of the capital, together with another military leader, Bernardo O'Higgins.

O'Higgins was another product of the ruling elite. He was the illegitimate son of a former governor, Ambrosio O'Higgins, an Irishman who had emigrated via Spain and Peru to Chile, where he became one of the most effective governors. An affair with a lady of Chillán, Doña

Isabel Riquelme, produced Bernardo, who was sent to Lima and then England for education.

Back in Chile, O'Higgins was elected a deputy to the Congress. He then distinguished himself as a military leader, and took over command of the army in 1813 from the more impetuous José Miguel Carrera. But by the end of the year the war was going badly. A truce was negotiated. Both sides were exhausted.

In March 1814, the Treaty of Lircay was signed. But the Carrera brothers and their troops rebelled and took the government again. O'Higgins set off to overthrow the new regime, but before he and the Carreras clashed came the news that a new royalist army had disembarked at Talcahuano. Divided and unprepared, the patriots met them at Rancagua on October 1, and were soundly beaten. O'Higgins and the Carreras all fled together to Argentina.

Spain back in charge

Ironically, it was the Spanish reconquest which finally convinced the Chileans that independence was their only option. The Spaniards tried to turn the clock back to 1810. Every reform the patriot governments had made, from allowing free trade to abolishing slavery, were all annulled by the royalists.

There was direct persecution of patriots. Many were sent into internal exile – one group was banished to a cave on Juan Fernández Islands. Nationalists in the public prison in Santiago were shot. The rest of the citizenry had to prove their loyalty to the Crown. Patriot public servants lost their jobs, others, their property. Heavy fines were exacted from all wealthy citizens. Chileans were not allowed to travel without permission, or carry arms. Public festivals were banned, a very unpopular move, and the gaming houses were closed.

Meanwhile, the remains of the patriot army, led by O'Higgins, had joined forces with the Argentine General José de San Martín and spent the next two years in Mendoza preparing to invade. A spy network kept the patriots in touch with sympathizers in Chile. Its leader was Manuel Rodríguez, a young lawyer who helped form guerrilla bands to harass the Spaniards. Rodríguez became a national folk hero; the

tales of his clever disguises and narrow escapes from the Spaniards passed into legend. On one occasion he took refuge in a Franciscan monastery and, disguised in a monk's robes, showed his pursuers around the convent to prove he was not there. Another time he dressed as a beggar and politely helped the Spanish governor to alight from his carriage. Even if they were not all true, the stories helped to keep up people's spirits.

Triumph for the nationalists

By 1817, O'Higgins and San Martín were ready, and their 3,600-strong "army of the

Andes" crossed the Andes. On February 12, they defeated royalist troops at Chacabuco, then entered Santiago in triumph, welcomed by vast crowds of Chileans.

The first job was to set up a new government. O'Higgins was named *director supremo*. On January 1 1818, the new regime declared the independence of Chile. But there was still fighting to be done. The royalists counterattacked with a new force from Peru, and took Talca. The patriots soon recovered and inflicted a final defeat on the Spaniards at Maipo on April 5 1818. That settled Chile's future.

But O'Higgins continued to fight for the independence of the rest of South America, not

---

LEFT: Bernardo O'Higgins, who led Chile to independence.

RIGHT: clergymen, early 19th century.

least because Chile would never be secure while the royalists held Peru. A navy was formed under Lord Cochrane, a Scot, with ships begged and borrowed from all parts and mostly foreign officers and sailors. In 1819, the new force patrolled the coasts of Peru, disrupting the enemy's supplies. At the end of the year, the navy took Valdivia, which was one of the few remaining royalist strongholds in Chile.

On August 20 1820, the army of the Andes, now mainly composed of Chileans but led by

RAPID CHANGES

In the first 13 years following independence, the Chileans tried out five different constitutional formulas, and went through 11 changes of government.

eventually died in 1842, but his body was not brought back to Chile until 1869.

The other revolutionaries fared worse. Two of the Carrera brothers were shot by the Argentines in 1818; then José Miguel too was shot, in Mendoza, Argentina, three years later. A secret society, known as the *Logia Lautarina*, formed originally by O'Higgins and San Martín in 1815, was said to have given the orders for their executions. Only Javiera Carrera survived and returned to Chile after the downfall of O'Higgins.

the Argentine San Martín, set off for Peru. With the fall of Lima and the final defeat of the Spanish, Chile's independence was assured.

Tribulations of the new republic

Once independence was secure, the Chileans had to work out how to replace two and a half centuries' rule by an absolute monarch with a republic. Most of the trial constitutions and reforms introduced were received quite peacefully but were not always popular. In 1823, O'Higgins ran into determined opposition from the land-owning aristocracy. He was forced to resign and went back to Peru, where he lived the rest of his days dreaming of return. He

Manuel Rodríguez, who had been closer to the Carreras than to O'Higgins, presented a problem for the new government. He was a headstrong, popular leader. O'Higgins tried to send him into gilded exile in the United States as a diplomat. Rodríguez refused, and ended up first in prison and then, in 1818, shot – "while trying to escape," said the official report.

But most of the decade was taken up with the struggle between Conservative landowners and the Church against the Chilean Liberals, who were strong in the towns, and among the intellectual elite. The Liberals hung on to the government until 1829, when they lost control of Santiago and the administration.

Finally, in 1833, the Conservatives were able to impose an authoritarian model of government that lasted until the next century. On paper, the president was all-powerful and Congress was a sideshow. Congress sat for only four months, while the president could veto laws, and had personal representatives in each province. The president could also veto electors, giving him enormous influence over the election of congressmen and of his successor.

Conservative values

The real leader of the Conservative movement, though he never ran for president and preferred to rule from behind the throne, was Diego Portales, best-known until then as a businessman.

It was Portales who organized the highly centralized Chilean system of government. Like other leaders of the independence movement, he was committed to liberal ideas in the abstract but argued that, in practice, Latin America was "not ready" for democracy. It was never made clear when the transition would take place or under what circumstances what came to be called the "enlightened despotism" would end.

As Portales explained: "The Republican system is the one we must adopt, but do you know how I understand it for countries like this? A strong, centralizing government whose men are true models of virtue and patriotism, and thus will strengthen the citizenry in the path of order and virtue. When morality has been established, then comes a true liberal government, free and full of ideals, in which all citizens can take part." Portales was all for democracy, in other words, but not yet.

While the Congress was writing the new Constitution, Portales was busy imposing the authority of the central government. He himself was minister for the interior, foreign affairs, the army and the navy. He purged the army of its rebel leaders, and exiled some to Lima. The military academy was reorganized; officers were to return to the professional, non-political status they held before Independence. To encourage this, Portales reinstated a system of local militias, directly loyal to the government.

A successful campaign stamped out banditry in the countryside. Economic and financial reforms reduced the size of the army and the civil service and brought in better book-keeping and fiscal controls. Such was Portales' influence in these years that in 1833 the British consul wrote home that "Every measure of the government originates with him (Portales) and no state body dares carry out any order without his express approval..."

Portales was murdered by political opponents in 1838. The organizational model he had established, however, lasted for nearly a century. By and large, the deeply conservative Chilean bureaucracy was better organized and less corrupt than others in the region – on the

other hand, Portales' expressed desire to extend democracy to Chilean society as a whole would only be fulfilled much later and in the wake of major social conflicts.

Stability and prosperity

Chile developed through the 1800s in largely stable conditions, though violence and social unrest erupted in the 1850s as the undemocratic manner of selecting presidents came into dispute. Reforms of the electoral system in the early 1870s temporarily resolved the issue.

Throughout most of the 19th century, a strong state oversaw an economic growth which was concentrated in overseas trade and

---

LEFT: Valparaíso, one of the world's busiest ports by the late 19th century.
RIGHT: southern market town in the 1860s.

copper and silver exports. Like its neighbor Argentina, Chile encouraged European immigration; in the south, for example, German immigrants came to control some of the larger and most profitable estates, while European dominance of trade ensured that the British and French occupied key positions elsewhere in the economy. The British led the shipping business. In 1825, 90 British ships called at Valparaíso compared with 70 from the US. Fifteen years later, the number of British vessels had doubled, while the number from the US continued to fall. By 1875, Britain took 70 percent of Chile's exports and sold it 40 percent of its imports.

Market forces

Much of Chile's growth came from copper exports. In 1826, 60 tons were shipped out of the country; by 1831, that was up to 2,000 tons, and by 1835, it was 12,700. By 1860, copper represented 55 percent of all Chile's exports. However, copper sales taught Chile about the dangers as well as the benefits of joining the world economy. The industrial revolution in Britain had boosted demand for copper in the 1830s. But industrial slumps in Europe in the 1850s and 1870s hit Chile hard. From then on, the daily price of copper on the London Metal Exchange became a national obsession.

Another problem that Chile faced for the first time in this period was the cost of being so far from its markets. In the 1840s, Chile found a profitable new market for its wheat and flour in California, at the height of the gold rush. Its exports leapt more than 70-fold in three years. But by 1854 the North American farmers were back on top, and Chile's sales slumped. When the gold rush started in Australia a little later, Chilean farmers could not compete in price with their Californian rivals.

For the rest of the century there was a steady flow of migrants from the countryside and its decreasingly profitable farms, to the towns and the mining centers of the north.

Rail, cables and banknotes

Transport was a problem internally. The first railway line was planned in 1845, from Copiapó to the little port of Caldera. An energetic North American, William Wheelwright, organized the finances from the private sector and by 1851 the first 81 km (50 miles) were inaugurated. Another line from Valparaíso to Santiago was finished in 1863. A telegraph line linked the main port with the capital in 1852; by 1876 there were 48 national lines, and one each to Argentina and Peru. In 1853, Chile introduced postage stamps, just 13 years after Britain.

Getting a banking system organized was a major task. There was a physical shortage of coins and paper money – the first bank notes began to circulate in 1839. In the mining sector the owner-entrepreneurs started to use their own trade bills as a form of exchange, and to coin lead tokens to pay their workforce. Their logical next step was to set up a bank. By 1850, there were 60 operating, including the Banco de Chile. The government regulated their currency issues, but did not produce its own.

Already by the 1840s, contemporary chroniclers were writing about the effects of a period of stability and prosperity. Wealth was conspicuously displayed. There were fine new houses in Santiago, such as the Palacio Cousiño. There were two theaters, a school of painting, and several literary magazines – and not just in Santiago, but in La Serena, Valparaíso and Copiapó, too.

In 1843, the University of Chile was founded for research and debate. The Instituto Nacional was the only higher education center, but there were schools for music and art. In 1860, primary education was made free and a state responsibility. At this date only 17 percent of the population was literate, but 60 years later the figure had risen to a creditable 50 percent.

War with the neighbors

In the first half of the 19th century, the northern desert area close to the Peruvian and Bolivian borders had attracted little attention. But from the 1850s onwards, deposits of natural fertilizers (guano and nitrate) were discovered there. Guano became a major source of income for Peru, and Chile and Bolivia disputed deposits along the coast north of Coquimbo. By 1874 Peru and Chile had agreed for both to exploit

and the day of his death, May 21 (*see box below*) is a national holiday.

The Chilean army marched to the Peruvian capital, Lima. Peru had to sue for peace; the Treaty of Ancon, signed in 1883, gave Chile Tarapacá and the towns of Arica and Tacna for a 10-year period. Bolivia ceded Antofagasta in 1884, thereby losing its only exit to the sea.

Since then, successive Bolivian governments have pressed the Chileans to give them even just a strip of coast for a port. Peru eventually resigned its claim to Arica in exchange for Tacna in 1927. But Peruvian army officers still swear an oath to recover Arica.

the guano, but the labor was mostly Chilean.

In 1878, new disputes broke out, this time over nitrate deposits. In 1879, Chile occupied Antofagasta, which until then was Bolivian territory. When it discovered that Peru and Bolivia had a secret defense pact, Chile declared war on both its neighbors. The ensuing War of the Pacific resulted in Chile gaining a future source of wealth, nitrate, and its best-loved national hero, Captain Arturo Prat. Today, his statue graces the plaza of even the smallest village,

LEFT: Captain Arturo Prat, a national hero.
ABOVE: mine workers in the northern deserts became the backbone of Chile's union movement.

DEATH OF A HERO

The story of Arturo Prat's death is in the best naval tradition of heroic defeats. His ship, the *Esmeralda*, was trapped in the bay of Iquique by the two biggest battleships of the Peruvian fleet, the *Huascar* and the *Independencia*. Prat refused to surrender and his ship resisted the enemy fire for two hours, until the *Huascar* rammed it. Sword in hand, Prat leapt into the *Huascar* with a handful of men, and was cut down. The Peruvian commander, Admiral Grau, was gentlemanly enough to send back the captain's sword and a letter he had written to his wife. It earned him equally generous treatment when the Chileans captured the *Huascar* later that year.

Nitrate boom and bust

One result of the war with Peru was that Chile now controlled the nitrate deposits of the north. Taxes from the new nitrate mines were the primary source of income for the Chilean state for many years thereafter.

The man who made the most money out of nitrate, however, was not a Chilean but an Englishman, John Thomas North. During the War of the Pacific, he bought up cheap title deeds to some of the best nitrate deposits. Then, back in England, he raised money on the stock market to work the mines. "Chile saltpeter" caught the British public's imagination. The

Power struggle and civil war

The power struggle between president and Congress had been muted during the 1860s and 1870s by a series of mild-mannered presidents and minor reforms. However, the key issue remained – the president's power to elect the Congress that he wanted.

Congress was not much more than a debating society, although it could block effective government. Presidents played off party factions against each other to buy support. By the end of the century the factions, now more like organized parties, were becoming harder to pacify with crumbs of power.

shares sold like hot cakes and North became a famous figure. " He's the most important man in England at the moment" wrote one of his competitors, " with the possible exception of [Prime Minister] Gladstone."

But by the 1890s the nitrate bubble had burst. There was overproduction, and prices plummeted. Early in the next century, a cheaper substitute was invented. Attempts to cut production failed, the price went on falling and the industry declined, until by the 1930s only a handful of offices were still producing. Once-bustling camps and villages such as Humberstone still stand today, now deserted and ghostly witnesses to Chile's past *(see page 197)*.

Under President José Manuel Balmaceda, the issue came to a head. Balmaceda faced a factious Congress, made some politically-inept appointments, and reacted to criticism by trying to assert his presidential powers. He finally lost his majority in Congress. When he tried to rule without it, and refused to convoke a special session to approve the military budget, the navy rebelled. Congress and the rebels organized an army and defeated government troops at the battles of Placilla and Concón, seizing Santiago. Balmaceda took refuge in the Argentine embassy, where he committed suicide. ❑

ABOVE: Santiago shopping arcade, late 19th century.

King of Patagonia

O relie-Antoine de Tounens was a mediocre lawyer who lived the first 33 years of his life in provincial France. In 1859, he packed his bags and sailed to the remotest corners of southern Chile, where he was to gain an eternal place in the annals of failed dreams: for a brief but glorious period, Tounens found himself king of the native Mapuche and Patagonian people.

The inspiration for this singular plan appears to have been a popular epic work by the 16th-century Spanish poet Alonso de Ercilla praising the virtues of the then unconquered Araucanians:

> Robust and beardless,
> Bodies rippling and muscular,
> Hard limbs, nerves of steel
> Agile, brazen, cheerful,
> Spirited, valiant, daring,
> Toughened by work, patient
> of mortal cold, hunger and heat.

Tounens reasoned that these exemplars of Rousseau's "Noble Savage" fantasy would elect him the king of their nation. Landing after an arduous sea voyage in the middle of Chile's northern Atacama desert, the Frenchman exchanged letters with the Mapuche *cacique* (chieftain) Manil and, encouraged by the positive response, headed south of the Bíobío River. With him were a translator and two other Frenchmen, one already appointed Minister for Foreign Affairs; the other Secretary of State for Justice in Tounens' future kingdom.

By a bizarre stroke of fortune, the *cacique* Manil had recently died, muttering that a bearded white stranger would lead his people to freedom. The new *cacique*, Quilapan, welcomed Tounens – who promptly prepared a document that would establish constitutional monarchy. The native Patagonians on the other side of the Andes (now Argentina) also agreed to accept the Frenchman as their king.

Drunk on power, Tounens left his new kingdoms for the Chilean port of Valparaíso, where he drew up a constitution for "La Nouvelle France." He was soon humiliated to learn that neither the Chilean government nor his French compatriots back home would recognize his rule. Nine months later, he returned to Araucania with a servant, Rosales –

RIGHT: Frenchman Orelie-Antoine de Tounens, who declared himself king of Araucania and Patagonia.

the man who would play Judas to Tounens' messiah. This time the foreign king was bent on war and the Frenchman announced that he would organize a native army to enforce the frontier with Chile.

News was sent back to the Chilean authorities, and the Frenchman was taken more seriously. Rosales lured Tounens into a trap: army officers jumped the king and dragged him off to a cockroach-infested jail in the nearby town of Los Angeles. After several weeks of dysentery, Tounens agreed to leave Chile.

The "king" was deported to France, but returned to South America to reassert his authority. Each time he was intercepted by the police and sent back to his family. In 1878, he died in the obscure

French village of Tourtoirac. But this was not the end of the kingdom of Araucania and Patagonia. Since the Tounens family had left no successor, a French champagne salesman, impressed by the history, decided to assume the vacant throne as *Achille Ier*. The title is now claimed by a French lawyer Philippe Boiry to whom it was entrusted by his friend Antoine III, the descendant of a friend of Tounens. In July 2004, Boiry caused a small stir when, to the annoyance of many indigenous Chileans, he presented medals to a Mapuche lawyer and student for their contribution to the cause of autonomy from Chile. But Boiry, now in his seventies, has no descendants and may well be the last King of Patagonia. ❑

A CENTURY OF UPHEAVALS

*From democracy to military rule and back to democracy – the 20th century saw
extraordinary reversals in Chile's political, social and economic arenas*

The civil war of the 1890s had tilted the balance of power in favor of the Congress and against the presidents, who were reduced to refereeing the fights for cabinet posts among the parties. But by this time there were new actors on the political scene. The railways had made travel easier and the towns were growing, and with them a new cultural and social life. A new middle class was organizing in the recently founded Radical Party. A strong force within it were the freemasons, whose lodges were political debating centers.

A new working class was forming too. Industry had grown up in the early and mid-century in specific centers – everything from biscuit and pasta factories in Valparaíso that supplied passing ships, to breweries started by German settlers in the south. The new railways needed workshops, and the growing towns needed textiles, shoes, soap and furniture. Business boomed, as did the numbers of urban artisans.

It was getting ever harder to scratch a living in the countryside, so many peasants were drawn to the nitrate mines of the north. Once there, they were often trapped, earning low wages paid in tokens that could only be exchanged for goods in the company store. Schools, a police force and courts were practically non-existent. Alcohol was easier to come by than water in the northern mining camps of the pampas.

Birth of the trade unions

It was in these harsh conditions that the modern Chilean trade union movement was born, evolving out of the early mutual aid societies. The miners formed the basis for Chile's early political movements, anarchist at first and later socialist. One figure stands out in that early history of working-class organization. Luis Emilio Recabarren, a former printworker, traveled the country as a union organizer. He got an audi-

ence among the miners for his political message by publishing newspapers which carried news from other parts of the country. They helped the immigrants isolated in the pampa to keep in touch with their homes, and also provided a means of communication between groups of workers in the cities, the mines and

the countryside, who until then had been isolated from one another. In 1912, Recabarren founded the Chilean Socialist Workers Party. After the Russian Revolution in 1917, it was the basis of the Chilean Communist Party.

Recabarren traveled to Russia, and met Lenin and Trotsky as well as trade union and political leaders from across the world. He was elected to the Chilean parliament twice during this period, though he was never allowed to take his seat. Although he was a key figure in the early history of the Chilean left, Recabarren's relationship with the Communist Party was always difficult. Political difficulties may well have been the cause of his suicide in 1928.

PRECEDING PAGES: demonstrators say "yes" to Pinochet, 1988.
LEFT: Santiago's Paseo Ahumada in the 1930s.
RIGHT: lumberjacks take strike action.

Desert slaughter

The massacre at Santa María de Iquique has come to symbolize the struggle of Chile's mineworkers in the early 1900s.

Santa María de Iquique is a remote mining town in northern Chile. In 1907, the miners went on strike for better pay and conditions *(see page 193–4)*. When an envoy was sent from central government to speak with them, the miners and their families gathered in the town center to hear what he had to say. Four and a half thou-

DRAMATIC PORTRAYAL

Luis Advis and his folk music group, Quilapayún, performed a famous oratorio based on the tragedy at Santa María de Iquique, which was first presented in 1969 *(see page 89).*

dent. But, said the witness, "There was a moment of silence as the machine guns were lowered to aim at the school yard and the hall, occupied by a compact mass of people who spilled over into the main square... There was a sound like thunder as they fired. Then the gunfire ceased and the foot soldiers went into the school, firing, as men and women fled in all directions."

The army general later reported that there had been 140 victims. The eyewitness quoted talked to doctors and oth-

sand of them were crammed into the local school, and 1,500 more were in Plaza Manuel Montt. An eyewitness gave a chilling account of what happened as squads of soldiers began to appear in the plaza.

"On the central balcony... stood 30 or so men in the prime of life, quite calm, beneath a great Chilean flag, and surrounded by the flags of other nations. They were the strike committee... All eyes were fixed on them just as all the guns were directed at them. Standing, they received the shots. As though struck by lightning they fell, and the great flag fluttered down over their bodies."

Most thought that was the end of the inci-

ers involved, and estimated the figure at 195 dead, and 390 wounded. Others reported many more.

Social inequalities

Experiences like these, combined with the organizing work of Recabarren, laid the foundations of Chile's strong trade union tradition. At one stage, before and during World War I, sections of the ruling classes gave some consideration to the implementation of basic social welfare legislation – the nitrate industry, after all, was booming as a result of the war. But the discovery of artificial nitrates had a powerful impact on Chile, putting a swift end to the boom *(see page 194)*, and all such proposals were shelved.

Agriculture was stagnant, dominated by huge landed estates whose owners lived either in town or in Europe, and had little interest in raising productivity or modernizing. Import figures for 1907 show the ruling class's priorities: 3.7 million pesos were spent on importing agricultural and industrial machinery, while 6.8 million went on the purchase of French champagne, jewels, silk and the latest perfume from Paris. As tax revenues from nitrates declined and the foreign debt grew, increasing numbers of ordinary Chileans found themselves without work or the possibility of it, and facing poverty and collapsing living standards.

Power struggles

In conditions of growing social conflict, there often emerge leaders who claim to bridge the conflicting interests of all social classes. In Chile, that "figure above society" was Arturo Alessandri, the son of an Italian immigrant.

Typically, his rhetoric was nationalist and deliberately vague, enabling him to appeal to different sections of Chilean society at the same time. His election to the presidency in the early 1920s did not give him the power over Congress he aspired to, and in deepening conditions of crisis he turned to the younger and more restless sections of the army.

The result was a military coup in 1928, which gave military Caudillo Colonel Carlos Ibáñez del Campo dictatorial powers. His models were Mussolini and Spain's José Primo de Rivera, and he was a fierce critic of the traditional political structures, especially the parties, some of whose leaders he "invited" to leave the country. But he was even more fiercely anti-communist, and had communists and union leaders arrested and deported. It was a return to authoritarianism such as Chile had not seen since the years of Diego Portales.

In a sense, the coup brought an end to a system of power which had observed the democratic rules but within a limited framework, in which power was simply exchanged between sections of the ruling classes. Chile has a reputation for a long democratic tradition; yet this was pushed aside in the 1920s, as it would be again in the 1970s, with considerable ease.

Ibáñez set about creating a powerful state sector of the economy, establishing the national airline and the daily government newspaper *La Nación*. This was an attempt to shift resources into new areas of the economy, placing them under national control and overcoming the resistance of the traditional ruling classes, using the state as an instrument of economic control.

Recession and social unrest

It was a bad time to be increasing state expenditure. With the Wall Street crash in 1929 and the world recession that followed, the Chilean

economy went into a crisis. Nitrate sales had long been declining, and now the expanding copper industry was also hit as the Great Depression squeezed its markets. There was widespread unemployment and social unrest. The government set up an emergency employment program, and printed money to pay for it. Inflation rose, and so did the protests.

Ibáñez was forced to resign. He left for exile in July 1931, but his elected successor was promptly overthrown by a military-civilian junta. In June 1932, a "Socialist Republic" was installed by Colonel Marmaduque Grove. Grove belonged to a group of radical young officers whose aim was to bring about a redis-

LEFT: nitrate workers, Antofagasta.
RIGHT: Arturo Alessandri, who had two shots at leadership.

tribution of wealth, particularly through land reform, that would set the economy to work again. The new republic lasted only one hundred days, however, before Grove was exiled to Easter Island and Arturo Alessandri returned with a draconian program in October 1932. He purged the army of dissident elements, clamped down on trade unions, banned strikes and closed down the opposition press.

Although Grove's social experiment had achieved very little, some proposals had reached the statute book: 40 years later, President Salvador Allende would begin to implement some of the changes that Grove had envisaged.

Recovery and reform

By the late 1930s, economic activity had resumed as the United States economy began its recovery under the Roosevelt New Deal. A new Chilean government, elected in 1938, offered a program of mild economic and social reform. Headed by a Radical, Pedro Aguirre Cerda, it enjoyed the support of both the Communist and the Socialist parties, but disputes later broke the alliance. Aguirre Cerda's elected successor, another Radical, quickly outlawed the Communists.

The Radicals boosted the state sector of the economy substantially and usefully, with a steel industry and a nationwide electrification pro-

gram. But in the countryside, government intervention had a negative effect. Strict price controls on farm produce meant that the landowners had little incentive to invest and produce more. Public opinion was beginning to sense that farming would simply never take off under ruling-class ownership and that the only hope was to take away the land and give it to those who could produce.

The other conflict that began to loom was the ownership of the copper mines. The main deposits had always been owned and worked by US corporations. During World War II, and later in the Korean war, the US government bought copper from these North American-owned corporations at a special low price. That meant a substantial loss of tax revenues for the Chilean state. Control of such a major source of national wealth was bound to become an issue.

The caudillo returns

By the late 1940s, party infighting and petty corruption had again paved the way for a "strong man." Carlos Ibáñez was returned to power by the electorate in 1952, demanding "a fundamental change of direction," and brandishing a symbolic broom with which he would sweep away politicking and corruption. He had the support of a redoubtable figure, María de la Cruz and her Feminine Party of Chile – women got the vote, finally, in 1949 and promptly strengthened the conservative forces.

Ibáñez had the personal charisma to get himself elected, but no organized support. He tried to get the Constitution reformed to give more power to the presidency, failed, and sat out the rest of his term in political impotence. In 1958, Arturo Alessandri's son, Jorge, succeeded the old general, elected almost entirely on the strength of his father's name. Since then, no president from the political right has been elected in Chile.

The Christian Democrats

The center and the left were now grouped in two easily definable camps. In one were the Socialist and the Communist parties – full-blooded Marxist-Leninists who talked of armed struggle to overthrow "the bourgeois state", but who were actually engaged in building up their electoral strength to win it by peaceful means.

Their rival, proposing very similar reforms in, for example, land ownership and nationalization of the copper mines, was the Christian Democrat Party. It developed in the 1930s out of a movement started by a group of young Catholics from within the Conservative Party, initially with vaguely fascist leanings, who called themselves the Falange Nacional. By the end of the 1950s their ideas had been modified to Christian socialism and they were growing rapidly among both the middle and working classes. They had strong links to the Catholic Church and a comparably strong anti-communist message. There was not a vast difference between the programs of the two camps

In the early 1960s when the influence of the Cuban revolution was sweeping through Latin America, the Christian Democrats throughout the region looked like the best answer to the Marxist threat. The Chilean Christian Democrat Party was the first of its kind in Latin America to get into government, in 1964, with a good deal of North American financial support. The following year they won a solid ma-

> **KISSINGER'S WARNING**
>
> US Secretary of State Henry Kissinger condemned the Allende reform program, saying that he did not see why the United States should stand idly by "and let a country go communist due to the irresponsibility of its own people."

jority in Congress, with party leader Eduardo Frei becoming the first president in Chilean history to have at least theoretical control of both the executive and the legislature.

Success went to their head, and they boasted that Christian Democrats would govern for the next 30 years (like their Italian counterparts). But the Frei government made two powerful enemies: the old land-owning class, which opposed its attempt at land reform; and the military, who felt underpaid and unappreciated. An army general, Roberto Viaux, led an uprising in 1969 to protest against their conditions.

The old political right, which had helped vote Frei into office, now withdrew to reform itself into a new party, the Nationals. Tensions within Frei's own party led to a split in 1969, and his leftwingers, who felt that the reforms had not gone far enough, went off to join the Marxists.

The Allende years

In 1970 a leftwing coalition known as Popular Unity put forward as their candidate a middle-class doctor turned socialist senator, Salvador Allende. Allende won his fourth attempt at the

LEFT: Turri Clock, Valparaíso.
ABOVE: Dr Salvador Allende.
RIGHT: General Augusto Pinochet.

presidency by a paper-thin margin (36.3 percent of the votes). One of the first electoral promises he honored was to give every poor child in Chile a pair of shoes, and to start a program of free milk distribution in the schools.

But the new government faced formidable enemies in the United States. President Nixon's government pumped in approximately US$8 million in covert financing over the next three years to boost the opposition and to help, for example, to keep the anti-Allende publishing group *El Mercurio* in business.

At home the government had some early successes. It got all-party support in Congress, in owner-drivers were opposed to a government proposal to create a state transport system.

Doctors, shopkeepers and bus owners joined in, and industrialists staged lockouts. Workers in dozens of small factories reacted by taking over their workplaces. Neighborhood committees set up their own retail networks, bringing goods direct from the factories. By this time the opposition had convinced itself that Allende was out to install a full-blooded Marxist state. The far left of Allende's own Socialist Party encouraged this view – ironically the communists were moderators in the unruly coalition, committed to a "peaceful road to socialism."

1971, to nationalize the copper mines. But Allende's decision not to pay compensation to the North American owners sparked an official US boycott of non-military aid and credits for Chile. The US government also tried to ban Chilean copper from world markets.

Social discontent

The political tension grew. When Fidel Castro of Cuba visited Chile in November 1971, upper and middle class women held the first "march of the empty saucepans" to demonstrate against food and other shortages. A year later, the shortages were worse, and the lines got much longer when the truck owners went on strike. Many

The tanks roll in

In March 1973, despite the growing chaos, the government won an increased majority (44 percent) in the parliamentary elections. The opposition decided that it could not wait until the next presidential elections, which were scheduled for 1976. In late August, Congress declared the government unconstitutional. Days later, on the morning of September 11, tanks rolled into the streets of Santiago, and the military took over the radio stations and announced a curfew, calling on President Allende to resign.

Besieged in the presidential palace with only a few advisers, Allende refused to resign. Photographs from the palace show him in a helmet and armed with a machine gun given to him by Fidel Castro, and the popular image remains of Allende fighting to the end before being cut down by the Army's bullets. In his final broadcast to the nation, he ordered his supporters not to resist, yet he himself refused an offer of a safe conduct to the airport and exile. Allende's doctor testified that he died by his own hand, alone, in the ruined palace which the airforce had bombed, but the truth may never be known.

Pinochet's rise to power

The Chilean coup sent shock waves around the world. For some, the 1970 elections had proved

two years as its undisputed head. And it was he who was largely responsible for the violence that followed the coup. The military took power quickly, pursuing and detaining all those who had led the trade unions, popular organizations, student groups and cultural movements most identified with the Allende regime.

The descent into brutality

The particularly brutal murder of the singer Victor Jara *(see page 88)* came to symbolize thousands of other, equally violent deaths, as the foreign journalists who were herded into the National Stadium (turned into a prison) together

the possibility that social change could occur peacefully, gradually, and via the ballot box. That hope now lay in ruins. Chile's reputation as a haven of democracy in a sub-continent given to resolving its political problems by violent means had now lost its legitimacy – though in fact military intervention had been a feature of 20th-century political life in the country.

Though the coup was led by a junta of the heads of all the armed forces, it was Augusto Pinochet who would emerge over the following

LEFT: the bombing of La Moneda, the presidential palace, during the 1973 coup.
ABOVE: demonstrations against Pinochet.

with Jara and other suspected leftwingers to suffer beatings and torture, would later testify. Thousands of people were murdered, many more were tortured and hundreds of thousands went into exile to escape persecution or, in some cases, in search of work, as factories, government institutions, schools and universities were reopened under direct military control.

All opposition activity was banned. The last demonstration in Chile for some 10 years was the funeral of Chile's great poet Pablo Neruda, who died just two weeks after the coup. The 3,000 mourners who marched between ranks of soldiers through the streets of Santiago shouted slogans against the military and carried placards bearing the names of Neruda and Allende. Thereafter there would be no more public expressions of hostility to Pinochet until the 1980s.

Initially, the churches provided refuge for those who could not find asylum in foreign embassies. From its formation in 1976, the Vicariate of Solidarity, organized by the Catholic Church, helped the victims of repression to find legal aid and became a focus for protests against human rights abuses that continued to occur in the years following the coup.

> **TURBULENT TIMES**
>
> The Italian film *Il Postino* was based on the novel *Ardiente Paciencia*, by Antonio Skármeta, which depicted the weeks following the 1973 Pinochet coup.

Free-market economics

By 1977 it was clear that Pinochet's regime had its own economic as well as political agenda. The crude anti-communism of the earlier years now combined with a new economic philosophy of neo-liberalism, or complete openness to the world market – ideas advocated by Milton Friedman and a group of his Chilean acolytes known as the "Chicago Boys" *(see page 61)*. The low-wage open economy that they advocated, with its savage reductions in public spending, would become familiar throughout Latin America from the 1980s onwards. But Chile was its first test case.

In the late 1970s, the new economic philosophy seemed in its own terms to have succeeded – there was a consumer boom, and foreign firms were investing heavily. New exports such as wine and fruit were beginning to find markets abroad, and the electrical goods assembled by poorly paid Chilean workers for US-based corporations were sold throughout Latin America.

The other side of the coin was the deepening poverty of a majority of the population, but this was concealed behind a curtain of repression while the "Chilean miracle" was celebrated. Thus 75 percent of those who voted in the 1978 referendum supported Pinochet as he concentrated more and more power in his own hands. The 1980 Constitution, drafted by a Chilean of known fascist sympathies, consolidated Pinochet's power and control over Chilean life.

Crisis and disintegration

The years 1982–3 brought a crisis in the Chilean economy which threatened to drive down even further the living standards of the majority, as well as to end the boom of the previous decade. In 1983 trade unions again began to call strikes and there was widespread protest as the gross domestic product (GDP) collapsed. All political organizations remained illegal, and most of the left-wing groups had been destroyed after the coup. In this new climate of protest, however, they began to reorganize.

The Communist Party had taken a moderate line under Allende, and had argued after 1973 that the coup happened because things had gone too far too fast in the Allende years. The party now turned in a radical direction as a new generation of young people joined its ranks. By 1985, the creation of the Manuel Rodríguez Patriotic Front marked a commitment to armed struggle, which culminated in the failed attempt to assassinate Pinochet in 1986.

Thereafter the old enemies came together in a series of agreements to build a joint campaign for a "No" vote in Pinochet's 1988 plebiscite, which was designed to confirm him in power for another eight years at least. In the event, and to the dictator's evident surprise, 54 percent of the Chilean people voted "No."

Elections followed in 1989, amid intense negotiations at a number of levels. The pace and direction of the return to democracy had to be agreed on by businessmen and trade unionists, Christian Democrats and Communists who supported the "No" campaign – people whose purposes were very different. The hopes for a peaceful transition led the campaign into a series of talks with Pinochet. While he yielded the presidency, and formal power, it could hardly be said that he relinquished control.

No regrets

The 1980 Constitution remained in force; the judiciary was dominated by Pinochet's appointees; a block of senators would continue to be

In effect this meant not only that Pinochet remained immune from responsibility for his actions, but also that the fundamental shape of Chilean society would remain as it was at the point when Pinochet finally ceded the presidency to the newly elected Christian Democrat Patricio Aylwin, in March 1990. The deeply unequal distribution of income would remain, and those who had grown rich in the Pinochet years would be protected. The privatized industries would not be returned to the state, nor would the broad program for a welfare state to which Allende had been committed be revived. In exchange, Pinochet agreed to allow the transition of power

nominated directly by the armed forces, giving them a controlling voice in parliament; the financial gains Pinochet had made as president and the economic power accumulated by the armed forces would remain untouched. Pinochet stayed on until 1998 as head of the army and, while a commission of investigation would seek the truth about the "disappeared" and the human rights abuses that had occurred under his rule, there would be neither revenge nor restitution.

LEFT: campaigning for a "No" vote to Pinochet.
ABOVE: socialist supporters march through Santiago in the closing weeks of a turbulent century.

to take place. Small wonder that he continued to figure large in Chilean political life – and that he should say in a 1995 speech that "he had nothing to regret and would do everything again in exactly the same way if he had to."

The question was whether the main danger facing Chilean democracy was Pinochet or the possibility of a new social movement growing up from below. Certainly the right in parliament felt no serious threat from the new government, and vetoed every new initiative, however mild. It took four years for a new labor code to be established, and a number of other social reforms were simply filibustered out. Living standards improved only slowly for the majority and, for many people, they still had not reached their 1970 levels by the end of 1998. Nonetheless the Aylwin and Frei governments did take some measures to redress poverty, achieving a slight increase in taxation, and introducing some new welfare provisions.

Chile remained, however, a deeply unequal society in which the transition to democracy left virtually intact the previous distribution of wealth and power as well as the political influence of those around Pinochet. The memories of the 1973 coup and its aftermath were sufficiently fearsome for the suggestion of renewed military intervention to silence parliament.

End of the party for Pinochet

Thus it was that Pinochet could display such absolute confidence and certainty when, in March 1998, he retired as commander-in-chief of the army, at the age of 82. He had already been named *senador vitalicio* – a senator for life – and in this capacity was given effective immunity from prosecution for crimes against human rights committed in Chile during his regime, for which there were some 200 cases pending in the Chilean courts.

It was with the same confidence that he departed for Britain in September 1998 for medical treatment. Pinochet's period in power had largely coincided with the governments of Margaret Thatcher in Britain, and her relationship with him had always been cordial and admiring – as had US President Ronald Reagan's with them both.

In the meantime, a series of cases had been brought before courts elsewhere on behalf of the families of Pinochet's non-Chilean victims. Many of them referred to a period early in the 1980s, when Pinochet had collaborated with the military regimes of Argentina and Uruguay in the pursuit of their political enemies. The operation (Operation Condor) was run by the notorious head of Pinochet's secret police (DINA), Manuel Contreras. Until December 1998, he was the only leading member of the Pinochet government in jail, having been sentenced to 7 years for his part in the murder in Washington of Allende's ex-Foreign Secretary Orlando Letelier.

Among the cases pending was one brought before a Spanish court by a team of lawyers including Joan Garcés, ex-adviser to Allende. While Pinochet was in London, the Spanish Justice Ministry initiated extradition proceedings with Britain. Other governments made similar requests and he was obliged to remain in London while the legal issues were debated. An extraordinary chain of events was set in motion, as the House of Lords in London confirmed by a majority that he had a case to answer under international law, and later overturned their own ruling when it was revealed that one of the Law Lords had links with the human rights group Amnesty International. Meanwhile, journalists and commentators began to revisit the experience of Chile in 1973, while those Chileans still in their countries of exile even after 1990 emerged in demonstrations.

During March 2000, the British Home Secretary agreed to the release of Pinochet on the grounds of ill health, opening the way for his return to Chile. The local courts subsequently removed his immunity from prosecution, but then declared that the former dictator was unfit to stand trial. Finally, as a footnote to this turbulent century, the former dictator was again stripped of immunity from prosecution in 2004. This time the lower court ruling was upheld by the Supreme Court, carrying no right of appeal and thereby unblocking the path to a human rights abuses trial. ❑

LEFT: military parade on the anniversary of the coup.
RIGHT: Stock Market building, Santiago.

AN ECONOMIC MIRACLE?

One of the world's first experiments in free-market economics,
Chile has since anchored its growth in free-trade agreements

For almost 17 years after the 1973 coup, Chile was ruled by a military dictatorship, committed to crushing even the most limited aspirations for social reform. Its recipe was free-market policies and the "trickle-down effect" – the theory that wealth created by the private sector would flow down and benefit the workers. These policies were imposed by a military dictatorship in a country without a Congress, without a free press and with restricted labor organizations – ideal, if abnormal, conditions for such an experiment. The "scientists" were economists, most of whom had studied at the University of Chicago, at the feet of Milton Friedman, the guru of free-market economics. They were dubbed the "Chicago boys," a nickname that stuck.

They made some bad mistakes, even on their own terms. In the late 1970s, the finance ministry fixed Chile's exchange rate for more than two years, and took all the controls off bank lending. Dozens of companies and individuals took out large dollar-denominated loans that local banks financed through international borrowing. When the government finally had to devalue the peso, there was a near-fatal bank crash. As a result, the state had to bail out most of the private banks, but many companies went bankrupt, mortgage repossessions soared, and an economic recession followed, lasting until the mid-1980s. The high unemployment and economic hardship of this period were key factors in mounting discontent with the dictatorship.

An example to the world

But Chile weathered the storm, and by the late 1980s was able to show nicely balanced books and an orderly, flourishing economy with a growing export sector and a lot of interest from foreign investors. It now had a model that other countries in the region were being actively encouraged to copy, not least by their bankers.

PRECEDING PAGES: rich Chileans relax after a polo match, Santiago; Lota, a Central Valley coal town.
LEFT AND RIGHT: the Santiago Stock Exchange.

In the 1980s, a leading "Chicago boy", Joaquín Lavín, who became mayor of Santiago's Las Condes district in the 1990s and, in 2000, narrowly lost the presidential election, wrote a book about the changes he saw in Chile. Called *The Silent Revolution*, it was a paean of praise for the economic model, and it

became a bible for many businesspeople and right-wing politicians. Lavín wrote enthusiastically, for example, about the new fruit export business, which developed during the military government; and he picked out the region of Copiapó in northern Chile as a prime example of a place where workers were making good money in a new, modern industry.

This was an area where the military government was sure that it would win a majority of votes in 1988, when it held a national plebiscite to vote President Pinochet another eight years in power. But here, and throughout the rest of Chile, the majority of voters apparently felt that "the economy may be doing fine but I'm doing badly" and the dictatorship was defeated.

In Copiapó, the mayor told a national newspaper, after the vote: "I was sure we (the government) were going to win here with 58 percent of the votes, but now I realize people don't sell themselves for a plate of lentils. It's not enough to give them houses, they have to feel they are participating."

The other side of the coin

The other side of Lavín's Chile was presented by Eugenio Tironi, a left-wing sociologist. In answer to Lavín's *Silent Revolution*, he published a book called *The Silence of the Revolu-*

and scratched a living collecting waste paper and cardboard for recycling, or from selling goods illegally on the streets. The military government made great play of the improvement in the infant mortality rate, but Tironi argued that there had also been a dramatic increase in the many diseases created by poverty, such as mange and other parasitic infections.

A second group to suffer, he said, were young people. They were "the left-overs", the "too-many-of-them", as one local rock group described itself and its generation in a popular song. For most of the 1980s, young people made up the biggest single group of unem-

tion: the other side of modernization, in which he described the social effects of the dictatorship's economic policies. He wrote about the phenomenon of "two Chiles" – "a society in which two groups co-exist practically without touching each other; a modernizing tendency for an elite which is more and more integrated into the international world; and a tendency towards the ever-increasing impoverishment of a majority, which relies increasingly on state help."

Tironi singled out four groups in Chile as having suffered most from the policies of the "Chicago boys." First, the lowest-income groups, who lived in makeshift, overcrowded homes on the outskirts of the capital, Santiago,

ployed. The third group to lose out under the military, Tironi suggested, were the workers, who lost the possibility of organizing collectively to defend themselves.

Tironi also argued that the middle class, a large sector in Chilean society, had mixed fortunes. Some professionals in the private sector became part of the Chilean elite, but others fared badly. Tironi highlighted the fate of teachers. Once respected figures, they became poorly paid, overworked drudges, with scant resources for their own or their pupils' cultural enrichment.

The two different worlds depicted by Lavín and Tironi still, to some extent, exist today, despite the vast increase in prosperity brought by the sustained economic growth of the 1990s. Lavín's Chile, or at least his Santiago, is what most foreign visitors see: gleaming office blocks, well-stocked shopping malls, modern banks with automatic cash machines, and efficient telecommunications services.

Tempering the military legacy

Once democracy was restored in 1990, one of the new government's challenges was to attempt to reduce the huge gap between the very rich and the very poor, and to restore the standard of living of the middle classes, without upsetting Chile's

Allende's socialist government had regarded foreign investment with deep suspicion.

With the grudging assent of the right-wing political parties, the Aylwin government raised corporate and income taxes to finance improvements in national health and education services. These had been squeezed of resources by the "Chicago boys", for whom state-run enterprises were anathema.

The new government also battled some fairly timid labor reforms through Congress to help improve wages and working conditions, and give the unions more strength to defend their members. These were much more

healthy balance of payments and finances.

The new center-left government, led by President Patricio Aylwin (1990–94), accepted the main tenets of the macroeconomic policies of the "Chicago boys". Even the Socialist Party admitted that "the market has the main role in assigning resources" and that a mixed economy with "all forms of property" is the best recipe for sustained growth. A member of the Socialist Party became minister of the economy, and part of his job was to attract ongoing foreign investment. Twenty years earlier, Salvador

controversial than the tax increases. The business community insisted that low wages for miners, forestry and industrial workers were crucial, if Chile's exports were to remain competitive in world markets. However, labor leaders argued that, without stronger unions, the workforce had no defense against routine abuses such as permanently renewable short-term contracts.

The Aylwin government did much to redress the worst social inequalities inherited from the military dictatorship. It increased teachers' pay, and poured money into the resource-starved national health service, which most of the popu-lation use.

LEFT: World Trade Center, Santiago.
ABOVE: life in an impoverished Santiago *población*.

Improvements to infrastructure

President Eduardo Frei, a son of the 1960s Christian Democrat president, succeeded President Aylwin in 1994, heading a government of the same center-left coalition. President Frei, a civil engineer by profession, paid less attention to social issues and his government concentrated on projects like improving roads and airports (usually through private concessions), and on privatizing ports and water companies, as well as launching a major school and criminal justice reforms. These reforms improved infrastructure and increased productivity as the key to competitive exports and sustained future growth.

President Ricardo Lagos was elected in 2000 and heads the center-left coalition's third government. A moderate socialist, he has sought to combine economic growth with greater social justice and to extend the benefits of increased prosperity not only to the poor, but also to provincial Chile. Despite slower economic growth from 1999 through to 2003, owing mainly to the weakness of international export markets, his government has, for example, introduced unemployment insurance and has embarked on a major reform of public and private health services in a bid to increase their efficiency and to achieve greater equality of access to care.

Future challenges

A national census, carried out in 2002, revealed a radical improvement in material welfare since the previous census a decade earlier. By 2002, 96 percent of Chile's homes had access to electricity, up by a fifth on 1992, and 91 percent had drinking water, representing an increase of more than a quarter. Similarly, 82 percent had a refrigerator, as compared with 55 percent in 1992, while 79 percent had a washing machine, as compared with 48 percent a decade earlier.

But for many Chileans, their democratically chosen governments have not lived up to expectations. As the country became better off, the number of people living in poverty dropped from 5 million in 1990 to just over 3 million by 2000; however, income distribution, which gives the richest tenth of the population about 42 percent of the national income, failed to improve.

According to the government, the foundations for ongoing export-led growth are in place. A free-trade agreement between Chile and the European Union came into effect in February 2003, followed at the beginning of 2004 by the implementation of a similar agreement with the United States. And, before it ends its term in 2006, the Lagos government hopes to seal an agreement with the giant Chinese market, a key purchaser of Chile's main commodity exports, led by copper.

By 2006, the government aims, through a targeted program, to have eradicated extreme poverty, and to have put a total end to the shanty towns that were once common on the outskirts of cities. However, it recognizes that an improvement in income distribution remains a challenge.

Although the economy is expected to show strong growth between 2004 and 2006, progress on income distribution will necessarily be slow, depending mainly on long-term projects, such as improving standards in state primary and secondary schools, which still fall far below those of the private schools attended by the elite.

In the meantime, however, material welfare will continue to increase, but many Chileans may continue to feel that they are still being left by the wayside. ❑

LEFT: the consumer society in full flush near the shops of Plaza de Armas, Santiago.
RIGHT: the main post office, Santiago.

THE CHILEANS

In a land where the "melting pot" has well and truly melted, social hierarchies are still firmly in place, but the contradictions are fascinating and change is afoot

For centuries lonely travelers have made brief visits to Chile that have stretched into lifetimes. Maybe that's because the Chileans are among the most contradictory and intriguing of Latin America's peoples. They are inherently careful and cautious – quite unlike their more effusive and spontaneous Argentine neighbors. Yet it was Chile that, in 1970, elected the socialist government of Salvador Allende beguiled by its promise of radical economic and social change, an experiment that ended in the tragedy of the 1973 military coup.

And the contradictions have continued. Chile is – as Isabel Allende points out in her nostalgic autobiographical book *Mi Pais Inventado* (My Invented Country) – the end of the line and about as far away as you can get from the world's main consumer markets. Yet, over the last twenty years, Chile has used international trade to build one of Latin America's most successful economies.

Chileans take great pride in this achievement and in their modern economy, and are avid users of the Internet and eager foreign travelers. Yet – another contradiction – the country remains an island of social conservatism that critics sometimes dub "Victorian Chile". Until recently, it was one of only a handful of Western countries not to have a divorce law.

For most of its history, Chile was cut off from the rest of the world by the Andes mountains in the east, the Atacama desert in the north, the Pacific Ocean on the west, and the Straits of Magellan and Antarctica in the south. Even during its period as a Spanish colony, Chile was on the periphery, an outpost that looked towards the Empire's center of operations in Peru.

Isabel Allende, in fact, describes her home country as an island. And that is key to understanding not only Chile's social conservatism,

but also many other aspects of the national character, including a fierce pride in all things Chilean. She advises foreign visitors "not to question the wonders they will hear about the country, its wine, and its women, because the foreigner is not allowed to criticize; for that, there are fifteen million Chileans, who do it all the time,"

Chile's roots

Chileans are primarily *mestizo*, the product of unions between the country's original peoples, especially the Mapuches of the south, and the Spanish colonizers. Chileans' great admiration for patriotic symbols, like the Spanish *conquistadores* and the great Mapuche guerilla fighters, is the source of another striking contradiction. They idolize both the conquerors and the natives who resisted them.

In the wealthy areas of Santiago and luxury vacation spots in southern Chile, shopping centers and resorts often have names of native origin. However, the native peoples themselves mostly live in poverty, whether it be in tradi-

---

PRECEDING PAGES: flea market find.
LEFT: chess break, Santiago.
RIGHT: a *huaso*, or Chilean cowboy.

tional rural communities or in the cities to which many have migrated. In addition, urban Chileans know surprisingly little about the country's indigenous cultures. In fact, they are likely to tell you they were "poor", especially by comparison with the Inca and Aztec cultures, and not really worthy of interest.

Physical beauty in Chile, as in many other Latin American countries, is associated with being tall, thin, and fair. By contrast, the Mapuches are brown-skinned with strikingly black hair, and tend to be short and stocky. Skin color in Chile is, in fact, synonymous with class – the whiter your skin, the higher your class.

New arrivals

A mixed bag of surnames bears testimony to the variety of settlers who followed the Spanish to Chile and eventually formed small foreign enclaves within the larger population. Ethnic groups include the Germans, immigrants from the former Yugoslavia and, more recently, the Spanish (exiled during the Civil War), the Arabs, the Italians and the Jews.

The German "colony" has played an important although sometimes ambivalent role in Chilean society *(see page 244)*. In the 18th century Ambrosio O'Higgins decided that the solution to Chile's perennial problem of col-

There are still many Aymara and other native communities high up in the northern Andes or on the border with Bolivia, while almost 400,000 Mapuches *(see page 79)* continue to live around the southern city of Temuco. Reduced to small patches of land, generally of poor quality, the Mapuches suffer from many of the ills of native peoples throughout the Americas. Those who haven't moved to the cities usually live in large extended families, cultivating wheat, corn, potatoes and vegetables.

Others combine farming with traditional handicrafts: woven ponchos, wood carvings, handmade ceramic pots and baskets can make a significant contribution to family economies.

onizing the lush but harsh territory of the Lake District was to import people from Europe. This idea was not implemented until the 19th century, when a presidential adviser, Vicente Pérez Rosales, began the task of recruiting Germans. In 1853, they founded the city of Puerto Montt on the shores of the Gulf of Reloncaví.

By 1860, more than 3,000 immigrants had built homes along Lago Llanquihue, and in Osorno, Río Bueno, La Unión and as far north as Valdivia. By 1900, 30,000 German colonists had cleared the native forests, planted crops and created small towns. Today, German surnames are still common, as is the language, and the area is famous for its sausages, cakes and pastries. Many small farmhouses offer *küchen* to passers-by.

British immigrants were also important in the nitrates industry and the construction of railroads, as well as in shipping and banking, particularly in the port of Valparaíso. Chileans have a great admiration for the British and like to call themselves the "English of South America" in reference to their phlegmatic temperament and lack of "tropical" excitability.

In 1998, that admiration faced a tough test

> **URBAN LIFE**
>
> Eighty-seven percent of the Chilean population lives in cities.

A small country

When one lives in Chile, one quickly realizes that in spite of the huge distances from north to south, it's a small country as far as the people are concerned. The same surnames crop up again and again in Chilean history – even today, a person's surname can help or hinder a career.

Chilean politics is rife with influential families wielding power publicly or behind the scenes, generation after generation. Even the democratic congress, which was elected in - December 1989 after 16 years of military rule,

among Pinochet supporters when the former dictator was arrested in London, where he liked to indulge in the pleasure of having tea with Margaret Thatcher (a bond built during the Falklands War when Chile provided discreet support to British troops). For a brief time, whisky was outlawed as a socially acceptable drink in these circles, but the general's supporters often returned from trips to visit him in London with conspicuously new Burberrys and, once the general was safely home, the incident was soon forgotten.

LEFT: romance on the Plaza de Armas, Santiago.
ABOVE: bringing in the coal, Lota.

was full of the brothers, sisters, sons and daughters of past and present leaders.

And although Santiago has a population of over 5 million, it's common to bump into friends and acquaintances, even if you haven't been there very long. That is partly because the people you'll meet tend to frequent just a few areas of the city, principally in the Las Condes and Providencia districts.

Newspapers also reinforce the small-town feeling. *El Mercurio*, the *grande dame* of the Chilean press, has a large section of social pages – at weekends, they take up more space than international news – in which the same faces appear time and again in events that range from the opening of art exhibitions to embassy cocktail parties.

That is also a reflection of the closely-knit nature of the Chilean political, business, and intellectual elite. Most of its members went to the same private schools and to the same universities, live in the same neighborhoods, and even take holidays in the same places.

It was this privileged upper class that felt most threatened by the reforms promised by the Popular Unity's experiment with socialism in the early 1970s and reacted with the violence that finally culminated in the military coup. For them, democracy was acceptable only so long

are where most of the working class lives.

Over the last ten years, increasing prosperity has gone a long way to reduce poverty – although it has made no dent on the country's extremely unequal income distribution. Around 3 million people countrywide, out of a population of 15 million, still live below the poverty line. However, shanty towns, once common on the periphery of large towns and cities, are gradually being eradicated and replaced by state-subsidized housing, often taking the form of the large and bleak apartment blocks that you'll see alongside any of the main roads into the city. These are cramped affairs but do, at least, have all the basic services.

as it did not upset the status quo – that is, the unequal social order.

If you're in Santiago long enough, you'll soon realize that the city is unusually segregated. There are virtually no areas in which different classes live side by side, and a person's home address is an almost fail-safe guide to social extraction. The moneyed elite, which has gradually moved out towards the mountains, now tend to live in La Dehesa or Vitacura, while Las Condes and Providencia are upper-middle-class territory, and nearby La Reina and Ñuñoa are popular with less conventional, but successful professionals. The west of the city and the densely populated southern outskirts

Winds of change

Beneath this rigid surface, social change is afoot in Chile, even if not apparent at first sight. The prosperity of the 1990s, when GDP almost doubled, laid the foundations of a new middle class. Materially ambitious, it apes the consumer habits of the moneyed elite, but has little time for their social conventions.

The development of this new class was temporarily halted in the late 1990s, when the Asian financial crisis brought high unemployment to Chile. But, as growth again gathers speed, it once more promises to become a force for a positive change.

The La Florida district of southern Santiago,

with its gleaming new malls and fast-food restaurants, is typical of this burgeoning middle class. Families tend to be small – two or three children at most, rather than the five or six that are common in La Dehesa – and both parents usually work. Money is tight and consumer borrowing, mainly through store cards, is high, but these families are buying their own homes, are ambitious for their children, and have a stake in the future.

Young people, both from this new middle class and from the moneyed elite, are another important force for change. More open to new ideas than their parents, they avidly follow

The Catholic church

In a national census in 2002, 70 percent of Chileans identified themselves as Roman Catholics. A much smaller number attend Mass regularly, but the country's exceptionally conservative Catholic church is still very powerful.

The Opus Dei and the Legionnaires of Christ, two bastions of conservatism within the Catholic church, are strong and very active in Chile. They control private schools and universities and have a great deal of influence in the business community and the media. In addition, the center-left government coalition is loath to flout the church because of the debt

Friends, Sex and the City, and other American soaps on cable television, and their life style has changed enormously since democracy was restored.

Ten years ago, most young people lived at home until they married. Today, they are marrying later and frequently move out to live on their own as soon as they have secured a job. And, increasingly, couples live together, something that was unheard of, and would have been considered shameful, only a few years ago.

LEFT: lunch with the family, alfresco.
ABOVE: young dancers in Santiago.

of gratitude it feels for the protection that some priests provided for victims of the dictatorship's human-rights abuses.

That helps to explain why divorce was not legalized in Chile until mid-2004 and then only in the teeth of fierce opposition from the Church. Previously, an ad hoc annulment system existed, based on the fiction that a marriage was invalid due to some administrative irregularity. However, that required the consent of both parties. The fact that just over half of children in Chile are born out of wedlock is partly the result of so many second partners being unable to obtain the freedom to remarry.

Abortion, even when a mother's life is at

risk, is illegal in Chile, although many abortions do in fact take place, either in expensive private hospitals, where they are disguised as some other operation, or in unregulated backstreet clinics. And, although the morning-after pill is now available on prescription, there was a great fuss when it was introduced.

Gay people also still have a hard time in Chile. Although tolerance reigns among young people, few gays come out, mostly for fear of hurting their families, or of being discriminated against at work. But now, at least, they

A YOUNG COUNTRY

Twenty-six percent of Chileans are under 15 years of age.

vasive. For generations it was customary for men to have two families – one with their wives and one with their mistresses. And today, the outskirts of cities are full of motels (some without so much as a sign to identify them) dedicated to renting beds, by the hour or the night, to couples desperate for a little sexual recreation.

The only difference is that Chileans are more discreet or, depending on your point of view, more hypocritical than in many other countries. Foreigners planning to settle in Chile are often given a piece of advice that sums up local lore:

have their own newspaper, *Opus Gay* (the name is a deliberate play on Opus Dei).

Chilean families

In keeping with Catholic morality, Chileans set a high value on the traditional family or, at least, claim to. Most like to think they're very attached to their families; certainly, families play a major role in the weekly rituals of visits, telephone calls, and Sunday lunches.

However. Chileans are no more, or less, faithful to their partners than in other countries. In general, the machismo of Chilean men is less obvious than that of other Latin American males. However, while subtle, it remains per-

behave as badly as you like, just don't make the mistake of talking about it.

Girls in Chile nowadays get just as much schooling as boys and tend to perform slightly better and, although a slightly smaller number of girls than boys go on to university, female university students are more likely to graduate than their male peers. However, in 2000, the United Nations Development Program found that only 37.6 percent of women in Chile were economically active, as compared with 48.1 percent in Colombia, 43.8 percent in Brazil and 39.4 percent in Mexico.

Moreover, in Chile, relatively few women reach positions of power either in the private or public sector. Under President Ricardo Lagos, 5 out of 15 Cabinet ministers are women, up from 3 out of 21 under his predecessor, President Eduardo Frei, but only 15 of the 120 seats in the lower house of Congress, and 2 of the 48 Senate seats are held by women. Similarly, few women occupy board seats in large companies and no major company currently has a female CEO.

A hard-working country

Chile has worked hard for its economic success and expatriate business people posted to Chile are often surprised by the long hours put in by their Chilean staff. Schools start at eight in the morning so many parents, after dropping their children off, are in the office by half past eight and usually stay there until at least seven. Nor do Chileans indulge in long lunches – unless business is being discussed, an hour is the norm.

Overseas executives frequently complain that they find it embarrassingly difficult to head for home at half past five, or whatever is their usual time. That is perhaps also one reason why so few Chilean women work, despite the availability of domestic service.

Chileans are often very late for social appointments, but for business meetings, they are rarely more than 10 minutes behind schedule. And, in one of the keys to Chile's success in attracting foreign investment, they are reliable. Their word is their bond and corruption, although it certainly exists, is scarce by Latin American and even international standards. In many neighboring countries, taxi drivers will happily tell you the amount of the bribe expected for different traffic offenses; in Chile, an attempt to bribe a policeman is more likely to get you arrested.

Chile's economic success is the source of some irritation among neighboring countries. Immigration, particularly from Peru, is common, with immigrants often taking jobs as, for example, live-in maids that most Chileans now shun.

Folk traditions

Scratch any Chilean, no matter how urban, or sophisticated in appearance, and you'll find someone superstitious and sentimental about the country's folklore. September is the best month for observing Chile's folk traditions, as Chileans dust off their ponchos and handker-

LEFT: happy bakers.
RIGHT: Mapuche woman.

chiefs and get ready to celebrate Independence Day on September 18.

For children, the traditional pastime is kite flying; for adults, it's lots of *chicha* (fermented grape juice) and *empanadas* (savory turnover); and for just about everybody it means at least one visit to the *fondas*, eucalyptus-roofed shelters that suddenly crowd empty lots, turning them into improvised dancehalls.

The *cueca* is Chile's official national dance and September is also the best time to catch a glimpse of everyone from the national president down, strutting their stuff and doing some serious flirting as men, women and chil-

dren stomp the floor in the traditional one-two rhythm, twirl their handkerchiefs and generally go after each other in what is supposed to be a stylized imitation of mating chickens.

You'll also see *cumbias*, *corridas*, rock and jive, since cultural influences from more northerly countries are also strong.

Each of Chile's various regions has its own version of the *cueca* and there's also a kind of class division between the *cueca patronal* (boss's *cueca*), characterized by the women's elegant dresses and men's colorful ponchos and shiny black boots with silver spurs, and the *cueca campesina* (peasant's cueca), whose performers are far more simply dressed and go barefoot. The dance's formal gestures and rather strict stereotyping between the aggressive, strutting male and the shy, fluttery female have changed over the years and young people's versions of the dance often challenge more traditional versions. Chile's folk traditions are more than skin deep. They include a wide variety of folk music which varies from the Andean music of the Altiplano (high plain) prevalent in the north, to the music of Chiloé towards the south, and various ethnic songs and dances, particularly of Yugoslavian origin, around Punta Arenas.

> ### LONG LIFE
>
> The average life expectancy in Chile is 77 years of age.

Payadores are grassroots poets and musicians, who engage each other in witty, passionate poetic duels whenever they meet. This may be during a barbecue in the Andes mountains or in a smoky city café.

Folk traditions include stories about each region's original inhabitants, be they human, ghostly, godly, mythical or immortal. Popular beliefs have blended with grassroots medical knowledge to create different kinds of faith healers. *Mal de ojo* (evil eye) is still considered a common cause of stomach and other health problems and the person most equipped to cure it is still the *curandera*, whose knowledge of herbal – and magical – medicine works more frequently than skeptics might care to believe. Maybe it's not surprising that in a country of such intense geological activity, earthquakes are central to Chileans' mentality. Popular wisdom has it that every (democratic) government in Chile gets welcomed into office by an earthquake – an act of God which was conspicuously absent after the 1973 military coup.

Meaty gatherings

One of the most cherished social events among all age groups is the *asado* – a huge steak or roast cooked over hot coals, not to be compared with the rather squalid (at least to Chileans' eyes) hamburgers and hot dogs that you might find at North American or Australian barbecues. This ceremony usually occurs either in someone's backyard or in a park. While the men compare recipes and worry about how the meat is shaping up, the women prepare huge tomato, potato and other salads. Everyone drinks abundant quantities of red wine, and the meal ends with sweet desserts or whatever fruit is in season (or both).

Chileans generally like foreigners and treat them well, but foreigners here remain so all their lives. Unlike some other New World countries, where the population consists mainly of immigrants, it often takes several generations for a family of foreign origin to become accepted as Chileans. Perhaps the best source of behind-the-polite-smile information about Chileans are Chilean writers. Chile may be a small country, but when it comes to literature it's a giant. Two Nobel prize-winning poets, Gabriela Mistral (1945) and Pablo Neruda (1971) have plumbed Chileans' contradictions and aspirations through their work, which is widely available in English translation.

Chilean novelists have participated in the "boom" in Latin American literature. José Donoso, Jorge Edwards and, more recently, Ariel Dorfman, Isabel Allende, Poli Délano and Antonio Skármeta, have explored Chilean events and psychology in books with universal appeal, enhanced in many cases by prolonged experience abroad. Allende's books are all available in English either through inclusion in anthologies or translation of full books. ❏

LEFT: relaxing over drinks in an urban bar.
RIGHT: harvesters in the Lake district.

THE MAPUCHES

*Unconquered until the late 19th century, the native people of the Araucanía
now struggle to maintain their culture in cities as well as in their homelands*

*What we've achieved
with the civilization
they say they have given us
is to live squeezed together
like wheat in a sack*
—Lorenzo Colimán

The Mapuche people, in their myriad mythologies, believe in a perfect balance between the positive and negative forces present in every act. Ngenechen, the positive god, represents the forces of life, creation and love. His counterpart is Wekufu, god of death and destruction. It is in these terms that the Mapuches understand the meeting of European and American cultures 500 years ago.

For Native Americans and their descendants, the arrival of Christopher Columbus meant the destruction of the delicate balance of forces which had until then sustained their culture, their way of life, their language, their habitat, their religion and their people. Wekufu's spirit threw its mantle over the world's boundaries, leaving Ngenechen unable to keep up his end of the balance.

The Spanish passion for gold overwhelmed the "love of god" or "loyalty to the crown" that they used as excuses to commit abuses against indigenous peoples. The Mapuches, living in the continent's extreme south, were not exempt from this treatment. But their reaction was a long and often successful resistance to the theft of their lands and the violation of their traditions.

A hierarchical society

The Mapuches, or "people of the earth," were used to living from the earth's fruits and from hunting. They lived in scattered settlements from the Aconcagua Valley in the north, as far south as the Island of Chiloé. They also inhabited most of what is now Argentine Patagonia.

The Mapuches had, and still have today, a relatively hierarchical society based on family

LEFT: Mapuche woman in traditional clothes, Temuco.
RIGHT: young musician.

structures. Women played a major role in the mystical and mythological aspects of society. Only *they* were allowed to communicate directly with the gods, and their functions were distributed according to the type of forces they represented. The gods of life, for example, would communicate with women called the

Machi; those of death, with the *Kalku*. Music always accompanied their rituals, particularly percussion instruments like the *kultrun* and the *trompe*, and wind instruments like the *trutrucas* and wooden whistles. Oratory skills were of prime importance to the Mapuches and their language, *Mapudungun*, reached truly poetic heights as it captured extensive images within its sounds.

Freedom-lovers

During the first 100 years of war between the Mapuches and the Spanish the northern limit of their territories was reduced to the Bíobío River, a border that remained established for more than 300 years. The cross and the sword could not defeat the lances of the naked-chested Mapuches, and the Spanish Crown was finally forced to negotiate. It recognized borders and established trade and transport agreements between the territories.

Many historians who defend the Spanish cause speak of the Mapuches as belonging to a "military race" or being a "fierce people". Nevertheless, the testimony of friars who accompanied the Conquest indicates that the Mapuches were peaceful and friendly. It

HALF MAN HALF BEAST

When the Conquest started, the Mapuches believed the Spanish attacker and his horse were one creature, unbeatable, a god which had come to conquer them.

became convenient for pro-Spanish historians to paint the Mapuches as "ferocious warriors" in order to justify their side's defeat. But the Mapuches are and were a peaceful, humble people, dedicated to their land and their traditions. The reasons for the long struggle are not to be found so much in their "warrior virtues" but rather in a profound dignity and immense love for their land and their freedom.

Their devotion to their own cultural values led the Mapuches to acts of great heroism and impassioned resistance. They quickly learned about their enemy and its weapons, and developed the tactics necessary to defend themselves.

Perhaps the most striking reason for the

Spaniards' inability to conquer the Mapuches was that, unlike the Incas and Aztecs, they had no central authority. Their political and economic organization was based on the family. The family head was the polygamous *cacique* (pronounced "ka-see-kay"), or *lonko*. He could have as many as 10 wives, forming an extended family group of up to 500 members.

The *lonko* developed his prestige through the accumulation of wealth and the wise advice that he gave to youths inclined to fight among themselves. Faced with a warlike situation, the Mapuches chose a *toqui* as their leader, and their peacetime authority was the *ulmen*. Both were chosen for their gifts for public speaking and their decision-making abilities.

Alliances between *caciques* were established to develop economic activities like the gathering in of breeding stock, hunting and fruit collection, and the benefits were shared among the participating members.

This loose organization meant that the Spanish could not seize control through capture of a single political leader. The Mapuches didn't have villages to harass and destroy. While they weren't nomads in the strict sense of the term, they lived in *rucas* or huts, which they moved from place to place according to need.

Lautaro the liberator

When the Spanish began their advance they were fast and efficient, but when the Mapuches realized that these horsebacked attackers were only human they began to develop unique military strategies to defend their land. Lautaro, a Mapuche who was barely 20 years old, escaped from the Spanish camps where his intelligence had caused him to be trained as the page of the *conquistador* Pedro de Valdivia. He was chosen as *toqui*, leader of the *caciques*, to lead the war against the invaders.

Lautaro – who now knew the language, weapons, tactics and weaknesses of the enemy – taught his warriors to ride. They became better horsemen than the Spaniards. He also developed two combat tactics which today are recognized as the beginning of guerilla warfare in this continent. The first was "mounted infantry" where each rider also carried along a foot-soldier holding onto the horse's tail. This allowed rapid movement of large parties of fighters. The second and more devastating tactic was the constant replacement of squadrons: each group fought ferociously for 15 to 20 minutes before being replaced. The Spanish soldiers labored under their heavy armor, and finally yielded to the waves of native fighters who, fresh and rested, gave them no respite.

These tactics led to enormous victories for Lautaro, who not only killed Pedro de Valdivia himself, but also secured for his people all the southern territories, burning and destroying the Spanish forts until, after four years of victorious campaigns, he reached the gates of Santiago.

dreams of freedom for his people. The *conquistadores* appeared wearing the armor of their period, but they carried machine guns and wore dark glasses – a clear reference to the Chilean military government's political police, who were active at the time.

The last uprising

The last general uprising of Chile's indigenous peoples took place in 1881. This time it was directed against the now-Chilean republic, which was doing everything possible to take over the southern lands. Mapuche *huerquenes*, messengers especially educated for eloquence

During Lautaro's northward push, many Yanaconas, another indigenous people who had until then formed part of the Spanish troops, joined Lautaro's forces. One of these betrayed Lautaro, killing him while he rested in his tent the night before the great assault on the capital. This was a terrible blow to the Mapuches, who decided to retreat southward, where they continued to defend "their" border for 300 years.

In 1985, a distinguished Chilean playwright, Isidora Aguirre, presented the play *Lautaro* in which this historic character has prophetic

LEFT: a Mapuche *cacique* on horseback.
ABOVE: traditional weaving.

and good memories, began to travel through mountains and valleys, bearing knotted red cords around their wrists. Every day they undid one knot. When these were all gone, the *caciques* simultaneously attacked the forts, towns and missions of the Chileans. With hindsight this was an impossible attempt given the Chileans' superior weaponry, but it demonstrates once again the Mapuches' dedication to their independence and freedom.

The army, fresh from its victories in a war against Peru and Bolivia, suffocated the bloody rebellion and from then, the Mapuches became farmers of small, individual plots. Their land was now the poorest in Chile.

Integration and adaptation

Throughout the 1880s, the indigenous territories shrank. A decree made Araucanía (the Mapuche territory) property of the state, and a colonization process began in which the native people received very little for their land. Along with this, a process of cultural transformation began. It was a time of fear, disease, hunger and loss of identity as the Mapuches became an ethnic minority within Chilean society.

> **POWERFUL FRIENDS**
>
> The Workers' Federation of Chile (FOCH) became the Mapuches' voice in Santiago, declaring them "brothers in the suffering of the poor of city and country."

The 20th century saw three reactions to this

process. The first, encouraged by missionaries, was to press for the total integration of the Mapuches into Chilean society. Education and evangelization would "absorb" the Mapuche culture. This later became the policy of the 1973–90 Pinochet dictatorship, which decreed an Indian Law that allowed the Mapuches to split their collectively held land into small farms with individual titles. With no access to credit or technology, many were forced to sell their land to wealthy landowners.

The second reaction was a modified form of integration which, in 1914, inspired one group of Mapuches to develop a special school which taught Spanish but valued indigenous cultural

traditions. The children of several *caciques* studied here. This tendency continues to exist, and there are many Mapuche groups that try to keep their traditional culture alive. The third reaction was to reject any integration and seek to recover their stolen lands and culture. The first attempts were led by Manuel Aburto Manquilef, a descendant of *caciques*, who mobilized huge numbers of Mapuches in search of their own identity. This movement insisted that the central problem was the seizure of the Mapuche lands. Its activists revived the rites and traditions of the *malones* (meetings to listen to dreams and predict the future) and *machitunes* (collective prayers to the gods). It organized many congresses and made the native voice heard in Santiago.

One of the great merits of this group was its ability to find allies within other social movements of the period. Its leaders had the vision to recognize that the problem wasn't simply between Mapuches and *huincas* (the name that the Mapuches gave to the Spanish invader), but rather between the wealthy and the poor. This led to the Mapuches' own struggle being more generally recognized as one of the social problems of the 1930s.

The Workers' Federation of Chile (FOCH) became the Mapuches' mouthpiece in Santiago, helping them to participate in mainstream politics through the Democratic Party and eventually through elected representatives in the House of Deputies.

However, under the Pinochet dictatorship, Mapuche organizations were heavily repressed, and many native people were arrested and "disappeared".

An Indian Peoples Law was passed by the new democratic government, but failed to live up to the expectations of the Mapuches who, in the 1990s, found a new enemy – the expanding forestry industry. As well as occupying land claimed by Mapuche communities, the industry has, according to many communities, dried up their water supply, as well as depriving them of access to the woods that are their traditional source of fuel, medicinal plants and food.

Another focus of protest in the 1990s was the construction of the vast Ralco hydroelectric dam on the upper reaches of the Bíobío River. The reservoir, which began to be filled in mid-

2004, will flood land belonging to some of the last remaining communities of Pehuenches, a branch of the Mapuches.

The border lands today.

A national census in 2002 found that Chile's indigenous population – of which the Mapuches are by far the largest group – reached just under 700,000, representing 4.6 percent of the total population. Many Mapuches have migrated to the cities, particularly Santiago, where they often form tight-knit communities, notably in the La Pintana district of southern Santiago, and keep traditional customs alive.

insufficient income to cover basic food needs).

Considerable progress has been made since 1990 in taking basic services, particularly electricity, to indigenous communities, and in improving roads. However, the intensely proud Mapuches – who consider themselves the "true Chileans" – resent their lack of political status. Chile is the only Latin American country that does not afford its Amerindian minorities constitutional recognition, and no Mapuches – or, indeed, members of other ethnic groups, sit in Congress. Moreover, their lack of say, even at a local government level, in decisions that affect their lives also means that too many well-

In a recent initiative, the national health service has, in some of these areas, begun to offer Mapuche remedies for minor ailments.

However, almost 400,000 Mapuches still live in communities south of the Bíobío River and Araucanía has one of the country's highest poverty rates. A survey in 2000 found that almost a third of the population was below the poverty line, as compared with 16 percent in Santiago, and that just over one in ten was extremely poor (defined as a family with

intentioned government initiatives have failed dismally to achieve their objective.

A few radical Mapuche organizations remain active, and violence occasionally flares up in Araucanía, directed mostly against forestry companies or local *huinca* farmers. Most communities, although they do not directly support these organizations, defend their methods as a useful tactic in the struggle for greater recognition.

The fire in Chile's south has not yet gone out. The spirits of Ngenechen and Wekufu still wander, caressing *canelo* trees and araucaria pines – the Mapuches' sacred trees. They still seek a balance between life and death, good and evil. And justice. ❏

LEFT: traditionally dressed Mapuche woman in a village near Temuco.
ABOVE: family with traditional Mapuche house.

A CULTURAL RENAISSANCE

After contributing to the downfall of the Pinochet dictatorship, the arts in Chile have helped the country to come to terms with the traumatic events of that period

To be seventeen again
After living a hundred years
Is like deciphering signs
Without the wisdom of experience
Suddenly to again become
As fragile as a second in time
To again feel deeply
Like a child before God
That is what I feel
At this fertile time.

—Violeta Parra

The moving simplicity of Violeta Parra's voice, accompanied by a lone guitar, echoes through each of her recordings, bearing testimony to the inspiration of a woman who sang to life, but succumbed to death. Her song *Gracias a la Vida* (Thanks to Life) – composed ironically after one of her suicide attempts – is one of Latin America's best-loved songs. It has since been recorded by artists of the stature of Joan Báez, Argentina's Mercedes Sosa, and Cuba's Omara Portuondo, the female star of Buena Vista Social Club. Violeta Parra's influence marked the development of popular music in Chile from the 1960s onwards and her offspring have continued to play a prominent role in the arts.

A tragic star

Violeta was born in the south of Chile. Her family was poor, but artistically prolific. It produced not only Violeta, but also such different and imposing figures as her brother Nicanor (Chile's "anti-poet" and a many-time Nobel candidate), and Roberto, the creator of a new style of *cueca* (Chile's national dance) and the author of *La Negra Ester* (Black Esther), the play seen by the largest number of people ever in Chile's history.

Violeta received little recognition during her lifetime, either from critics or the public. Her

PRECEDING PAGES: Chile's social struggle seen in art.
LEFT: jazz concert in the Bellavista district, Santiago.
RIGHT: Violeta Parra.

work was characterized both by the incomprehension with which it was met, and by the irrepressible creativity seen both in her music and her tapestries, which have been exhibited in the Louvre art gallery in Paris. The appreciation of her work outside Chile led Violeta to settle in France for two years, a period during which she

VIOLETA PARRA
(CHILE)

toured Europe. But, in 1965, she returned to Chile where, apparently overwhelmed by frustration, isolation, and an ill-fated love affair, she committed suicide in 1967, depriving the country of one of its most lucid voices.

Music of the turbulent 1960s

The social upheaval of the 1960s was a propitious moment for Violeta to pioneer a quest to rediscover Chile's musical roots. At that time, a stylized vision of traditional folklore predominated, based on an idealized image of the countryside and farm life. This was reflected in the jingle-like versions of traditional songs, sung by city-bred *huasos*

(Chile's typical small farmer), which Chilean radios played, interspersed with *Nueva Ola* (New Wave) music that imitated overseas stars. Violeta not only toured the countryside, rescuing songs and rhythms that were in danger of extinction, but also revitalized urban lyrics, using them to refer to current events. For the first time, the *tonada* and the *trote* (traditional musical expressions in the north of the country) spoke of social injustice, inequality, and class struggle.

The *Peña de los Parra*, founded by Violeta and her children, Angel and Isabel, in 1965, served as a stage for many of the musicians

Worker), *Te Recuerdo Amanda* (I Remember You, Amanda), *Luchín* (Little Luis), and *El Derecho de Vivir en Paz* (The Right to Live in Peace), pay tribute to the dispossessed and the working class, and it was through his work that university students came to know the New Song movement.

In 1966, Jara became the artistic director of a new group, Quilapayún (Three Bearded Men), founded by the brothers Eduardo and Julio Carrasco, and Julio Numhauser. Jara's musical knowledge and theatrical experience helped to transform this group into an icon of the New Song movement. With their black flowing pon-

who followed in her footsteps. Located in central Santiago, at Carmen 340, this modest, but vibrant club became the headquarters of a new type of music: *La Nueva Canción Chilena* (Chilean New Song). Patricio Manns, author of *Arriba en la Cordillera* (Up in the Mountains), as well as Isabel and Angel Parra, were prominent in this movement, from which Victor Jara, a key figure in Chilean popular music and an icon of the struggle against social inequality, was to spring.

Victor Jara, a young actor and theater director, shared Violeta's humble beginnings, as well as her deep social concerns. His songs, such as *Plegaria a Un Labrador* (Public Prayer to a

GRACIAS A LA VIDA
BY VIOLETA PARRA

Gracias a la vida, que me ha dado tanto
Me dio dos luceros, que cuando los abro
Perfecto distingo, lo negro del blanco
Y en el alto cielo, su fondo estrellado
Y en las multitudes, la mujer que amo

Thanks to life, which has given me so much
It has given me two eyes, which, when I open them
I can clearly distinguish black from white
And in the infinite sky, its starry depths
And in the crowds of people, the woman I love.

chos, they epitomized the masculine force of Latin America's folklore repertoire, and were soon followed by Inti-Illimani, a group that also collaborated closely with Jara.

Violeta's suicide, at the age of 49, in *La Carpa de la Reina*, her tent-home in Santiago's La Reina district, which also served as a music club and cultural center, did not silence her voice. Her compositions continue to be regarded as a pinnacle of Latin American folklore.

A fertile time

The political polarization of the late 1960s, and the election of Salvador Allende's Popu-

State support for the arts was reflected in the creation of the Dicap label, which produced recordings of many popular songs. This was the period when Luis Advis composed the Cantata Popular Santa María de Iquique, performed by Quilapayún, which recalls the massacre of miners that took place in the Santa María de Iquique school in 1907, an event that was ignored by history books, but engraved in the memory of northern Chile.

The 1970s saw the emergence of a new strand of the New Song movement, when a younger generation took the elements and instruments of Latin American folklore and

lar Unity government, proved fertile ground for the New Song movement. Recognized as the voice of the Allende government, left-wing artists became exponents of the official ideology. So much was this the case that one of Victor Jara's songs was used each day to start the transmissions of the state television channel. And both Quilapayún – with *El Pueblo Unido* (The People United) as the battle hymn of the Popular Unity coalition – and the Parra family were a staple part of government ceremonies.

LEFT: dancing the *cueca*, Chile's national dance.
ABOVE: instruments for sale.

TE RECUERDO, AMANDA
BY VICTOR JARA

Te recuerdo Amanda, la calle mojada
corriendo a la fábrica, donde trabajaba Manuel
La sonrisa ancha, la lluvia en el pelo
no importaba nada, ibas a encontrarte con el
con el, con el, con el ...

I think of you Amanda, in the wet street
running toward the factory, where Manuel worked
With a broad smile, the rain in your hair
Nothing mattered, you were meeting up with him,
with him, with him, with him ...

merged them with rock music. The result was revolutionary and *Todos Juntos* (Together), sung by Los Jaivas, became a symbol to an entire generation – so much so that, in 1999, when Chileans were asked to vote for their favorite song with which to greet the new millennium, this was the title they chose.

Originating from Valparaíso and influenced by the hippy movement, Los Jaivas are recognized as the founding fathers of Chilean rock. Together with Los Blops and Congreso, they formed a generation whose careers in Chile were cut short by the military coup of September 11, 1973.

After the 1973 coup

The seizure of power by the armed forces meant the death or exile of the icons of the New Song movement. Inti-Illimani and Quilapayún were performing in Europe at the time of the coup but Victor Jara, who was immediately arrested, was brutally tortured and shot in the *Estadio Chile* (Chile Stadium) – now known as *Estadio Victor Jara* – but not before he had written the poem *Somos Cinco Mil* (We are Five Thousand) in reference to the number of prisoners with whom he shared his last hours. His mutilated body was identified by his British wife, Joan Turner, in the morgue. Angel Parra also suffered at the hands of the dictatorship,

first as a prisoner in the National Stadium and then in the Chacabuco concentration camp, where he composed the *Oratorio de Navidad* (Christmas Oratorio). Los Jaivas emigrated to Argentina and then France, where they were joined by Quilapayún and Illapu, a group that had become famous thanks to their song *Candombe para José* (Candombe for José).

World attention

This exile had unanticipated consequences for Chilean music. Awakening the sympathy of the countries where they were granted asylum, these groups sang songs of protest against General Augusto Pinochet to an international audience. As a result Inti-Illimani, for example, sold more than a million records in Italy alone. But, while their music was acclaimed abroad, cultural repression reigned in Chile as the military attempted to stamp out any hint of ideological opposition. Records made during the Popular Unity government were banned, and music was strictly censored under the guise of a supposed patriotism that brought about a revival of sentimental *huaso* songs, performed by groups such as Los Quincheros and Los Cuatro Cuartos.

The growing discontent felt by many Chileans found an echo in the work of exiled artists, which was smuggled into the country, and the New Song movement was kept alive as a vehicle for expressing – between the lines – opposition to the dictatorship. Groups such as Schwenke y Nilo, Huara, and Sol y Lluvia peppered their songs with contemporary references that escaped the military's grasp.

Into a new era

In the 1980s, in France, Los Jaivas launched *Las Alturas de Macchu Picchu* (The Heights of Macchu Picchu), a conceptual album that set to music the words of Chilean poet, Pablo Neruda. The acclaim with which this album was received was such that the group was allowed to return to Chile to perform at massively attended concerts.

It was at this time that Los Prisioneros, a band from San Miguel, a working-class district of Santiago, made its appearance. Mixing punk, rock, and techno music, with the angry lyrics of its vocalist, Jorge González, the trio was a phenomenon in its own right. Songs like *La Voz de los Ochenta* (The Voice of the Eighties), *El Baile de los que Sobran* (The Dance of the

Excluded) or *Muevan las Industrias* (Get the Industries Moving), spoke of discontent with the system and openly complained about lack of opportunities. Despite the efforts of the dictatorship, the band became a reference point for an entire generation, as cassettes were passed from hand to hand. Los Prisioneros also opened the way for many other new bands, which took their place in the late 1980s, when they broke up.

The end of the most brutal period of the dictatorship gradually permitted the return of exiled musicians, who became influential in the protest movement that, in 1988, culminated in

The return of democracy brought with it a new generation of musicians. Los Tres, a band from Concepción in southern Chile, led by Alvaro Henríquez and including Angel Parra, a grandson of Violeta, were in the forefront of this generation. Mixing the rockabilly of Chuck Berry with the lyrics of Roberto Parra, Los Tres – the first Chilean group to record an unplugged session for MTV – gave new popularity to the *cueca*, freeing it from the stigma it had acquired when harnessed to the dictatorship's efforts to foster patriotic support.

By dint of combining pop with Anglo-Saxon esthetics, another Chilean band, La

the "No" vote against General Pinochet. These musicians, turning their guitars on the dictatorship, were a key feature of the demonstrations that, in the run-up to 1988, encouraged increasing numbers of Chileans to show their previously mute opposition to the regime.

The end of the dictatorship brought a weakening of the New Song movement. Once Pinochet was no longer in power, many of the rallying calls that had made these groups so popular became an anachronism. It was time for renovation.

LEFT: Victor Jara.
ABOVE: Chilean group Inti Illimani in concert.

Ley, successfully launched an international career, triumphing in Mexico, becoming popular in the United States, and going on to win a Grammy award.

Thanks to Tiro de Gracia, hip-hop and rap also made a re-appearance in Chile. This group, from an extremely poor background, became a top-seller with its album *Ser Humano* (Human Being). Overseas influence was apparent in the Brazilian rhythms of Joe Vasconcellos (the former drummer of Congreso) while Gondwana, filled the radios with reggae. This growing diversity was further expanded by Chancho en Piedra (funk) and Lucybell (rock).

The turn of the 21st century brought the

appearance of Los Pettinellis (led by Alvaro Henríquez, formerly of Los Tres), Los Bunkers, and the return of Los Prisioneros who, on two consecutive days, filled the 70,000-seat National Stadium. Violeta Parra's music also returned to the rankings with *Arriba Quemando el Sol* (Up Where the Sun Burns), part of an album recorded by the country's main young bands as a tribute to her.

In 2003, both old and new musicians joined together to mark the anniversary of the deaths of Salvador Allende and Victor Jara. The two concerts – in the National Stadium and in the Victor Jara Stadium – served to demonstrate

1919 documentary *Recuerdos del Mineral de El Teniente* (Memories of the El Teniente Mine) and, in 1926, Pedro Sienna, an actor, producer and director, made the film *El Húsar de la Muerte* (The Hussar of Death) about the life of Manuel Rodríguez, one of the heroes of Chile's independence from Spain. Other films made in this early period include *Sueño de Amor* (Dream of Love) in which Chilean pianist Claudio Arrau played the role of Franz Liszt.

In the 1940s, Corfo, Chile's economic development agency, which had been created in 1938 to promote industrialization, supported film making through its subsidiary, Chile Films. The

that Chile's collective memory, and its music, today have a common root. This was further underlined in February 2004 when, on the stage of Viña del Mar's annual song festival, Los Pettinellis played a rock version of the anthem of the Popular Unity government, *El Pueblo Unido*, while giant screens showed images of Allende and Pinochet. A few days later, Inti-Illimani played for the first time at this mainstream festival.

A moving image of Chile

Film making in Chile dates back to the early 20th century when Salvador Giambastiani and his wife, Gabriela von Bussenius, made the

company boasted what were then South America's most advanced studios and, in its heyday, produced films like José Bohr's *La Dama sin Camelias* (The Lady without Camellias), Adelqui Millar's *Tormenta en el Alma* (Torment in the Soul), Eugenio de Luigoro's *Memorias de un Chofer de Taxi* (Memories of a Taxi Driver), and René Olivares' *Yo Vendo unos Ojos Negros* (I Sell Black Eyes).

In 1949, the film *Esperanza* (Hope) by Argentina's Francisco Mujica and Eduardo Boneo marked the beginning of the studios' decline and, throughout the 1950s, its output reached an average of only one film per year.

However, in the early 1960s, the University

of Chile set up its Department of Experimental Cinema and, tapping into special state subsidies, triggered a revival of activity. The box-office successes of this period include *Ayúdame Usted Compadre* (Help Me, Mate) by Germán Becker, which was seen by 370,000 movie-goers, while *Tres Tristes Tigres* (Three Sad Tigers) by the now-famous director Raúl Ruiz was, despite critical acclaim, seen by only 17,000. In 1969, *Caliche Sangriento* (Blood-Stained Nitrate) by Helvio Soto challenged the official version of the 19th-century War of the Pacific, focusing on the economic interests that triggered it, and was considered offensive by the establishment.

In 1970, Miguel Littin directed a key film in Chile's cinema history: *El Chacal de Nahueltoro* (The Jackal of Nahueltoro). This recounts the true story of a man who, while under the influence of alcohol, murdered his partner and children. The incident caused considerable public commotion at the time, not only because of the brutal nature of the crime, but also because of the murderer's fate. A man of virtually no education, he changed dramatically while in prison, acquiring schooling and reformed attitudes. However, despite this, the courts showed no mercy and he was executed by a firing squad. Littin's film was a success both with spectators and critics.

During the Popular Unity government, only nine films were produced, despite state incentives. It was in this period that Raúl Ruiz made *Palomita Blanca* (White Dove) – although it was not screened until 1993 – and Patricio Guzmán, a documentary-maker who has recorded much of Chile's recent history, made *El Primer Año* (The First Year).

After the military coup, many filmmakers were forced into exile while those that remained in the country mostly made commercial advertising. Nonetheless, seven full-length films were shot in Chile between 1973 and 1985. These include *A la Sombra del Sol* (In the Shadow of the Sun) by Silvio Caiozzi and Pablo Perelman, *Julio Comienza en Julio* (Julio Begins in July) by Silvio Caiozzi, and *Los Hijos de la Guerra Fría* (Children of the Cold War) by Gonzalo Justiniano.

Since the return of democracy, film production has boomed. Initially, films tended to focus on politic issues, such as *La Frontera* (The Frontier) by Ricardo Larraín, about the relegation to remote areas of the country used by the dictatorship to punish its opponents. However, an increasing number of films have gradually sought to depict the everyday life of Chileans. Examples of this type of film include *La Luna en el Espejo* (The Moon in the Mirror) by Silvio Caiozzi (for which Gloria Münchmeyer won the Best Actress Award at the Venice Film Festival in 1990); *Johnny Cien Pesos* (Hundred-Peso Johnny) by Gustavo Graef-Marino, based on the true story of a hold-up in

Santiago that went wrong and ended with hostages taken; and *Historias de Fútbol* (Football Tales) by Andrés Wood. More recently, this movement also produced *Taxi para Tres* (Taxi for Three), directed, written and produced by Orlando Lübbert, which received the best-film award at the San Sebastián Film Festival in 2001.

Reflecting social change

Films made in recent years have also begun to mirror changing attitudes towards sex and, by challenging taboos, have helped to push back the frontiers of public discussion. The success of *El Chacotero Sentimental* (The Sentimental

LEFT: musicians perform at a political rally.
RIGHT: poster for the protest group Quilapayún.

Teaser), based on a radio phone-in in which young listeners talk about their sex life, and the more recent *Sexo con Amor* (Sex with Love) are a clear sign that Chileans are avid to see themselves portrayed on the screen with their behavior, and its virtues and defects, stripped naked.

Chile on stage

The theater in Chile has survived in the face of constant difficulties. Its inventiveness allowed it to survive the dictatorship and even to serve as a channel for veiled criticism, particularly by the Ictus group. And, since the return of democracy, it has taken on a new lease of life,

Local playwrights, such as Ramón Griffero, Marco Antonio de la Parra, Egon Wolff, Juan Radrigán, and Benjamín Galemiri, regularly stage plays and, as audiences become better acquainted with the theater, are expanding the range that is on offer. However, barring a few theaters, such as the new Matucana 100 Cultural Center, located near western Santiago's Quinta Normal museum area, infrastructure remains precarious.

One of the few Chilean playwrights to have triumphed abroad is Ariel Dorfman, whose *La Muerte y la Doncella* (Death and the Maiden) was made into a film in 1994 by Roman Polan-

thanks to initiatives like Teatro a Mil (Theater for a Thousand Pesos). Because of its accessible price and its focus on comedies and other plays with a ready appeal, this annual event draws an audience far wider than that of traditional theater productions.

Prominent local theater groups include La Troppa. Its three members, Juan Carlos Sagall, Jaime Lorca and Laura Pizarro – who reject the traditional hierarchical authority of a director – have worked together since the mid-1980s. After their first great success, *Pinocchio*, the group went on to stage *Gemelos* (Identical Twins), a play about war that brought them recognition in Europe.

ski. This play tells the story of the encounter of the protagonist (Signourey Weaver in the film) with her former torturer.

However, perhaps the most venerated figure of Chilean theater is Andrés Pérez. A director and choreographer, he studied for six years at the Théâtre du Soleil in France, before returning to Chile to found and direct the Gran Circo Teatro, which mounted many memorable productions. However, Pérez, who died of Aids in 2002, is most remembered as the director of *La Negra Ester,* Chile's most popular play ever. ❑

ABOVE: rappers performing at an open-air concert.
RIGHT: mural near Pablo Neruda's Bellavista house.

A TASTE OF CHILE

Chile, the home of the potato and the strawberry, is enriching its once rather bland fare by rediscovering the indigenous origins of its cuisine

Pablo Neruda's *Oda al Caldillo de Congrio* (Ode to Conger Eel Soup) is a recipe in verse that lingeringly savors each step in making this rich and fragrant soup from the "giant eel with snow-white flesh," Flavoured with potatoes, onion and garlic, this is one of Chile's most traditional and best-loved dishes. The poet was mistaken on one count: *congrio* isn't – despite the common belief in Chile – an eel at all, but a fish known internationally as kingclip. But Neruda's ode – as do the many others he wrote about the simple joys of Chilean food – makes no mistake about the satisfying pleasure of a steaming bowl of *caldillo*, especially on a cold winter day.

Congrio, with its springy white flesh, is also popular *frito* (fried), when it is traditionally served with *ensalada chilena* (a salad of sliced tomato and blanched onions). "If you visit Chile without trying *congrio frito*, you haven't really been there," warns Chilean chef, Carlo von Mühlenbrock.

In Santiago, the Mercado Central, the city's old fruit and vegetable market by the Mapocho River, is a good place to try *congrio*. At the main restaurant, Donde Augusto, you'll find excellent *caldillo* and *congrio frito* at very modest prices, as well as *corvina* (sea bass) and a variety of the shellfish that flourish in the cold Antarctic waters that are carried up the Chilean coast by the famous Humboldt Current.

Another of the treats not to be missed in Chile is the *cordero* (lamb) that is raised in the far south of Chile around the Magellan Strait. It has a special taste attributed to the sea winds that feather the grass with salt, and to the fact that, in this area's virtually virgin pastures, the land is free of pesticides and insecticides. Unfortunately, though, lamb is not very popular in Chile (most of the Magellan lamb goes straight for export) and, except in Patagonia, it tends only to be served in more expensive restaurants.

PRECEDING PAGES: color at Santiago's fish market.
LEFT: prawns for sale.
RIGHT: *pescados y mariscos* for main course.

Chile is also famous for its farmed salmon which, over the past twenty years, has developed into a major export industry. Salmon is rarely absent from a restaurant menu in Chile and is widely considered to have a pleasanter, less strong taste than that of Norwegian or Scottish salmon. However, the jury is still out on whether

– as Chileans will tell you – it contains lower levels of antibiotics and hormones than the farmed salmon of other countries.

Chile's fresh fruit is also not to be missed if you visit in spring or summer. Too infrequently served in restaurants – on the grounds that fruit is not a "real" dessert – it is a delight. If you visit the Sernatur tourist office on Santiago's Providencia Avenue, you'll find an excellent fruit and vegetable market just around the back of the building.

In summer, the roads are lined with stalls offering the pick of the season: blackberries, plums, strawberries, peaches, apricots, cherries, melons, kiwis and, as autumn approaches, the famous Chilean grape, sweet and luscious. And, during a winter visit, don't neglect to try the *chirimoyas* (custard apples), a sweet and fragrant fruit grown mostly around La Serena, and best eaten just with a dressing of freshly squeezed orange juice.

Indigenous roots

Scientists believe that the potato originated in Chile, probably on the islan of Chiloé 13,000 years ago, before spreading to the Andean Altiplano where the Spanish *conquistadores* found it in the mid-16th

PAEAN TO SOUP

The 19th-century traveler Edward Revel Smith described the *cazuela* as "the best dish that can be had in Chile, and one which, I believe, can be had nowhere else."

not previously reach consumers. As well as being sold in Santiago's main supermarkets, they are now served in a number of restaurants, including Carlo von Mühlenbrock's Osadía.

Von Mühlenbrock is in fact one of the leaders of a new generation of Chilean chefs that has rebelled against the international, and frequently undistinguished, fare that was until recently standard in most Chilean restaurants. "Restaurant owners used to think that local dishes weren't chic; they scorned

century. Even today, the potato forms a staple part of the islanders' diet as, for example, in *milkao*, a traditional flat bread made with grated potatoes that are fried in lard. And, on the smaller islands of the archipelago, many varieties have survived, some with graphic names like the long thin black potato that is known as *mojón de gato* (cat's dung).

It was, therefore, all the more surprising that, until recently, only one standard variety of potato was sold in Chilean supermarkets, or served in the country's restaurants. But that is changing; a firm called Papas Arcoiris (Rainbow Potatoes), based in Puerto Varas, has begun to rescue and market varieties that did

them as rustic and not sophisticated enough," he recalls. But that is also changing. Until a few years ago, most Chileans had never heard of merkén, a Mapuche seasoning. However, thanks to research by von Mühlenbrock and other like-minded chefs, it is now a common feature of restaurant menus. A red spicy paste that the Mapuches spread on bread or use to liven up stews, it is made from red chili peppers – traditionally smoked by being hung above the cooking fire in Mapuche homes – which are then ground to a powder with cilantro (coriander) seeds, garlic and salt, and mixed with water when needed.

Another popular addition to restaurant menus

are *piñones*, the fruit of the monkey puzzle trees, and the staple diet of the Pehuenches, the branch of the Mapuches who live in the Andes mountains. The Pehuenches use *piñones* to make bread, or simply eat them boiled, much like chestnuts, which they resemble in taste, although not in their long, thin shape. Today, you can find *piñones* served as a garnish alongside a piece of meat or, in Osadía, as part of a pine nut and blueberry tart.

Beans and sweet corn

The Chilean word for beans – *porotos* – is believed to originate from the language of the

usually eaten with chopped tomatoes and Chile pepper but, in the countryside, it sometimes comes with a beefsteak *(bifstek)* on top.

Sweet corn, which is known as *choclo* (the Quechua name for corn) is also used in many other Chilean dishes, but the most famous are *humitas* and *pastel de choclo*. *Humitas* are the Chilean equivalent of the tamales found in many other Latin American countries, with the difference that they contain only mashed corn – no meat as is often the case in other countries – and are always wrapped in corn leaves and not, for example, banana leaves. *Humitas* are usually served with *ensalada chilena* and finely

Quechua people of the Andes, but beans were also an important part of the Mapuche diet. Through a project Recomienda Chile (Chile Recommends) that brings together a local NGO, leading chefs, and Mapuche women, different varieties of beans – each of which have a different use in traditional Mapuche cooking – are being saved from extinction and catalogued.

Beans are popularly eaten in Chile as a rich summer soup known as *porotos granados*. This is made from shelled haricot beans, pumpkin, onion and sweet corn, seasoned with basil, and is

chopped chili pepper, although some Chileans prefer to eat them with sugar.

Pastel de choclo has a minced-meat base that includes quarters of hard-boiled egg, olives, and sometimes a piece of chicken, and is covered with a mashed corn layer. It is, in fact, much like a cottage pie, with corn replacing the potato. Raisins are often added to the meat base and sugar is sometimes sprinkled over the corn top before it is put in the oven to brown.

The Spanish legacy

The popular *empanada* – a savory pastry turnover – is found in most Latin American countries, although the name varies, and has a

LEFT: food cooked on a spit, *à la brasa*.
ABOVE: *humitas*, a local specialty.

definite Spanish origin. In fact, it traces its roots back to the hollowed-out loaf of bread that European farm workers used to carry their midday meal to the fields.

In Chile, it is most commonly filled with *pino* – the same mixture of minced-meat, onions, hard-boiled egg, olives and raisins that is used in *pastel de choclo*. In this version, it is baked in the oven, but there is also a tasty fried version, with a flakier pastry, that is filled with cheese.

Another Chilean favorite, *cazuela*, is a winter dish. It starts with a meat *(carne)* broth in which potato, pumpkin, corn and peppers are cooked. The dish arrives at the table as a sea

big fire in the middle of a rustic, checkered table-clothed room, complete with a guitar-playing *huaso* (horseman). This is a good place to try a *prieta,* a Chilean blood sausage. If you simply order a *parrillada*, you'll get meat grilled (possibly at the table). It is also quite common to order pure entrails if you like them.

Post-conquest influences

Chileans consider – with some justification – that their cuisine is a poor relation to Peruvian and Mexican cuisines, undeniably the most varied and interesting in Latin America. The difference, says Carlo von Mühlenbrock, is

of steaming soup, with large vegetable and meat islands, under which a bed of rice is discovered. As well as beef, this is often made with chicken or turkey and, in the latter case, is sprinkled with *chuchoca* (milled corn that is similar to Italy's polenta). This is a very hearty and is usually cheap *(see box on page 100).*

While not considered as fine as Argentine meat, Chilean cattle produce very credible steaks, which are served up in restaurants known as *parrilladas*. The *parrilladas* cook every type of meat over a charcoal grill – anything from a steak to a sausage or chop. In some of the *campesino* (farming) areas, you can find great cheap *parrilladas*, usually with a

explained largely by the lack of post-Conquest influences in Chile. The lack of the African influence that is so clear in Peru reflects the fact that few black slaves were taken to Chile and those that were did not, except in the far north, survive its harsher climate. And the Chinese immigration that, in Peru, merged with the local cuisine, to produce the *chifa* cuisine, was virtually absent in Chile.

In addition, argues von Mühlenbrock, Chilean society was less permeable to outside influence, perhaps partly because of its difficulty in establishing control over Mapuche lands. That also explains, he says, why there are so few regional variations in Chilean food.

"An *empanada* is an *empanada* from Arica to Punta Arenas because that's the way Chileans wanted it to be," he notes.

In fact, only two post-Conquest influences have played a significant role in the development of Chilean food – Italian and German cuisine. Italian immigration into Chile was small, but pasta is a common main course in restaurants and homes, a custom probably learned through Argentina, where Italian immigration was far more important and pervasive than in Chile.

The German influence is seen most strongly in the Lake District of the south, which is traditionally made by slowly boiling up a mixture of milk and sugar, flavored with a vanilla pod, until it thickens and turns a light caramel brown. By far the best way to sample *manjar* is in *dulces de La Ligua*, cakes of sponge or meringue filled with *manjar*. La Ligua is just off the PanAmerican Highway traveling north around an hour and a half out of Santiago, and the *dulces* are well worth the detour, although they can also be acquired in bakeries in Santiago.

A day of dining

Breakfast is *desayuno*. In most *residenciales* this will simply be bread with jam and butter

where most settlers from Germany arrived in the 19th century. This may explain the importance that cabbage now has in the Mapuche diet and it is certainly reflected in the widespread use of the word *küchen* to describe any sort of fruit tart.

Küchen is, in fact, one of the few traditional sweet pastries in Chile. However, in the sweet line, *manjar* is very popular. Similar to Argentina's *dulce de leche* (which literally translated means sweet milk), *manjar* is

LEFT: *cazuela*, a favorite dish.
ABOVE: clouds of steam rise from a *curanto* casserole, Chiloé.

(mermelada and mantequilla) and coffee or tea. Coffee will almost certainly be instant. *Café con leche* (with milk) is milk coffee; if you want just a little milk, ask for *un café cortado*. Tea lovers should prepare for a hard time in Chile. Asking for a cup of tea usually gets you a tea bag in a cup of hot, but not necessarily boiling, water. Beware, also, of asking for milk. This will almost certainly be warm and in a larger quantity than you anticipated.

A fuller breakfast can be ordered anywhere that serves *desayuno* (though rarely before 9am). Eggs and toast *(huevos con tostadas)* should be no problem. Fried eggs are *huevos fritos*, scrambled are *revueltos,* poached are *pasados,* hard-boiled are *huevos duros,* and soft-boiled are *a la copa.*

Lunch *(almuerzo)* is served after 1.30pm and can run until around 4pm. Set lunches *(colaciones or menú del día)* are usually very good value, and give you the opportunity of trying something typical without having to know what to order. As a starter, you'll be served something like tomatoes, cooked beans and cheese, before a main dish of perhaps *porotos granados* or *pollo con arroz* (chicken with rice), and then there may be a little *postre*

PUKKA CUPPA

For a decent cup of tea, try Le Flaubert in Santiago's Providencia suburb (Orrego Luco 0125) or the lobby of the city's Hyatt Hotel.

(dessert). Tea and coffee, or a soft drink, is usually part of the deal.

In Chile, late afternoon, between 5 and 7pm is, somewhat confusingly, the time for *onces* (elevenses). These usually include tea, coffee, sandwiches and cakes, to bridge the gap between lunch and dinner, which is rarely eaten before 9pm. The name is said to come from the British custom of having "elevenses," a late-morning snack. An alternative theory is that this used to be the time when the man of the house would sneak off for a peaceful drink of *aguardiente,* the local firewater, the name of which contains 11 letters.

As in most Latin American countries, dinner *(cena)* isn't served until after 8.30pm, and usually runs on until late. If you don't drink coffee after dinner, try an *aguita* or *yerba,* a fresh herb tea found everywhere.

Health issues

Health-conscious travelers may find Chileans' liberal use of sugar and salt quite disturbing. In this case, the phrases *"sin sal"* and *"sin azúcar"* (without salt/without sugar) should be slipped into your vocabulary.

The only really serious food-related health hazard is *marea roja* (red tide), a toxic alga that infects shellfish and can be fatal. Restaurants are perfectly safe because of strict controls on the transport of products from the areas, mostly in the south of Chile, where infections occur. However, you should not gather your own shellfish, or buy them from artisan fishermen on quaysides or beaches.

Water contamination in Santiago's market-garden region has been cleared up and serious food-borne illnesses like cholera, typhoid fever and hepatitis have been virtually eradicated. Raw salads and strawberries (traditionally a hazard because they grow near the ground) now represent no danger at all. The exception is *berros* (watercress), which harbors a nasty parasite, and should be avoided everywhere, unless you can be sure it was grown under hydroponic conditions.

Although coffee-drinking habits have evolved in recent years, instant coffee is still ubiquitous in Chile, especially in cheaper restaurants where, after dinner, you may be asked to spoon instant into your cup, which the waiter will then fill with hot water. To avoid a surprise, specify that you want *café café* or *café de grano,* the two usual terms for real coffee.

Vegetarians used to have a hard time in Chile, but that is changing. Santiago now has some excellent vegetarian restaurants, such as El Huerto, or its lower-priced La Huerta sister-restaurant, in the Providencia district, and the same is true of most other cities and large towns. In addition, most restaurants carry a small selection of vegetarian alternatives. ❑

LEFT: chef displays his latest creation.
RIGHT: mussels and seaweed hung up to dry in Angelmó, Puerto Montt.

FRUIT OF THE VINE

*Immensely popular worldwide, Chilean wines are still seen as new and exotic,
yet they are made from grapes with an ancient European pedigree*

Chileans have been making fine wines for more than a century, and have probably boasted about them for almost as long. Their great selling point, as every Chilean schoolchild knows, is that the best wine is produced from vines which can trace their ancestry straight back to cuttings brought over in the

middle of the 19th century from France by some enlightened Chilean vineyard owners.

Before that era, the Spanish *conquistadores* had grown vines, legend has it, by planting the pips of the raisins they had brought over with them from Spain. This was the origin of what is known as *país*, or "native" wine, the equivalent of California's "mission" wine. Winemaking was also an essential part of the activities of the Jesuit missionaries, who settled in the country throughout the 18th century.

French roots

A century later, an affluent landowner, Don Silvester Ochagavía, decided to improve the qual-

ity of his vines and went to France. It was a timely visit, as Ochagavía brought back cuttings not long before a plague of the dreaded *phylloxera* beetle began to chew away at the roots of the parent stock in Europe, and nearly destroyed the wine industries in France, Italy and Germany.

The European growers saved their vines by eventually grafting tougher, beetle-resistant American stock on to them. But while the European vineyards were being replanted, several out-of-work French enologists went to Chile, together with their vines, to give technical advice on planting and wine-making.

The *phylloxera* blight never reached Chile, cut off as it is from the rest of the world by natural barriers – the Pacific Ocean, the Atacama Desert and the Andes. So Chilean vineyard owners boast that their vines grow naturally, ungrafted, from original European stock. Wine buffs argue about whether this makes any difference to the wine's taste. It certainly does make a difference to the economics of the industry, because ungrafted vines can go on producing for three or four times longer than the grafted stock that now dominates in Europe.

Señor Ochagavía brought cuttings of Cabernet Sauvignon vines, which is now the most common type used for red wine *(vino tinto)*. It is usually produced as a 100 percent unblended wine, though it is sometimes blended with Merlot grapes, or occasionally with Malbec. At around the same time, someone – it is not known who – also brought cuttings of Carmenère from its Bordeaux homeland. The plant and its wine are similar to Merlot, but with subtle differences – so subtle, in fact, that until the late 1990s, when a sharp-eyed (or nosed) Frenchman spotted it, it was marketed as Merlot. DNA testing proved that it was Carmenère and it has become a Chilean signature because of its rarity value. White wine comes from Chardonnay grapes and from Sauvignon Blanc. Señor Ochagavía brought his cuttings of the Sauvignon Blanc vine from Bordeaux rather than the Loire Valley, and the flavor is softer and less pungent than the Loire valley variety.

Changing tastes

By the 19th century, Chilean wine growers already had the best vines and an excellent place to grow them – the long Central Valley, with its ideal temperate climate, hot sunny days and cool nights, and the right type of soil for the vines to flourish. But it is only since the late 1980s that they have really begun to make consistent top-quality wines that sell successfully in Europe, the United States and Asia, and are even making inroads into the giant Chinese market.

LESS WINE, MORE BEER

At the beginning of the 1970s, the average Chilean drank 50 liters (106 pts) of wine a year; by 2000, this figure had dropped to 15 liters (32 pts) per person, in favor of beer and soft drinks.

prises decided to test their reputations by trying to sell in a big way to the outside world. That meant changing the heavy, full-bodied wines – with the strong tannin taste that Chileans were used to – and going for the lighter and fruitier unblended wines *(varietals)* that are popular in the United States and Europe. That meant investing in new equipment. For example, red wine was traditionally matured in big, old casks of *raulí*, the native oak, which masks the taste of fruit. The vineyards that decided to go

Local consumption of wine, however, has been dropping steadily since the 1970s, although there is an emerging wine-drinking culture among the middle and wealthy classes. Even so, beer and fizzy drinks have become far more popular, and wine consumption is well below that of other European wine-producing countries and much less than neighboring Argentina.

Modernizing for export

In the 1980s, the future looked bleak for wine producers. However, some of the bigger enter-

for export markets had to import very expensive small casks, made from French oak, each of which lasts for only three or four years before it has to be replaced.

The investment for making good white wine was even larger, since white wine needs more careful handling. The grapes have to be picked in the cool hours of the morning, not in the heat of a summer afternoon. It's also important to pick them when they are not too ripe, or the wine will lack acidity, at least for non-Chilean tastes.

Vineyards have installed computerized pneumatic grape presses, which don't crush pips, and stainless-steel tanks, in which the temperature of the fermenting juice can be rigidly controlled.

LEFT: a worker tying vines in the Santa Rita vineyard.
ABOVE: harvesting Malbec grapes at Viu Manent.

Visiting vineyards

The *vendimia*, or harvest, takes place between early March and mid-April – the farther south the vineyard, the later the picking starts. The Spanish-owned enterprise of Miguel Torres, which has its winery down near Curicó, holds a festival for the *vendimia* around mid-March. In recent years, the *vendimia* in Santa Cruz, in the Colchagua valley, has also won acclaim for the quality of its tastings and activities.

Public visits to most of the vineyards in the off-season are usually limited to the bottling plant, the original cellars – some of them, like those of the Santa Rita winery, near Paine, built

hour's drive toward San Antonio, and could be combined with a visit to the resorts of Algarrobo or Las Cruces, or the port of San Antonio. Tours run from Monday to Friday starting at 10am. Again, booking is advisable (tel: 02-372-2850).

The **Cousiño Macul** winery, one of the oldest in Chile, still has land on the outskirts of Santiago. Grapes have been grown there since vines were planted by its first owner, Juan Jufré, one of the *conquistadores* who came with Pedro de Valdivia. The winery has been in the Cousiño Macul family since 1856, and the person most responsible for its development was the daughter-in-law of the first Cousiño, Doña

by the Spaniards in the 18th century – and the grounds of the winery. This kind of tour takes only about an hour, so you might plan a visit as part of a day out in the countryside around Santiago. Tastings are usually included in the tour, and most wineries have added elegant sales rooms and, in some cases, restaurants.

Concha y Toro, for example, which is by far the biggest single wine producer, and exporter, has its plant located in the direction of the Cajón del Maipo, about an hour's drive southeast of Santiago. A tour of the plant and old family estate might be included in a weekend trip to the mountains, but requires a booking (tel: 02-476-5000).

Viña Undurraga is near Melipilla, about an

Isidora Goyenechea, who had the cellars built and brought over an enologist specially from Bordeaux to produce quality wine. The vineyard, where organized tours are available, is sited in the Andean foothills, a quiet haven of trees and vines about 45 minutes' drive from the city center. However, the company is gradually moving out of Santiago, driven away by air pollution, and most of the land will soon be given over to a housing development.

The Colchagua Valley, south of Santiago, also offers organized tours of its vineyards, located in the heart of Chile's most traditional agricultural region. Tours start in Santa Cruz, 178 km (110 miles) from Santiago, and range from a half-day visit to a two-day package that includes an overnight stay in the Santa Cruz Plaza Hotel (tel: 02-470-7474). Bookings for the wine tour can be made through the hotel or directly with the Ruta del Vino (Wine Route) office (tel: 72-823-199). Santa Cruz can easily be reached by taking the train to San Fernando and a *colectivo* from the station. A century-old railway line linking San Fernando with the coast has been re-opened and renamed "Tren del Vino" (The Wine Train). Visitors can ride the train – hauled by a refurbished 19th-century steam engine – through the Colchagua Valley, stopping off to visit state-of-the-art wineries and taste their wares.

If you want to take some Chilean wine home, try one of the big supermarkets chains, such as Jumbo or Líder, in upmarket areas of Santiago such as Providencia, Las Condes, Vitacura or Avenida Kennedy. These stores offer large wine selections at good prices. But, if you want expert advice, you'd be better off in one of the specialized wine shops in the El Golf area. El Mundo del Vino, in Isidora Goyenechea, is one of the best and the staff are generally well informed.

The bigger producer-exporters are Concha y Toro and its subsidiary, Santa Emiliana and Santa Rita, which also owns Viña Carmen and San Pedro. However, Chile has almost 300

Informal tours

Wine buffs might enjoy a visit to the **Restaurant Enoteca**, otherwise known as Camino Real, on Santiago's pleasant wooded Cerro San Cristóbal, where you can sample a range of Chilean wines at about US$1.50 a glass. The restaurant is open from 10.30am–11pm. If you arrive unannounced, there will be no expert on hand to comment on or recommend wines. But if you want to take sampling more seriously, you can make an appointment and, with several days' notice, arrange for a private tasting session (tel: 02-232-3381).

LEFT: vineyards in the Valle del Elqui.
ABOVE: wine tasting at William Cole Vineyards.

wineries and there is also a wealth of small boutique-style vineyards, such as Miguel Torres and Los Vascos, which produce mainly for export.

Most of the wine-making areas are located in the Central Valley to the south of Santiago. To the north, most of the vines are for growing table grapes, with the exception of the *pisco*, a pink Muscatel-like variety which is distilled to make the spirit of the same name *(see page 187)*. The Valle del Elqui, near the pretty northern town of La Serena, is the most famous *pisco* area. Two main brands are distributed nationally, but if visiting the valley or La Serena it is worth tasting and shopping around for local brands, which have the finest taste and smell of ripe grapes.❏

WILD CHILE

Chile's wide range of climatic zones gives it an unusually diverse flora and fauna – but sadly, much of it is endangered

With the world's driest desert in the north and the continent of Antarctica in the south, it is not surprising that Chile's climate is divided into extremely different zones and that within that, the wildlife varies tremendously. Add to this the country's huge extension of ocean (the 320-km/200-mile territorial limit is almost twice the width of Chile at its widest point) on the west and the lofty Andes on the east, and you have a world of differences packed into one long strand of a country.

Chile's wilderness areas hold few dangers for the intrepid camper or hiker. There are no bears in the mountains, no poisonous snakes and only two kinds of poisonous spider (the corn spider or *araña del trigo*, with a red splash on a black body, and the brown corner spider, *araña del rincón*), which you're unlikely to run into. Way up in the mountains there are wildcats and pumas, but they usually avoid people.

Unfortunately, while Chileans are generally proud of the numerous species endemic to their country, many of these are in danger of extinction, including the world's smallest deer, the *pudú*, and the *huemul*, the large, royal-looking deer which appears on the Chilean coat of arms. On Chile's island territories (Easter Island and particularly the Juan Fernández Islands, sometimes called the southern Galápagos) are species that, developing in isolation, have formed their own unique gene pools.

The far north

The soils of Chile's northernmost desert regions are dry, and the climate is harsh, but the coastal areas teem with seals and all kinds of birds: seagulls, pelicans, petrels, penguins and *jotes* (vultures). High up in the Andes, disguised among the low shrubs and rocks, is the occasional herd of *huemules* deer, hard to find but protected (at least in theory) in the national

parks. Parque Nacional Lauca *(see page 206)* is the only area in Chile where the *huemul* is easily spotted at dawn or dusk, maybe hiding amongst the *queñoa* trees.

Chilean flamingos can be seen picking bugs out of the mud around altiplano lakes. The Andean flamingo and the James flamingo are

also often seen in the salt marshes south of Parque Nacional Lauca. Conservation groups are working to protect flocks from collectors who gather the flamingo eggs to sell as food. Females only lay one egg at a time, and flocks have decreased from 75,000 to 7,000.

At least 150 other bird species have been noted in the park, one of the most obvious being the giant coot, a turkey-sized bird that builds huge nests up to 2.4 meters (8 ft) wide, floating or resting on piles of stones in water.

Mountain cats, wild ducks, *ñandúes* (ostrich-like birds), owls, eagles and condors also add life to the dry landscape of Chile's far north, at 3–4,000 meters (9,800–13,000 ft) above sea

PRECEDING PAGES: llamas near Volcán Lincancábur, San Pedro de Atacama.
LEFT: finding a ñandú nest, Magallanes.
RIGHT: tiny Darwin's frogs.

level. The *vizcacha* or Andean rabbit is endemic to the Andes. Its fluffy tail, tufted ears and long whiskers give it a rabbit-like appearance, but this rodent is actually a relative of the chinchilla and guinea pig. *Vizcachas* are quite easy to spot as they run around, popping out from behind rocks during the day.

High in the altiplano (over 4,500 meters/ 14,800 ft) is one of the world's last reserves of wild chinchilla. The French naturalist Claude Gay described the chinchilla as "one of Chile's most beautiful animals" and said they were easily tamed. They live in extensive caves dug under the ground, and come out only at night,

found the occasional hollow covered with the only sparse grasses capable of resisting the extreme saltiness of the soil. Climbing slightly higher into the mountains, around 2,200 meters (7,200 ft) above sea level, cacti appear, accompanied by birds, some insects and lizards – the main life form capable of surviving in the area.

The camelids

All over the northern territories and in many parts of the south are herds of the animals most closely identified with (and arguably best adapted to) the extreme conditions of the altiplano: llamas, vicuñas, guanacos and alpacas.

so their eyes are extremely sensitive to the light. The chinchilla is an endangered species: in the early 20th century, an average of 350,000 chinchilla skins were exported per year. According to Chile's Committee for Defense of Flora and Fauna (CODEFF), these wild chinchillas are particularly important because most existing animals have been born and bred in captivity, with the resulting damage to gene pools which results from excessive in-breeding. These last, wild chinchilla are key to the renewal of breeding animals and have been studied by professors at the University of Chile.

In the broad plains formed between the coastal and Andean mountain ranges can be

CAMELID SPOTTING

Visitors to Chile will almost certainly spot a few camelids on their travels, but few will be able to say with certainty whether the wooly deer-like creatures are llamas, guanacos, vicuñas or alpacas. Here's how to tell them apart and impress your travel companions.

The guanaco and llama are the largest of the camelids, being almost twice the size of the vicuña and alpaca. The guanaco has rust-colored fur with a dark head and tail. Vicuña have creamier colored fur. Alpaca and llama may be a combination of black, grey, white, rust or cream, the alpaca being slightly smaller and with a fatter, often shorter neck.

All relatives of the camel, these four species are hard to tell apart, though the llama and alpaca are long-haired (and valued for their wool).

Claude Gay described guanacos as "animals with gentle, timid and very curious personalities... They're very sociable and live in herds of many females with one male... They're hunted for their edible flesh and because exceptionally strong lassos can be made from the skin of their neck... Their only form of defense is spitting at people who try to come near them: at the slightest provocation they lay their ears back and fling saliva mixed with other matter which doesn't cause the least damage."

Jorge and Talinay, full of trees more commonly found further south (particularly the cinnamon and *olivillo*). The vegetation hums with abundant insects, including dragonflies, butterflies and beetles, which in turn sustain a sizeable population of lizards and non-poisonous snakes. Wild donkeys live in the Andean foothills.

From this region down towards Santiago, the climate, while still dry, is considerably more generous toward plants and animals. The climate in these regions is among the most pleasant in the world. The average temperature for the area is around 14°C (57°F) all year round, and mists blown off the ocean condense on the

Towards the Norte Chico

South of Parque Nacional Pan de Azúcar (*see page 191*) there is enough humidity to permit the growth of a large variety of cactus, many of which are valued abroad. Over the years ruthless hunting has reduced the herds of guanacos and the number of *vizcachas* and chinchillas as well. Colorful beetles of all kinds are noteworthy throughout this region.

Thorns, shrubs and small trees, along with wild flowers like the Cordilleran violet and chamomile, give way to the forests of Fray

coastal mountains, ensuring sufficient moisture to support a wide variety of flowers, trees and other vegetation necessary to maintaining animal life. However, the landscape pays dearly for those years when the moisture is not sufficient: huge dunes have formed and have begun to creep steadily into formerly fertile areas, turning them into semi-deserts, which may be virtually impossible to recover.

In these more temperate regions, sea swallows and cormorants join the bird species more common farther north, and farther inland there are thrushes, turtledoves and partridges along with the other species named above. Wasps, scorpions (although their sting is painful, it is

LEFT: Andean condors.
ABOVE: penguin family, Otway Sound, Magallanes.

not dangerous), *tábanos* (horseflies), and both black and large hairy spiders form part of the insect population, while frogs and toads join the lizard and snake community.

The central region

From the early days of the Spanish conquest, Chile's fertile Central Valley region, where Santiago is located, became the main area of settlement and agriculture. As a result, the main animals of the area are people and about the only wildlife you'll find is in the zoo.

As you travel farther south, the landscape changes and with it the different animals which

inhabit it. In the lush forests which cover a large part of the southern region are rabbits, hares, *coipo* and mice, wildcats and other small animals. The *coipo*, a sort of Chilean beaver, is hard to see in the wild because it usually only comes out at night. Many of the animals which formerly populated the coast have been virtually wiped out by indiscriminate hunting, particularly the different species of seals which once thrived in the area.

Birds with names such as *huairavo, piquero, pollito de mar, pinguera, chucao, run-run* and *becacinas* populate the forests, and the lizards are joined by four-eyed toads, the cowboy toad and different kinds of frogs. One of the more unusual is the Darwin's frog. It lays eggs, which are then swallowed and tended by the male, who, upon their maturation, "gives birth" through the mouth to the young tadpoles.

The insect community includes a fascinating beetle, the *madre de la culebra* (snake's mother), which is a couple of centimeters or more in length, with long claws. Praying mantis, colorful "stink bugs" of a bright metallic blue and different kinds of butterflies also thrive under the trees – although they, like all species, have been affected by the wholesale cutting and burning of Chile's native forests and have not adapted well to foreign species like the lodgepole pine, which have been used for reforestation in some regions.

Longtailed snakes (which look very similar to North American garter snakes) and short-tailed snakes feed on mice, toads and small birds. They're about 8 cm (3.15 inches) long at birth and can grow to 2 meters (7ft). They are not poisonous.

RESOURCEFUL REPTILES

Chile's varied landscapes are home to 76 species of lizard and six species of snake. Unlike most Chilean wildlife, reptiles are common throughout the country – except in Magallanes. Many are endemic to Chile. The history of their development has been extremely difficult to trace, but the sparse evidence available indicates that lizards go back about 70 million years in Chile.

Chilean lizards live in the desert, on the coast, in tropical forests, in the heights of the Andes and on the Patagonian and southern steppes. Some lizards have been found at altitudes of up to 4,900 meters (16,000 ft). These species live in underground burrows and have evolved special adaptations for keeping warm by absorbing more radiation from the sun.

Some lizards reproduce by laying eggs, while others give birth to live young. Sizes range from 10 cm (4 inches) from nosetip to tail, and up to half a meter (1.6 ft) long, as is the case with the Chilean iguana.

Lizards play a key role in the ecology, living on flies, crickets, locusts and other insects, and thus controlling the insect population. Birds and several of Chile's snakes in turn live on the lizards. None are dangerous: they prefer to get away if approached by humans. They will only bite when there is no alternative.

Condors inhabit the high peaks of the *cordillera*, and Chile's mountain forests also provide homes for wild ducks, mountain partridges and tricahue parrots. *Felis colo colo* (mountain cats), which are peculiar to Chile, are an altogether unnerving sight – their physical appearance is exactly that of the marmalade domestic cat, but they live in the wild, surviving on partridge, hare, rabbit, mice and birds.

The Lake District

Between Lago Vichuquén and the coastal village of Llico is the Reserva Nacional Laguna Torca. Graceful black-necked swans crowd the

to concentrate as far from human inhabitants as they can get, and are very difficult to spot.

The *pudú*, a tiny reddish deer which is endemic to Chile, lives in thickets in the densely forested areas between Chillán and Isla Chiloé, and is almost impossible to spot in the wild. Also found in this region is the *llaca*, the only marsupial left in the southern Andes. It spends its life in the trees and feeds on fruit and insects. In winter it goes into a state of semi-hibernation, just lazing around in the trees.

Chile's smallest and rarest fox is the Darwin's or chilote fox. The destruction of its natural habitat has put it in danger of extinction. It

lake, feeding on aquatic plants and laying their eggs on floating nests. Upon hatching, the white offspring climb on to their parents' backs. Along the coast, colonies of penguins and swamp cormorants can be seen.

Farther south, the climate becomes increasingly damp and rainy and the species change somewhat as a result. However, considerable deforestation in the area has severely cut back on what would otherwise be a numerous population of wild animals. There are still some foxes, *pudús*, wildcats and pumas, but they tend

LEFT: flamingos in flight, Magallanes.
ABOVE: the *culpeo* (Chilean fox).

has, however, been sighted recently on Isla Chiloé and in the forests north of Osorno.

The Lake District is home to one of the world's largest beetles, the stag beetle, which grows as long as 9 cm (3½ inches) and lives in the oak and *coigüe* forests of this southern region. Woodpeckers and hummingbirds are common in the forests of the region, especially near wild fuchsia (bleeding hearts). Dolphins appear in the coastal areas, where whales were once hunted virtually into extinction.

Magallanes and Tierra del Fuego

High up in the most isolated southern parts of the Andes are small herds of *huemules*, which are virtually extinct, and now protected. But Chilean TV documentaries have revealed that even in supposedly protected national park areas, illegal human settlements where cattle are raised are competing with the endangered deer.

In Chile's southernmost region, sea lions can be sighted along with seals and dolphins. Beavers (introduced from abroad), muskrat and *coipo* are also common here, along with petrels, albatross, cormorants and other sea birds. Foxes, guanacos, pumas and skunks roam the pampas of Tierra del Fuego.

Magellanic penguins can be seen in colonies at the Otway Sound, 60 km (37 miles) north of Punta Arenas, and on the island reserve of Monumento Natural Los Pingüinos, near Punta Arenas. Magellanic penguin skins were once heavily sought after by indigenous people in the area for food and clothing and penguin eggs provided an important source of food. Other birds scouring the beaches and fishing the coastal shelf waters are blue-eyed cormorants, pintado petrels, wandering albatross, brown skuas, pink-footed shearwaters, chinstrap penguins, gulls, oyster-catchers and steamer ducks.

Within the chilly Antarctic waters, the delicate food chain depends first on marine zooplankton (arrow worms, microscopic crusta-

PUMAS – LIONS OF THE MOUNTAINS

Chileans who live in the mountains frequently see pumas (*felis concolor*, but popularly known as *leones* – lions), particularly in winter. But pumas rarely attack people, unless they are cornered. The presence of guanaco may indicate that pumas are nearby, as guanaco make up 55 percent of their diet. Guanaco skeletons found in remote areas often have dislocated necks, a sign of the work of this powerful mountain lion. Pumas also feed on hares, *vizcachas* and *huemules*, attacking domestic animals only occasionally.

Despite this, hunting has seriously reduced their numbers. In 1980 the government banned the hunting of puma; in response, many sheep farmers have since switched to raising cattle as their sheep were being increasingly ravaged by pumas.

A solitary animal, the puma reaches maturity at two or three years of age, and usually has two kittens per litter. Pumas and their relatives are found throughout Chile, and indeed, are among the few animal species found throughout the Americas, from Canada right down to the Strait of Magellan. The elusive puma grows up to 1.5 meters (5 ft) in length and stands 63 cm (2 ft) at the shoulder. It has a light brown coat with a white muzzle, and is hard to see, but its human fist-size footprints are fairly common.

ceans and shrimp-like krill). These zooplankton thrive in the nutrient-rich Antarctic water and feed the ecosystems of the continental shelf. Small marine species in the area depend on marine zooplankton for survival. There are hundreds of endemic mollusks, starfish, sea urchins, sponges, jellyfish and other marine species that have adapted to the extreme temperatures and harsh conditions.

A little higher on the food chain are an estimated 25 species of octopus and squid, along with five fish families. Toward the top of the food chain are seals (Weddell, elephant, Ross, and leopard), fur seals and sea lions,

There are an estimated 380,000 whales, belonging to 28 species, in the Antarctic Ocean. The blue whale, 20–30 meters (66–98ft) long and weighing over 100 tons, consumes about 40,000 kilos (88,000 lbs) of zooplankton each day. An estimated 10,000 are all that are left of more than 200,000 blue whales that existed in 1800. Ruthless exploitation in the 18th and 19th centuries put them on the endangered list.

Orcas (killer whales) also inhabit the waters of southern Chile. They are particularly fond of eating sea lions, tossing them into the air with their tail fins to stun them before moving in for the kill. ❏

which, with their thick blubber and fur, are all well adapted to the cold Antarctic water. Unfortunately, hunting in the 20th century reduced their populations, but an international treaty now protects them.

The Weddell seal is the deepest diver, reaching depths of 600 meters (1,968 ft), with the ability to hold its breath for over an hour. Fish, shellfish and squid make up the bulk of the seal's diet, but the leopard seal will also feed on penguins and other seals.

Far Left: the Chilean southern-ringed kingfisher.
Left: a giant red-headed woodpecker.
Above: a *vizcacha* makes itself cozy.

PERILOUS PENGUINS

Chile has nine species of penguin, the largest of which is appropriately called the Emperor. These penguins can grow as tall as 1.2 meters (4ft), and are characterized by a yellowish orange patch on both sides of their chests. They live in colonies of up to 5,000.

The most common species is the Magellanic penguin, which nests in sandy burrows in colonies of up to several thousand birds. If frightened, it hastens back to its burrow using its flippers as another pair of legs, and making a braying call like a donkey. Though seemingly tame, these penguins have been known to bite. Be warned if you see one pointing its beak towards you and hissing.

ADVENTURE ACTIVITIES

Chile's great outdoors is unusually tempting, and there are many ways to enjoy it, whether on skis, on a surfboard, in a boat or on foot

With over one third of the nation's population living in the capital Santiago, it is easy to find somewhere in Chile to get away from it all. But Chile offers more than remote and pristine wilderness. Its dramatic, untamed and highly varied landscape makes it a land of adventure.

The options are as varied as the country's many geographical zones. In the north, the vast empty desert can only be crossed in four-wheel drives. The heart of the Andes must be reached either on foot or on horseback. There are volcanoes to be climbed and rivers to be rafted, while the glacier-riddled islands of the southern archipelago can often only be visited on organized boat trips.

The season for adventure tourism is summer: November to March. This is when the weather stabilizes, save on the Andean high plain, at the northeastern border with Bolivia, where electric storms are common. Do not expect rain in the desert, even in the foothills. Some parts of the Atacama Desert only see rain every 30 to 50 years. From there to Santiago, rain rarely falls between October and March.

The spectacular alpine and coastal wilderness of southern Chile attracts visitors from October through April. The town of Pucón is a good base from which to organize hikes, climbs, river rafting, mountain biking and horseback riding into the nearby national parks of Huerquehue and Villarrica.

Chile's many volcanoes offer treats for hikers, while thrill-seekers scale the sheer rockfaces of central Patagonia, whose main attraction is Parque Nacional Torres del Paine. Here are great opportunities to hike or go horseback riding past towering granite spires and azure lakes, amid roaming guanaco and *ñandú* (rheas).

PRECEDING PAGES: dawn display at El Tatio geysers near San Pedro de Atacama.
LEFT: reaching the Torres del Paine.
RIGHT: fly-fishing in the Lake District.

Northern jeep excursions

The Chilean Norte Grande presents a wide selection of geological phenomena and archeological sites, from ancient civilizations as well as the much more recent remains of early 20th century nitrate mining "ghost towns" *(see page 197)*. However, vast distances between sites

and roads that are often barely distinguishable tracks make traveling difficult. Some of the sites are very hard to find and are often spread over large distances, so usually the best option is to pay for a driver or organized excursion. These are available in the coastal towns of Arica, Iquique and Antofagasta, and in Calama and San Pedro in the interior, and are usually comprised of small groups traveling with a guide in a four-wheel-drive vehicle. The Explora hotel, near San Pedro de Atacama, organizes visits and other activities for its guests; it is pricey, but a good way to see the area's attractions comfortably in a short time.

The main rule of thumb in the desert is to

never leave the road unless you know exactly where you are going. It can take hours of pushing and shoving in the blazing sun to free a vehicle bogged down in the sand. It is also important to take a large supply of fresh water along. Even up in the mountains where it is possible to find streams, a high mineral content often makes the water brackishly saline and generally undrinkable.

The desert can be very cold after the sun goes down, especially if there is a wind. In fact, it will probably be freezing should you arrive early in the morning to see the geysers go off in El Tatio or wildlife around Lago Chungará – take

in Santiago or in the south. Riding skills are not required either, as, given the terrain, most of the trip is a walking tour. The guides for these trips are *arrieros*, men who run cattle herds over the Andes or take them up to pasture after the spring snows melt. Many have learned the trails from their fathers and grandfathers before them. Their tales, related around the campfires as the beef sizzles on the spit, are worth learning Spanish to understand, and there is usually a musician to liven up the evenings.

The Andes reach their highest point in the hemisphere on Mount Aconcagua, just to the north of Santiago, in Argentina. The trails

warm clothing with you, even if it seems a ludicrous prospect in the cloying heat of the desert. Prepare also for the effects of altitude if you are embarking on a trip to El Tatio or the high Altiplano. Headaches are likely, so take aspirin along with you. Queasiness is also a symptom. Altitude problems can strike unexpectedly, and rest is the best remedy. In serious cases sufferers should immediately return to lower levels.

Horseback riding

Exploring the many nooks and crannies of the high Andes from the back of a horse is not as difficult as you might think, and there are many places hiring horses or organizing treks, either

nearby wind diagonally up huge steep hills topped by barren rock whose colors often betray their mineral content: green for copper, white for gypsum or lime, red for clay.

Some excursions include visits to lagoons, which are not marked on road maps, such as Laguna Negra and the twin Lagunas del Yesillo, whose surfaces support floating blocks of snow. *Piuquenes* (wild geese) make their nests in the lake that bears their name. The atmosphere is so dry and clear it seems you could see to the end of the world if the snow-capped peaks were not blocking your vision. And the overwhelming silence of the cordillera makes all human achievement and modern metropolitan life seem very small and distant.

The Astorga family (tel: 02-861-1303) offers trips departing from their Cascada de las Animas (Waterfall of Souls) resort in Cajón del Maipo. Activities include trekking and horseback excursions as well as white-water rafting and kayaking on the Maipo River. Accommodation in cabins is available at the resort, which has a swimming pool and specializes in vegetarian food (although meat dishes are also served).

SPECIALIST OPERATORS

There are various Chilean and foreign travel agencies who specialize in many of the activities mentioned here, based in Santiago and around the country. See Travel Tips, pages 351–54.

White-water rafting

The mighty Bíobío River in central Chile used to be one of the most exciting rivers to run in all the Andes before part of it was destroyed by the vast Ralco hydroelectric dam. Now only the rapids on the very upper reaches of the river remain. Nearby, indigenous communities run campsites amid spectacular scenery.

The Futaleufú River, southeast of Chaitén, in Aisén, is Chile's white-water paradise. Depending on the water level, the river's rapids are rated grade 4+ on the international scale of 1 to 6, while upstream, the Inferno Canyon and Terminator sections can reach grade 5+, and this is not a trip to be attempted by anyone but expert kayakers with guides. Shorter excursions on other rivers, such as the Claro, Palena or Petrohué, are not quite as wild as the Futaleufú, but every bit as exciting, and can be easily arranged. Relaxing day trips floating down stretches of the Trancura river can be organized in Pucón; the upper reaches of the river are stunning, with a backdrop of high volcanoes, while in the lower part, it becomes calmer, but "bouncy".

Climbing a volcano

Chile has 55 active volcanoes, and some of them can be climbed. The Llaima and Villarrica volcanoes are the most active in Chile, with a record of ten eruptions each during the last century (Llaima erupted as recently as 1994). A strong eruption in these volcanoes or in the nearby peaks of Quetrupillán, Lanín, or Mocho-Choshuenco can cause a chain reaction in the

LEFT: a horseback trek in the Maipo River Canyon (Cajón del Maipo), southeast of Santiago.
RIGHT: paraskiing in the Valle Nevado, one of five ski centers east of Santiago.

area. This is what happened in the mid-17th century – the Mapuches tell of how they were forced to move out of the area because of the extensive volcanic activity. The age of the forests – not more than 250 years old – in the valleys between Freire and the mountains, confirms the folk memory. More recently in 1971, the town of Coñaripe was buried below a terrifying slide of mud, ash, lava and tree trunks caused by volcanic activity; while the last time a lava flow reached the banks of Lago Villarrica was 1908.

If you care to take on one of these roaring giants, agencies in Pucón organize hiking tours right up to the very crater of Volcán Villarrica (2,840 meters/9,320 ft). Walking up the conical mountain takes you through one of the centers of the Pacific "Ring of Fire", surrounded by volcanic peaks. Here and there are emerald and sapphire lakes. Sometimes you hear some of the dark, hidden underground groans of Mother Earth, and feel a few tremors and shakes. To stare down the 100-meter (330-ft) drop into the crater of hellishly boiling molten lava is a sight that few will forget. Here, the subterranean noises reach a roar and the stench of sulfur can be almost overpowering.

The ascent of the western face of Volcán Villarrica takes around four hours, thanks to a ski-lift that cuts the climbing distance. The descent of the volcano takes about two hours. The climb is strenuous, but anyone who is in reasonable health and physically fit should be able to make it. It is also possible to ascend other volcanoes such as Osorno, near Lago Llanquihue. The ascent of this particular volcano, however, is quite a bit more difficult and requires climbing gear.

EXPEDITION ADVICE

A good source of information and guides is the Federación de Andinismo in Santiago, whose members often organize expeditions for both professionals and amateurs. *See Travel Tips page 351 for more details.*

short-distance vessels are rather lacking in safety measures and have a tendency towards dangerous overcrowding during the peak season. The calmest part of the day for navigation tends to be early morning and sunset. On these journeys, it is a good idea to take your own life jacket and water, and a sleeping bag to put over the bare mattresses or reclining chairs on the freighters. Other recommended items include woolen pants, socks and a heavy sweater or fleece jacket. Rubber boots are best

It is also possible to climb Ojos del Salado, the world's highest volcano, in the heart of the Atacama Desert, surrounded by green lagoons that are home to colonies of flamingos. Although a period of acclimatization is needed, the ascent is not difficult and there are two mountain shelters on the route.

A good source of information and guides is the Federación de Andinismo in Santiago, whose members often organize expeditions for both amateurs and professionals.

Sailing the southern channels

There are a number of boats that visit the archipelagos of southern Chile. In many cases, small

for going ashore. Stops are often made in pristine, uninhabited environments and where the clear, unforested land tends to be marshy at the water's edge. Here, birds who have no fear (or knowledge) of humans will sometimes hop on to your shoes, to pull at the laces, presumably mistaking them for hefty worms.

The most luxurious cruise boats are those of Skorpios (tel: 02-231-1030; fax: 02-232-2269) for trips from Puerto Montt or Puerto Chacabuco to Laguna San Rafael by way of the Campo de Hielo Norte (Northern Ice Field), or from Puerto Natales to Puerto Edén, visiting the glaciers of the Campo de Hielo Sur (Southern Ice Field). Navimag runs regular scheduled freighters on rather spartan voyages between Puerto Montt and Puerto Chacabuco, near Coyhaique; or through the windswept Golfo de Penas to Puerto Natales. Navimag has branches in Santiago (tel: 02-442-3120; fax: 02-203-5025), Puerto Montt, Coyhaique, Puerto Chacabuco, Puerto Natales, and Punta Arenas.

Cruceros Australis (tel: 02-442-3110; fax: 02-203-5173) operates the *Mare Australis*, a comfortable ship that navigates the Patagonia Channels from Punta Arenas to Ushuaia in Argentina, past Tierra del Fuego, passing through the Straits of Magellan and the Beagle Channel and its glaciers at the very southern

gradually disappear at high tide, particularly around the time of the full moon. More than one camper in the Cahuelmo fiord has had to keep warm in the thermal tubs carved into the hillside after he and all his gear were soaked at 2am, when the full moon's tide came in. Short, yellow, wild flowers with bunches of tiny concave petals mark the highest tide level.

When camping in dense forest it is worth bringing a machete to clear the site. Ferns and the gigantic leaves of the *nalca* vie with the native bamboo *quila* and towering trees for ground space. Hanging flowering vines twist up trunks bearded by thousands of varieties of

tip of Chile. On the way back, it visits the penguin sanctuary on Isla Magdalena, which is inhabited by 40,000 breeding pairs of Magellanic penguins from October through March.

Camping in the sodden south

For those who wish to camp on the banks of the fiords, beware of the large differences between low and high tide in the area. Grass-covered islands in the rivers, which are common at the inland extremes of fiords, can

multicolored lichens. Where the forest canopy allows sufficient light, one finds bushes of the native blue *calafate* berries and red *murtillas*.

Tours are available that pass the small hamlets of Isla de Chiloé, through the Guaiteca Archipelago, to return through inland fiords passing the great San Rafael glacier. This enormous field of ice calves, with bomb-like explosions, into Laguna San Rafael. The melting icebergs become top heavy and roll over, to expose the most incredible translucent shades of lavender, powder blue or emerald green, like floating jewels. Pehuén Expediciones (tel/fax: 65-635-254) offers excursions into the surrounding areas of both insular and continental Chiloé.

LEFT: the view from Volcán Villarrica.
ABOVE: the crater of Villarrica, one of several still-active cones in Chile that can be climbed.

Hiking in Torres del Paine

Several companies offer trekking excursions in the most beautiful national park in the country, Parque Nacional Torres del Paine *(see page 301),* which was created in 1959 and declared a Biosphere Reserve by UNESCO in 1978.

The park itself is centered around the amazing "towers" and "horns" of rock, sculpted by glaciers, which point heavenward like daggers ripping at the sky's fluffy white belly. Here, the visitor will not only see some of the

most incredible and beautiful Chilean landscapes, but will also experience everything that comes under the title "weather" – from cloudless skies to deafening thunderstorms, often in a time lapse of only 24 hours.

While there are log-cabin refuges along the trails, these huts provide little more than a roof overhead, and the distances between them are sometimes a hike of as many as seven to eight hours. For those visitors wishing to hike alone, a tent is a necessary precaution, as weather conditions can slow the hiker down, and rivers can swell, making it necessary to postpone a crossing. And *please* take out your own garbage – garbage is often the only sign that one is not

the first explorer to set foot in this unblemished, primeval territory. Big Foot Expediciones (tel: 61-414-611; fax: 61-414-276) is one of the many companies offering hiking trips in this region.

Sea kayaking

The fiords and majestic mountains of northern Patagonia make a spectacular backdrop for sea kayaking. The Canal de Dalcahue (Dalcahue Channel) is a good area for beginners to practice before heading out to the other islands off Isla de Chiloé. Altué Sea Kayaking (tel: 065-641-110) organizes trips that last from one to eight days. Around the Golfo de Ancud (Gulf of Ancud), in northern Patagonia, particularly Hornopirén and the fiords of Comau, Quintupeu and Cahuelmo on the eastern side, are glacial valleys, thermal hot springs and temperate rainforests, with dolphins, sea lions and penguins. Yak Expediciones (tel: 09-436-0760) organizes sea and river kayaking trips, as well as rafting excursions.

Fishing

Wild rainbow and brown trout and six species of Pacific salmon may be the reward for a fishing expedition anywhere in the south of Chile. Four-to eight-pound (2–3.5kg) trout are a rule rather than an exception. Some say that the trout are so abundant you have to keep the smaller fish from jumping into your boat with a stick – which may or may not be another fisherman's tale. Contact local hotels or travel agencies for organized excursions.

Skiing and snowboarding

Chile has some of best long ski runs in the world. Most runs are at altitudes of around 3,000 meters (9,843 ft) and there is an abundance of natural snow, particularly "champagne" snow blown in from the Antarctic storms. Resorts stretch from just north of Santiago all the way to Patagonia. Portillo, near Santiago, is one of the most famous ski resorts in South America. Valle Nevado, also near Santiago, is a modern resort built in 1988 and the seat of snowboarding world cups *(see page 169).* Heli-skiing, paragliding and parascending are also available here. The best time to visit is June through October.

Termas de Chillán, situated 80 km (50 miles)

WEBSITE FOR SKIERS

If you have access to the worldwide web, visit:
www.mtnresorts.com
for information on Chilean ski resorts and facilities.

east of Chillán on the slopes of Volcán Chillán (3,122 meters/10,243 ft) is famous for its thermal springs. There are plenty of groomed runs, but if you want to get away from the crowd, it is easy to find virgin powder runs.

To reach the extreme runs, you can either hike up the mountain or go for the easy (and pricey) option and take a helicopter. A special park has been set up for snowboarders to show off their freestyle moves. Other attractions at the resort are snowmobile and helicopter tours. After a long, hard day on the snow, you can relax in the thermal baths. The season runs from June to September only.

page 282) often attracts cyclists along its unpaved road. Pared Sur (tel: 02-207-3525) organizes regular excursions to different parts of the country, including Easter Island, ranging from a weekend to a full week.

Surfing

Many spots along the coast of Chile are acquiring a worldwide reputation as surfing centers, with good conditions virtually all year round. Powerful reef breaks near Iquique and Arica in the north attract big crowds. Farther south, the water becomes colder and a 3x2 wet suit will be needed.

Mountain Biking

There are endless places to go biking, particularly in southern Chile, and this is one way to explore Easter Island, but it's probably best to bring your own bike if you want to go any distance in Chile.

If you go biking in the desert north, where trails pass through the salt flats, national parks, and indigenous villages, it's essential to carry water supplies. The Carretera Austral that runs from Puerto Montt to Villa O'Higgins *(see*

From the Santiago region the coastal shelf is more abrupt and swell conditions pretty consistent. Pichilemu, a popular beach resort just south of Santiago, has become internationally known as a surfing center.

Paragliding

The fast-growing sport of paragliding *(parapente)* has also caught on in Chile. A hardcore of paragliders soar through the sky near Santiago or launch themselves off the ski slopes at resorts like Antillanca in the south. At Iquique in the north and in Maintencillo, a sea resort north of Santiago, there are paragliding schools *(see Travel Tips page 352).* ❏

LEFT: embarking on one of the well-marked trails in Parque Nacional Torres del Paine.
ABOVE: coming down to earth gently on a paraglider.

THE SKILLS AND THRILLS OF THE RODEO

The horse is the star of Chile's national sport, demonstrating skills of patience and agility, with the help of its close companion, the huaso

The stocky Chilean horse, or *corralero*, is the inseparable companion of the horseman, or *huaso*. This working pair still dominates in the movement of stock in the Chilean countryside. The *huaso* and his horse are also the protagonists in one of Chile's national sports – the rodeo.

Most rodeos are held between September and May. The most famous is the Chilean Championship, held at the end of March in Rancagua, in the Central Valley. In a semicircular arena, or *medialuna*, a pair of riders and their mounts attempt to chase and maneuver a steer to a padded section of wall. Here it must be stopped and held by direct horse-to-steer body contact. The curved shape of the corral means the horse must learn to gallop sideways, an extremely difficult task. The *huasos* must work in close, fast coordination, one chasing the steer, the other hemming it close to the wall. This exercise produces spectacular shows of horsemanship, with horses spinning about on their back legs, changing direction, rearing and galloping as they track the steer about the ring. Riders earn *puntos buenos* (good points) or *puntos malos* (bad points) depending on where they hit the steer, if brute force is used (the rougher, the more bad points), and their appearance.

▷ **COUNTRY STYLE**
It's not just the riders who dress for the occasion. Here, a couple of *cueca* dancers wear traditional *huaso* costume at a rodeo in the Central Valley.

▷ **CORNERING A STEER**
Unlike Australian and American rodeos, in Chile there is no roping or riding of wild beasts, although the animal still gets knocked about somewhat.

△ **BESPOKE SADDLERY**
A well-stocked *talabartería*, or saddlery, will offer an impressive selection of hand-made leather tack and carved wooden stirrups.

▽ **PARTY TIME**
At the end of the rodeo, the prizegiving takes place. The horses rest, but the winning *huaso* is in for a long night of dancing and feasting.

DANCING WITH THE DEVIL

After the excitement of a rodeo, a hearty meal of beef and beans is knocked back with red wine. Then out from the pockets come the handkerchiefs for the *cueca*, Chile's national dance. The *cueca* is an intergral part of the event, and a *huaso* is not roundly accomplished if his cuban-heeled boots don't do a coordinated stomp. To begin the *cueca* (pronouced like "quaker"), the man first advances toward his female partner in a courting fashion. She, keeping her distance, establishes the pattern of pursuer and pursued. Folklore has it that the dance is inspired by a rooster stalking a hen. As the courting continues, both partners hold their handkerchiefs aloft and flick them about as they step in a smooth, shuffling manner. The dance must be accompanied by festive music and a crowd of clapping onlookers, spurring the man on in his hot pursuit.

The *cueca* produces such a high-spirited response that Chileans believe even the devil himself can't help but uncrumple his scarf and join in with a young *señorita*.

△ **SERIOUS SPOKES**
A *huaso's* Cuban-heeled boots sport large spoked spurs, ensuring a melodic jangle when he walks. He also wears finely plaited, tasselled leather leggings.

▷ **SADDLE SOAP**
Appearance is so important that *huasos* may have their *sombrero* (hat) ironed beside the ring, to ensure a flat rim during competition.

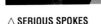

PLACES

*A detailed guide to the entire country, with principal sites
clearly cross-referenced to specially drawn maps*

Despite its elongated shape, Chile is one of the easiest countries in South America to travel around. Domestic flights connect the country's major cities; modern passenger buses run to almost every minor town (and depart punctually every time), and passenger boats link remote locations in the far south.

Almost all travelers flying into Chile arrive in the bustling capital of Santiago. At the country's midway point, Santiago is the logical base for exploring – many visitors leave their luggage in one of the capital's hotels and make excursions into the far-flung provinces.

Just a 90-minute drive away is the capital's colorful port city, Valparaíso, stretching across a mountain-encircled bay, while neighboring Viña del Mar is one of Chile's most popular beach resorts. Irregular flights from Santiago also reach the Juan Fernández Islands, famous as the temporary home of the Scottish sailor whose experiences inspired the creation of the fictional *Robinson Crusoe*.

The landscape north of Santiago becomes progressively drier as it extends toward the hauntingly beautiful Atacama Desert. Many travelers fly directly to Calama, support town for the spectacular Chuquicamata copper mine, before heading for the oasis village of San Pedro de Atacama. In the vicinity are ancient pre-Columbian ruins, thermal springs, salt flats and dramatic geyser fields. The city of Iquique contains relics of its days as a mining capital, while nitrate ghost towns are scattered in its hinterland.

Most of Chile's many vineyards are located south of Santiago in the lush Central Valley. Farther south, beyond the Bíobío River, lies Chile's most famous attraction, the Lake District. A spectacular region of rivers, volcanoes, forests and lakes, its attractive resort towns and remote mountain villages attract thousands of visitors.

The fishing port of Puerto Montt marks the end of the Lake District. South of this point, the landscape becomes wilder and travel more unpredictable, although boat cruises through the southern archipelago are popular. Aisén is the vast province of woods and glaciers opened up over the past 20 years by the Carretera Austral highway. Then come the vast sheep plains of Magallanes and Parque Nacional Torres del Paine, considered the most dramatic mountain region in South America and home to Chile's most awe-inspiring glaciers. At the southernmost tip of the country is the windswept island of Tierra del Fuego, shared with Argentina.

Chile's most remote outpost is Easter Island, situated 3,790 km (2,350 miles) west of the mainland. Despite its location, this mysterious speck of land covered with ancient statues continues to attract and intrigue visitors from all over the world. ❑

PRECEDING PAGES: an aerial view of Mount Aconcagua and the surrounding Andes; Volcán Payachata, Parque Nacional Lauca; a warning to drivers on the open road, Llanqui, Atacama. **LEFT:** tall cacti in the Andean foothills.

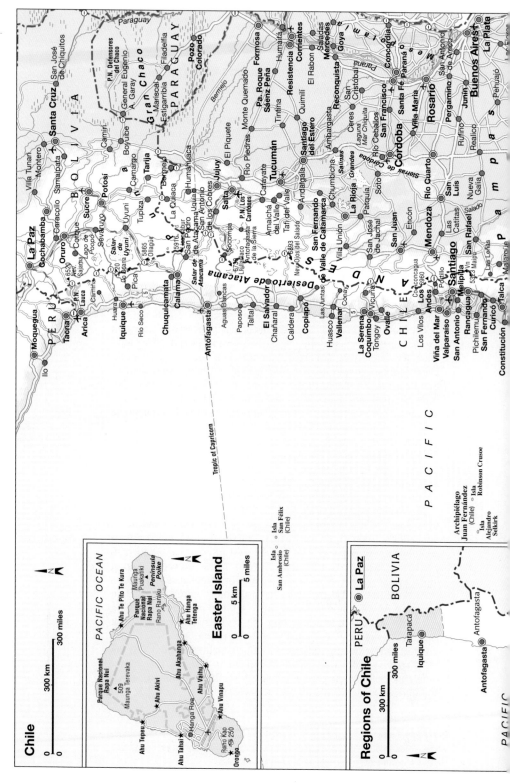

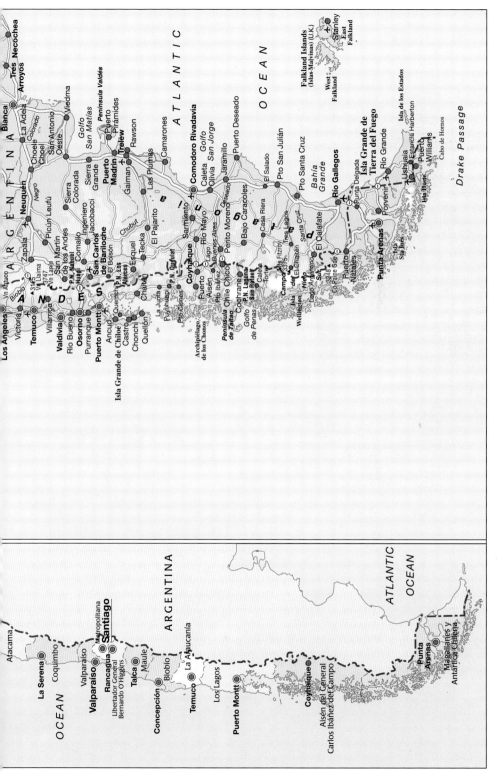

SANTIAGO

Elegant colonial architecture, bustling pavement cafés and colorful street performers give Chile's capital city a cosmopolitan feel

Santiago

When Chilean children draw or paint, in the background there is almost always a stylized line of snow-capped mountains. In Santiago, it is easy to see why. Rising immediately alongside the city, the Andes are a constant presence, albeit a shadowy one in the city's habitual smog, but still engraving themselves on the minds and subconscious of *santiaguinos* from birth. For the visitor, they not only impress with their beauty (above all when bathed in the rose-colored light of a clear sunset), but also serve a very practical purpose: it is hard to lose your bearings in Santiago.

So long, that is, as the smog does not cloud your vision. Air pollution is a serious problem in Santiago, whose streets are often clogged with motor traffic. The pollution is worsened by the city's almost windless location between the Andes and nearby hills, making one wish fervently that the Spanish *conquistador* Pedro de Valdivia had been forewarned about the internal combustion engine before siting Santiago here in 1541. But this is the only real drawback to a gently attractive and unpretentious city, whose people, though less effusive than others in Latin America, are friendly and always ready to welcome foreigners, and which is endowed with an ideal Mediterranean, or Californian, climate.

Santiago is also one of the most manageable capitals in Latin America for the first-time visitor. It is a big city, yet it has an almost provincial atmosphere. Standing in the compact few blocks and narrow streets of its center it's hard to believe you are at the heart of a conurbation of more than five million people. The city's sprawling extension gives it a feeling of spaciousness, despite the mountains; only in the center is there much of the sense of pressure and density characteristic of most cities of this size. The rest is residential suburbs: leafy avenues and sophisticated shopping malls in the plush *barrio alto* (high neighborhood), and vast swathes of well-tended middle-class neighborhoods and poor working-class areas – labyrinthine networks of tiny adobe and wooden dwellings, and bleak state-subsidized apartment blocks.

PRECEDING PAGES: hilltop view of Santiago. **LEFT:** La Moneda landmarks. **BELOW:** statue of the Virgin, Cerro San Cristóbal.

A European touch

Many visitors are struck by the European feel of Santiago, with its tidy grass verges and elegantly fading colonial buildings, but after almost three decades of free-market economics, the North American influence is more apparent in newly developed areas: the old buildings of the city center were built by European architects, inspired by Paris and Rome, but the smoked glass and marble of the new *barrio alto* offices transport the visitor to Chicago or Houston, rather than a European capital.

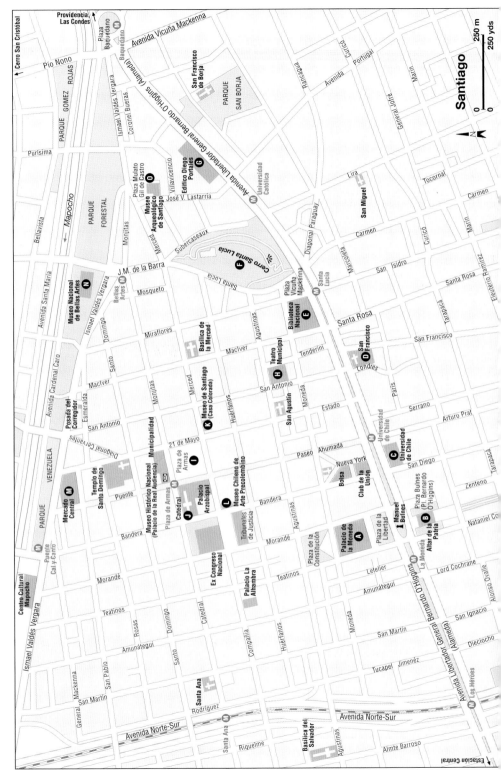

Santiago

250 m
250 yds

Getting around the city is easy. A brief glance at a map – there's an excellent A to Z booklet that comes with the Santiago phone book, as well as those you can pick up at bookshops and kiosks – will reveal just how straightforward the city is. You're almost bound to enter the city along the **Avenida Libertador Bernardo O'Higgins**. This broad avenue, named after the Chilean-Irish independence hero and father of the republic, has been the city's main thoroughfare since a fork of the Mapocho River was filled in before independence to create it. It is known universally as "the Alameda" (a word of Arab origin meaning an avenue with trees and spaces for recreation).

If you enter Santiago on the old road from the airport, rather than taking the newer ring road, your first main point of reference will be the imposing wrought-iron of the **Estación Central**, the city's only remaining functioning railway station. Surrounded by the hue-and-cry of one of the city's most popular and active commercial sectors, the station is well worth a look.

Map on page 146

The heart of Santiago

The ugly concrete telecommunications tower run by the company Entel announces the beginning of the city center proper. A block farther on, the Alameda broadens, and the low form of the presidential palace, **La Moneda **, rises to the left. La Moneda, so called because it was originally designed by the Italian architect Joaquín Toesca as the country's mint, was built between 1788 and 1805. Between 1846 and 1958, Chile's presidents lived there, sharing the premises with the mint until 1929. Squat by comparison with the high ministerial buildings around it (Toesca designed it low to resist earthquakes), many consider La Moneda one of the finest examples of colonial public buildings in the sub-continent.

Monument to Chile's indigenous peoples, Plaza de Armas.

BELOW: old and new in the Plaza de Armas.

The building's tragic international fame came with the military coup led by General Augusto Pinochet on September 11 1973, when much of its interior was destroyed by rocketing from Air Force Hawker Hunters and its image, smoke and flames belching from its northern side, leapt onto the world's front pages and TV screens. It was here that the deposed president, the socialist Dr Salvador Allende, almost certainly committed suicide during the onslaught. The newly restored palace was re-inaugurated in 1981 as the seat of government. The patios of the palace are open to the public (Mon–Sat 10am–6pm, Sun 10am–2pm; identification document required), and guided tours of some of the beautifully restored rooms, with their prime collection of Chilean painting, can be arranged by appointment (tel: 02-690-4000).

In front of the palace's main entrance, in the **Plaza de la Constitución**, former presidents Jorge Alessandri and Eduardo Frei, the father of President Frei who was elected in 1993, and Salvador Allende stare at each other from their pedestals on opposite sides of the square. The plaza was remodeled by General Pinochet, who built underneath it a complex network of meeting rooms, offices, an emergency war room and a television studio for making broadcasts to the nation, all known popularly as *"el bunker"* – the entrances are visible on three sides of the square. On the west side of the plaza is what was the luxury **Hotel Carrera** which, as from 2005, will become the Ministry of Foreign Affairs. It was from the upper stories of the Carrera that the bombing of La Moneda during the 1973 coup was filmed.

Back across the Alameda is the **Plaza Bernardo O'Higgins**, more generally known as the Plaza Bulnes (after the 19th-century General and President Manuel Bulnes, whose statue is in the center of the Alameda). This square is dominated by the **Altar de la Patria** , a structure erected by General Pinochet to house a marble urn containing the remains of O'Higgins. The altar is topped by an equestrian statue of the Liberator and a permanently lit "flame of liberty," intended by Pinochet to celebrate national values and his coup. This divisive monument blocks an impressive view from the palace down Avenida Bulnes and will soon be moved to an army barracks as part of a plan for a new civic plaza, which includes the construction of an underpass for this section of the Alameda. In the center of the Alameda to the west is another statue, this time of O'Higgins' partner in the Chilean campaign and later liberator of Peru, José de San Martín.

BELOW: Plaza de la Constitución.

The Plaza O'Higgins is flanked to the east by the headquarters of the armed forces and the Carabinero police. Every other day at 10am, a green-uniformed, jackbooted detail of the Carabinero palace guard, a special unit whose members are selected for their height, marches from the Carabinero HQ to La Moneda in an impressive changing-of-the guard ceremony.

Buildings of the colonial era

Continuing along the Alameda, past the **Banco del Estado** on the left (believed to have been the largest building in Latin America on its completion, in 1945), is the **Club de la Unión**, Latin America's oldest and plushest gentleman's club, membership of which is still a much-prized goal for Chile's male conservative elite. The building, inaugurated in 1925, is lavishly decorated inside in Louis XIV and XV, gothic and other European styles. All the club's tableware was specially imported from France, Spain and England, and it has an excellent collection of Chilean art. Opposite, on the southern side of the Alameda is the yellow-washed central campus building of the **University of Chile ⑨**. The building, begun in 1863, was designed by Lucien Henault, one of the contracted French architects who founded the neo-classical style which dominated Chilean public architecture of the time and hence much of the profile of Santiago's city center. Outside is a statue of the university's founder, the Venezuelan exile Andrés Bello, one of the continent's great intellectual figures of the 19th century.

Back on the north side of the Alameda, beyond Calle Bandera, is the **Paseo Ahumada**, a busy, fountain-bedecked pedestrian walkway that bisects the city-center from north to south. This is the natural entry to the center, to which we'll return shortly. Meanwhile, on the other side of the Alameda again, is one of Santiago's best-known landmarks: the red-washed colonial church of **San Francisco ⑩** (open Mon–Sun, closed Sun pm), the oldest in the capital. Franciscan friars built the first church on this site in 1572 to house the "Virgen del Socorro" (the Helpful Virgin), which Pedro de Valdivia himself brought to South America, firmly attached to his saddle. The original adobe church was destroyed by an earthquake in 1883 and was replaced by a stone church, the nave of which survives, that was completed in 1612. The Church's distinctive tower was added in 1860. The "Virgen del Socorro", of Italian or Spanish origin, was declared the patron of Santiago by the *conquistadores* after she was said to have saved them during the first major Amerindian attack in the Mapocho val-

Map on page 146

TIP

In the Banco de Chile, on Ahumada between Agustinas and Huérfanos, the old wooden cash desks are still in use.

BELOW: poised to accompany the changing of the guards, La Moneda.

ley by appearing before them and throwing dirt into the attackers' eyes. Much-venerated, she can still be seen above the church's main altar.

Inside the church, note the wooden ceiling, built in the first half of the 17th century. Its original Mudéjar-style decoration was replaced in a 19th-century neo-classical restoration. The attractive cedar-wood choir stalls are the oldest in Chile. The museum in the adjacent Franciscan monastery (open Mon–Sat 10am–1pm and 3–6pm, Sun 10am–2pm; entrance fee) has a fine collection of Chilean and Peruvian colonial art. The museum also holds a facsimile of the Nobel Prize medal given to the Chilean poet Gabriela Mistral, who died a lay member of the Franciscan order.

Gabriela Mistral (1889–1957) was the first person in Latin America to be awarded the Nobel Prize for Literature, in 1945.

Behind the square outside the church is the quaint **Barrio París-Londres**, two short streets named after these European capitals, whose houses, designed as a whole by a group of architects in the 1920s, jumble together imitations of styles ranging from neo-classical to Mudéjar and Gothic. The next structure of note is the **Biblioteca Nacional** ⑤, which occupies the main part of a block on the northern side of the Alameda. The imposing building, in late 19th-century French style, opened in 1924 and contains one of Latin America's largest national libraries and archives, with a reading room open to the public and free concerts, talks and film shows (open Mon–Sat, closed Sat pm.)

Landmarks of character

Beyond the Biblioteca is one of Santiago's most curious and historically significant sites, the **Cerro Santa Lucía** ⑥. It was here, on what was then a rocky outcrop known by the indigenous people as Huelén (Pain), that Pedro de Valdivia and his 150 men first encamped, and Valdivia decided to found the city.

BELOW: the highly ornamented Terrazo Neptuno, Cerro Santa Lucia.

He renamed the *cerro* (hill) after the saint of the date on which he reached it, December 13 1540. In 1872, the great historian and intendent of Santiago, Benjamín Vicuña Mackenna, began to transform the hill into the baroque maze of pathways, gardens, fountains and squares which it is now.

Don't be startled by the cannon which is fired from the Cerro to mark noon (weekdays only). Together with the **Parque Forestal** by the Río Mapocho, the Cerro is one of the city's best-loved venues for lovers and strollers. A lift has recently been installed on the west side, on Calle Santa Lucía.

At the foot of the Cerro, on the Alameda, is a fine mural in homage to Gabriela Mistral, representing the poet herself and the main themes of her work. A few yards farther on, a smooth rock is set in the skirt of the hill, engraved with an extract of a letter sent by Pedro de Valdivia to Emperor Charles V in 1545, extolling Chile's climatic virtues.

The Cerro marks the end of the city center as such, and the start of the last stretch of the Alameda. On its north side is the vast and, to many, hideous **Diego Portales building** ⑦, erected in record speed and constructivist style in 1972. General Pinochet's government made it the HQ of the military junta, and now it is the Defense Ministry. Across the road is the Carabineros' church, the small neo-gothic **Iglesia de San Francisco de Borja**, and in front of it a monument to members of the police force who were killed in the line of duty. Immediately afterwards is the Crowne Plaza Holiday Inn hotel, located opposite one of the city's best art cinemas, the Cine Arte Alameda.

Yards farther on, the Alameda ends at the junction with Avenida Vicuña Mackenna and the Plaza Italia (also referred to as Plaza Baquedano), centered on the equestrian statue of General Manuel Baquedano, commander of the Chilean army during the War of the Pacific against Peru and Bolivia. This spot marks the end of central Santiago and the beginning of Providencia and the *barrio alto*. It is therefore a good point to retrace your steps and return to the Paseo Ahumada (by metro, three stops to Universidad de Chile). In the Universidad de Chile station, the giant murals are by Chilean painter, Mario Toral.

Map on page 146

Shopping and business

If the Alameda is the center's main thoroughfare for motor traffic, Ahumada is the pedestrian hub. Everyone – shoppers, businesspeople and street artists – seems to converge there. Business gossip is exchanged in cafés like the Haiti, where mini-skirted young women serve *espresos* and *cortados* (black and white coffee) with glasses of mineral water. Crowds press past the Paseo's many and varied shops, banks, department stores and well-stocked newspaper kiosks.

Elegant interior of the Correo Central.

To the left of Ahumada is the *barrio cívico,* a few blocks built in the 1930s around La Moneda in rigorously utilitarian style and densely polluted by the throng of horn-hooting buses crawling along Calle Bandera, beside the Club de la Unión. This area holds the **Intendencia** (corner of Moneda and Morandé), the **Stock Exchange** (Calle La Bolsa, just behind the Club de la Unión), the **Banco del Estado**, the **Central Bank** and most ministries.

BELOW: rooftop refreshment.

Uptown from Ahumada, three blocks along Calle Agustinas, is the 17th-century church of **San Agustín**, site of an interesting wooden crucifix above the northern altar carved in Peru in 1613 (open Mon–Sun; closed Sun pm). Beyond the church is the **Teatro Municipal** . Designed and restored by French architects – its original plans were approved by Charles Garnier, the architect of the Paris Opera – the theater opened in 1857. Housing the city's symphony orchestra and ballet and opera companies (all of them considered among the finest in the continent), the theater has played host to artists from Sarah Bernhardt to Placido Domingo, who appeared there in 1990. Opposite the theater is perhaps the city's finest example of the influence of late 19th-century French architecture: a house built by the millionaire wine-producing family of French origin, the Subercaseaux, now occupied by the air force officers' club and a bank.

Street life and sacred art

Ahumada ends in the **Plaza de Armas** ❶, the city's historic center. Originally traced out by Pedro de Valdivia in 1541, it takes its name from the weapons held in the fort built in the square to shelter the first settlers at night. Thereafter, the plaza was used for all public activities from troop parades and religious processions to hangings. It is always a hive of activity: shoe-shiners, portrait painters, and pentecostal preachers ply their trades, while sweet and peanut vendors sell from their traditional *barquitos*, or "little boats," mounted on bicycle wheels, and photographers attract your custom with ancient, brightly decorated tripod cameras. On Friday and Sunday mornings and Thursday and Saturday afternoons, a very good police band plays on the bandstand on the eastern side of the plaza; the rest of the time, the bandstand is used for chess matches.

BELOW: statue of Santiago's founder, Pedro de Valdivia, just outside the Municipalidad.

The **Cathedral** (open Mon–Sun, closed Sun pm), on the west side of the plaza, is the fifth on the site. Its predecessors were destroyed by earthquakes in 1552, 1647 and 1730, while the first was burned down in an attack by native people shortly after Pedro de Valdivia built it. Work on the present building began in 1747, but the final design was by Joaquín Toesca, who was brought from Italy for this task, moving on later to La Moneda – though the twin towers were not added until 1899 by another Italian, Ignacio Cremonesi. The cathedral's internal decoration bears the somewhat heavy imprint of the Bavarian Jesuits who created much of it, although some of their work, and important local handicraft adornments, were destroyed by clumsy restoration carried out by Cremonesi. Those buried in the cathedral include the four Carrera brothers, partners and rivals with O'Higgins in the country's liberation from Spain *(see page 34)*, and Diego Portales *(see page 37)*, considered by many as the founder of Chile's 19th-century conservative state. On the left side of the cathedral is the entrance to its **Museo de Arte Sagrado** (open Mon only, 10.30–1pm and 3pm–6pm; free of charge).

After the Conquest, the land along the northern face of the Plaza was owned by Pedro de Valdivia, who lived in a house on the site now occupied by the **Correo Central** (Central Post Office). In 1541, however, the house was burned down in an attack by native people; later Valdivia sold the land to the Royal Treasury in order to finance further expeditions south. Two centuries later, the post office site saw the city's first, and reputedly magnificent, theater. Chile's first stamps, printed in England, were sold here in 1857 (a plaque with a facsimile of the stamps can be seen on the outer wall on Calle Puente) and the present building was finished in 1902.

Palaces and museums

Next door to the Correo Central is the Palacio de la Real Audiencia, now the **Museo Histórico Nacional** (open Tues–Sun; closed Sun pm in summer; entrance fee, except Sun), which was inaugurated in 1808 to house the sessions at which the Spanish Crown's representatives heard local reports and dispensed justice. This purpose was short-lived, however, and two years later the building was used for the swearing-in of the first revolutionary government junta. The first Congress met here and the palace was the seat of government until President Bulnes moved to La Moneda in 1846. The museum, which contains some 12,000 pieces from pre-history until the 1930s, moved there in 1982 and is well worth a visit.

The last building along the plaza's northern edge is the **Municipalidad** or Town Hall (open Mon–Fri 9am–2pm). Formerly the Palacio Consistorial, it was designed by Toesca for the colonial *cabildo* and opened in 1790. The facade was replaced in the 1800s by the present neo-classical design, and restored again after the 1985 earthquake. High on the facade, and in the wrought-ironwork above the entrance, you can see the red lion coat of arms granted the city by the Spanish Crown after the first *cabildo* met. In front is an equestrian statue of Pedro de Valdivia donated by Chile's Spanish community in 1986.

Map on page 146

BELOW: evening diversions in the Plaza de Armas.

On Calle Merced, at the southeast corner of the square, is the striking red-washed **Casa Colorada**. Built in 1769, this is the best-preserved colonial house in the city. It was the residence of the president of the first revolutionary junta, Mateo de Toro y Zambrano and, for a time, of Lord Thomas Cochrane, the maverick Scottish admiral hired by O'Higgins to command naval operations against Spain. Now it houses a tourist office and the **Museo de Santiago** (open Tues–Sun, closed Sun pm; entrance fee, except Sun), dedicated to the history of the capital. This has didactic models of the city, but few real exhibits. Plaza de Armas has only one pavement café (that serves dreadful coffee) but, behind the Casa Colorada, there is a small plaza, sheltered from the city noise, with a new restaurant that is a good place for a coffee or light lunch.

Two blocks westwards, the excellent **Museo Chileno de Arte Precolombino** (Bandera 361; open Tues–Sun, closed Sun pm) occupies what used to be the Real Aduana (Customs House). Access is by way of an arcade built through the building on the corner. This museum, widely recognized as the best and most important in Santiago, surprisingly has no coffee shop, but the City Hotel, opposite on Compañía, is a handy alternative, and also serves reasonably priced lunches.

Immediately west are the Law Courts, and across Calle Compañía is the neo-classical grandeur of what was the pre-1973 Congress Building (now the Foreign Ministry). Previously, this was the site of the Jesuit headquarters (hence the name of the street, after the Compañía de Jesus), until they were expelled from the country in 1766; and later of a church which burned down in 1863, at the cost of 2,000 lives. This disaster, one of the worst of its kind on the continent, led to the formation of the city's first fire brigade, whose headquarters is nearby at Calle Puente 978 – the bell in its fine tower still tolls

The tall CTC telephone company's corporate building on Plaza Italia is designed in the shape of a cell phone.

BELOW: the ornate facade of Estación Mapocho.

every time a fireman, who are all voluntary in Chile, is killed. Also close by is the curious **Palacio de La Alhambra** (Compañía 1340; not open to visitors), begun in the 1860s and later transformed into a miniature copy of the famous Mudéjar palace of the same name in Granada, Spain, complete with mock-Arab furniture made in Paris.

Wrought-iron splendor

Back in the Plaza de Armas, if you're feeling hungry and like seafood, you can do no better than walk north along Calle Puente (the continuation of the Paseo Ahumada) to the **Mercado Central**  (open Mon–Sun till 5pm). This, together with **La Vega**, on the other side of the Mapocho River, is the city's central market. Bustling with the character of such markets around the world, both the interior and the exterior of this elegant structure are worthy of attention. Designed in Chile but built in England; the market was inaugurated in 1872 by Vicuña Mackenna as the site of a National Exhibition to celebrate the thrusting and confident economy of the time. It is full of cheap eating places, and above all *marisquerías* where cheap and abundant portions of Chile's remarkable seafood are served, considered by many the best in the world.

Figure, Museo de Arte Precolombino.

Here, too, is the fine, copper-roofed shell of what used to be Santiago's second railway station, the **Estación Mapocho**. Opened in 1912, and designed by another of Chile's leading French architects, Emile Jécquier, this once served as the terminus for trains arriving from the coast, but it is now used as an arts and convention center. Its ornate facade looks across the **Parque Venezuela**, with its green-tinged monument to the navy, down the long vista of the **Parque Forestal**.

BELOW: statue in the huge wrought-iron Mercado Central.

Map on page 146

An artistic park

The Parque Forestal, which is generally referred to by Chileans as their Bois de Boulogne, was laid out by the French landscaper Georges Dubois in the late 19th century. The idea was to make use of the wasteland left over after the canalization of the Mapocho in its now characteristic stone course. Looking at the generally narrow flow of the Mapocho (a name which in Mapuche means, "river which loses itself in the land," in reference to its partially subterranean course west of Santiago), it is hard to believe that it is capable of swelling suddenly with torrents of melting snow or rain from the Andes. In the past, flooding caused several disasters and was dealt with first by wide stone embankments, or *tajamares* (built by Toesca), then by the present channel.

Planted with varieties of native and imported trees, the park contains several small squares and monuments to figures such as Columbus, Bach, the god Pan and the seminal Nicaraguan modernist poet, Rubén Dario (opposite Merced 230), who wrote his most important work, *Azul*, while exiled in Chile in the 1890s. A block from the Mercado Central, in a square off Calle Esmeralda to the right, is another fine colonial house, the **Posada del Corregidor**, one-time bar and center of Santiago's bohemia, now a museum (open Mon–Sa,; closed Sat pm; entrance fee). The house never in fact belonged to a *corregidor* (official), despite the whim of a later owner who placed the coat of arms of one of the city's best-known such officials, Luis Manuel de Zañartu, on the wall.

Halfway along the park, close to the northern tip of the Cerro Santa Lucía, is the **Museo de Bellas Artes** Ⓝ (open Tues–Sun; entrance fee, except Sun), the country's principal art gallery. Designed by Jéquier as an approximate copy of the Petit Palais in Paris, it contains permanent displays of contemporary and past

Chilean art as well as hosting visiting exhibitions. As from 2005, the University of Chile's collection of Chilean art from the first half of the 20th century (currently in storage) will be housed in the **Museo de Arte Contemporáneo** in renovated premises in the back part of the building. Further along still is the extraordinary **Palacio Bruna**, another turn-of-the-20th-century mansion designed in part by one of Chile's leading poets, Pedro Prado, who studied architecture without ever graduating. It is now occupied by the National Chamber of Commerce.

Shortly before you reach the *palacio*, a few steps backtracking along Calle Merced takes you to Calle José Victorino Lastarria and the pleasant cafés of the **Plaza Mulato Gil de Castro ⓞ**. The **Museo de Artes Visuales** (open Tues–Sun; entrance fee) in the plaza holds a small but choice private collection of Chilean painting and sculpture from the 1960s onwards. Nearby is the **Biógrafo** art cinema. The Parque ends with the extravagantly symbolic **Fuente Alemana**, representing Chile and its wealth of natural resources. This monument was presented by the country's German community in 1910 for the first centenary of Independence, and its fountains serve as an impromptu bathing pool for schoolchildren. Note too the strange art-deco house, complete with mythological beast, at Merced 84.

Elevated views

We are now back at the **Plaza Italia**, shadowed on the left by the looming shape of the **Cerro San Cristóbal** (named after St. Christopher by the Spanish because of the landmark it offered to travelers). To reach the Cerro, cross the river by the **Pío Nono bridge** and proceed past the 1930s pile of the University of Chile's Law School up Calle Pío Nono. At the far end is the entrance to the **Parque Metropolitano**, the park containing the Cerro's attractions. You can tour the

Map on page 146

BELOW: young artist painting at the Museo de Bellas Artes.

Mural for peace.

Cerro completely by car, a minibus service, or on foot. But a more picturesque route is to ascend by the 60-year-old funicular (open daily; 10am–7pm, closed Mon am; 10am–8pm weekends), following in the footsteps of Pope John Paul II, who rose to bless the city during his 1987 visit in his bullet-proof "pope-mobile."

Perched halfway up the hill is the **Zoo** (open Tues–Sun), and at the top there are lookout points and the **Santuario de la Inmaculada Concepción** (shrine of the Virgin Mary). In front of the nearby chapel is a tree from the Basque town of Guernica, planted by Chile's Basque community. The 14-meter (46-ft) high statue of the Virgin, dating from 1908, is frequently the focus of religious ceremonies.

From here you can take a ten-minute ride in the Swiss cable car (open Mon–Fri 10.30am–6.30pm, closed Mon am, weekends 10.30am– 7pm), opened in 1980, along the length of the Cerro and linking the hills to the end of Avenida Pedro de Valdivia, in Providencia, with an optional stop on the way at the Tupahue gardens and public swimming pool. Other attractions in the park include cafés, restaurants, Chilean and Japanese gardens, a wine-sampling center and exhibition (Enoteca), and another open-air swimming pool. Tickets can be purchased for part or all of the round trip at the foot of the funicular and at the end of the cable-car. This trip is particularly worthwhile for its view of the snow-capped Andes if you happen to be in Santiago in winter, after a day of rain has washed the city's air clean of smog.

From Plaza Italia, you can also take the metro (Line 5, southbound) to the **Museo Interactivo Mirador** (Sebastapol 90, La Granja), an interactive science museum that children enjoy enormously (open daily 9.30am–5.30pm). From the Mirador metro station, *colectivos* (communal taxis) run to the door of the museum. The visit is also an opportunity to get a glimpse of one of Santiago's working-class suburbs.

BELOW: romance in the park.

Artists' quarter

The area between the Cerro and the Mapocho is the closest Santiago gets to a bohemian *barrio*, **Bellavista**. This is a mixed residential and artistic neighborhood with lots of charm and interest. Nobel poet Pablo Neruda had one of his houses, La Chascona, here *(see page 181)*. This house is now open to the public (Fernando Márquez de la Plata 0192; Tues–Sun 10am–5.45pm).

Bellavista's main streets, apart from Pío Nono, are Purísima, running parallel, and Antonia López de Bello, cutting across laterally. A great variety of restaurants are scattered through the *barrio*. There are also several theaters, and at night there is considerable street life with musicians and handicrafts sold from the pavement. Calle Bellavista itself has a string of more tourist-oriented shops specializing in Chile's national stone, lapiz lazuli.

Bellavista is skirted along the Mapocho by Avenida Santa María, the fast route uptown to the wealthy neighborhoods of **Las Condes**, **Vitacura**, **La Dehesa** and **Lo Curro**. The last is home to the huge and unmistakable modernistic presidential residence built by General Pinochet, but never occupied after the scandal it produced; now it is the army's country club. Along the way, Santa María crosses under the Américo

Vespucio loop road, which from here provides a rapid freeway connection around the north of the city to Arturo Merino Benítez airport – a useful way of avoiding the city-center for trips between the airport and the upper *barrio alto*.

Embassies and ice creams

Across the river from Bellavista, Avenida Providencia runs uptown from the Plaza Italia. In Plaza Italia, the Telefónica building has a ground-floor art gallery that puts on excellent exhibitions (open Tues–Sun 10am–8pm; free). Several squares cluster around the point at which the Alameda becomes Providencia, with monuments to several historical figures, including the Cuban independence leader José Martí and the hero of Chile's Independence war, Manuel Rodríguez. Between Providencia and the river are the long Parque Balmaceda, with children's amusements and the Café Literario, a new bookstore and coffee shop.

Near Salvador metro, a long metal monument, erected in 1980, celebrates Chilean aviation. Buildings of interest in the area include the **Casa Matriz de las Hermanas de la Providencia**, a convent of the Sisters of Providence which is a Canadian order (Providencia 509); and the colonial-style church of **Nuestra Señora del Carmen**, built in 1892 by a local landowner out of gratitude for victory in the civil war of the previous year. The main tourist office, Sernatur (Providencia 1550), is located farther eastwards, with a fruit and vegetable market just behind it. Treat yourself to a drink in the nearby **Phone Box Pub**, in a quaint pedestrian cul-de-sac, which also has a second-hand English-language bookshop. Avenida Providencia continues on through the shopping and residential area into Avenida Apoquindo, its continuation under another name, now the site of some of the city's most modern office blocks. ❑

Map on page 146

The government tourist service, Sernatur, has its main office in the old Providencia fruit and vegetable market (Providencia 1550).

BELOW: the coastal mountains, seen from Cerro San Cristóbal.

SANTIAGO EXCURSIONS

Map on page 164

The countryside around Santiago is perfect for day-trips, with numerous outdoor activities possible, from wallowing in hot mud to wine tasting, skiing to sunbathing – all amid gorgeous surroundings

Santiago

On an average day the jagged peaks of the Andes loom mistily over the eastern end of Santiago, a distant yet overbearing presence. In fact, you can travel within a day, by car or bus, far up into the mountains beside the winding course of the **Río Maipo**. This rushing torrent sweeps the loose earth of the mountains downstream toward the rich, agricultural plains of Chile's central valley region, pouring itself finally into the Pacific, 4 km (2½ miles) south of San Antonio. The Maipo Valley, or **Cajón del Maipo** as it's called in Spanish, is a popular weekend venue for *santiaguinos* anxious to escape the relentless pace of the city streets for a few hours of fresh air and relaxation.

For the sedentary the canyon offers an easy but visually seductive drive towards the mountains' heart; and for the more active, depending on the season, there are plenty of opportunities to swim (in open-air pools), ride horses, picnic, hike, camp or cabin overnight. The river is too rough for regular canoeing or kayaking, but agencies like Cascada Expediciones (tel: 02-861-1777 or fax: 02-861-2222) offer raft rides all year round. You must be over 10 years old (or more, depending on the time of year and river conditions) and know how to swim.

There's also a surprising variety of wonderful country restaurants, with varied menus that include traditional Chilean foods, espresso coffee and *küchen* that would be a credit to any German pastry chef. The delicious home cooking draws heavily on the canyon's almond, walnut and cherry orchards. The canyon's economic base depends largely on tourism, but prices tend to be reasonable and the Chilean flavor of the area remains distinct.

PRECEDING PAGES: a rare glimpse of traditional farming, near Santiago. **LEFT:** near San José de Maipo. **BELOW:** new votive temple of Maipú, framed by ruins of the old one.

Home cooking by the roadside

Driving up the winding road, especially on weekends, you'll see white flags and small tables by the roadside, piled with round breads of more than 30 cm (1 ft) in diameter or jars containing intriguing liquids. The white flags mean someone is selling something they've prepared in their kitchen: bread cooked in ashes, often in the traditional ovens of baked mud; jams made with local walnuts, almonds and berries; fresh honey; the ubiquitous *empanadas*, as common in Chile as the hamburger is in the United States. The sight of the sellers' bread with *chicharrones* (dried pork) evokes nostalgic enthusiasm from most Chileans, especially those who have spent part of their childhood in the country.

Toward the summer's end (February), you may be lucky enough to have a prickly pear, or *tuna,* fall at your feet. This visually unappealing fruit should be handled carefully, to avoid the prickles. When peeled, it will yield a mouthful of melon-like flesh, full of pips small enough to swallow. Prickly pears are as

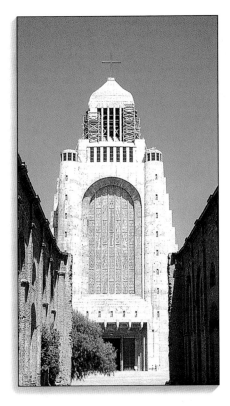

common as apples in Chile, where they droop like large, green teardrops on cactus arms. *Tuna* are particularly popular crushed and blended into refreshing juices, with the pips filtered out.

Exploring the lower Andes

Strung out along the road are stopping points affording spectacular views of the canyon itself, as well as small towns and villages, campgrounds, parks and an obelisk marking the site where, in 1986, the Manuel Rodríguez Patriotic Front (one of the country's Marxist guerilla groups) staged a daring ambush of General Augusto Pinochet's cavalcade, which almost put an end to his dictatorial rule. If you're a racing enthusiast, plan your first stop at the canyon's mouth in **Las Vizcachas ❶**, where a private club houses a racecourse used by both cars and motorcycles. Unfortunately, the rest of the facilities, including a large swimming pool and pleasant picnic area, are not open to the public.

As you pass through **La Obra** you will be able to see craftspeople working at the roadside with the pale pink stone that characterizes the area and is popular for terraces and other building projects. A few kilometers before La Obra is the sales room of the Cavas del Maipo where, at weekends, you can visit the vineyard, taste and buy wine. Just past La Obra is **Las Vertientes**, a small town with a gorgeous swimming pool surrounded by grass and flowers, where you can spend the day swimming, lying in the sun and munching on sandwiches.

Silver boomtowns and ski resorts

San José de Maipo ❷, approximately 25 km (16 miles) from Santiago, is the canyon's main town, founded in 1791 after silver deposits were discovered in

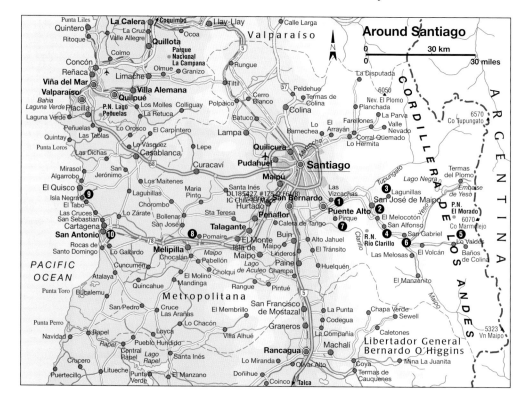

the surrounding area. The town's buildings are constructed in the adobe and straw common to the region. This is a pleasant place to stretch your legs, enjoy the fresh air and absorb some of the tranquility of a traditional Andean town. On the outskirts of San José, a narrow gravel road sheers off from the main highway and begins climbing up to **Lagunillas ❸**, a ski resort perched on a mountain peak, overlooking an immense bowl formed by part of the Cordillera. Good nerves and a head for heights are recommended for this trip, but it is worth it, especially during the ski season.

Map on page 164

A New Age retreat

If you prefer to continue along the canyon, you will pass through the towns of **El Toyo** and **El Melocotón** before reaching **San Alfonso ❹**. This village sits in a generous hollow, which was carved through the Andes by the river itself. The people who live around the village are a curious mixture of old country-dwellers and New Agers attracted by the area's spectacular natural setting, the peace, and the proximity to Santiago.

La Cascada de las Animas (Waterfall of Souls), a camping and picnic ground, captures this peculiar mix. It has a wonderful circular swimming pool and handmade cabins built with local materials, and belongs to a family who once owned most of the land on which the town now sits. The sons and daughters of the original *latifundista* have established a community based on New Age ideals and sensitivity to the natural environment. The result is that the park and campgrounds are maintained extraordinarily well and the trail rides organized by family members (usually over weekends and for week-long periods) provide an excellent opportunity to explore some of the remoter areas of the Andes.

Colored grasses for sale in the pottery town of Pomaire.

BELOW: preparing the day's catch on the coast.

Concha y Toro wine vat.

BELOW: mud baths close to the Argentine border.

Other activities offered by the community include guided walks and rafting on the river. For more information or to reserve a cabin in La Cascada de las Animas, tel: 02-861-1303.

For the less adventurous or for those with less time, the Hostería Los Ciervos serves excellent meals in a garden lined with lush, well-kept plants and, if the weather is cold, has a cozy dining room with the purple abundance of a bougainvillea visible through a window.

San Alfonso is a good stopping and turning point for a leisurely day. However, it's also possible to start early in the morning from Santiago and head straight up the canyon 70 km/44 miles (the last 14 km/9 miles on a gravel road may be difficult in winter) to **Lo Valdés** ❺. The road passes the rather run-down hot springs of **Baños Morales** and continues up past a checkpoint (the Chile-Argentine border is near), to the **Refugio Alemán**, a comfortable inn with a good restaurant, a spectacular view of snowy peaks and a deep natural pool, surrounded by fossils from the period when the Andes were under the sea. Baños Morales is also the entry point to the **El Morado National Park**, where a three-hour hike through majestic scenery will take you to the San Francisco glacier. The park is administered by CONAF, the national park service, and basic camping facilities are available.

A further 11 km (7 miles) on are the **Baños de Colina**, hot springs which are open to the public from September, where the water reaches temperatures as high as 60°C (140°F). The drive (feasible only in summer) takes you through a spectacular moonscape, completely different from the rest of the canyon, and the baths themselves are arranged in smooth, natural pools on terraces carved into the mountainside. At the source, hot water steams out of natural caves into the hottest bath, which in turn jets into pools further and further down. The further away from the source the pool is, the more bearable the temperature. In the second pool, you can rest your elbows on the edge and gaze down the valley at the mountains' extraordinary shades of gray, green and subtle pinks, as your body soaks in warm, sulfurous luxury.

On the Argentine frontier

Another alternative is to turn left at **San Gabriel** ❻ (before El Volcán) and follow the **Río Yeso** up to the Yeso dam, high up in the Andean cliffs. You'll have to stop at a control on the way and leave your identification at the checkpoint, because this is a pass to Argentina. The round trip from Santiago is 170 km (106 miles), 65 km (40 miles) of it on a dirt road, so it's a good idea to carry a picnic lunch.

To return it's possible to retrace your steps as far as El Toyo and then cross the Maipo River and follow the other side of the canyon back down to the Las Vertientes bridge. Here you can cross and retrace your path to Santiago, or carry on through **Pirque** ❼, a picturesque country town with a public sales and tasting room of one of Chile's most well-known vineyards, run by the Concha y Toro company. You can tour the huge vats where wines are stored and matured and peer through the gloom and dust into the "devil's locker room" where one of the company's top wines,

El Casillero del Diablo, is aged. The original country estate and family mansion can be seen from the road, surrounded by the smaller cottages of the vineyards' workers. The main house, which appears on some of the labels, was built around 1875, at roughly the same time that the French landscape designer Gustavo Renner was designing the surrounding park.

A car gives the most flexibility for traveling up and down the canyon, allowing plenty of time for visiting anything which catches your fancy. However, buses run regularly from Santiago up the canyon, some of their routes ending in San José, Pirque, Puente Alto and, in January and February, there is a daily bus up to Baños Morales (weekends only in winter).

A village of potters

It is easy to catch a bus from Santiago that will drop you off at the crossroads to **Pomaire** ❽, a town where clay pottery is the sustaining activity for almost the entire population. The road to the town, about a half hour's walk from the highway, stretches between an avenue of trees and green fields.

In 1985, an earthquake razed the original adobe homes and they have mostly been replaced by simple wood houses. The reddish clay once common in the town is now virtually exhausted and the raw material for the pottery is mostly imported from other parts of the country, but the magic of this small village is still potent.

Designs are primarily traditional, including *miniaturas*, small figures inspired by country stories and religious beliefs; decorative work and, perhaps most beautiful, the utilitarian oven-proof clay pots of all shapes and sizes, ideal for many Spanish and Chilean dishes. A shapely, sensual parade of vessels are dis-

Map on page 164

Brown pelicans inhabit the Chilean coast from Arica down to Isla de Chiloé.

BELOW: the beach front, San Antonio.

Map
on page
164

Pottery at Pomaire.

BELOW: soaking up
the sun at a Pacific
resort.

played for sale, with names like *pailas, fuentes, tinajas, maceteros*; all are considerably more enticing than the one English word that sums them up: pot.

You can easily spend an enjoyable day wandering up and down Pomaire's two main streets, trying in vain to resist the temptation of taking at least a *chanchito* (a peculiarly Chilean pig pot) or an old worn-out clay shoe, back to your homeland to hold plants or trinkets. Tucked in between the potteries are small plant stores and greenhouses, along with restaurants offering an excellent selection of Chilean-style meals, which range from the ubiquitous *empanadas* to *cazuela*, a stew made with a variety of vegetables and containing a piece of beef, chicken or, most traditionally, turkey.

Down to the Pacific

If you're traveling by bus, the round trip to and from Pomaire is probably enough for a good, full day. If you're using a car and you don't mind driving back to Santiago after dark, you have the option of carrying on to **Isla Negra ❾** on the coast. Returning from Pomaire to the new Autopista del Sol ("Highway of the Sun"), continue along this stretch until just before San Antonio, where you turn north to head toward the popular seaside resorts of **Cartagena**, **Las Cruces** and **El Tabo**. (Be careful to take the old coast road, rather than the new tolled highway.) Cartagena was one of the resorts that became popular in the early 19th century, with the arrival of the railway from Santiago.

All of these resorts are lovely places with long sandy beaches, particularly agreeable in the spring or fall, when the sun is a little more merciful. But Isla Negra, a little farther up the coast from all three, has a special quality. It is unclear whether this is because Pablo Neruda, one of Chile's influential most poets, chose to live there, or whether he chose to live there because it is so special. Neruda's favorite house *(see page 181)* overlooks a particularly rough stretch of Isla Negra's beach, where the waves crash against humped rocks rising abruptly out of the white sand like children's castles.

You can easily lose an hour or two, hunched on the humped rocks, gazing out over the restless, changing landscape that cast its spell on so much of Neruda's work. Alternatively, you can walk along the beach, searching for mussels, starfish, clams and barnacles on the damp, naked rocks.

From here it's a short trip back down the coast to **San Antonio ❿**, a working port with the grime of hard labor in evidence and fishing boats moored in the harbor. There are several good restaurants in San Antonio, but the *picadas*, as the Chileans call them, are right on the harbor itself: these are where the fishing people themselves like to eat. Here you'll get huge platefuls of your favorite shellfish or fish dish, with a fresh Chilean salad, rice or French fries, at very reasonable prices.

If you're looking for slightly more comfortable surroundings, then try the Juanita (Antofagasta 159), which also serves all of Chile's most traditional fish dishes at very affordable prices. The drive back to Santiago takes about an hour and a half, all on the Autopista del Sol. ❑

Andean Ski Resorts

There are five ski centers near Santiago: Portillo; Valle Nevado; Farellones; La Parva and Lagunillas. All of them are located in the same area about 50 km (31 miles) from Santiago except Portillo, which is 164 km (102 miles) away, close to the border with Argentina. Skating is also possible on the green Laguna del Inca lake, just above Portillo, which freezes over in winter.

The road to Farellones winds narrow and steep through the cordillera, following most of the Mapocho River canyon deep into the Andes. This is an excellent day trip whatever the season, but snow chains are required in winter (they're available for rental where the road begins). Careful driving is essential at any time of year. Access to the road is controlled by the police in winter and drivers are only allowed to head up until noon, but it's best to start early in the morning. Cars can begin the return descent only after 2pm. Warm clothes are essential, whatever the temperature in Santiago when you leave. Snow usually begins in June and lasts until September, making the area popular with ski enthusiasts from the Northern Hemisphere, who can ski during their summer holidays.

Farellones provides excellent conditions, and equipment rental and classes can be arranged in the town itself. It has four well-equipped slopes extending to altitudes of 3,333 meters (10,935ft), and which are suitable for skiers of variable experience. Group and private classes are available.

Even if you're not a skier, it's well worth making the trip to Farellones. The view from the road as you ascend higher and higher, the pure sky, the clear air, and the chance to enjoy the Andes from the inside out all make the drive worthwhile. On the way there you'll have a bird's-eye view of El Arrayán, a small town perched on the edge of Santiago, made up of the kind of houses architects design for themselves. You'll also see La Ermita, with its characteristic chapel, and the nearby hydro-electric station that supplies one of Chile's main copper mines, La Disputada.

Near Farellones is the hamlet of La Parva, situated at 2,816 meters (9,239ft), with a spectacular view down the valley toward Santiago. La Parva usually enjoys snowy conditions until well into October and you can ski as high as 3,630 meters (11,910 ft).

Also near Farellones is Valle Nevado, a modern ski center opened in 1988. The turn-off, 2km before Farellones, takes you 10 km (6 miles) deep into the mountains. There are three luxury hotels and a luxury apartment building, providing services as varied as video movies, a discotheque, a French restaurant, a gymnasium, a pool room, sauna, whirlpool bath and a snack bar. Stores sell and rent ski equipment and clothing, and there is a day-care center and a medical center equipped for any emergency. The highest point you can ski is 3,670 meters (12,040 ft) above sea level.

Skiing in Chile is an expensive activity, and prices of equipment and accommodation are similar to those of any developed country.

More information on Farellones, La Parva and Valle Nevado can be obtained from the Sernatur Tourist Office in Santiago (tel: 600 7376 2887). ❑

RIGHT: ready for action at Valle Nevado.

VALPARAÍSO AND VIÑA DEL MAR

*The port and its neighboring beach resort
are steeped in history, but it's the unusual ascensores
that scale Valparaíso's hills that will leave a lasting impression*

Map
on page
184

Valparaíso and Viña del Mar may sit side by side on Chile's Pacific coast, but when it comes to urban character, they are worlds apart. One of the first Chilean cities founded by the Spanish in 1541, Valparaíso was Santiago's thriving port for centuries. It is spread along some spectacularly steep hills, with stairways and streets winding up past splendid aging buildings many built by the British in the 19th century, when the port was virtually run from the city of London.

Viña, on the other hand, is a tourist city of steel, glass and neon. Traditionally the reserve of the well-off, it is now middle-class territory and a pleasant enough place to relax, but Valparaíso holds the attractions of its wild and varied history. And, although the poverty that followed the opening of the Panama Canal is still apparent, Valparaíso is now being smartened up again, particularly since UNESCO declared its historic center a World Heritage Site in 2003.

Three bus companies run a shuttle service to Valparaíso and Viña from the Pajaritos metro station in Santiago and this is by far the easiest – and cheapest – way to visit them. A car is more of a liability than a help on Valparaíso's steep hills and there are regular bus and train services between the port and Viña. The 90-minute bus journey from Santiago will take you through the vine-draped Casablanca Valley, where sea breezes help to produce some of Chile's best white wines.

From Santiago you enter **Valparaíso ❶** along Avenida Argentina. On Wednesdays and Saturdays, this avenue's central walkway becomes a city market, groaning with vegetables and fruit, fresh fish and shellfish, dry goods and spices. On Sundays it is home to a vast fleamarket, or *feria persa*.

Upon reaching Avenida Pedro Montt, a former horse race track, the Congress Building rises up imperiously. For some, this is the symbol of the new Chilean democracy, but for most, the exile of Congress to Valparaíso, dictated by the outgoing military government, is just one more reminder of this painful period. The splendid old Congress building in Santiago is now used by the Ministry of Foreign Relations.

The foundation of a great port

The sea has shaped Valparaíso's history since its foundation, four and a half centuries ago. Before the Spanish arrived, the region was inhabited by the Chango people, who fished the bay and called it Quintil. In 1536, Juan de Saavedra sailed down from Callao in Peru to meet a supply ship for Diego de Almagro's earlier foot expedition to Chile. The bay's

PRECEDING PAGES: view across Bahía de Valparaíso. **LEFT:** houses climb the hills above the port. **BELOW:** the popular Cinzano cafe in Valparaíso.

beauty flooded him with such nostalgia for his distant homeland that he named it after his hometown in Spain.

In 1547, Pedro de Valdivia, the founder of Santiago and Governor of Chile, would find himself here, isolated, impoverished by wars and discouraged by the lack of news and support from the crown. With characteristic (and very Chilean) ingenuity, he called on colonists wishing to return to the more developed Northern colonies to load their fortunes (built through the exploitation of gold reserves using native slaves) and themselves onto his ships. About 20 families boarded. On the last night before setting out, under the pretext of a final goodbye banquet in the port, Valdivia set them all ashore where they cheerfully set to consuming wine and meats in huge quantities. But as the feasting reached its height, Don Pedro weighed anchor and set out with the gold, leaving a beach full of furious victims.

Valparaíso went on to become the main port for the growing city of Santiago. This made it a tempting target for pirates, mostly of English or Dutch origin, and the port had to build strong fortifications to repel the attacks, which continued through most of the 16th and 17th centuries. Its defensive towers and forts not only discouraged potential attackers but also acted as a strong stimulus to trade and the warehousing of merchandise. Soon the English stopped raiding and became the largest trading partner of the newly independent Chile, buying up large parts of Valparaíso.

Revolutions, uprisings and riots

Occasionally laid waste by earthquakes and tidal waves, Valparaíso also became notorious for political disturbances. Two of the city's governors died tragically within 20 years of each other. The first was the powerful "king-maker"

Valparaíso's importance as a port declined in the early 19th century, when the opening of the Panama Canal meant that boats no longer had to travel round Cape Horn.

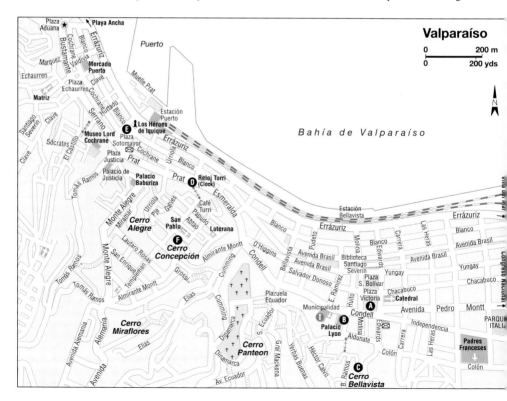

Diego Portales, who was shot to death on his way to Quillota in 1837, during a brief military uprising. The other was an army general, killed on September 18 1859, during a civil uprising at the doors of the La Matriz church, during a religious ceremony giving thanks for Chile's independence.

But, by the early 20th century, the old port had begun to assume its present look. Builders battled the sea for a few extra meters of earth for the *costanera* (coast road) and the railway line. European-style buildings marked the skyline and the old street of trade became the financial and banking center for all the maritime and port activity. The growing population began to spill out of the city's basic "plan" – as the lower part of the city is called – and the incredible feat of building on the cerros (hills) began. Each individual builder found his or her own techniques for fighting gravity and resisting earthquakes, creating a unique city of winding streets, stairways, walks and lookout points which began to string together the different hills, each one separated by the abrupt ravines that characterize the area.

To conquer the hilltops, the *ascensores* (funiculars or cable cars) were introduced, and remain the main form of transport up the city's hills. No visit to Valparaíso is complete without a trip in an *ascensor* – appearances aside, they've proven a secure means for traveling up the hills, while affording spectacular views of the bay.

Map on page 174

Exploring the city

The best way to see Valparaíso is on foot and, to build up the necessary strength, the Vitamin Service Café, on Pedro Montt, near the **Plaza Victoria Ⓐ** is a good place to start. Across from the café, at one side of the **cathedral**, is the house

BELOW: dining room with a view, atop Cerro Artilleria.

A bus adds a splash of color to the imposing city center.

house where General Augusto Pinochet spent his youth. Nothing suggested the prominent role that Pinochet, a mediocre student at the old Sacred Hearts School, would play in Chilean history. In the center of the Plaza sits the lovely **Neptune Fountain**, a war trophy that was stolen from the Peruvians in 1879.

A block along Calle Condell is the neoclassical **Palacio Lyon** , once the mansion of a wealthy family, that now houses the city's natural history museum and municipal art gallery. At the bottom of Calle Huito, which runs alongside the Palacio, the Ascensor Espíritu Santo (the Holy Spirit Lift), one of the city's 15 funiculars, will carry you up to **Cerro Bellavista** ● and its **Museo a Cielo Abierto** (Open-Sky Museum), a collection of murals painted on the sides of houses, some of them by leading Chilean artists. Along Calle Ricardo Ferrari, you will reach **La Sebastiana**, one of the homes of Chilean poet Pablo Neruda (Jan–Feb, daily 10.30am–6.50pm; Mar–Dec, daily 10.10am–6pm, entrance fee). Although Neruda actually used this house relatively little, many visitors find it the most attractive of his four homes, partly because they are allowed to wander through it without taking a guided tour, but also because of the spectacular view over the Bay of Valparaíso that Neruda could enjoy from his bed.

Alternatively from the Palacio Lyon, continue along the narrow, curving Calle Condell – on which buses race at great speed, contributing to the air pollution of this lower part of the city – to Plaza Aníbal Pinto, with two landmarks of the city's gastronomic history: the old **Bar Cinzano** and the **Café Riquet**, the traditional place to tuck into (an enormous) tea. From there, Calle Esmeralda, leads to the **Turri Clock** ●, Valparaíso's equivalent of Big Ben. This is where

BELOW: a popular Valparaíso beach.

Avenida Prat, the city's financial heart, begins. The British influences are so obvious here that it's hard to believe you're in a Latin American city. At Cochrane

Map
on page
174

851 is the **Bar Inglés** (English Bar), a wood-paneled reminder of the city's past. At the end of Esmeralda you'll find yourself in the open expanse of **Plaza Sotomayor ⑤**, overlooked by the gray-washed Naval Headquarters. The Plaza is dominated by the Monument to the Heroes of Iquique, who died in a key naval battle in the 19th-century War of the Pacific (page 39). In a crypt under the monument, naval hero Arturo Prat and his crew are buried (open daily 9am–5pm). The handicraft stalls on the nearby pier, Muelle Prat, are tawdry, but this is the departure point for boat trips out into the bay, with a magnificent view of the port's amphitheater of hills. On New Year's Eve, you can enjoy Valparaíso's unique fireworks show on the water: all the ships anchored in the harbor sound their horns together to welcome the New Year.

Arturo Prat, Chile's most important naval hero (see page 39) is buried under the Plaza Sotomayor.

A prosperous past

To the northwest of the Plaza is **Cerro Playa Ancha**, one of the city's largest in both size and population. Residents proudly call this the "People's Independent Republic of Playa Ancha". Valparaíso's naval school is here, as well as the hospital, a cemetery and the education, medicine and biology faculties of the University of Valparaíso. A walk around Playa Ancha is also a reminder of the port's better days of fine but unostentatious buildings that populated the hill, little by little. Walking down the Paseo 21 de Mayo gives the city's best view of the bay and the whole port area. In the distance you can see Viña del Mar.

In Caleta El Membrillo, a restaurant run by the Fishermen's Co-operative serves up a variety of local specialties, in particular, fantastic shellfish and fish which, eaten with a glass of wine, give the sensation of a perfect world. However, this is definitely a place to keep a close eye on your possessions.

BELOW: the Naval and Maritime Museum.

From Plaza Sotomayor, you can also take the Ascensor El Peral (opposite the law courts) to **Cerro Alegre** which, along with the neighboring **Cerro Concepción** ❻, is part of the area declared a World Heritage Site. At the top of Ascensor El Peral is Paseo Yugoslavo, one of a number of similar short promenades that look out over the bay, with the Museo de Bellas Artes (Fine Arts Museum) housed in Palacio Baburizza. This has an excellent collection of Chilean painting and the setting is magnificent but, unfortunately, the museum has been closed for renovation for several years and no date has yet been set for its re-opening.

From the Paseo Yugoslavo, it's a short walk down and up again to Cerro Concepción, also accessible by the Ascensor Concepción (close to the Turri Clock). This was the residential area preferred by the British in the late 1800s, and it is still a haven of attractive buildings, broad avenues and sea views, principally from Paseo Atkinson and Paseo Gervasoni. From there, it's a short walk back down to Plaza Aníbal Pinto.

Both of these hills have become fashionable places for a weekend home and, as well as tasteful renovation, this has brought a sharp increase in property prices. However, they are full of small, moderately priced restaurants and tiny art galleries of varying quality·

Another side of town

As a general principle, the hills of Valparaíso become poorer, the higher you climb. And some are, indeed, very poor. However, during daylight, they are perfectly safe: their people are generally warm and welcoming – much more so than in Santiago – and they will be only too happy to share their love of their city, and its many attractions, with you. And, although the streets twist and

In 1834, Charles Darwin climbed Cerro La Campana, east of Valparaíso, which is now a national park. The adjoining Parque Nacional Ocoa is one of the last reserves of the native Chilean palm.

BELOW: Valparaíso's busy port.

turn, it's not easy to get lost, as the sea is always there as the ultimate landmark.

It's worth going up the **Ascensor Polanco**, on the eastern side of Avenida Argentina. This ingenious *ascensor*, built in 1915 and now a National Monument, is a feat of engineering. Reached by a walk through a long, narrow but well-lit tunnel, it rises vertically through the heart of the hill, before emerging into daylight at the top of a tower that is connected to the hilltop by a suspended walkway. The poverty here is apparent and the contrast with the monumental Congress, although now muted by new blocks of high-rise apartment buildings, gives some idea of why, when it was built in the late 1980s, the ostentatious Congress building seemed so out of keeping with its surroundings. From here, you can walk north towards **Cerro Barón**, so-called because a European Baron once built his castle there, and then on to **Cerro Los Placeres**, literally "the hill of pleasures." This hill is virtuously protected by the imposing Castle of Don Federico Santa María, today a university which bears his name.

Valparaíso is a good base for daytrips by car to **Parque Nacional La Campana** and the region's interior cities. Quilpué, Limache, Quillota and San Felipe are all small towns whose buildings recall colonial times. Plazas and squares full of palm trees, the peaceful, slow pace and a climate especially kind to the elderly make these towns particularly agreeable for relaxing.

The glittering resort

Just northeast of Valparaíso is the adjacent resort haven of **Viña del Mar ❷**. Viña is an affluent city, with elegant hotels, a casino and numerous good restaurants, all set in wide palm-lined avenues. It was born as Valparaíso's seaside resort in the mid-19th century, when the two were connected by railway. In

Maps:
City 174
Area 184

TIP

Viña del Mar's annual song festival, held every February, takes place in the Quinta Vergara, one of Chile's most beautiful parks.

BELOW: graffiti and ships in an informal Valparaíso café.

**Maps:
City 174
Area 184**

*A Valparaíso
police officer.*

BELOW: casino hotel
in Viña del Mar.

spite of some industrial development (principally textiles, mining and metal), its major source of income is still tourism. The Cerro Castillo palace, on a hill overlooking the city, is the summer home of Chile's presidents.

If Valparaíso is the city where Augusto Pinochet grew up, Viña is the city that sheltered the remains of Salvador Allende, the Chilean president who died, allegedly by suicide, amid the relentless bombing of the Airforce's Hawker Hunters during the 1973 military coup. His tomb in the Santa Inés cemetery remained unmarked until 1989; but was always covered with fresh flowers placed by admirers. On 4 September 1990, exactly 20 years to the day after he was elected president of Chile, Dr Allende's remains were finally moved to his permanent resting place, in a mausoleum in Santiago's general cemetery.

Fall is the best time to see Viña, when summer tourists have abandoned it and only its inhabitants remain. Avenida Perú is the perfect place to stroll along the shore, enjoying the sunset. For those with a car, the northbound coastal road is lovely on a clear day. One by one the resorts of Reñaca, Cochoa, Higuerillas and Concón appear, surrounded by rocky outcrops and reefs where you can see sea lions, pelicans, cormorants and, with a bit of luck, a penguin looking for the island across from **Cachagua**, a small town 60 km (37 miles) north of Viña del Mar. **Concón**, at the mouth of the Aconcagua River, has very good restaurants serving traditional seafood *empanadas* and tasty fish dishes and sauces.

On your way back to Santiago from Viña, climbing Cerro Agua Santa, you will have a clear view of Valparaíso. If you pass this way in the dark, you can enjoy a view from the crest of the hill of the marvelous firmament of lights of both Valparaíso and Viña. By night the two very different cities can barely be distinguished, blending together in a clandestine love affair. ❑

Memories of Pablo Neruda

A winding street leads to a modest bungalow, with a rough stone face that sets it apart from its showy neighbors. But where the inside should begin there's a leafy patio of ladders and stairs leading to rooms of glass scattered among gardens, terraces and mosaics. This is La Chascona ("woman with tousled hair") on Cerro San Cristóbal in Santiago. Pablo Neruda, the poet who won the Nobel prize in 1971 and died shortly after the military coup in 1973, built the house for his lover Matilde Urrutia while he was still married to his second wife, the painter Delia del Carril. He named La Chascona for his lover's rebellious hair.

Neruda was an avid collector of books, shells, paintings, wines – and houses. By the time of his death he had four: La Chascona; Isla Negra (*see page 168*); La Sebastiana in Valparaíso and La Quinta Michoacán (in Santiago). Neruda's home in the 1930s and 1940s, La Quinta is the only one of his houses not open to the public.

Friends called Neruda a spontaneous architect: his houses just grew. "In Isla Negra everything flowers," Neruda wrote. "The sea flowers all year round. Its rose is white. Its petals are salt stars." This is the place where Neruda and Urrutia are now buried, after being moved there in 1992 from Santiago's General Cemetery.

Neruda's thirst for life and his love for poetry were tempered by his sensitivity to the poverty around him. He joined the Communist Party in 1943. While alive, he dedicated his work to the daily struggles of Chileans. In death, he left his wealth to them. "Neruda didn't collect things in order to hoard them, but rather to share them," said Juan Agustín Figueroa, head of the Neruda Foundation. "He always imagined that his things would become the heritage of the people of Chile."

Upon the deaths of Neruda, Delia del Carril and Matilde Urrutia, the four houses were to go to the Communist Party, for use as cultural centers. But after the 1973 coup,

the military confiscated their goods. Military patrols repeatedly sacked La Chascona and La Sebastiana.

This didn't stop Matilde from holding Neruda's wake there, and his funeral became the first march against the regime. From then until her death in 1985, she and a small group of lawyers, writers and artists waged silent war against the military's bureaucracy. Matilde spent her last years in La Chascona, repairing the house and organizing Neruda's library, papers and writings. After her death, the Foundation published her memoirs and made La Chascona its headquarters.

The military confiscated the house in Isla Negra, but Matilde never gave up possession. After a lengthy struggle, the government recognized the Foundation. Today, visitors can tour La Chascona, while the Isla Negra house has been turned into a permanent museum by the government. Tours can be arranged through the Neruda Foundation in Santiago (tel: 777-8741) or at Isla Negra (tel 35 461284), or it can be visited independently (open Tue–Sun). ❏

RIGHT: Pablo Neruda.

EL NORTE CHICO

*Chile's "Little North," the area just north of Santiago, is a dry,
mostly flat region of wide Pacific beaches, deserted mining
settlements and spectacularly starry night skies*

Map
on page
184

Santiago

Hop on a northbound bus in Santiago and, in just a few hours, the crush and
bustle of the city will be replaced by windswept coastal expanses and
empty, arid desert. As most long-distance buses in Chile travel at night,
you will probably be treated to views of northern Chile's extraordinarily clear
night skies, which are so exceptional that the region has five major observatories. Maybe it's not surprising that this region is also on the map for international
UFO-spotters.

Chile's long, skinny north is unofficially split into two regions: for convenience, the southernmost part is known as El Norte Chico (The Little North), and
the northernmost part as El Norte Grande (The Great North). This terminology
reflects the awe inspired by the extreme conditions and vast extension of the Atacama Desert, beside which the dry scrublands closer to Santiago seem a pale
imitation. But both regions are characterized by expansive Pacific beaches and
resort towns, and both regions bear the scars of Chile's mining enterprises, with
the skeletons of old mines open to visitors *(see page 197)*. The two areas contain petroglyphs and other archeological remains of ancient desert cultures.

The clearest night skies are seen in El Norte Chico, where four of the main
observatories, along with several smaller ones, are located. Pisco, Chile's
piquant grape brandy, is produced in this region,
which was also the birthplace of the Nobel prize-winning poet Gabriela Mistral.

LEFT: Laguna Verde,
on the Altiplano.
BELOW: a woman
scythes her crops.

El Norte Grande, covered in the next chapter, is a
geological wonderland of geysers, hot springs, salt
lakes, strange desert formations and snow-tipped volcanoes. The abundant remains of the Atacameño cultures, including mummies, textiles and ancient
structures, can also be seen here.

Chile's north is harsher territory than its lush, picturesque south. The north is utilitarian; it provides
much of the country's wealth, and has also frequently
been used as a dumping ground for the politically
inconvenient. Much of the north was annexed by
Chile late in the game; in 1884, Chile defeated a confederation of Peru and Bolivia in the War of the
Pacific to take control over the flourishing nitrate
mines. This "white gold," a key ingredient in the production of fertilizer, provided fabulous wealth for several decades while copper and silver mining already
flourished in the provinces closer to the capital. Later,
a vast copper mine was developed at Chuquicamata,
part of the captured spoils.

The distances from the northern deserts to Santiago
and the few transport options available encouraged
the idea of a journey north as a sort of banishment –
whether it was self-imposed exile in the pursuit of
spiritual or material gain, or literally an attempt by

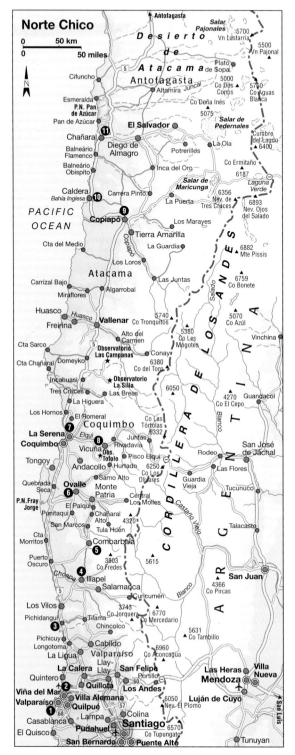

Norte Chico

0 — 50 km
0 — 50 miles

N

PACIFIC OCEAN

Antofagasta
Salar Pajonales
Desierto de Atacama
Vn Lastarria 5700
Vn Pajonal 5500
Plato de Sopa
Antofagasta
Cifuncho
Co Dos Conos 5000
Co Aguas Blanca 5760
Altamira
Juncal
Esmeralda
P.N. Pan de Azúcar
Pan de Azúcar
Co Doña Inés 5075
El Salvador
Salar de Pedernales
Chañaral
Diego de Almagro
Balneário Flamenco
Potrerillos
La Ola
Cumbre del Laudo 6400
Balneário Obispo
Inca del Oro
Co Ermitaño 6187
Caldera
Bahía Inglesa
Carrera Pinto
Salar de Maricunga
Laguna Verde
Nev. de Tres Cruces 6356
Copiapó
Los Marayes
Nev. Ojos del Salado 6893
Tierra Amarilla
Cta del Medio
La Guardia
Mte Pissis 6882
Los Loros
Atacama
Las Juntas
Co Bonete 6759
Carrizal Bajo
Algarrobal
Miraflores
Huasco
Huasco
Vallenar
Co Tronquitos 5740
Freirina
Alto del Carmen
Co Azúl 5070
Cta Sarco
Domeyko
Observatorio Las Campanas
Co Los Mogotes 5380
Vinchina
Incahuasi
Observatorio La Silla
Conay
Co del Toro 6380
Tres Cruces
Las Breas
6050
La Higuera
Co El Cepo 4270
Guandacol
Los Hornos
El Romeral
Co Las Tórtolas 6332
La Serena
Coquimbo
Elqui
Juntas
Coquimbo
Vicuña
Rivadavia
San José de Jáchal
Tongoy
Obs. Tololo
Pisco Elqui
Rodeo
Andacollo
Hurtado
Co Los Olivares 6250
Las Flores
Quebrada Seca
Ovalle
Samo Alto
Guardia Vieja
Tucunuco
P.N.Fray Jorge
Monte Patria
Central Los Molles
Punitaqui
El Palqui
San Marcos
Chañaral Alto 4320
Tula Huén
Talacasto
Cta Morritos
Combarbalá
Puerto Oscuro
3803 Co Fredes
5615
Illapel
San Juan
Salamanca
4366 Co Pircas
Choapa
Cuncumén
Blanco
Los Vilos
3743 Co Jorquera
Pichidangui
Tilama
6770 Co Mercedario
Chincolco
Pichicuy
5631 Co Tambillo
Longotoma
Cabildo
6960 Co Aconcagua
La Ligua
Valparaíso
Llay-Llay
La Calera
San Felipe
Las Heras
Villa Nueva
Quintero
Quillota
Portillo
Mendoza
Viña del Mar
Villa Alemana
Los Andes
Valparaíso
Quilpué
6050 Nev. El Plomo
Luján de Cuyo
Colina
Casablanca
Pudahuel
Santiago 6570
El Quisco
Lampa
Co Tupungato
San Bernardo
Puente Alto
Tunuyan

others to get the unlucky subject out of the way. The central male character in Isabel Allende's famous novel *The House of the Spirits*, published in 1985, makes his way north early in life to slog out a miserable living in the nitrate mines. He manages to accumulate capital and returns to lay a now-credible claim for the hand of his chosen fiancée. But he never goes near the north again for the rest of the book.

Bustling cities

Unlike his southern cousin who receives the urban visitor with shy admiration and enormous instinctual hospitality, the northerner must be convinced that the newcomer is worthy of his confidence or even his notice. The cities of the north bustle; those of the south doze. But this does not mean there is no room for friendliness or hospitality here – an initial brusqueness can often be an abrupt opening to further communication, leading to unexpected warmth and humor.

The north is the birthplace of the Chilean left. Away from the moderating influences of intermediate social forces such as small landowners, professionals and shopkeepers and the ideological grip of "leading families", the northern laborer was face to face with the company.

Along with this history of class conflict, Chile's north is also associated with military feats and heroism dating from the earliest colonial campaigns against Inca rule. Near San Pedro de Atacama are the ruins of the last stand of the Incas who had ruled the area for less than a century. The great naval battle of Iquique of 1879 was key to the defeat of the Peruvians in the war for control of the desert; it is commemorated in a national holiday every May 21.

Arica, the border city facing Peru, is physically dominated by the El Morro Hill, another famous battle site from the Peruvian war. On the Peruvian side is the site of the La Concepción battle where an entire Chilean battalion was wiped out to the last man rather than surrender. The soldiers are honored in the Santiago metro station Los Héroes. The desert cities of Arica, Iquique and Antofagasta tend to have a noticeable military presence, being frequently visited by soldiers on leave from lonely outposts in the mountain border stations or local barracks.

Age-old mining traditions

The Diaguitas culture moved into the El Norte Chico region from across the Andes around AD 900 and flourished until the Inca conquest 500 years later, quickly followed by the arrival of the Spaniards. Ceramic work of this group is considered among the best in the Americas, and the black and white geometric designs on a red base are widely copied in Chilean decoration. Both La Serena and Ovalle have anthropological museums with excellent artifacts. Mineral smelting and the need for domestic fuel wiped out most native woods throughout the desert. The ore grade in the early mines was always at least 25 percent and could reach 50 or 60 percent. (Modern large-scale copper mining works with ore with a copper content of only 1 or 2 percent.)

Driving north from Santiago, the Central Valley vegetation soon disappears, to be replaced by hardy thorn trees. Signs of inhabitants become fewer and fewer, and lands are no longer enclosed in farm plots or ranches. The highway descends to the coast where a series of popular beach resorts are located, far enough from the capital to retain their small-town dimensions. Long stretches of deserted beach are surrounded by rocky cliffs. Pichicuy and **Pichidangui** ❸ ("pichi" means "little" in the Mapuche tongue) have white-sand beaches with strong surf; the latter's church is built on a promontory over the sea. A bird sanctuary with abundant sea life is located in between at the **Los Molles** rock gardens, where underground caverns produce a thun-

Map on page 184

A rather large bottle of pisco.

BELOW: the beach at La Serena.

derous roar. Nearby is the **Governor's Chair**, at 695 meters (2,280 ft) the country's highest sea cliff; it can be viewed from Valparaíso in good weather.

To make a pisco sour, mix three parts pisco with one part lemon or lime juice, sugar, one egg white and crushed ice.

Copper country

A few kilometers off the highway is the lively tourist town of **Los Vilos** which is full of rustic seafood restaurants and artisans who carve in *guayacán*, a durable wood once plentiful in the district. The **Bodegón Cultural** (Cultural Warehouse), which opened in 2002 in the restored 19th-century Customs building, holds regular art exhibitions in summer, and has a pleasant coffee shop. A sculpture park, created by a local architect on the cliffs, is open to the public and worth a visit.

North of Los Vilos is the Choapa River valley and with the city of **Illapel ④**, its principal urban center. Illapel, like many northern towns, had a mining boom and bust and has since returned to its original agricultural economy. Some 18th-century construction is preserved, both in the town and on the road to Salamanca, giving an idea of how rural estates were built around a central courtyard. A typical mansion has an adobe first-floor which blocks the heat and a wooden upper floor with balconies surrounding the inner patio. Sometimes the adobe walls are painted brightly.

The entire zone is arid and mountainous but has some surprisingly green valleys and attractive river beaches with excellent trout fishing. It is good for camping off-season when the sun is not so strong. The old north-south road which followed the Inca route and predates the Pan-American Highway can be taken from Illapel up a severe climb through the narrowest part of Chile, in which the sea is only 80 km (50 miles) from the Argentine border. The view from the top just before **Combarbalá ⑤** is superb, with views of the snow-

BELOW: an Aymara near the border with Bolivia.

Map
on page
184

topped Andes. *Pirquineros,* independent miners, are plentiful in the zone where the soil has a reddish tinge due to its copper content. The town of Combarbalá has used the color and geometrical schemes of the Diaguitas people in the design of its central plaza. A whitish, marble-like stone particular to the area, called *combarbalita,* is cut and polished by the artisans to make miniature figures.

Petroglyphs and pisco

The next valley to the north is the **Limarí**, with the city of **Ovalle 6** at its center. The surrounding area is an agricultural zone traditionally dependent on the city of La Serena to the north, but recently the expansion of irrigation has added new lands for export grapes and a burst of unevenly distributed prosperity. Five km (3 miles) southeast of Ovalle is the Monumento Arqueológico **Valle del Encanto** (Enchanted Valley National Monument), which is rich in archeological treasures (open daily 8am–7pm; entrance fee). There is evidence of a hunter-gatherer civilization here dating back 4,000 years, though the bulk of the artifacts are from the Molle culture of around AD 700. This idyllic valley contains over 30 petroglyphs – designs carved into rocks – as well as 20 "piedras tacitas", groups of circular indentations hollowed out of flat rocks in the river bed. Sadly, some of the most interesting petroglyphs have been hacked off and whisked away to European museums.

Parque Nacional Pan de Azúcar.

To the north of Ovalle is the **Recoleta Reservoir**, a popular lake resort. En route the junction of the Grande and the Hurtado rivers from a high altitude can be seen. Farther towards the cordillera along this route is the **Monumento Natural Pichasca**, with gigantic rock formations and petrified wood. Many of the hamlets in this region, lying along the original north-south route through the mountains, were Inca outposts ruled by a representative of the empire.

The town of **Hurtado** is known for its dried fruit, figs, quince jelly and nuts, as well as its flower farms of dahlias and chrysanthemums. From here, the mountains can be crossed straight north toward Vicuña *(see page 189)* on an unpaved road which offers a panoramic view of both the Andes and the next valley north, the **Valle del Elqui**.

BELOW: a tranquil spot in La Serena.

Rare gems

Just southeast of Ovalle is the giant **La Paloma reservoir**, responsible for much of the new agricultural wealth of the region. Planted with stands of trees, it presents a refreshing spectacle in its dry setting. At the end of the difficult gravel road is the small village of **Las Ramadas** whose hills nearby contain one of the two known lapis lazuli mines in the world (the other is in Afghanistan). This semi-precious blue stone is worked into a variety of pendants, earrings and decorations, and sold in artisan markets throughout the country.

Back on the Pan-American Highway is a turn-off for **Parque Nacional Fray Jorge**, a dense green forest which is surrounded by near-desert. This concentration of plant life is the result of an almost constant ocean fog which hugs the hillside. In nearby **Tongoy** (town names now begin to be Quechua in origin,

rather than Mapuche), the beaches are among the finest in Chile, composed of extremely white pulverized conch shells. Tongoy is also one of the best places to try the local scallops, served in the innumerable beachside restaurants.

City of serenity

The comfortable, slow-paced northern city of **La Serena** ❼ was the first settlement established by Pedro de Valdivia as part of his plan to secure the region for Spain. As such, it became an important hotel center from the beginning of the colonial period to receive travelers making the long trek across the desert. Religious orders also built receiving houses for their missionaries, and the city still has 29 churches; the oldest ones have remarkable stone façades. The discovery of silver in 1825 led to an upsurge of prosperity and a construction boom, though most of the original buildings were superseded by an ersatz "Spanish colonial" style imposed in a 1940s urban renewal scheme.

Chile's two species of carnivorous plants, known as Fox's Ear, grow between La Serena and Copiapó.

All the landowning families of the Limarí, Elqui, Huasco, Choapa, and Copiapó valleys had their own residence here, and La Serena retains an old-money reputation. The city's inhabitants have been mocked for being so laid-back as to be barely alive. La Serena's **Museo Arqueológico** (open Mon–Fri 9.30am–5.45pm, Sat 10am–1pm and 4–7pm, Sun 10am–1pm; entrance fee, except Sun and holidays) has an excellent collection of Diaguitas artifacts, and the cemetery provides an ample view of the river valley from above. Along with the tomb of native son and Chilean president Gabriel González Videla and relatives of Gabriela Mistral is a stone honoring officials of the Salvador Allende Unidad Popular government, who were shot in the days after the 1973 coup. González Videla's house on La Serena's main square is also a national monu-

BELOW: irrigated valley near Vicuña.

ment and museum (open Mon–Fri 10am–6pm, Sat 10am–1pm; entrance fee). Several kilometers of fine beaches can be seen from the Cerro Grande which towers high above the city, and is accessible by a dirt road.

Map on page 184

The sister city of **Coquimbo** is a small port, active mostly at the height of the fruit export season in December and January. Some elaborate woodcarving, the handiwork of foreign carpenters, can still be seen on a few buildings. These craftsmen arrived as the mining industry grew, since local tradesmen did not know how to build on the scale required. Shipped in from abroad were Oregon pine (neither pine nor from Oregon) and a sturdy species of bamboo from Ecuador, which could be planed to form a solid surface. These materials and techniques were used to build the region's churches, most of which have a high central bell tower and have survived severe earthquakes.

The starriest skies

The sleepy village of **Vicuña** ❽, east of La Serena in the Valle del Elqui, was the birthplace of Gabriela Mistral *(see page 190)*, and houses a **museum** of the famous poet (open Jan–Feb daily except Sun pm, Mar–Dec Mon–Fri 10am–1pm and 2.30–6.30pm, Sat 10am–1pm and 3–6pm, Sun 10am–1pm; entrance fee). From Vicuña, the road continues up to **Monte Grande**, where she is now buried. This is also Chile's main pisco-producing area, and plants can be visited without appointment.The outlying hills of the Valle del Elqui are the haunt of a variety of esoteric movements and guru-led communities, in part, no doubt, due to the great clarity of the night skies and the sensation that, as the title of a book about the zone suggested, *Heaven is Nearer*. North of La Serena the Pan-American Highway cuts back towards the interior, but a side spur leads to the

BELOW: the natural rock arch of "La Portada," near Antofagasta.

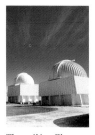

The striking El Tololo observatory, Valle del Elqui.

BELOW: Gabriela Mistral bust, in the Vicuña museum.

interesting beaches and fishing villages at **Temblador** and **Chungungo**, the last being the name of a local species of otter.

Bethlehem Steel ran the world's largest iron mine between 1914 and 1954 at **El Tofo** 10 km (6 miles) in from this part of the Chilean coast, and its abandoned remains can still be seen. Also nearby is the Camanchaca Project: here the heavy mist that rolls in from the sea (called *camanchaca*) is captured and condensed on fine netting to provide a water supply. The atmosphere in the mountains here is excellent for astronomical purposes as the air is particularly clear and populated areas are sparse. With 300 nights a year suitable for sky photography, it is one of the Southern Hemisphere's most popular observatory spots (Mount Palomar in the United States has 215). The observatories at **Cerro Tololo**, **La Silla**, **Las Campanas** and **Gemini South** can be seen from the highway, and from Cerro Grande in La Serena. Visits are possible by appointment.

The area just north of La Serena is the transition zone between the transversal valleys, where agriculture is still possible, and the Atacama Desert, where it is frankly inconceivable. The Copiapó is the last river to make its way down from the mountains to the sea. North of here, any mountain flows evaporate into nothing along the way, with the one exception of the Loa River, which flows past the Chuquicamata copper mine (and becomes seriously contaminated). The Andes now divides into two parallel ranges, trapping the melting snows in an interior basin to form enormous salt flats, a phenomenon repeated all the way north into Bolivia. These deposits have great commercial potential for the concentrations of lithium, potassium and borax. In the central plain, followed by the Pan-American Highway, an occasional wet winter brings the desert into flower the following spring. This rare and short-lived display is an unforgettable sight.

GABRIELA MISTRAL

Vicuña is the birthplace of Gabriela Mistral, one of Chile's greatest poets. An austere, rather than popular heroine, Mistral is treated in Chile like the precious mineral commodities that are unearthed from the dry, surrounding hills – a resource to be claimed and honored for its undeniable value, but not in itself a source of joy or pleasure. Awarded the national literary prize six years after winning the Nobel prize, she was mistrusted as an eccentric during her life and was never one of the darlings of Chile's literary elite. A schoolteacher by profession, she spent much of her life abroad, first in Mexico, where she participated in educational reform and, later in life, as Chilean Consul in different countries.

Her first book of poetry, *Desolation*, was published in New York, the city where she died. The themes of her work are displacement, separateness, the difficulty of romantic love in a world ruled by a punishing God.

Further up the Valle del Elqui from Vicuña is Monte Grande, the village where Mistral spent most of her childhood under the watchful eye of her elder sister, the local school- and postmistress. The school is now a small, very pleasant museum. Here too, on a rocky outcrop overlooking the valley, Gabriela Mistral is buried.

Salt lakes and flamingos

Copiapó ❾, the capital of the region, is now a grape-growing zone *par excellence*, the result of enormous investments in earthmoving and irrigation. As these grapes are the first to ripen and hit US supermarkets around Christmas, they are worth the expense. From Copiapó it is possible to drive eastwards through the desert to the salt flats, an extraordinary trip if correct precautions are taken: wear warm clothes; bring food, water, and petrol; and register your route and the duration of the trip with the local *carabineros* (police).

The **Salar de Maricunga** salt flat is impressive for its setting near the Andes, including the world's highest volcano, Ojos del Salado (6,893 meters/22,615 ft), which last erupted in 1956. For a longer stay there are cabins in Parque Nacional Nevado Tres Cruces, a bit farther along the road. Near the Argentine border, the **Laguna Verde** lake is apparently dead, but flamingos live in the salt flat, contentedly picking bugs out of the oily ooze in the rocks. Explorer/conqueror Diego de Almagro used this crossing from Argentina in his ill-fated 1536 journey: he lost most of his men en route in the frigid passes. Legend has it that half-frozen survivors often pulled off a couple of toes along with their boots.

Bahía Inglesa, near Copiapó, is said to be the most beautiful beach of the north, but there are many bathing spots along the Pan-American Highway, which returns to the shore for a long stretch between **Caldera** ❿ and **Chañaral** ⓫. The latter port was severely polluted by wastes from the Anaconda copper mine at Salvador, which was later nationalized. Deposits from the copper mine are now diverted to a newly inaugurated desert site, ending 60 years of contamination. Bahía Hedionda ("Stinky Bay") takes its name from this unfortunate history. North of Chañaral is the wildlife refuge **Parque Nacional Pan de Azúcar**. ❑

Map on page 184

BELOW: a shepherdess minds her flock.

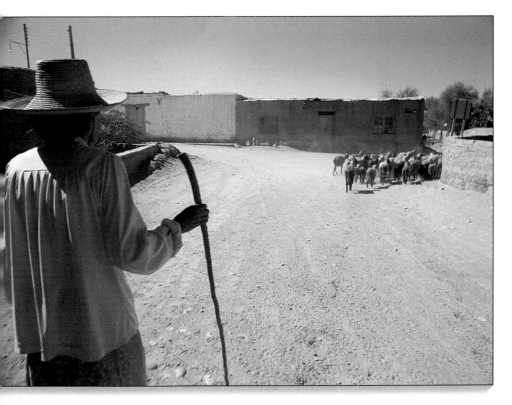

CHILE'S BURIED TREASURE

The seeds of class struggle were sown in Chile's austere mining settlements of the early 20th century – today, the abandoned skeletons of these enterprises leave a haunting impression

Map on page 202

Santiago

Mining has had a long and turbulent history in the Chilean north. In prehispanic times, the brief rule of the Incas in this region led to the importation of Peruvian agricultural and metallurgical techniques by settler-rulers who collected tribute in towns along the "Inca Road." Later, Spanish settlers gathered in agricultural oases, dabbling occasionally in gold and silver mining when there were discoveries. In the early 1800s, hundreds of tiny copper and silver mines sprang up. This mining activity was the precursor to the industrial transformation that occurred after independence. Much of the mining activity around Copiapó was owned and operated by Chileans rather than foreigners, creating a new industrial class.

Mining activity also stimulated railroad construction, the first in all of Latin America. The giant railroad equipment works at Mejillones near Antofagasta, second only in size to a California factory, functioned until the 1970s; it has since been dismantled. As the railroads were not primarily for human transport, which would have implied a north-south orientation, they began at ports and led inland, often to now-abandoned sites.

By the mid-19th century, El Norte Chico was the economic, intellectual and cultural center of the country, and the great families often had industrial interests here to complement their agricultural estates in the south. Liberal ideas flourished, and the Radical Party of Chile was founded in Copiapó in 1863 by two industrialists shortly after a serious rebellion against the conservative capital. The wife of one moneyed mine owner died horribly when her Paris gown became entangled in the equipment of a new foundry they were inspecting. Another important Chilean fortune was made in the zone by Agustín Edwards whose grandson and namesake later founded the *El Mercurio* newspaper chain. In 1879, Chile went to war with Peru and Bolivia for the territories of the far north and the wealth of the nitrate mines.

LEFT: display at the Chuquicamata Mining Museum. **BELOW:** mining town mural.

The seeds of class struggle

Mining firms sprang up not on fertile, inhabited lands with previous residents and a social history, but on the desert pampas, in the middle of absolutely nowhere. The company built the housing, the company stocked the stores, the company decided who worked, for how long, at what rates, and what he did with his wages (miners were often paid in *fichas,* tokens only valid for company goods). Into this starkly polarized environment, the seeds of Marxism arrived from Europe, where proletarian consciousness was in its early heyday, and found propitious soils.

Class antagonism was sealed permanently by the notorious 1907 massacre at Santa María de Iquique

Monument to miners, Chuquicamata.

(see page 46) where some 2,000–3,000 peacefully striking workers and their families were gunned down in cold blood by government troops. The incident is thought to be the worst example of mass slaughter in a labor dispute in world history. The revered grandfather of Chile's union movement, Clotario Blest, who died in 1990, remembered as a child listening to men having just fled from the north discuss the killing and the impact of their stories on his parents and other working people.

Birthplace of radicalism

As a mining-dependent region, the Chilean north has always been marked by a traumatic dependence on the ups and downs of commodity markets thousands of kilometers away. In the 19th century, Chile's oligarchs converted the country into virtual single-product dependence on saltpeter, and the mineral eventually accounted for 51 percent of the country's overseas income. But the boom collapsed overnight: a German-invented synthetic nitrate eliminated the need for the raw material, and by the end of World War I, Chile's "desert gold" had become almost obsolete. As late as the 1960s, Chileans visiting the Santa Laura "ghost town" could observe trains sitting on abandoned sidings, their cars loaded with nitrate ore, which had suddenly turned to lumps of irrelevant rock.

BELOW: miners in the northern desert region became the backbone of Chile's union movement.

The ebb and flow of the nitrate business was accompanied by massive migrations of workers, first north to work the mines, then south in unemployed droves, seeking new lives and bursting with the ideas of unionism, class struggle and socialism. This newly active, radicalized working class contributed to the end of oligarchic rule in 1925. An industrial working class, which had taken centuries to evolve in Europe, had been formed in a few decades.

At the time of the 1973 coup, the army felt it necessary to execute selected political prisoners and thereby intimidate the community out of any attempts at resistance. However, in the 1989 elections that marked the end of 16 years of military rule, communist and socialist candidates retained a substantial portion of their historical strength in the north, despite the heavy repression of the intervening period.

Map on page 202

Chuquicamata: a colossal copper mine

The emptiness of the surrounding desert conceals to some degree the scale of the colossal open-cast copper mine of Chuquicamata. Smoke from its concentrating and refining plants and its gigantic "cakes" of waste rock or "tailings" can be seen kilometers away. But only upon closer approach does the true size of Chuquicamata – or Chuqui, as it is fondly known – become obvious.

Tours leave from the visitors' center at 9.45am on weekdays and are a highlight of any trip to the north, no matter how small your interest in mining. An identification document is required, and early arrival is recommended owing to limits on tour size. The first thing that strikes you are the special trucks that load and carry the mineral loosened by dynamite explosions from the terraced sides of the vast pit. The wheels alone are nearly 4 meters (13 ft) in diameter, and drivers sit another 2 meters (6 ft) above them, reducing all other traffic to Lilliputian status. Regular-sized trucks circulate with flags on long poles in order to alert the big-truck drivers to their presence. One important job of the small vehicles is to water the roadways to ease wear on the giant tires, which cost US$12,000 each.

The "charge" or "feed" of copper ore is first crushed and broken into gravel-

BELOW: Chuquicamata, one of the world's largest open-cut mines.

Map on page 202

Coat of arms on an old nitrate train, Iquique.

BELOW: crane, Chuquicamata.

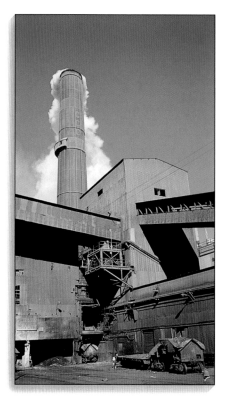

sized pieces, and then mixed with water and further mashed into a more manageable paste. This is agitated with chemical agents in flotation cells, resulting in the separation of the metal-rich concentrate from the unwanted mud. The concentrate has about 35 percent copper purity. This is then smelted in a series of ovens in order to produce copper anodes or "blister" with about 99.3 percent copper content. Both the concentrates and blister are then sold to overseas clients, in particular to China, South Korea and Japan.

Environmental hazards

The mineral molybdenum, as well as some gold and silver, are recovered from the ore. But there are also less attractive byproducts. Sulfur is released from the sulfate ores, although the gas is captured and converted into sulfuric acid to be used in some copper refining processes. The Chuqui ore also contains alarming traces of arsenic. Union leaders charge that arsenic poisoning is rampant among workers and suggest that the surrounding area, including Antofagasta's water supply, is contaminated with arsenic escaping from the plants. One tragicomic tale is told there about the retired worker who traveled to Spain with his wife and suddenly died. His spouse was arrested on suspicion of poisoning him when the forensic specialist found high levels of arsenic in his blood.

Though increasing attention is being paid to environmental issues, a lot still remains to be done. Copper is the cornerstone of Chile's economy and the five divisions of the state-owned copper company Codelco, of which the Chuquicamata is the largest – produce 35 percent of the country's 5.5 million metric tons of fine copper. Chuquicamata is responsible for nearly half of that. Despite a diversification of exports over the past two decades, copper still brings in 40 percent of Chile's foreign exchange.

Ore grades at Chuquicamata, while still attractive by world standards, have been falling for years. This requires the mining and treatment of more and more ore to produce the same amount of copper. Continued expansion of the mine has slowly engulfed the town of Chuquicamata, which was once several times larger than neighboring Calama, but is now being dismantled, partly also because of high pollution levels.

Codelco originated in the 1971 decision of President Allende to nationalize the country's most important industry, with unanimous support from Congress. The military regime, after Allende's overthrow in 1973 compensated the US companies that had been expropriated by nationalization, but kept the mines in state hands, establishing Codelco as a national concern in 1976.

Among Chilean workers, the copper miners are an elite group with relatively handsome wage and benefit packages. Although there are sharp distinctions in the workforce – the result of subcontracting out many mining jobs to reduce permanent staff and cut costs – the town of Calama is still full of dark-skinned, burly workers sitting down to drinks and ample meals with an air of satisfaction usually reserved for the puissant, blue-eyed classes of Santiago. Most of the staggering wealth produced by Chuqui is absorbed by the rest of the country, but enough of it remains to give this desolate outpost in the wilderness a chance to entertain itself. ❑

Ghost Towns

The collapse of the nitrate or saltpeter market at the end of World War I was so sudden that the mining towns, which had no other reason to exist, were abruptly abandoned *(see page 194)*. Now the north is dotted with these town shells, most of which have been thoroughly sacked, even including their graveyards. A few, however, remain and have been converted into historical monuments.

Mining camps were known as "offices," referring to the offices of the purchasing agents, who bought everything mined within a certain radius. Virtually anyone determined and hardworking enough could be a miner, since the earliest production method consisted of simply digging up the readily visible *caliche* (nitrate ore), grinding it, and selling it at the "office." When the best ore, which had a grade of 50–60 percent, was exhausted, the office simply moved elsewhere.

More complicated processes which could utilize lower-grade ore led to more permanent settlements. These offices are identifiable by waste piles of gravel built up into cake-like constructions. Many are visible from the highway between Antofagasta and Calama, and south of Iquique. A small roadside marker gives the history of each site.

The best-preserved ghost town is Humberstone Office on the turn-off from Pozo Almonte to Iquique. Established in the mid-19th century, it had a population of 5,000 and provided an unusually varied existence for its inhabitants. A few *tamarugo* trees remain standing around the plaza, and the town's theater with its seats, the church and the market are still intact.

The abandoned frames of workshops and homes are spread out over a large area; everything is covered with dust and battered by the steady desert wind. The air of recent habitation is genuinely spooky, as if the inhabitants had suddenly fled without warning. Nearby is Santa Laura Office, where a processing plant and administrative complex are preserved. Both offices, which were recently acquired by a private foundation, are gradually being restored and are open to visitors daily 9am–6pm. However, guided tours are available only at weekends.

Along the Antofagasta-Calama road just past Carmen Alto is the Chacabuco Office, which is also being restored, and the nearby Salinas railway station, site of an abandoned 1872 drinking-water plant which used solar energy. Of the other offices visible from the road, only the walls of the homes, in general, remain.

Between Antofagasta and Tocopilla are the only functioning nitrate centers, Pedro de Valdivia and María Elena. These are both owned by the Chilean Chemical and Mining Company SOQUIMICH, which was returned to private ownership during the military regime. The nitrate market has perked up considerably with the renewed demand for natural fertilizers, and iodine can also be recovered commercially as a byproduct. SOQUIMICH is, in fact, one of the world's leading producers of iodine. In María Elena, the street plan is based on the Union Jack. ❏

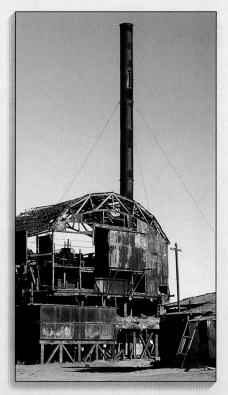

RIGHT: The "ghost town" of Santa Laura.

EL NORTE GRANDE

Chile's far north, or "Great North", is an area of spectacular beauty, with Pacific beaches, deserts, volcanoes, lakes teeming with wildlife, and the remnants of ancient civilizations

Map on page 202

Santiago

he Atacama Desert is located in the same latitude belt as other deserts in the Southern Hemisphere whose dominant high-pressure systems prevent storms from moving in. Chile's twin mountain ranges aggravate the situation; no precipitation has been measured in this desert since the Spanish colonization, giving it the title of driest spot on earth. The Altiplanic Inversion occurs around the summer equinox (December 21) when strong evaporation generates sometimes violent rain and hail storms in the mountains, and the water rushes down the dry gorges. These storms last until March, and serious flooding makes many roads impassable.

The extraordinary dryness is responsible for great archeological treasures, such as the famous Atacama mummies, which predate the Egyptian varieties by several thousand years. All sorts of artifacts are easily preserved, and new finds occur regularly. The excellent Le Paige Museum in San Pedro de Atacama, founded by a Belgian Jesuit, Gustavo Le Paige, has 380,000 objects. A 2,800-year-old site called Tulor has been unearthed nearby (open daily 8.30am–7pm; entrance fee).

Water is obviously a major logistical problem, not only for personal use but also to satisfy the enormous demands of modern mining. Huge investments have been made in pipelines to bring Andean waters to the coast or to mining outposts. At the Conchi bridge north of Chiu Chiu (near San Pedro), six pipelines come together. The first known industrial use of solar energy in the world was in a water desalinization plant built in 1872 at Carmen Alto near Antofagasta. Pollution from mining and smelting has been rife, but not all industrial intervention has been a disaster: the Salado River was diverted to Chuquicamata in 1951, removing its unwanted salts from the Loa, which runs all the way to Antofagasta. (Unfortunately, the Loa now has high levels of arsenic.)

PRECEDING PAGES: Salar de Atacama, a vast dry salt lake. **LEFT:** colonial church at San Pedro de Atacama. **BELOW:** llamas crossing, near San Pedro.

Desert metropolis

Antofagasta ❶ is the fourth-largest city in Chile and the most populous of the desert. It is still the main port for export of minerals from the state-owned Chuquicamata mine and the giant Escondida copper mine, controlled by BHP Billiton, an international mining company. However, an alternative port is gradually being developed in nearby Mejillones, mostly to relieve road congestion in Antofagasta. Antofagasta's 20-km (12-mile) beachfront gives it a fresh, gracious air despite the unrelieved brown of the hills. A financial dispute and property seizure here in 1879 sparked the War of the Pacific, which ended Bolivian control of the town and lands to the east. This portion of Chile is the widest, measuring 355 km (221 miles) from

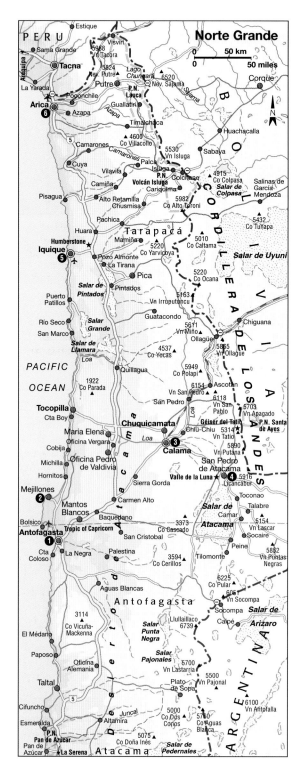

Andes to sea. The Andean peaks reach 6,000 meters (19,700 ft) while the highest peak of the entire coastal range is **Mount. Vicuña Mackenna** to the southwest at 3,114 meters (10,217 ft).

In Antofagasta, the excellent **Museo Regional** (open Mon–Fri 9am–5pm, Sat and Sun 11am–2pm; entrance fee, except Sun and holidays) relates local history and anthropological details about the surrounding desert. There are two universities, and students flock to the beach at sunset all year round.

Some 13 km (8 miles) north of the city is the famous **La Portada**, a huge rock eroded into an arch by the sea. Across a peninsula to the north is the town of **Mejillones ❷**, which started out as the northern railroads' mechanical shop, producing wagons and locomotives. One of the most sheltered bays in the area, it now houses thermal power plants and other industries, as well as port facilities.

Northeast of Antofagasta are the **Chuquicamata** mine and the next-door service town of **Calama ❸**, which has long superseded the older Chiu Chiu in importance. Most travelers only stay in Calama overnight to visit the mine *(see page 195)*, since the town itself has little to offer besides streets full of cheap bars and strip joints.

Chiu Chiu, however, was the prehispanic crossroads at the fork of two rivers. It fulfills the stereotype of a desert oasis, a green speck in the midst of a hostile brown sea, and has a 1675 church whose construction borrowed elements of the Atacameño indigenous culture.

The road toward San Pedro de Atacama crosses the Plain of Patience, whose name soon begins to make sense: the landscape between two distant ridges appears not to change at all for tens of kilometers. An advertised alternative route to San Pedro though the **Valle de la Luna** (Valley of the Moon) is not advised for small cars as sand accumulated on the road can trap them, and this is definitely not a place where you'd want to be stuck.

Center of activity

The oasis town of **San Pedro de Atacama** is a popular base for exploring the north's most spectacular sights. A dry salt lake, the **Salar de Atacama**, stretches beyond the town to a distant row of snowcapped volcanoes – including Licancábur which, at 5,900 meters (19,360 ft) is one of the highest extinct volcanoes in the Andean chain. Many travelers find the town a good place to relax. It has a restored adobe house on one side of the plaza that is universally called Pedro de Valdivia's residence but is now thought to be prehispanic in construction. Opposite is a 16th-century church, one of the oldest in Chile.

San Pedro's **Museo Arqueológico Gustavo Le Paige** (open Mon–Fri 9am–noon and 2–6pm, Sat and Sun 10am–noon and 2–6pm; entrance fee) is regarded as one of the best in South America. Founded by the former village priest after whom the museum is named, it has an unusually wide array of pre-Columbian artifacts, all excellently displayed. Particularly fascinating are the ancient mummies, of both children and adults, preserved in the dry desert air, and the deliberately deformed skulls. Many pre-Inca groups warped the shapes of their children's heads using flat stones and tightly bound ropes, for esthetic or religious reasons.

Southeast of San Pedro is the village of **Toconao**, past a plantation of *tamarugo* trees which provide a tiny seed for animal pasture. A forest service guide can be hired here to drive to **Lago Chaxa** and observe pink flamingos. The entire Salar de Atacama can be circled in a two-day trip, passing through impressively desolate landscapes and curious desert outposts. Pozo 3 is an oasis near San Pedro, turned into a commercial swimming pool and picnic area.

Three kilometers (2 miles) northwest of San Pedro, at **Quitor**, are the ruins

Woven hat from the northern desert, made around 1,500 years ago.

BELOW: ancient geoglyphs in the Valle de Azapa.

of a 700-year-old pre-Columbian fortress. This was where the native peoples made their last stand against the invading Spaniards under Pedro de Valdivia. Some of the fortress has been restored, and it is worth exploring the turret where the last native chief of the north lived; the view from the top is breathtaking.

Thirty-two kilometers (20 miles) northeast of San Pedro are the hot springs called the **Termas de Puritama** (entrance fee). You can get there on a local tour; an alternative is to hire a bicycle in San Pedro, but take plenty of water and protect yourself thoroughly from the desert sun. At the end of your journey you will be welcomed by a choice of steaming pools to wallow in, as well as a few waterfalls for a natural shower.

Desert winds and geysers

The famous **Valle de la Luna** is about 8 km (5 miles) from San Pedro. As the name suggests, this is a haunting landscape of colored gypsum, clay and salt, without a hint of organic life to be found. The valley is at its eeriest at sunset, while under a full moon the beams reflecting off the salt crystals of the region make it a truly spectacular sight.

But perhaps the most interesting excursion from San Pedro is the one that leaves at 4am to visit the daily show of at least 100 geysers at **El Tatio**, which burst forth just before sunrise every morning. As they exit the frozen earth with strange gurgling subterranean sounds, they thrust their columns of steam high into the air. Some are wide, boiling pools, while others resemble mini volcanoes with cones of bright yellow mineral deposits. The display dies down at about 10am until the next morning. The visitor can bathe in a huge pool of tolerably hot thermal waters before returning. However, it is a good idea to be the first

The clocktower in the middle of Antofagasta's Plaza Colón is a miniature replica of London's Big Ben, down to the chimes. It was erected by British residents in 1910 to celebrate the centenary of Chile's independence.

BELOW: Valle de la Luna (Valley of the moon).

Map on page 202

back down the mountain before others scare off the wildlife around the Putana River, where sulfur is extracted from the volcano of the same name; or to bathe in the purifying waters of the thermal Purifíca River which surfaces in a brief, concealed stretch of narrow canyon not far from the base of the mountains.

Big beaches and big dunes

Traveling north toward **Iquique ❺** takes you past numerous geoglyphs carved into the hillsides. The best collection is in the **Reserva Nacional Pampa del Tamarugal**, 48 km (30 miles) south of the turning to Iquique (open daily 10am–5pm; entrance fee). This is also the zone of nitrate ghost towns. The detour to Iquique is close to **Pozo Almonte**, 47 km (30 miles) across a plateau which abruptly ends with a breathtaking view over the city. Iquique looks like it should be in Saudi Arabia rather than South America. Between it and the 600-meter (1,968-ft) cliffs lies a huge sand dune whose dimensions only become clear from below – this is a popular venue for the extreme sport of sand skiing. Iquique's golden era was the nitrate heyday from 1890–1920, when European opera singers appeared in the elegant **Teatro Municipal** and adjourned to a replica *Mudéjar* palace, now the **Centro Español**, across the plaza, for a late meal. After the collapse of nitrate mines, fishmeal (a fish powder used to feed livestock and farmed fish) came into its own, but has recently declined, largely as a result of over-exploitation.

The **Museo Regional** (Baquedano 951; open Mon–Fri 9am–5.30pm, Sat and Sun 10am–5pm; free entry under review) is worth visiting, with archeological artifacts and a model Aymara village. The nearby **Museo Naval** on Avenida Centenario is also worth a visit (open Tues–Sat, closed 2–4pm and Sat pm;

Pica, near Iquique, is famous for its tiny lemons, used to make Chile's best pisco sour.

LEFT: church in Iquique.
BELOW: Cocha de Pica thermal baths, near Iquique.

Map on page 202

Mural, Iquique.

BELOW: *Mudéjar* style of Iquique's Centro Español.
RIGHT: the geysers of El Tatio at full moon.

entrance fee). But the main interest is in the range of stately 19th-century mansions that are kept as national monuments; many are clustered around Plaza Arturo Prat, with its clocktower and Corinthian columns. The whole center has been declared a National Monument.

About 70 km (44 miles) east of Iquique is the village La Tirana, the site of the Virgen del Carmen religious festival. This annual event takes place during mid-July and goes on for a week. The festival has dance groups composed of virginal maidens and men disguised as devils. The whole experience is a compromise between Catholic rite and indigenous animist influences.

On the northern frontier

Arica ❻ was the first port for exporting the fabulous silver wealth of Bolivia's Potosí mine. (In 1611 Potosí was the largest and richest city in the Americas.) But Arica's climate generated malaria, and the city was abandoned for other sites. Under Peruvian rule until the 1880s, Arica is now the international link to Bolivia (by rail and road) and Peru (by road). Its warm-water beaches make it a popular summer resort. A small church in the town center was built by the French architect Eiffel, better known for his Paris tower.

The **Museo Arqueológico San Miguel** (open Mar–Dec daily 10am–6pm. Jan and Feb daily 9am–7pm; entrance fee) is 14 km (9 miles) from town with an impressive collection of sand-preserved mummies older than their Egyptian counterparts. The Azapa valley in which the museum is located demonstrates the desert's fertility: given an adequate supply of water, brightly colored flowers grown commercially suddenly appear in the distance.

From Arica, passing the ancient geoglyphs near **San Miguel de Azapa**, and taking the inland road toward Lago Chungará, you pass through prehispanic and colonial villages with baroque churches and *pukarás,* or stone forts, used by native tribes from unrecorded times to defend themselves from invaders. As you ascend 4,500 meters (14,800 ft) into **Parque Nacional Lauca**, the mighty 6,000-meter (19,700-ft) high volcanoes Parinacota and Pomerape – sacred gods to the inhabitants of the high Andean plain – dominate the landscape. The ritual town of Parinacota, locked and abandoned for most of the year, is a center for the colorful religious festivals of the Aymara shepherds in the region, who otherwise rarely show themselves.

After passing the emerald waters of **Laguna Cotacotani**, one arrives at **Lago Chungará**, declared a Biosphere World Reserve by UNESCO. Wildlife teems all around the lake: the large flightless tagua-tagua make their nests on floating reed islands; the chinchilla-like vizcachas with their hopping scamper could be mistaken for fleeing gray hares; the sand-colored vicuñas often tag behind llama herds; the black-and-white *piquén* (Andean geese) will show themselves far from their nesting offspring as decoys; but perhaps most famous are the pink flamingos who dwell in the lake's shallows. Covering the rocks at this altitude like a green carpet is the pungent native lichen *llareta*, which grows a centimeter a year and has been used almost to extinction for fuel farther south. ❑

BLOOMING MARVELS IN THE ATACAMA DESERT

A mysterious, barren region of haunting beauty, spectacular natural phenomena and the well-preserved remains of ancient civilizations.

Chile's far north is made up of barren desert and scrubland, and the forbidding high plains of the Altiplano. No wonder most of the population prefer to live along the coast, in towns like Antofagasta and Iquique, famed for their architecture and expansive Pacific beaches. For the visitor, however, the mountain and desert regions present a series of awe-inspiring spectacles. The Atacama Desert is reputed to be the driest in the world, yet every decade or so a rare downpour (usually linked with the *El Niño* weather system) brings dormant seeds into bloom, in a phenomenon known as "The Flowering Desert."

The oasis village of San Pedro de Atacama *(see page 203)*, dominated by the Lincancábur volcano, is at the center of a region of immense geological interest, with huge salt lakes, hot springs and unusual desert formations. East of San Pedro the terrain ascends steeply to the Altiplano, where it meets Argentine and Bolivian territory. In this chilly region lie more hot springs, geysers and mountain lakes of ethereal beauty.

More natural and geological delights lie farther north of the Atacama Desert, toward Peru, where national parks like Lauca and Volcán Isluga, and Reserva Nacional Las Vicuñas are home to a variety of distinctive wildlife.

Some hardy travelers take the rail journey from Calama to Oruro in Bolivia. Rewards of this grueling trip include more Altiplano highlights, such as the immense salt basin of Uyuni, and Lagunas Verde and Colorado.

▷ **SHY VICUÑA**
The smallest and rarest of the camelids, the vicuña prefers the highest altitudes, mostly in northern Chile. Its fine wool has been prized since Inca times.

◁ SLEEPING GIANT
Volcán Licancábur (5,916 meters/19,4140 ft), presides over the ancient village oasis of San Pedro de Atacama, marking the place where the flat desert meets the chilly Altiplano.

△ FLAMINGOS IN FLIGHT
Flamingos are a common sight around Altiplano lakes. Three species of flamingo breed around Laguna Chaxa, south of Toconao (see page 203).

A NATURAL AND CULTURAL OASIS

The Atacama Desert has a restful quality – despite its inhospitable climate it comes as no surprise to learn that it has sustained human civilizations for thousands of years. Numerous ancient remains have been found in the area around the oasis of San Pedro, a tourist-dominated yet extremely pleasant hamlet with one of Chile's best museums, the Museo Gustavo Le Paige. The area's lack of rain has preserved ancient artifacts, including several mummies, which are displayed in the museum, along with pottery, jewelry, fragments of woven cloth and other items. It all provides a fascinating insight into what life was like before the arrival of Europeans. Also in the region is Pukará de Quitor, a 12th-century fort. San Pedro is also a good base from which to explore the surrounding desert, with numerous tours available from the village, for instance to the Valle de la Luna, a lunar landscape of eroded salt-rock formations.

△ CAMELS OF AMERICA
The largest of the camelids, llamas thrive in the barren desert conditions of the Atacama region.

◁ STEAMY PERFORMANCE
The geysers of El Tatio, 4,300 meters (14,100 ft) above sea level, give early-morning performances only.

▷ FLOWERING DESERT
Every 10–15 years, a downpour brings the Atacama Desert into bloom. It's such a rare event that knowledge of some of the flora is very scant.

JUAN FERNANDEZ ISLANDS

Map
on page
214

Famed as the temporary home of the real-life Robinson Crusoe, the inaccessibility of these small Pacific islands makes them natural biospheres replete with abundant endemic wildlife

Most people have never heard of the 18th-century Scottish sea dog named Alexander Selkirk or the **Juan Fernández Islands**, 650 km (404 miles) off the Chilean mainland. Yet they are part of our popular mythology. Try to imagine being marooned on a desert isle and you will probably see a man dressed in goat skins, flintlock at the ready, scanning the horizon for passing ships. His island – unlike the barren, windswept rocks where most mariners were washed up – has plentiful wood, crystal waters, abundant food and no wild beasts. The scene is from *Robinson Crusoe*, of course. But although Daniel Defoe set his classic novel in the Caribbean, he based it directly on Alexander Selkirk's real-life adventures on Chile's tiny Pacific possession.

The foul-tempered young Scotsman spent four years and four months on the largest of the three deserted Juan Fernández Islands. Finally rescued by a group of English privateers, Selkirk was clad in goatskins and could barely speak, croaking rather than talking. He had made himself two wooden huts with fur-lined interiors and had become incredibly fit from chasing wild animals around the rocky shores. The marooned sailor became a minor celebrity on his return home and – with the more debauched side of his character being carefully tidied up – inspired one of the most enduring classics in the English language.

The inhabitants of the Juan Fernández Islands today certainly aren't shy about this unique claim to fame. Selkirk's island was renamed **Isla Robinson Crusoe** in the mid-1970s while another, which the Scotsman never visited, was renamed **Isla Alejandro Selkirk**. Hotel and street names in the islands' only township refer insistently to the shipwrecked hero, and a disproportionate number of males on the archipelago have the Christian name of Robinson.

These unsubtle grabs at attention might suggest that the islands are something of a tourist trap. Nothing could be farther from the truth. Thanks to some spectacular transport difficulties, the archipelago is one of the least visited places in Chile. And while there are several fascinating excursions relating to Selkirk's adventures there, the most lasting pleasures lie elsewhere; the archipelago is a unique wilderness area, declared a Biosphere Reserve by UNESCO in 1978; while its people maintain an unusual serenity and striking indifference to the lures of the outside world.

PRECEDING PAGES:
the view from
Selkirk's Lookout.
LEFT: giant clawless
lobsters provide
income for the
islanders.
BELOW: a yacht
pulls into harbor.

The real-life Crusoe

While Daniel Defoe's fictional hero was shipwrecked in a tropical storm (and so, in his more meditative moments, saw the Hand of God at work), the real-life mariner Alexander Selkirk could only blame himself for his predicament: Selkirk actually asked to be let off his ship in the middle of nowhere. As sailing mas-

A good catch.

ter of the *Cinque Ports*, a privateering vessel making a circumnavigation of the globe in 1704, the quarrelsome Selkirk found himself constantly at odds with the ship's captain. Feelings finally came to a head over some poor repairs which had been made to a leak in the hull: Selkirk snapped that, if the boat was to go down, it would be without him. The captain agreed to land the Scotsman at the nearest island with a few supplies.

Selkirk stubbornly held to his demand until the very last moment. Sitting on the shore of Mas Á Tierra (as the island was then known), watching his former shipmates row back to their ship, the enormity of his decision struck him. Marooning was considered by pirates to be the ultimate punishment, far worse than walking the plank. A slow death by starvation or dehydration was the usual result. Most were put ashore with only their sea chest and a pistol with one ball; tales abounded of ships' crews finding a lone skeleton with a shattered skull and a rusting pistol clenched in one hand.

Selkirk is said to have plunged into the ocean and chased after the departing rowboat, screaming madly that he had changed his mind. "Well I have not changed mine!" spat the captain. "Stay where you are and may you starve!"

Goats, rats and feral cats

This indecorous scene was the beginning of four years and four months of isolation for Selkirk. He spent most of his time reading the Bible. A journalist who interviewed the Scotsman in a London tavern after his return to England noted that he believed himself "a better Christian while in this solitude than ever he was before, or than, he was afraid, he should ever be again."

Yet in the beginning, Selkirk hardly took his fate philosophically. For several

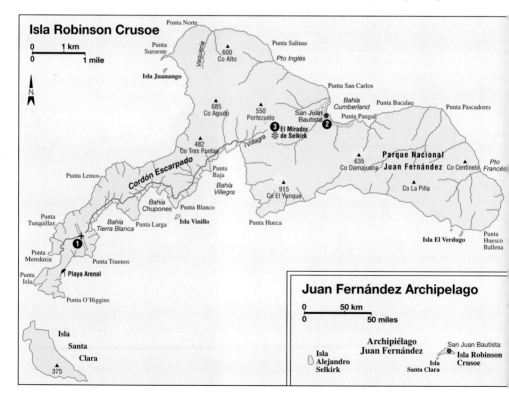

Map
on page
214

weeks after the marooning, he apparently wandered the coast, wailing and staring at the empty horizon. He simply could not believe that his shipmates would leave him there to rot on the shore. It took him 18 months to accept his fate, tear himself away from the shoreline and explore the rest of his island prison. At least Selkirk was not starved for animal company. Every night he heard the "monsters of the deep" whose cries were "too terrible to be made for human ears" – which, it turned out, were sea lions that had come up to shore. Eventually Selkirk overcame his fear, and learned how to climb behind these ponderous beasts and crack their skulls with a single blow of his hatchet.

Domestic animals had been introduced during an ill-fated attempt by the Spaniards to colonize the island following its discovery by the navigator Juan Fernández in 1574. Wild goats became the Scotsman's staple food: after his ammunition ran out, he chased them on foot with a knife and became an impressive athlete. He even chased goats for sport, marking their ears as a record. However, this diversion had its dangers: on one occasion Selkirk grabbed a goat just as it was leaping off a precipice. He was able to use the beast's body to cushion his fall, but was knocked unconscious for at least a full day. After this debacle, he decided to raise goats in a compound.

Wild rats were less amusing animal neighbors, invading Selkirk's hut by night to nibble his feet and tear his clothes. The Scotsman tamed feral kittens and laid them around his bed as a defense. Apparently he also taught some of his cats and kids to dance. "Thus best we picture him," intones the early 20th century poet Walter de la Mare, "praying aloud, singing and dancing with his kids and cats in the flames and the smoke of his allspice wood, and the whole world's moon taunting and enchanting him in her seasons."

The three Juan Fernández islands are believed to be the result of three separate volcanic eruptions.

LEFT: Selkirk's memorial plaque.
BELOW: the fictional Robinson Crusoe.

Return to civilization

Charming as these bestial balls must have been, Selkirk did not waver in his attempts to escape the island. Every day he climbed up to a lookout to survey the horizon. On two occasions ships actually pulled into the bay and Selkirk thought himself saved – only to discover that they were Spanish barks that would have taken him as a slave to the mines of Peru if they had caught him. (On the second visit, Spanish sailors even fired on the maroon and chased him into the bushes, but were no match for Selkirk's superhuman speed. The Scotsman hid up a tree until the danger had passed.)

Finally, after 52 months of isolation, Selkirk spotted the English *Duke* and *Duchess* lowering anchor on the island with 50 scurvy-ridden sailors. Brought on board, the goatskin-clad Selkirk cut an extraordinary figure, but disbelievers were soon silenced when William Dampier came forward to recognize the maroon and confirm his story.

Despite romantic reports to the contrary, Selkirk appears to have had few qualms about returning to his old life of privateering and debauchery. Appointed a mate on the voyage, he took part in the pillage of various Spanish ports before returning with the profits to celebrity in London and his home town of Lower Largo in Fife, Scotland. He was no doubt gratified to learn that the captain and crew of the *Cinque Ports*, after dumping him at Juan Fernández, had spent the last four years in a festering Lima jail, having been captured by the Spanish when the vessel foundered, just as Selkirk had predicted.

Drinking and whoring soon took its toll on Selkirk, sapping his unnatural fitness. He even became sentimental for his island prison, noting to one journalist that "I am worth eight hundred pounds, but shall never be so happy as when

The Juan Fernández native eagle lives only on the small Isla Alejandro Selkirk. It visits the other two islands, but never settles on them; no one knows why.

BELOW: barbecue on a fishing boat.
RIGHT: island girl.

I was not worth a farthing." The Scotsman may have gone a little batty: he reportedly dug a cave in his parents' backyard to hide in, ran away to London with a milkmaid, dumped her, then signed on for another privateering expedition. He caught a fever in the tropics and died on board in 1723, at the age of 47. Selkirk never knew that his marooning on Juan Fernández – extended by Defoe to 28 years and with a Man Friday thrown in – would become a legend.

Map on page 214

A remote destination

Getting to the Juan Fernández Islands today can seem as complicated as it was for Alexander Selkirk to get off them 300 years ago. Flights are generally confined to the summer months (October through April) when two companies operate the route. The frequency of flights depends, though, on demand, and getting a confirmed departure date requires luck and dedication. Even in summer, flights can be postponed for several days, depending on weather conditions.

The flights depart from Santiago's Tobalaba or Los Cerrillos airports early in the morning, leaving the capital behind in a bed of smog. Two and a half hours later, the tiny green specks of Juan Fernández appear, looking as tall as they are wide. For years it was considered impossible to build an airstrip on this rugged terrain, but in the 1970s something looking like a giant ski-jump was blasted through a far corner of the largest island. From the **airstrip ❶**, a jeep heads down a 45-degree angled road to the sea, followed by a 90-minute journey in an open fishing boat to town. On a fine day, the water is clear and blue, with schools of fish zigzagging below and the obese Juan Fernández seals sunning themselves by the shore. The boatmen often smoke succulent lumps of fresh cod caught on the outward journey and share them around with bread and water.

BELOW: farewells on the jetty.

The township of **San Juan Bautista** ❷, where almost all of the archipelago's 600 inhabitants live, is located roughly where Selkirk spent his enforced leisure time. Set beneath forest-covered fists of stone with their peaks always lost in gray mist, it has only a few, unpaved streets, a small museum-library, a handful of restaurants, a bar, a soccer field and one small cemetery with ship's anchors above many of the graves. With motor vehicles few and far between, the only noise is the never-ending howl of the wind.

Along the shore are tiny fishermen's huts, looking like the bathing machines at late 19th century beach resorts. This is a lobster town and not poor, although prices of goods imported from the mainland are high. Despite the soporific calm, Bautista is crowded with monuments to war. Eighteenth-century Spanish cannons, dug up from excavations above the town, are set into the footpath, along with a series of green pillboxes built to defend the island against Peruvian warships during the 19th-century War of the Pacific. Most curiously, along the path running north from the town is a spot where famous gun shells can be seen embedded in the cliff side. They were fired by the British warships *Glasgow* and *Kent* at the German cruiser *Dresden* when it tried to retire here for repairs in 1915, during World War I. The captain blew up the ship rather than surrender.

Fifty native fern species grow on the Juan Fernández Islands. The largest can reach a height of five meters (16 ft).

In Selkirk's footsteps

The classic hike from town follows Selkirk's path to **El Mirador de Selkirk** ❸ – the lookout used by the marooned sailor every day to scan the horizon on both sides of the island. Start early, at about 8am, to arrive before the mists roll in. The path runs through crops of introduced eucalyptuses into higher forests of indigenous trees. It passes the remains of an old Spanish fort, and a turning leading to a rock with carvings on it from 1866 – sailor's graffiti showing a ship and giant fish. The trail becomes a corridor through rainforest before revealing a knife-shaped peak.

The saddle of the mountain is the only place from which to view both sides of the island: the lush green Juan Bautista side to the east giving way to dry brown swirls and jagged peaks on the northern side of the mountain. A plaque commemorating Selkirk's ordeal was erected here by the crew of a British warship in the 19th century. It has more recently been joined by a small memorial from one of the mariner's descendants from Largo in Scotland.

On the return journey, call in at the **Caves of the Patriots**, where 300 pro-Spanish soldiers fled in 1814 after Chile's declaration of independence. Unlike Selkirk, they couldn't stand the wind and rain in their huge but damp caves, so gave themselves up. Back on the shore, a number of other caves vie for the title of Selkirk's home – although for most of the time the mariner lived in his own hand-made huts.

Conservation drive

CONAF, Chile's national park service, is very active on the Juan Fernández Islands, protecting the endemic flora and fauna of the area that put the island on the UNESCO World Heritage list (in some areas of the island, only guided hikes are permitted). The plant life is unusually varied on the island, with 101 endemic

BELOW: unique flora of the islands.

Map on page 214

varieties including a range of enormous ferns, many of which look like they belong in Dr Seuss books. Of the endemic animals, the red Juan Fernández hummingbird is most famous for its needle-fine black beak and silken plumage.

CONAF spends most of its time trying to eradicate threats introduced by man: everything from mulberry bushes to the wild goats and feral cats descended from Selkirk's days. Rabbits were a problem, but they have been controlled by the simple solution of paying a trapper to catch and sell 150 a day (the islanders thought this a more humane solution than using the fatal viral disease myxomatosis). Biologists here regularly turn up new finds: a fern called *dendroseries macranta* that had not been sighted since 1907 was found not so long ago in a remote spot.

But one of the real pleasures of any visit to Isla Robinson Crusoe is just taking a seat by the wharf and watching the world go by, sipping on a beer and chatting with the islanders. Everyone will eventually mention that Juan Fernández is a paradise. And, although the archipelago doesn't boast the swaying palms or golden sands of most South Pacific islands, it does have plenty of other elements to make it a contender: beautiful scenery, good weather, plenty of food, no crime, no poverty, no racial tensions, no bad weather, no pollution.

The people of the Juan Fernández Islands are not a remote group being dragged into the 21st century, with a delicate society about to buckle under the strain. Everyone is descended from Chilean or European immigrants, and has grown up within a Western culture – albeit a detached version. The islanders take what they want from the modern world – medicine, music, radios or TV soap operas – and leave the rest. Perhaps that's why the half-familiar world of Juan Fernández is so beguiling: one admires the islanders' good sense but, already being a part of the outside world, can never share it. ❑

The sandalwood boom of the late 19th century deprived the island totally of its native sandalwood trees.

BELOW: sea lions on the lookout.

CENTRAL VALLEY

Vineyards and fruit flourish in the temperate climate of this lush, fertile region, yet until the late 19th century it marked the border to the wild, unconquered southern lands.

Map on page 222

Santiago

Running parallel between the towering Cordillera de los Andes and the lower coastal mountain range is the Chilean **Central Valley**. The area from Los Andes, just 80 km (50 miles) north of Santiago, to some 500 km (300 miles) farther south is the richest farmland in the country. Vineyards have been established here since the arrival of the Spanish *conquistadores* and, today, wine-making for export is among its most important activities. Similarly, most of the traditional agricultural activities of the old landed aristocracy, such as growing wheat, grain and fodder for domestic animals, have given way to the much more profitable cultivation of fresh produce for export worldwide.

Driving in springtime along the Pan-American Highway south of Santiago, fields of flaming orchards perfume the air and make a brilliant display. The dark, hot pink of peaches and nectarines, the lighter rose-colored cherry trees and the white flowering almond, apple, apricot or plum trees all proclaim the Central Valley's world-renowned fertility, as do the hundreds of road-side stalls offering freshly harvested produce.

Leaving the main roads is to take a step back in time to a simpler, slower-paced, infinitely more relaxing era. Never is this more true than during the Independence Day celebrations held annually on September 18, which offer an inside view to festivities in rural areas throughout the country. *Fondas* or *ramadas*, outdoor ballrooms with thatched eucalyptus leaf roofs, are erected all over the countryside. People gather from miles around to watch the competition between *huasos,* the Chilean cowboys; to dance the *cueca,* the national dance; to eat *empanadas* (meat and onion pies) and to drink *chicha,* fermented grape juice *(see page 130).*

Luxurious traditions

The busy town of **Rancagua ❶**, 87 km (54 miles) south of Santiago, is as much an agricultural center as the home of miners employed in El Teniente, the world's largest underground copper mine. The mine, and a heritage-listed workers' camp called Sewell, is at the end of the Carretera del Cobre (Copper Highway), which runs from Rancagua east and up into the mountains. The complex is not officially open to the public, although on occasion visits can be arranged with the owners, Codelco (tel: 02-690-3000). Yanguas, a Santiago-based tour operator, also organizes visits (tel: 02-774-0148).

Travelers may want to combine the trip with, or prefer to simply visit the thermal baths of **Termas de Cauquenes ❷**, 28 km (17 miles) east of Rancagua, in the Andean foothills. Used by native peoples long before the arrival of the Spanish, the first to lay claim to the medicinal waters were Jesuits. The baths were

LEFT: gathering Cabernet Sauvignon grapes.
BELOW: Sunday Mass.

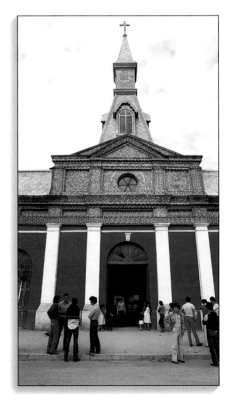

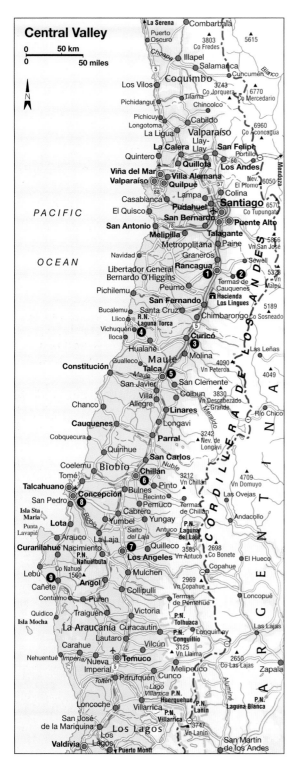

Central Valley

0 — 50 km
0 — 50 miles

frequented by the Chilean founding father Bernardo O'Higgins during rests from his revolutionary bouts against the colonial authorities, and in 1834, the British naturalist Charles Darwin wrote of the excellence of their waters.

The construction of what is today a hotel began in 1885. The huge high-ceilinged bathhouse with stained-glass windows leads up an enormous staircase to the dining and game-room area. Rooms and suites, some modernized, some still with wood-burning iron stoves are set around large open gardens or down the back overlooking the Cachapoal River. The surrounding hills are filled with *peumos*, a native tree with bright red edible fruit and shiny green leaves.

In their quest to compete with the smart new boutique hotels springing up all over the country, traditional establishments, such as this, have used top cuisine to draw visitors. In Chile, many argue that Swiss-born René Acklin, Chile's only accredited master chef, has done just that at the Termas de Cauquenes. Diners at the hotel's immense restaurant are transported back a century, with its fine old furnishings contrasting deliciously with the modern fare prepared in the kitchen.

Wine country

Once back on the main highway, the next city south of Rancagua is **San Fernando**, a bustling rural center, which is gradually succumbing to the advances of shopping malls, Internet cafes and smarter urban life. For the tourist, though, it serves simply as a reference for Santa Cruz, a charming little town 40 km (25 miles) towards the coast. Laid out around a traditional Spanish-style city square (Plaza de Armas), Santa Cruz has, since the late 1990s, transformed itself from a quaint, but lifeless, colonial town into a cosmopolitan hub for travelers from all over the world. No visit is complete without at least a night in the Hotel Santa Cruz Plaza, an impeccably restored colonial building, which has

44 tastefully decorated rooms, a landscaped swimming pool and gardens, and arguably one of the best restaurants south of Santiago. Its wine list is replete with the area's finest varietal whites and oak-matured reds, and tours of local vineyards can be arranged at the hotel *(see page 107, Fruit of the Vine)*.

Map on page 222

The town is also home to an excellent historical museum. Run by a not-for-profit foundation in a converted 18th-century estate house, the Museo de Colchagua houses the private collection of Carlos Cardoen, the hotel's owner (open Tues–Fri 10am–12.30pm and 3–6.30pm, weekends and holidays 10am–1pm and 4–6pm; entrance fee, except for hotel guests).

At the Museo San José del Carmen de El Huique in Palmilla, a 15-minute drive from Santa Cruz, visitors get a rare glimpse of 19th-century rural elegance as lived by the wealthy Errázuriz and Echeñique families, who settled there from northern Spain (open Wed–Sun 11am–5.30pm in summer; until 5pm in winter; Mass is said in what was the family chapel every Sunday at 11.30am).

Fish for sale, Concón.

Lakeside serenity

While the colonial town of Vichuquén can be reached by bus from **Curicó ❸**, there is so much to see in this interesting coastal area that it's worth hiring a car. The 110-km (68-mile) road that follows the northern bank of the Mataquito River from Curicó as far as Hualañé is a route of breathtaking scenic beauty, bordered by vineyards. But the cut-off route from the highway near San Fernando, through Santa Cruz, Lolol, San Pedro de Alcántara, Rarín and the coastal town of Llico, also has its own charm, revealing rolling hills and hidden, sleepy country towns.

Farther north, at the end of the main road west from Santa Cruz, is Pichilemu, Chile's surfing capital. This one-time rural center and fishing village has been transformed into a hip destination for surfers from around the world, most of whom stay in the beachside cabins dotting the unpaved road to Punta de Lobos and Bucalemu. Diehard surfers should ask around for details on how to reach "secret spots" farther north toward Navidad.

BELOW: sliding stop at the National Rodeo Championship, Rancagua.

The town of **Vichuquén** existed before the invasion of the Incas from Peru in the 15th century, who formed a colony there with the native Mapuches. The name of the town comes from the Mapuche language and means "the serpent lake." Time seems to have stopped still some 100 years ago along its orange tree-lined streets, where unhurried locals linger along the covered wooden sidewalks. The town's museum is worth a visit.

The main attraction here, however, is **Lago Vichuquén**, just 5 km (3 miles) towards the coast. Pine forests that grow in record time surround the summer houses that line the shore. Windsurfers and small sailboats cut silently across the mirror-like surface of the lake to explore the uninhabited Isla del Cerrillo that sits alone in the lake's center. There are two main hotels on the lake, both situated on the southern side. The Hotel Playa Aquelarre has spectacular views of the lake and the myriad species that make the area a bird-watchers' paradise. Binoculars and ornithological guides are provided for guests. At the nearby Hotel

Marina Vichuquén, the accent is on aquatic pursuits. There are also several camping grounds and cheaper lodgings around the southern end of the lake.

Just 3 km (1.7 miles) north of the lake is the **Reserva Nacional Laguna Torca ❹**. The lagoon is a nesting ground for black-necked swans and another 80 or so species of exotic birds. Great blue herons hide in the reed-lined banks. The S-shaped bodies of stark white herons wade through the shallows, while an enormous variety of ducks and the small, black *tagua* coots keep up a tremendous clatter of quacking.

The black-necked swans found on Lago Vichuquén lay their eggs in floating reed nests.

After a morning's bird-watching, stop in for fresh shellfish or fried *congrio* (kingclip) at the Residencial Miramar in **Llico** (tel: 071-198-3748). Returning to Vichuquén, an unpaved road forks off and runs south through a series of beachside towns famed for their seafood *picadas* (cheap restaurants). Locals and visitors alike say Donde Gilberto (tel: 075-198-3768), just before the town of Iloca, is the pick of the bunch. It also has reasonably priced accommodation offering spectacular sea views.

Seat of Chilean independence

Continuing south on the Pan-American Highway, **Talca ❺** is 60 km (37 miles) southwest of Curicó. An important urban center since its founding in 1742, Talca was the traditional residence of the landed elite. The older part of town, as in most Chilean colonial towns, surrounds the **Plaza de Armas** with its jacarandas, palms, magnolia trees, cedars and other conifers.

BELOW: rich river valley.

The **Museo O'Higginiano** (open Tues–Fri 10am–6pm, Sat 10.30am–2.30pm, Sun 3–7pm; entrance fee), on the corner of 1 Norte and 2 Oriente, was the childhood home of the Chilean hero and father of Independence, Bernardo

Map
on page
222

O'Higgins. The building was also the home in 1813 of José Miguel Carrera, who presided over the first governmental junta. Carrera declared Chile a sovereign, autonomous state in the 1812 Constitution, and also – with the help of O'Higgins – organized resistance to invading royalist troops from farther south *(see page 34)*. In one of the house's many salons, Bernardo O'Higgins signed the Act of Independence. The museum also features an important collection of paintings, sculpture, historical manuscripts and pre-Columbian artifacts.

Farther south on the highway is the town of **Chillán** . Repeatedly destroyed by earthquakes and rebuilt, most of its buildings are not more than 50 years old. In 1939, a night-time earthquake killed 15,000 and destroyed 90 percent of the town. Mexico donated a school to the city as part of the reconstruction. The Mexican muralists David Alfaro Siqueiros and Xavier Guerrero painted representative scenes of Chilean and Mexican history there in 1941. The Escuela Mexico (corner of Av. Bernardo O'Higgins and Vega de Saldías) still operates as a school, but staff welcome visitors who want to see the heritage-listed mural (open Mon–Fri 9.30am–12.30pm and 3–6pm in summer; Tues–Fri 9am–1pm and 3–6pm in winter; entrance fee).

Chillán's market, on Calle Maipón between Isabel Riquelme and 5 de Abril, is the largest and most vibrant in Chile. Here you can find handicrafts from all over the country as well as the locally made clothing that makes up the typical *huaso* dress: from the felt (for winter) or straw (for summer) flat-rimmed hats; and small dress ponchos in finely woven, bright colors, to the leather boots and carved wooden stirrups. The market is open every day, but is particularly lively on Saturdays.

Skiing and bathing on a volcano

The western-facing slopes of the **Volcán Chillán**, 80 km (50 miles) from Chillán, provide some of the finest open-slope skiing in the Andes from June through October. **Termas de Chillán**, named for its famous thermal springs, is the base for the ski resort. The resort, at 1,650 meters (5,413 ft) above sea level, has five "T"-lifts, one triple chair lift and two double chair lifts (one of them, at 2.5 km/1½ miles, is the longest in South America). An accomplished skier can stay on the slopes from morning to late afternoon and, as there is so much variety, need never cover the same trail twice. A series of pistes from the summit down to the wooded region around the hotel area connect to produce a 13-km (8-mile) run, also the longest in South America.

After a hard day on the slopes, there is no better way to ease tired muscles than to plunge into one of the four outdoor thermal swimming pools in the Parque de Aguas. The Gran Hotel Termas de Chillán, which reopened in 1996 after the old one burnt down, has 120 modern bedrooms, as well as sitting rooms with roaring fireplaces, a disco, and games and music rooms. The set menu is wholesome if not very imaginative, but delicacies are available at an additional cost in the Montañés restaurant.

A more modest, but very comfortable choice is the 48-bedroom Hotel Pirigallo, just half a kilometer

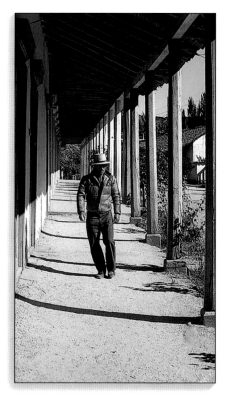

BELOW: the "Wild West" look.

away and run by the same owners. There are also five self-service apartment buildings, ideal for budget-conscious family groups.

Chillán's thermal baths have been famous for the past 150 years, while the ski resort has only developed within the last 25 years. Many visitors make the trip in the summer to hike to the geyser-like fuming springs of the thermal waters and to bathe in the medicinal muds nearby. Summer visitors often camp near the hotels or stay in the guest cabins or in the hotels in **Las Trancas** or **Recinto**; in winter, the villages also offer myriad cheaper alternatives to the pricey accommodation of the main hotel area. A trip in the chairlift reveals stupendous views of the towering volcanic crater and accompanying eternal snows of the Nevada de Chillán mountain range. Guided walking tours and horseback excursions are also available.

The road back from the hotel is lined with lush forest vegetation resembling that found in the Lake District farther south. Huge old oaks join firs, pines and the delicate, native *ñirre* trees set among giant ferns and red *copihues* – the fleshy, trumpet-shaped national flower that hangs from climbing vines. Two kilometers from the hotel you can visit an enormous natural cavern, the **Cueva de los Pincheira**. This was used as a hideaway by the Pincheira brothers and their followers, a group of royalist highway robbers who ransacked the area during the struggle for independence. The spectacular **Piedras Comadres**, colossal rock walls that drop straight down from their forest-covered heights, can be seen from the road.

Before the town of **Los Angeles** ❼, 80 km (50 miles) south of Chillán, the **Salto del Laja** waterfall can be viewed from the bridge that crosses the River Laja. The falls crash down some 15–20 meters (49–66 ft) from two wide arches

TIP

Visitors can go down the "Devil's Draught" coal mine, near Lota, in which Chile's best-known novel of mining life, *Sub Terra*, is set.

BELOW: a rich landowner's house near San Fernando.

into deep, enormous pools, to be swiftly conducted into the narrow river canyon further down. The area has numerous hotels, campsites and restaurants, some with swimming pools and recreational facilities.

Map on page 222

Gateway to the south

The country's second-largest city (even though, including the adjoining port of Talcahuano, it has only 580,000 inhabitants), **Concepción ❽** is located some 86 km (53 miles) off the Pan-American Highway. It lies at the mouth of the **River Bíobío**, the natural boundary between southern and central Chile, and is an important center for the country's forestry industry. Founded by *conquistador* Pedro de Valdivia in 1550, Concepción was the site occupied by the Real Audiencia: the political, military and administrative center of the Spanish colony from 1565 to 1573. The location of the city was changed a number of times due to repeated earthquake devastation, particularly in the mid-18th century, and attacks from the Mapuches. Its present location was settled in 1764.

Shrine on coastal road near Viña.

Repeated reconstruction following the natural disasters, combined with economic growth, have made Concepción a modern city with little remaining of its past glory, and many visitors would rather pass on through it. The city's pride is the **Universidad de Concepción** campus, with its open amphitheater and central green dominated by the University's watchtower. Nearby are the marble-fronted walls of the courthouse, and the railway station, above which is a mural depicting the history of the city. The **Casa del Arte** (Pinoteca), on the corner of Lamas and Larenas, houses an extensive collection of national paintings.

In **Talcahuano**, the battleship *Huáscar* can be visited. Captured from the Peruvian fleet during the War of the Pacific in 1879, it has been held as a tro-

BELOW: scooping up coal in Lota.

Map on page 222

Nahuelbuta means "the big cat" in the Mapuche tongue, a reference to the puma that lives in the mountains named after it.

BELOW: horsemanship at Pucón.
RIGHT: the Andean foothills south of Santiago.

phy of the victory that added the country's northernmost provinces and their rich mineral deposits to the national territory. Worth a visit in nearby Lota is the park created by the Cousiño family, the original owner of the area's now mostly disused coal mines.

One of these, the Chiflón del Diablo (Devil's Draught), is open to visitors as part of a tourist circuit created to help revive the formerly mining-dependent community. Visitors are lowered 40 meters (131 ft) down a shaft and guided through its tunnels as ex-miners relate anecdotes about the grueling life at the coal-face. Other attractions include the town's museum and the Central Hidroeléctrica Chivilingo, Chile's oldest power plant, with an interactive energy museum. Accommodation can be found in Lota at a number of basic, but friendly, hotels.

The Viña Macul vineyard is still owned and run by the Cousiño family, who built the Palacio Cousiño in Santiago. They also founded Chile's first forestry industry in the Colcura valley, near Lota, in 1881 to supply beams for use in their mines. Dark pine forests, a faster-growing crop than the native hardwood forests, run south along the road to Curanilahue, which is lined with timber-laden trucks. The cellulose plant for paper manufacturing in the beach resort of **Arauco** has contributed to the economic development of the zone. This industry is probably primarily responsible for the paving of the road south, which was taken by the Spanish conquerors as they explored the area between the coast and the Nahuelbuta mountain range.

Following this so-called Ruta de los Conquistadores, one arrives in **Cañete** ❾. This town has a frontier flavor that announces the beginnings of the Mapuche lands. It was here that the Mapuche *toqui* or warrior chief Lautaro surprised *conquistador* Pedro de Valdivia and put a dramatic end to his life *(see page 81)*. Cañete's **Museo Mapuche** (open Jan–Feb Mon–Sun 9.30am–5.50pm, Mar–Dec Tues–Fri 9.30am–5.50pm, Sat and Sun 1–6.30pm; entrance fee) displays a large range of native peoples' culture, including ceremonial and domestic artifacts, weapons, documents and photographs. A reconstruction of a traditional Mapuche *ruca* (dwelling house) can be seen behind the museum, though guides must be pre-arranged to be able to wander about inside (tel: 41-611-093).

From late December to mid-March, lodgings are available on the nearby **Lago Lanalhue** in the Hostería Lanalhue on the western side of the lake, and there are cabins, camping facilities and other basic accommodation around the lake. The summer months are ideal for activities such as windsurfing and fishing and the lake is also used for swimming and nautical sports.

There are also hotels and cheaper lodgings in the quaint neighboring town of **Contulmo**, settled by Prussians in 1868. The main square is surrounded by enormous linden and cedars, as well as native trees. The **Grollmus** house, a large wooden house built in 1923, and mill has 23 varieties of *copihue*, which bloom between March and April, and the remains of a small hydroelectric generator that used to supply the town with light. ❑

THE LAKE DISTRICT

Map
on page
234

Snow-capped mountains reflected in looking-glass lakes, quaint wooden hamlets steeped in healthy alpine air, fishing ports and old rural traditions – the Lake District is Chile's wonderland

Santiago

The Lake District exercises a near-mythic fascination on Chileans. The south symbolizes everything healthy, unspoiled and pure in Chile and its people. City folks, particularly in Santiago, look kindly on southerners as their own better selves, even while succumbing to the temptation to take advantage of their gullibility and innocence. The *huaso*, the typical small farmer, is the object of an ambiguous mix of derision and affection in Chile and, in popular folklore, he always comes from the abundant, fraternal south rather than the arid north where skeptical, wary individualism sets the tone of human relations.

Foreign visitors will be made to feel very much at home in the Lake District, where European influences of all kinds, including immigration, have long been welcomed. An early pioneer and champion of southern settlement and development, Vicente Pérez Rosales *(see page 244),* exemplified this eurocentrism when he announced in 1854 that "the word 'foreigner' has been eliminated in Chile. It is an immoral word and should disappear from the dictionary." Pérez Rosales was not thinking of Peruvians or Brazilians or other *mestizo* nations when he made the statement – he meant the Germans, Austrians, Swiss and Italians whose communities are still common in the south.

PRECEDING PAGES:
the famous falls
of Salto del Laja.
LEFT: lakeside rodeo.
BELOW: making hay.

Unfriendly encounters

However, native Mapuche roots are still not so far from the surface of southern Chile's collective memory. The south, where most of the country's rural indigenous population lives, was not fully dominated by the European-descended settlers until the second half of the 19th century. The first European colony at what is now the lakeside resort center of Villarrica, for example, was besieged by Mapuches in a 1598 uprising, collapsing without survivors in 1602, and was not re-established until a military mission arrived in 1882, nearly three centuries later.

In the interim, an uneasy state of semi-war prevailed. Early in the 1600s, the Bíobío River (which reaches the sea at what is now the port of Concepción) was established as the frontier between the Spanish colony and native lands, but the truce was violated annually in raids from one side or the other. Spanish mercenaries fought to capture Mapuches and sell them into slavery, while the Mapuches raided to plunder cattle and other goods or to punish the invaders. Regular peace conferences between the two sides usually ended in great celebrations of feasting and drinking and vows of friendship – which would invariably last only a few months before the next outbreak of hostilities.

Finally, commerce pacified the situation. A regular trade in cattle, woven goods, knives, arms and liquor

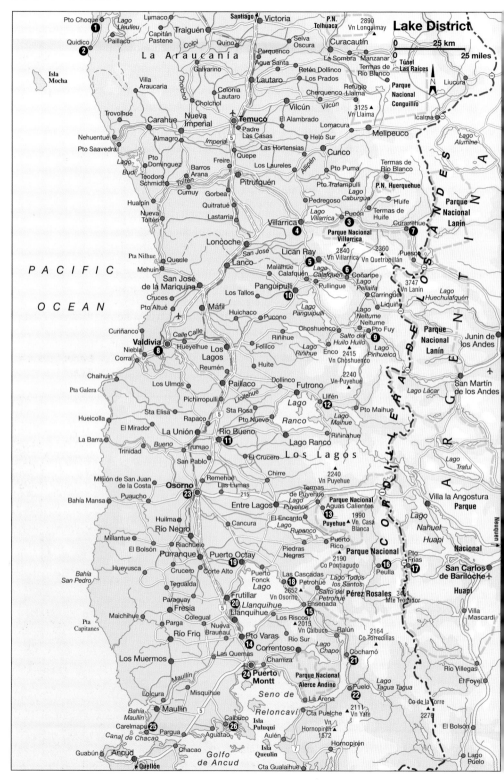

Map on page 234

developed, though violent outbursts between Mapuches and European soldiers, brigands, and shady dealers of all sorts continued to occur regularly. Naturally, the *mestizo* population grew steadily with the constant contact, and colonial garrison commanders preferred them as soldiers since they knew the area well and were notoriously impervious to hardship.

These hostilities meant that the Lake District was, until relatively recently, unexplored territory for those of European descent. Lago Colico, near Pucón, was the last of the big lakes to be discovered by Europeans, making its first appearance on maps in the early years of the 20th century. The great Lago Llanquihue near Puerto Montt was first sighted by Pedro de Valdivia in 1552, but Mapuche raids put it effectively out of bounds to Europeans until new waves of settlers began to arrive three centuries later.

Life in the outback

Chile's south is a more recently tamed version of the North American Wild West, and, in more remote areas, life revolves around horses, farm work and social events, lubricated with large quantities of wine or *chicha* made from fermented apples. Country families tend to live off seasonal sales of milk or a cash crop, or tourists, spending long months consuming the stores of grain they harvested themselves, while the men look for paying jobs in the larger towns and cities.

The rural areas are connected by an extensive network of local buses which transport schoolchildren, farmers and country residents returning from the larger towns with provisions. The buses are slow due to the terrain and the constant stops at every lane or farmhouse, but they are very cheap and reach many remote settlements. The first, and sometimes only bus tends to leave before dawn, so it is always prudent to inquire about schedules the day before traveling. As the terrain is ideal for backpacking and hiking, Chilean youth swarm southward in the summertime, many of them spending long hours on the highway awaiting motorists or truckers who will give them a lift. Most have the barest minimum of funds and camp wherever possible.

Gateway to the Lake District

The Lake District is generally considered to begin at the Toltén River, which empties into Lago Villarrica, but this is more a result of the area's fame as a resort region than strict topographic considerations. The characteristic combination of volcanoes and lakes actually begins farther north, around the area of Parque Nacional Conguillío, northeast of Temuco. This region is home to several volcanoes, including **Lonquimay** (2,890 meters/9,480 ft) which entered into full eruption in 1988 and blanketed the area with dangerous volcanic dust; and **Llaima**, which erupted in 1994. Lonquimay means "without a head" in the Mapuche tongue, referring to the volcano's flat top.

This is also Mapuche territory – the Mapuches' ancestors used the accessible mountain passes and gathered pine nuts from the ancient *araucaria*, or monkey puzzle tree, which is endemic to the southern Andes. There are male and female *araucaria* trees – biologists can determine their sex by examining their bark.

BELOW: the Bíobío River.

These rare coniferous trees, which take 500 years to mature fully and can live for more than 1,000 years, were endangered by logging activities until President Aylwin's government responded to environmental campaigners and prohibited their destruction in March 1990.

Temuco, founded in 1881, following an important treaty between the new republic and the Mapuches, is now a rapidly growing industrial town, and a good base from which to explore the northern Lake District. Its **Museo Regional de la Araucanía** (open Mon–Fri 10am–5.30pm, Sat 11am–5pm, Sun 11am–2pm; entrance fee) provides information on the native people and their history. The museum includes a Mapuche dwelling or "ruca", as well as displays focusing on more recent settlers. Mapuches from the surrounding countryside come to Temuco to sell their wares; the central market, although rather touristy, is a good place to buy local handicrafts and to try traditional dishes. The **Cerro Nielol** hill and forest park, where the national *copihue* flower grows in abundance, offers the best view of the city.

A new fast train service from Santiago to Temuco has cut travel time to nine hours and provides a good opportunity to see the gradual changes in climate and scenery on the journey south, with the Andes mountains rarely out of sight.

Source of the Bíobío

The town of **Lonquimay** and the land surrounding it lie to the east of the Andean cordillera, despite the general rule that the highest peaks mark the territorial boundaries between Chile and Argentina. However, **Lago Gualletué** south of Lonquimay provides the headwaters of the important **Bíobío River**, which then runs north for nearly 100 km (60 miles) before turning westward

BELOW: herding cattle.

toward the Pacific Ocean at Concepción *(see Central Valley map, page 222).* As this river was long considered the border dividing Spanish lands from unconquered Mapuche territory, Chile claimed the hydrographic basin.

Map on page 234

The main road to Lonquimay passes through the **Las Raíces** ("Roots") **Tunnel**. This was originally a rail tunnel, built in the 1930s as part of a plan (subsequently abandoned) to connect the Atlantic and Pacific oceans by rail. The access to the tunnel and the passageway itself are currently undergoing repairs, which are due to be completed in mid-2005. The tunnel is passable in all weathers (though large icicles form in winter). On the road to the tunnel from Curacautín there are several thermal baths, as well as the beautiful 50-meter (16-ft) Princess Waterfall and two huge volcanic rocks, Piedra Cortada and Piedra Santa, which were considered sacred by the indigenous people.

Roadside crafts.

Parque Nacional Conguillío can be reached from Curacautín in the north or Melipeuco in the south. Both routes skirt the snow-covered **Volcán Llaima** (3,125 meters/10,253 ft), and lead through virgin forests of *araucaria* and other Chilean species such as *coigüe* and *raulí*, as well as oak and cypress. Twelve-hundred year-old *araucaria* trees can be seen in Parque Nacional Conguillío, which was set up in 1950. Conquillío's prehistoric feel led the BBC to film parts of its 1999 natural history series *Walking with Dinosaurs* here. The park's popularity has brought about a serious erosion of vegetation and, in 2002, forest fires burned 1,633 hectares (661 acres) of the seldom-visited eastern section of the park. Three tiny lakes in the park (Verde, Captrén and Arco Iris) were formed by lava flows which blocked several rivers. The lakes are just a few decades old, and the trees that once grew on their beds can still be seen below the water. Volcán Llaima now has a small, modern ski resort on its slopes, at Los Paraguas.

BELOW: Petrohué falls and Volcán Osorno.

AN ACTIVE LANDSCAPE

Chile has 2,085 volcanoes, of which 55 are considered active. The entire country forms part of the Pacific "Rim of Fire" which stretches along the western coasts of North and South America, west to New Zealand and the western Pacific islands and up through Japan and the Kamchatka Peninsula.

Chile's volcanoes are doubly dangerous because of their eternal snows, which melt into rapid, devastating mudslides upon full eruption. The lava itself advances much more slowly but burns away everything in its path. These lava "runs" can be observed at Villarrica, Petrohué and Ensenada, and you can climb the Villarrica volcano for a peek down at the magma quite near the surface. Although some of the active volcanoes are considered semi-dormant, a strong eruption can always set off a chain reaction of volcanic activity, as happened in the 1960 earthquake.

The lakes are of glacial origin, their basins carved out by advancing ice, then filled by the melting ice as the glaciers receded. There is also evidence of tectonic influence, with earthquakes causing some lake basins to sink further while newly formed volcanoes sometimes shift the course of rivers as they rise up between them.

A private concessionaire manages the main campsite on the shores of the largest lake, Lago Conguillío, as well as several log cabins in a stunning location in an *araucaria* forest. December is the best time to visit, before the Chilean summer vacation crowds arrive in January and February.

Mapuche stronghold

On the coast, west of Conguillío, is the even more isolated **Lago Lleulleu** (in the Mapuche language, a repeated word has extra importance). The southern finger of the lake is the most beautiful, surrounded by virgin forests. Aside from the tiny community at **Puerto Choque ❶**, the only civilization nearby is at **Quidico ❷** on the ocean, which is popular in the summer for its excellent seafood and windswept beach. The end of the main road is just past **Tirúa** where Mapuche chiefs once charged a toll for land traffic between Concepción and Valdivia. According to legend, the bishop of Concepción was kidnapped and held here in 1778, only escaping when a rival chief won his freedom in a game of chance.

Next to the beaches at Viña del Mar and Reñaca, the area around Villarrica and Pucón is the most popular holiday resort in Chile. The two towns are the main urban centers on the end of **Lago Villarrica** which is dominated by the active **Volcán Villarrica**, (2,840 meters/9,320 ft), just an hour's detour from the north-south PanAmerican Highway. **Pucón ❸** could be called the "Viña of the South" for its success in attracting summer tourists, especially since the 1934 construction of the Gran Hotel Pucón by the Chilean State Railroad Company. (Guests arrived by train to Villarrica, then boated 25 km/16 miles across the lake to their lodgings.) It is now enormously popular amongst the Chilean middle

Chile's native parrots abound in the mountains around Conguillío and give campers a raucous early morning call.

BELOW:
Volcán Villarrica.

Map
on page
234

classes who are rapidly buying up the summer condominiums along the beach. Many flock to the area in the summer months, sunbathe on the beach, take part in noisy water sports on Lago Villarrica by day, and crowd the casino in the Hotel de Los Lagos by night.

Though it has become very commercial, Pucón provides all the services a tourist could want, including an excellent variety of restaurants, bars, and discotheques, and is extremely popular with backpackers.

The town is also a key center for adventure tourists and by far the most popular activity is the one-day hike to the lava-filled crater of Volcán Villarrica *(see page 125, Adventure Activities chapter)*. An increasing variety of water sports, including rafting, kayaking and hydrospeed, are also practiced on the Trancura River. Though the service offered by adventure travel agencies varies, most provide high-quality imported equipment and qualified guides trained to ensure international safety standards.

Skiing is available in winter at a resort owned by the Gran Hotel Pucón on the slopes of Volcán Villarrica. More relaxing activities include horseback riding, fishing, and visits to nearby hot springs and national parks.

The area around Pucón has also pioneered environmental tourism projects. **El Cañi**, east of Pucón, is one of Chile's first private parks. Its ancient *araucaria* forest growing on an extinct volcano became a reserve in 1992 with funding from Ancient Forests International and has been developed as a center for environmental education and scientific research. Though it requires a steep three-hour hike, reaching the summit rewards the climber with spectacular views of all the area's volcanoes on a clear day. Visits are best organized through the École hostel in Pucón.

Some Mapuche families living near Tirúa scratch a living by harvesting and selling the edible cochayuyo *seaweed that amasses along the seashore.*

BELOW: serene Lake Calafquén at Lican Ray.

Cultural resort

Numerous Mapuche communities are tucked away in the hills surrounding **Villarrica ❹**, and each summer a Mapuche cultural festival is held in the town. This includes a nightly demonstration of religious rituals. Some unusual craft work can be found among the stands, but most of the work has long been copied by artisans in Santiago and elsewhere.

One of the town's main streets is named after General Emil Koerner, the German military scientist who was hired in the late 19th century by President Balmaceda to reorganize the Chilean armed forces (he used the area for training). Koerner then betrayed Balmaceda to side with an 1891 insurrection fomented by local oligarchs *(see page 40)*. The oligarchs won, President Balmaceda committed suicide, and Koerner proceeded to reshape the army along Prussian lines, a model which remains largely in force today. His prestige led to a surge of pro-German sentiment which helped to stimulate a second wave of German immigrants, most of whom headed for the newly available lands in the south *(see page 244)*.

Mountain beaches

Just a short drive from Pucón to the north and northeast are lakes Caburgua and Colico, and, in the mountains of **Parque Nacional Huerquehue**, lakes Tinquilco, Toro and Verde. Rare outcroppings of "flywing" rock crystal usually observed only in the coastal mountain range 100 km (60 miles) to the west give some of Lago Caburgua's beaches white sand rather than the usual black sand that comes from the volcanic rock elsewhere in Chile's lake district. The lake is surrounded by densely forested hills, some areas of which can be explored on

BELOW: country store.

defined paths. Its waters flow underground, producing the springs at **Ojos de Caburgua**, a popular picnic spot. Access to the Huerquehue Park lakes is a serious 5-km (3-mile) climb. A public bus service takes visitors right to the park entrance, leaving Pucón at 8.30am and returning at 5pm.

Map on page 234

Puma live farther up in the mountains; these animals are rarely seen, but come closer to human civilization in winter when food is scarce. Pumas do not generally attack humans unless threatened, but still need to be considered dangerous animals. An 80-km (50-mile) route from Caburgua's north shore through the Blanco River valley can be hiked in about four days, ending up in the outpost of **Reigolil** (where a bus descends to Curarrehue twice weekly). A traverse from **Volcán Quetrupillán** to the village of **Puesco** through *araucaria* forests is increasingly replacing the circuit around Volcán Villarrica as the most popular hiking route in Parque Nacional Villarrica. Local tour agencies leave hikers at the beginning of the trek and there are public bus services back to Pucón.

South of Villarrica, a half-hour's trip on a paved highway leads to the rapidly expanding resort of **Lican Ray ❺** on Lago Calafquén. Wood furniture-making is becoming an important economic activity in this area and dozens of workshops have sprung up in recent years, particularly on the road from Villarrica to Lican Ray. Farther along the lake on a newly paved road is **Coñaripe ❻**, which retains the atmosphere of pre-boom Lican Ray. Regular buses do go this far, but Coñaripe is the end of the line before the rugged unpaved circuit around the lake, and the "back way" into Panguipulli.

The copihue, Chile's national flower.

Thermal baths proliferate across the area due to the constant activity in the volcanic belt that runs along the cordillera. Some, such as the **Termas de Menetué** or **Termas de Huife** farther east of Pucón are upscale commercial

BELOW: rural work, Maihue.

FRONTIER TRADITIONS

Rural traditions persist in many frontier towns of southern Chile. Men often wear flat-brimmed felt hats, and they are quick to invite visitors to drink a sweet wine that goes down with treacherous ease. On special occasions, a host family will kill a sheep or goat by plunging a knife into the neck and catching the blood in a pan filled with cilantro (coriander), where it is congealed with lemon juice to produce *ñache*, considered a great delicacy and pre-feast appetizer.

Grains are the traditional farm commodity, though the uncertainty of the weather makes farming risky. Potatoes are easily grown, but transport costs wipe out any chance of profit, so farmers usually consume them or use them as animal feed. Hops and sugar beet are also grown. Pasture is abundant, and many families earn a few pesos selling milk to the big dairy plants.

To fortify themselves for heavy farm work, the men breakfast on *chupilca*, white wine poured over toasted wheat, or *mudai*, a pasty, carbohydrate-rich juice made from cooked grains. Visitors should avoid giving offense by always accepting anything offered, even if they cannot bring themselves to sample it. When you've had enough, just leave the plate or glass untouched before you.

operations with eating and lodging facilities and bathing fixtures. Others, including the tiny **Termas de Ancamil**, just before Curarrehue, 45 km (28 miles) east of Pucón, are rustic, family-run affairs where one simply descends into the cave with a candle and bathes.

Border activity

The town of **Curarrehue ❼** is a typical southern frontier center where families often have relatives on the Argentine side and travel across the border to take advantage of work opportunities. Residents are mostly *mestizo* and sport lyrical Mapuche surnames such as Coñoepán, Colpihueque and Quirquitripay. The Chile-Argentine border in the south is lightly guarded, as the mountain passes are essentially uncontrollable. During the Pinochet dictatorship, many of these frontier towns smuggled people in and out who either could not move around legally or were in serious trouble for political reasons. Cattle-smuggling into Chile from Argentina causes occasional outbreaks of foot-and-mouth disease, which cannot be controlled in Argentina's vast ranches but has been basically eradicated in Chile.

The inhabitants of Chile's Andean foothills, like those surrounding Curarrehue, are unfailingly cordial, although sometimes shy in front of strangers. Passing horsemen are likely to invite those on foot to heave themselves up behind, and ox-drawn carts or even the occasional logging truck may slow down to allow villagers to climb on. Nor will they raise an eyebrow at discreet skinny-dipping, though they themselves are more reserved.

This friendly environment is not preserved, however, in the towns that have been turned into regular summer resorts. Here, the traditional generous welcome to strangers disappears behind a mask of indifference. Concerted efforts

BELOW: frying up lunch.
RIGHT: street musicians, Valdivia.

Map on page 234

and extra-gracious greetings usually manage to break the ice, but it's worth the effort to try a visit off the beaten path.

The Chilean government is currently planning to develop a tourist route in this area, called the *Ruta Interlagos* (Inter-lake Route), which involves upgrading sections of road and building some new roads that weave in and around lakes, national parks and other areas of natural beauty. The first stretch of the route will start in Victoria northeast of Temuco and will snake its way 300 km (186 miles) south skirting past national parks Tolhuaca and Conguillío and lakes Colico and Villarrica, before ending in Lican Ray.

Smaller roads will lead off toward areas of tourist interest such as volcanoes, lakes and hot springs. The first stage of the project, totaling 914 km (568 miles), is due for completion in 2005.

A slice of Germany

Valdivia ❽ is the best example of the urban face of Chile's south: sophisticated and festive, rainy and verdant, with a palpable German influence in architecture, cuisine and culture. Although usually treated as part of the Lake District, Valdivia is located at the crossroads of two rivers and is just a few kilometers from the sea, separated from the lakes by the coastal mountain range. The approaches to the city are marshy breeding grounds for unusual waterfowl. Named for the first *conquistador* to enter Chile from Peru, Pedro de Valdivia, the city was founded in the mid-1500s but had a difficult time of it for the first hundred years. It was taken over by a Dutch pirate in 1600 and, being on the Mapuche side of the Bíobío River dividing line between Crown and Mapuche territory, had to await the building of fortifications in the mid-1600s to achieve a measure

The Santuario de la Naturaleza Río Cruces, just north of Valdivia, is home to an astounding variety of river birds and plant life. The area was submerged under water in the earthquake of 1960.

BELOW: the waterfront, Valdivia.

German settlers

Millions of people emigrated from Germany in the 19th century, and many settled in Chile. The advent of steam-driven transport made overseas travel easier, and in the mid-1840s widespread crop failure and recession led to political turbulence and revolution in Europe, and triggered another wave of emigration.

German immigration to Valdivia occurred in two periods: a minor influx in the first half of the 19th century and the more important wave between roughly 1885 and 1910. The immigrants played an important role in commerce and industry, using technical knowledge brought from the old country. Some cultivated their new lands, although climatic conditions were not ideal. Others arrived as ironsmiths, carpenters, tanners, brewers, watchmakers, locksmiths and tailors.

Chile in 1850 was just emerging from three decades of political anarchy and economic stagnation, and distant provinces like

Valdivia were left largely to their own devices.

By 1900, a traveler claimed that upon entering Valdivia, he could not believe he was still in Chile. Many of the tradesmen had converted their shops into factories. Valdivia became Chile's prime industrial center, with breweries, distilleries, shipbuilding, flour mills, tanneries, a hundred lumber mills and, in 1913, the country's first foundry. Furniture-making was stimulated by the immense availability of beautiful native woods.

The wealth of the Germans of Valdivia was legendary in Chile until their luck changed, starting with the imposition of a heavy liquor tax in 1902 at the behest of Central Valley vintners. Unfavorable trade conditions wiped out much of the leather market. A great fire laid waste to the city in 1909 while the local merchant class was superseded by mine and estate owners from farther north, closer to the byzantine politics of the capital.

Beginning in the mid-19th century, the region around Lago Llanquihue was also heavily settled by German immigrants who disembarked at what is now the Seno de Reloncaví. Vicente Pérez Rosales, the indefatigable promoter of colonization in southern Chile, organized a solemn ceremony to formally establish Puerto Montt with a group of the recent arrivals, none of whom understood a word of Spanish. According to an account of the ritual, led by a Catholic priest, the Protestant settlers interrupted at what seemed to them an appropriate pause with a rousing chorus of *Hier Liegt vor Deiner Majestad* ("Here Before Your Majesty"). Despite the idiomatic complications, Pérez Rosales' project was a success in the long run.

Osorno is well-known as having been settled by Germans, yet the immigrants never actually numbered more than 10 percent of the total population of the region.

Chileans were also drawn to these new lands, generally uneducated and destitute people hoping to make a new start. The foreigners quickly established themselves as the dominant class, employing the *mestizo* citizens and directing economic development. Although the expected problems did arise on occasion, there is today no observable underlying ethnic tension. ❑

LEFT: German traditions in Puerto Montt.

Map on page 234

of security. The **Museo Histórico y Antropológico Mauricio van de Maele** (open Tues–Sun 10am–1pm and 2–6pm; entrance fee), on Teja Island in the middle of Valdivia, is housed in an old settler's mansion and includes Mapuche artifacts and period furnishings – providing an excellent insight into the prosperous lifestyles of the 19th-century German immigrants *(see page 244)*.

In 1960, Valdivia was the epicenter of the world's largest recorded earthquake, followed by a tidal wave whose effects can still be seen. Most of the old buildings were destroyed, but some European-style buildings remain by the waterfront. The **Museo Contemporáneo** (open daily Dec–Feb 10am–2pm and 3–8pm; Mar–Nov 10am–1pm and 2–7pm; entrance fee), also on Teja Island, is built on the ruins of the old Andwandter brewery.

Summer explosions

Valdivia has a popular week-long summer festival in February in which musical shows are staged on bandstands along the riverbank, boats parade down the river, and firework shows are presented on the last afternoon and night. There is also a film festival. Two required stops in downtown Valdivia are **Haussmann's Café** for its famous *crudos*, steak tartar pounded into a smooth paste and served on toast, and the Entrelagos chocolate and marzipan shop. Valdivia is also home to the **Kuntsmann brewery**, on Isla Teja, which brews three types of beer from German recipes. It includes a small beer museum and brewpub that, in the evening, serves up hearty portions of pork chops, *späetzle* and sauerkraut.

The city's long riverside walks are full of visitors throughout the season, as are the nearby beaches. The Parque Saval on Isla Teja has a riverside beach.

A highly recommended stop the **Feria Fluvial**, a lively fish market on the

Snacks for a sea lion, Valdivia.

BELOW: cruising and snoozing in Valdivia.

quay from which all the river cruises depart. Fat sea-lions come right up into the market, but be careful; they have been known to attack passersby.

Though swimming is possible in the rivers, most bathers head for the port villages of **Corral** and **Niebla**. Colonial-era fortresses are preserved at the latter site, which independence hero Lord Thomas Cochrane, a dashing Scots navy commander in the service of the Chilean rebels, took from the Spanish against heavy odds in 1820. For a bit of exercise, visitors can row from Corral to the tiny island of **Mancera**, Valdivia's military headquarters during the 18th century, to see its small church and convent.

River trips from Valdivia north to the Río Cruces Nature Sanctuary pass through the habitat of black-necked swans to the confluence of three rivers. Many make a stop at the indigenous Huilliche village of Punucapa.

South of Corral you reach **Chaihuín**, a fishing village with what some consider to be the most beautiful, untouched ocean beach in Chile and which is developing as an eco-tourism destination. Most of the original larch trees in the nearby hills have been cut and sold, but the place retains a frontier flavor.

Detours into the wilderness

The largely under-developed **Seven Lakes** district is among the least visited by vacationers due to a peculiar topographical layout and poor access. The district is named after seven lakes that all share the same river basin and include the large lagos Calafquén, Panguipulli and Riñihue, the smaller lagos Pellaifa, Neltume and Pirihueico, and Lago Lacar in Argentina. The lakes are generally bordered by heavily wooded cliffs with steep descents; roads are potholed and slippery at the best of times with difficult climbs and narrow turns through the mountains, which are often impassable in winter. Low-suspension vehicles will fare worst. However, the landscapes are spectacular, and local residents will guide visitors to even more extraordinary spots. These lakes are good for fishing and exploring, but not so good for bathing as beaches are few and far between.

BELOW: snorkeling for shellfish.

The circuit around Lago Calafquén is dominated by the seemingly ever-changing position of Volcán Villarrica to the north. Finally, **Volcán Choshuenco** (2,415 meters/7,923 ft) appears to the south. Recent lava flows can be observed from the highway shortly after leaving Lican Ray. From Coñaripe an alternative route leads to the small **Lago Pellaita** after a ferocious climb at **Los Añiques**. The way down leads through an agricultural valley to the Mapuche village of **Liquiñe**, which has some upmarket thermal baths.

From there, it is possible to drive along a logging track to **Lago Neltume** and **Puerto Fuy** ❾ on the finger-shaped **Lago Pirihueico**, which can be crossed in two hours on a ferry boat that connects to an international road to San Martín de los Andes in Argentina.

Panguipulli ❿ ("Town of Roses") was formerly the railway station that received logs dispatched from the interior via steamboats plying the lake of the same name. The construction of roads later superseded the lake transport system. The town is brilliantly decorated with rose bushes. As Panguipulli is located on

Map on page 234

the flat central plain rather than in the mountains, it tends to be hotter than other lake towns, and its beaches are somewhat less impressive.

On clear days, you should be able to make out Volcán Choshuenco, situated some 50 km (30 miles) to the southeast. The volcano itself can be climbed by motor vehicle up to the refuge after a trying, 80-km (50-mile) drive along the lake. To the east, about halfway to Puerto Fuy, is the **Salto del Huilo Huilo**, the highest and one of the most impressive waterfalls in Chile, which crashes down a deep vine-covered gorge into the River Fuy. Note that it is impossible to continue the circuit around Lago Riñihue out of season (and frequently in season as well) due to a severe, 7-km (4-mile) climb with terrible road conditions just after the tiny lakefront community of Enco. An approach can be made from the town of Los Lagos on the Pan-American Highway, passing through the town of Riñihue.

Fishermen's outposts

The enormous **Lago Ranco** and the smaller adjacent **Lago Maihue** have developed considerably as tourist centers in recent years. However, out of season they are very quiet. On the northern shore of Lago Ranco, the resort of **Futrono** is accessible by turning off the Pan-American Highway at Reumén. For foot travelers, buses to Futrono leave regularly from Valdivia and **Bueno River ⓫** all year round. Guided adventure tourism in the surrounding hills is still little developed, though Futrono has a network of rural tourism.

Many of the communities surrounding the lake originated as fishermen's hostels; a couple are now successful lodges serving upscale clients. The town of **Lago Ranco** itself is full of cheap tourist houses. The pebble beach and a hill behind the town give fine panoramic views. A small **museum** (Dec–Mar only,

Dried and bundled cochayuyo seaweed – a highly nutritious ingredient in local soups and stews.

BELOW: plowing the fields.

open daily) on the road leading to the beach has some interesting historical items. Boats can be rented when available. Activity after dark drops off sharply except for a pair of lakefront bars, although things are livelier during the summer festival.

The most beautiful and heavily settled part of the lake lies directly east along an unpaved road to the **Riñinahue** peninsula and the Calcurrupe River near **Llifén** ⑫ where the paving starts again. The road from Lago Ranco to Llifén is dotted with colonies of new summer vacation homes and crosses **Salto del Nilahue**, a double waterfall with a tremendous, roaring flow, especially in early summer. From the bridge over the Nilahue River, a tertiary road leads to the lower end of Lago Maihue and the hamlet of **Carrán**, named for the Carrán volcano which just appeared in 1957 and last erupted in 1979.

A Mapuche community near the southeast end of Lago Maihue and within view of **Volcán Puyehue** (2,240 meters/7,349ft) to the south, is said to preserve the purest indigenous traditions.

The 810-hectare (2,000-acre) **Isla Guapi** in the middle of Lago Ranco is also an indigenous colony with some 600 Mapuche and Huilliche residents. Huilliches were the original inhabitants, but Mapuches from Argentina colonized the island and now outnumber the original inhabitants. The penetration of evangelical groups has led many to fear the end of the Mapuche and Huilliche cultures on Guapi, but residents are not legally allowed to sell their ancestral lands which were divided and assigned to them individually under Chile's indigenous law of 1979. A ferry offers day-trips to the island from December to February. Out of season, the ferry makes only three return trips to the island a week.

BELOW: harvest time.

Lago Ranco can be completely circled crossing the new bridge over the Calcurrupe River, which replaced the old vehicle raft. A sturdy high-clearance

vehicle is recommended for the unpaved stretch from Llifén to Lago Ranco. The Caunahue River canyon just north of Llifén has a dramatic view. An alternative back route behind the line of volcanoes can also be taken, leaving from Llifén, though special permission to cross must be solicited at Arquilhue in the Blanco River valley. Farther up the valley are the beautiful Chihuío hot springs.

 Map on page 234

Lush forests in the shadow of volcanoes

Lago Puyehue is known to many travelers since it lies along the main route to Argentina from southern Chile. In wintertime when heavy snow covers the Andes mountains, bus and lorry traffic from Santiago sometimes has to detour nearly 1,000 km (600 miles) south to this pass, which is much lower and usually remains open throughout the year. The road has excellent views of the lake from gently rolling hills, then climbs to 1,300 meters (4,300 ft) through **Parque Nacional Puyehue** on the way to the famous resort of San Carlos de Bariloche on the Argentine side. The main town on the Chilean side is **Entre Lagos** ("Between the Lakes") on the western tip of Lago Puyehue, a former railroad center now heavily dependent on tourism. The beach in Entre Lagos is nothing special; camp grounds 10–15 km (6–9 miles) east on the international road are more interesting. Several international hotels give the area a certain cachet, but some visitors will head in the other direction for the same reason.

A detour toward Volcán Casablanca (1,990 meters/6,529 ft) leads to the open-air hot springs at **Aguas Calientes** ⓭. The park headquarters here make a good starting point for excursions. The road leads past several small lakes, through lush virgin forest, including an unusual temperate rainforest, and ends at a ski resort on the slopes of the volcano which can be climbed more easily than Vol-

BELOW: Lago Llanquihue.

cán Villarrica, farther north. Another topographic oddity is the existence of deciduous trees (beech) at the volcano's tree-line. At the top the views are very impressive even for this region, as the volcanoes Osorno, Puntiagudo and Puyehue can all be seen in a semi-circle.

As in other lakes, salmon-farming has been introduced in Lago Puyehue. Critics of the innovation, which is the basis of a thriving export industry, claim that the large concentrations of artificially fed fish will alter the ecological balance and that the inevitable escape of some fish from the underwater cages will threaten other native species. Sport trout fishermen are particularly worried that the ideal conditions of lakes and rivers will be endangered. The fish farms can be observed throughout the region, usually attended by one or two employees who circulate among the floating platforms.

The Termas de Puyehue Hotel is one of Chile's most traditional spa resorts, offering both thermal and mud baths.

The area around nearby **Lago Rupanco** tends to be exclusive and upscale, without the ready facilities for camping and day trips that abound around all the other lakes. Foreigners enjoy it for its extraordinary, mountain-ringed setting and superb fishing. (A well-known lakefront *hacienda* passed from hand to hand during the military regime, ending up for a time as the property of a Middle Eastern sheik.) The approach from Entre Lagos leads to a tiny settlement at **Puerto Chalupa**, which has a lovely beach. From the south, the road from **Puerto Octay** is a 25-km (15-mile) drive, with no public transport service. The beautiful campgrounds along the south shore of the lake are also virtually inaccessible without a vehicle.

BELOW: a small farm near Bueno River.

Lago Llanquihue is the grand-daddy of all the Chilean lakes. It is South America's fourth largest, covering some 877 sq. km (339 sq. miles) and nearly 50 km (30 miles) across from Puerto Octay to Puerto Varas on the south shore.

The lake has an oceanic feel, with breakers that churn higher in winds or rough weather and mini-climates in its interior that keep boaters and fishermen alert. The map on page 234 shows that, except for the narrow strip of land between Puerto Varas and Puerto Montt, the lake would be part of the ocean. The enormous national park at the eastern end of Lago Llanquihue stretching all the way to the Argentine frontier bears the name of Vicente Pérez Rosales, the promoter of foreign immigration to the region *(see page 244)*. It was Chile's first, established in 1926.

Map on page 234

Lago Llanquihue is one of the most visited sites in all of Chile, and tours of the district often start in Puerto Montt and then work back toward the north. **Puerto Varas** ⓮ is the main lakeside resort town and has one of Chile's few casinos. The beaches (the name of one, Niklitscheck, reflects a later immigration of Slavs, especially in the far south) run for several kilometers with rows of shops and restaurants and plenty of nightlife. The views from Puerto Varas across to Volcán Osorno (2,652 meters/8,701 ft) and Volcán Puntiagudo (Sharp-Pointed), 2,190 meters (7,185 ft), are breathtaking and summer activities abound, making it a fun place to hang out. The ease of transport and the plentiful accommodations to suit all budgets and tastes mean that all kinds of travelers gather at night to stroll the beach walks and rub shoulders.

Peak season is February; the views are just as fine in January, but the maddening *tábanos* are thickest then – irritating horseflies attracted to dark clothes and shiny objects, which love to buzz around your head in the sunshine. They don't come out in overcast weather, and since their life cycle is only a month, they disappear in early February. But before that they can easily ruin a day out.

Driving east from Puerto Varas the road curves and dips, providing countless views of the lake from every imaginable angle. Winds tend to whip across even on bright, cloudless days, so the air is likely to remain cool and tempt the unwary to overdo exposure to the sun. The notorious deterioration of the ozone layer, which becomes progressively worse as one moves closer to Antarctica, contributes to the potency of the sun's rays.

Numerous *hosterías* by the lakeside provide lodging and full meals, but they can be pricey. On a clear day, residents will come down from their rural domiciles and gather in lakefront soccer fields to watch a match in the strong breeze with the sparkling water in the background. **Volcán Calbuco** (2,015 meters/6,611 ft) is quite close on the right. This volcano's top was blown off in an 1893 eruption, leaving a jagged cone. About halfway to Ensenada is the **Río Pescado** (Fish River) which, not surprisingly, is famous for its good fishing.

Waterfalls in Black Rock

From **Ensenada** ⓯ most visitors head up the 16-km (10-mile) spur to Petrohué, stopping to see the unusual **Saltos del Petrohué**. These are a series of oddly twisting water chutes formed by a crystallized black volcanic rock which is particularly resistant to erosion. Volcán Puntiagudo's odd shape is also due to this erosion resistance: its central core is composed of the same crystallized rock which remains unaffected

BELOW: a fine day for a woodland ride.

Puerto Varas.

BELOW: the elegant Hotel Petrohué overlooks Lago Todos los Santos.

while the surrounding material erodes away. The water of the Petrohué River is bright green due to the presence of algae, a phenomenon repeated in **Lago Todos los Santos** (All Saints Lake), which begins at the town of Petrohué.

From the falls to the lake the road is cut by several riverbeds which will rise suddenly on a warm day with melt from Volcán Osorno. Eruptions from the volcano centuries ago diverted the River Petrohué's flow from Lago Llanquihue south to Lago Todos los Santos; signs of the earlier lava flows can be observed along with strange vegetation and insect life not found even a few kilometers away. **Petrohué** itself is nothing but a lodge, lakeside campground (the fishing is said to be great), and forest service outpost, but a large modern catamaran leaves from the dock for day trips on the lake. In the height of summer this area is plagued by two types of biting fly – the *colihuacho* and the *petro* (Petrohué is a Mapuche word meaning "Place of Petros"). The only relief from these pests is to shelter in the deep shade of the forests.

Small glaciers atop Volcán Tronador, "Thunder Mountain" (3,451 meters/ 11,322 ft), can be observed en route, and Volcán Osorno is even more imposing from the Lago Todos los Santos side than from Lago Llanquihue. The lake itself is narrow, with forested cliffs rising sharply on all sides. Lunch at touristic **Peulla** ⑯ at the other end is expensive. The famous **Cascadas Los Novios** (Bridal Falls) may be only a trickle if rain has been scarce, and the hamlet can be surprisingly hot. But the small beach is pleasant, and the river above is shady and fresh. Hiking excursions into the mountains from Peulla are excellent. It's possible to continue the same day to San Carlos de Bariloche in Argentina by taking the road to **Puerto Frías** ⑰, from where you pick up another boat.

Continuing the circuit from Ensenada back around Lago Llanquihue, the road is now paved except for a short stretch. The area, which was covered in an eruption some 150 years ago, nicely illustrates how plant life gradually returns after destruction by a lava flow; the borders of deciduous forest are abruptly marked on either side.

Map on page 234

Three km (2 miles) from Ensenada is the road to **La Burbuja** (Bubble) refuge on the volcano's slopes, well worth the 19-km (12-mile) climb. In clear weather, the sunset seen from the top is memorable, and the local refuge/ski center has overnight facilities. The road eases down to the town of **Las Cascadas ⓲** ("waterfalls"), but there is no public transport for this 20-km (12½-mile) stretch. Hitchhiking is easier in the afternoon, but never a sure thing. The road has more than the necessary twists and turns – locals explain that the original track was paid for by the kilometer, and their relatives ensured it was as long as possible.

Las Cascadas is the base for an attractive four-kilometer hike into the hills, but it's easy to get lost, so it's advisable to hire a guide from the town.

Symmetrical peak

Volcán Osorno, a perfect, snow-covered cone, dominates the view from the road. Skilled mountaineers can climb to the crater in about six hours, but quickly shifting clouds and hidden crevasses can be deadly even for the expert. Plentiful stories of people being lost there are intended to discourage freelance exploring. It is worth visiting one of the various farms set back up in the hills a few hundred meters, on the pretext of buying homemade cheese or marmalade – you should be able to get a wide vista of the lake and volcano together, and will understand why the original settlers went to the trouble of making these densely overgrown lands habitable.

BELOW: on the way to church for a confirmation.

Some settlers employed Chilotes, *mestizo* fishermen from Isla Chiloé farther south, to help with the backbreaking labor, sometimes abusing their trust to trick them out of fair wages. One whispered story even suggests the imported workers were often "lost" in the thick jungle in order to avoid paying them anything. Settlers dragged logs or their farm produce down to a dock to be picked up by the steamboat from Puerto Varas, sometimes going along to the town for provisions. But the frequent lake squalls could have led to financial disaster: in order to avoid capsizing, passengers would have to dump their recently bought goods overboard, package by package.

The only surviving pier from the epoch is at **Puerto Fonck** on the road that connects Las Cascadas with the road to Osorno. The long stretches of beach from Las Cascadas toward Puerto Klocker and Puerto Fonck are deserted. European settlers did not feel secure in the area until the Mapuche people were finally defeated in the late 1800s.

The Mapuche survivors were herded into undesirable lands deep in the mountains (both Andes and coastal ranges) where soils were poor and animal husbandry difficult. While the foreign and domestic settlers rushed in to conquer the wilderness, the orig-

Big chess match, Frutillar.

inal inhabitants suffered poverty, discrimination, and social decomposition with the attendant social ills that continue to plague these communities today.

The first tourist outpost

The idea of Lago Llanquihue as a vacation spot occurred as early as 1912 to a government functionary, Interior Minister Luis Izquierdo, who built a summer mansion on the Centinela Peninsula next to Puerto Octay with a group of his friends. The house remains in use today as the Hotel Centinela. Nearby, on the northern lakeshore, **Puerto Octay** is a popular resort town, and a bit less crowded than the southern side of the lake. The road along the lake heading south toward Frutillar has more spectacular views, and some stops of interest.

The tidy little town of **Frutillar** ⓴ has a famous classical music festival in the summer. It is actually two towns joined together: Lower Frutillar is 4 km (2½ miles) down a steep incline from Upper Frutillar. There are more houses up above, many of which offer summer lodgings at reasonable rates. Fixed-rate taxis will ferry you up and down if the walk is too tiring. Frutillar and other towns in the area are known for their shingled churches, which often appear in tourist brochures with the lake sparkling in the background.

A new road has opened up the **Estuario de Reloncaví** (Reloncaví Estuary), a finger of brackish water that connects with the Seno de Reloncaví (Reloncaví Sound). Fishing here is not what it used to be after years of commercial exploitation, but there are still plenty of unexplored inlets. This area and the region farther south are sometimes called "continental Chiloé" for the similarity in culture with Isla de Chiloé *(see page 261).* As the road winds down the glaciated Petrohué River valley onto the east shore of the Reloncaví, the characteristic

BELOW: Laguna Verde, Parque Nacional Vicente Pérez Rosales.

Chilote tiles begin to appear on many of the buildings. These are made from water-resistant *alerce*, Sequoia-related trees that live for hundreds of years and can resist forest fires. The wood is so valuable that *alerce* stumps are sometimes harvested and split for sale.

From Ralún, at the mouth of the Petrohué, a bridge crosses the river to **Cochamó** ㉑ farther south, a fishing town which has views of **Volcán Yate** (2,111 meters/6,926 ft), and **Puelo** ㉒. These towns are reminiscent of the isolated communities along the Carretera Austral highway which winds through the largely uninhabited archipelago region in the far south for more than 1,000 kilometers (600 miles).

Sleepy city

Of all the southern cities, **Osorno** ㉓ is the least interesting, partly due to the strange lack of street life. A business day in Osorno feels like a Sunday, and Sunday feels like a day of national mourning. The town was abandoned after the great Mapuche uprising of 1598, its inhabitants fleeing to establish protected outposts on the ocean inlets just north of Isla Chiloé. Osorno was not refounded until 200 years later, and it is still more of a market center for country residents than an urban entity. The cattle auction is perhaps its most impressive attraction.

City highlights include the interesting modern cathedral on the Plaza de Armas, and the **Museo Histórico** (open Jan–Feb Mon–Thur 9.30am–6pm, Fri 9.30am–5pm, Sat 9.30am–6pm; Mar–Dec, Mon–Thur 9.30am–5.30pm, Fri 9.30am–4.30pm; Sat 2–6pm; closed Sun; free), with displays on Mapuche history and the German arrival. Osorno's wooden houses have sharply angled roofs to handle the rain and snow, and when the storm clouds begin to threaten,

Map on page 234

BELOW: Cochamó Church, near Puerto Varas.

Map on page 234

the place has the air of a city in Quebec or northern New England. The 18th-century **Fuerte Reina Luisa** fort is derelict – the one at Río Bueno, 30 km (19 miles) north, is better preserved. It has a good view of the river, also known as El Gran Río, which carries off the water of four lakes (Maihue, Ranco, Puyehue and Rupanco) – making it the second-largest in Chile.

The countryside around Osorno, which is dotted with Huilliche communities, remains surprisingly poor, as can be observed from the aspect of travelers coming to and from rural areas at the bus terminal. All the cities in this valley are partly protected by the low coastal mountains known as the **Cordillera Pelada** ("bald" or "peeled" range) which blocks the ocean winds and allows the dry, southern winds to dominate.

Until 1930, the little fishing village of Maullín could only be reached by boat. Its name means "full of water."

Southern port center

The bustling, windy city of **Puerto Montt** ㉔ was connected by rail to the rest of Chile in 1912 and became the contact point for the rest of the south. It remains so to the present day, despite the loss of its railway line. It is an important fishing center; seafood at the harbor of Angelmó is famous. The port was completely destroyed in the earthquake of 1960. Boats leave from here for the long, slow trip down through the southern archipelago. (Puerto Chacabuco requires 22 hours, Puerto Natales three days.) The port is protected from the strong winds by **Isla Tenglo**.

BELOW: *araucaria* tree.
RIGHT: lakeside view to Volcán Osorno near Puerto Montt.

From the hills above the city there are fine views of the entire Seno de Reloncaví. Local boat trips can be arranged either in Puerto Montt or at La Arena where the estuary begins. From Chamiza, to the east of the town, it is possible to get close to **Volcán Calbuco** on the southern side of Lago Llanquihue. German settlers built an interesting Lutheran church in Chamiza next to two giant *araucaria* trees. **Parque Nacional Alerce Andino** has good facilities, and Lago Chapo is off the usual tourist beat. In the other direction is the port of **Maullín**, one of the few places this far south where it's possible to observe the open sea.

A peaceful rural site situated near Puerto Montt has recently thrown the archeological world into a frenzy, pushing back the possible date of human arrival in the Americas by thousands of years. During the 1970s, scientists discovered that the area around the Chinchihuapi Creek, known as **Monte Verde**, held human remains dating from 12,500 years ago. In 1998 more remains were found at the site, which suggest possible human occupation 33,000 years ago. The debate rages on.

Southwest of Puerto Montt is **Carelmapu** ㉕, one of the oldest settlements, dating from the Spaniards' flight after their defeat by the Mapuches around 1600. On its rough beaches, the original wild strawberries from which commercial strawberries were developed still grow, as in many other remote places in the south of Chile. An alternative route is the partially unpaved road that follows the bay southwest from Puerto Montt to Calbuco. This offers distinctive views of the volcanoes toward the north. **Calbuco** ㉖, like Carelmapu, predates Puerto Montt by some 250 years. ❏

ISLA DE CHILOE

This large, rainswept island is a culturally distinctive
area with its own music, dance, craft traditions and
a wealth of spellbinding myths and legends

Map
on page
262

Santiago

F
or a moment you think you've misheard, that someone has simply pronounced the word "Chile" and for some peculiar reason your ears have given it an extra "o". To some extent Chiloé is Chile in miniature, a peculiar time capsule that contains some of Chile's best and harshest traditions, shaping them into song, dance, crafts and a mythology which has become one of the main strands of the country's national identity. Much of "Chilean" folk music and dance was born in Chiloé's gentle summer fogs and harsh winters.

December, January and February are the better months for a visit to Chiloé, because the warmer summer weather makes it easier to travel within the main island and across to some of the smaller islands. In recent years, Chiloé has become something of a standard pilgrimage for the young and the not-so-young, so you may meet more people from Santiago than from the islands.

Chiloé's flood myth

A Mapuche legend tells the story of what may have been the formation of Chiloé as witnessed by the Mapuche and Chono peoples long before the Spanish reached the continent. It tells how the twin serpents Cai Cai and Tren Tren do battle. Cai Cai, the evil one, who has risen in rage from the sea and flooded the earth, assaults Tren Tren's rocky fortress in the mountain peaks, while the people try in vain to awaken the friendly serpent from a deep sleep.

Meanwhile Cai Cai has almost reached Tren Tren's cave, swimming on the turbulent waters. Cai Cai's friends, the thunder, fire and wind, help her by piling up clouds to bring rain, thunder and lightning.

Pleas and weeping don't wake Tren Tren. Only the laughter of a little girl, dancing with her reflection in the sleeping serpent's eye, arouses her, and she responds with a giggle so insulting that Cai Cai and her stormy friends fall down the hill.

Cai Cai charges again, all the more furious, shattering the earth and sewing the sea with islands. She makes the water climb ever higher, and almost submerges the mountain where her enemy lives, but Tren Tren arches her back, and with the strength of the 12 guanacos in her stomach, she pushes the cave ceiling upward, so that the mountain grows toward the sky. Cai Cai and her friends keep bringing more water and Tren Tren keeps pushing her cave roof higher until the mountain reaches above the clouds, close to the sun, where the evil serpent cannot reach it. Cai Cai and her servants fall from the peak into the abyss, where they lie stunned for thousands of years.

The waters gradually recede and the people are able to return to their lands, untroubled by either of the giant serpents, who continue sleeping. However,

PRECEDING PAGES:
pulling their weight
on moving day.
LEFT: *palafitos* on
Castro's waterline.
BELOW: the painted
spires of Castro
cathedral.

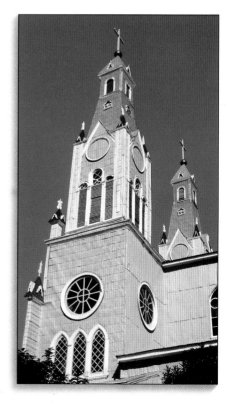

sometimes, it is said, Cai Cai has nightmares and an island appears in the ocean or the earth trembles a little. The legend may tell the story of an ancient earthquake which was accompanied by tidal waves and flooding, but it is also remarkably similar to scientific accounts of how the peculiar attributes of the area came about. These changes occurred gradually, over thousands of years, of course, but were no doubt punctuated with dramatic upheavals in a region which is so geologically active that even today, natural catastrophes occur every 30 or 40 years.

Birth of an archipelago

The island of Chiloé was once covered in impenetrable woods, which have gradually been cleared to make way for agriculture.

The scientists explain that over thousands of years, two giant tectonic plates forming part of the earth's crust clashed, producing the volcanoes characteristic of mainland Chiloé: Hornopirén, Huequi, Michimahuida and Corcovado. During the Ice Age, glaciers bore down upon the Central Valley region, carving a gap through the coastal mountains and pushing the valley farther and further below sea level. When the glaciers began to melt at the end of the Ice Age, the ocean poured through the openings located at the north and south ends of what is now the main island of Chiloé, to create the interior sea that now divides Chiloé from the mainland, turning what was previously the coastal mountain range into a series of islands which now form the archipelago of Chiloé. Toward the center of Isla de Chiloé, where the lakes of Huillinco and Cucao cut partially through the island's mountain range, the land drops to sea level, and many islanders fear that Chiloé may one day be cut in two.

BELOW: Vilopulli Church, near Chonchi.

Chiloé's **Isla Grande** (main island) is the second-largest island in Latin America, after Tierra del Fuego. Like a great ship moored off the Chilean coast it

seems to float, surrounded by several smaller constellations of islands called the Chauques, Quenac, Quehui, Chaulinec and Desertores. Some of these islands are so close to each other they are joined at low tide. The low mountains along the west coast of the main island are nevertheless high enough to stop the damp winds blowing off the Pacific, creating a slightly drier microclimate along the interior sea, where virtually all the settlements are located.

The interior sea, generally calm – at least as seen from the shore – can be difficult to navigate, especially for the many Chilotes who still rely on small rowboats or launches. As the tides roar in through the tiny channel of **Chacao** in the north (crossed by the mainland ferry; a bridge is mooted, but is a distant prospect) they eventually meet and clash with the tides pouring through the channel to the island's south, creating huge whirlpools and waves. In Cucao, on the Pacific coast, the difference between high and low tides is 2.5 meters (8 ft), while in Quemchi it is 7 meters (23 ft), because of the shallowness of much of the interior sea. These powerful tides leave shellfish and fish, a major source of food for the islanders, trapped on the beaches and in sea pools.

The making of the Chilotes

The first known inhabitants of the islands of Chiloé were the Chonos, a tough, seafaring people who have gone down in history for the creation of the *dalca*, a small, canoe-like boat built by binding several rough-hewn planks together. For centuries, the Chonos guided the Spanish and other adventurers through the intricate channels and fiords which honeycomb Chile's southern shores. They spoke a different language from the Mapuches or Huilliches (southern Mapuche), who began to invade the islands.

Map on page 262

Lago Cucao gets its name from the "cuca" heron that frequents its shores.

BELOW: lush landscape.

These invasions forced the Chonos to migrate farther and farther south. In the 1700s, the Jesuits pushed the Chonos and the Caucahues, a separate native group who had not been integrated into the Mapuche tribe, into small reserves on Isla Cailín, south of Quellón, and later the Chaulinec islands, where they eventually mixed with the other inhabitants. The Jesuit mission on Isla Cailín was the southernmost chapel in the Christian Empire.

Some straw-roofed rucas (*traditional Mapuche houses*) *still exist on the islands of Quinchao and Lemuy.*

When Alfonso de Camargo became the first European to see Chiloé in 1540, the archipelago's inhabitants were a mixture of Chono and Mapuche living scattered along the coast, which was at once their main highway, source of food, and the cradle for a wealth of legends and oral histories which are the backbone of Chilote culture to this day. The homes in which they lived were straw *rucas*, clustered near beaches and woods in groups of up to 400 people and known as *cabís*, led by *caciques* or chiefs. Using wooden tools, they farmed potatoes and corn in fields protected by fences which were woven using basket techniques, and they reaped the rich harvest of shellfish along the shores. They were also excellent weavers of llama wool.

Serfdom and rebellion

Thirteen years later Francisco de Ulloa's expedition formally "discovered" the islands, and 14 years after that, Martín Ruiz de Gamboa officially took possession of them, calling them Nueva Galicia. On February 12 1567, he founded the city of Santiago de Castro and for the next 200 years the Spaniards divided up the available land – and the people living on it – in what became known as the *encomienda* system, which was a kind of serfdom. The idea was that the native peoples worked for free in order to "pay tribute" to the king of Spain. This

BELOW: stilt houses are common in this wet region.

native labor system was used in the mining of gold in Cucao, the weaving of woolen cloth and the logging of *alerce*, a tough, fine wood native to Chile (which is today in danger of extinction). In the early years, the products of Chiloé brought considerable wealth to the Spaniards who had taken possession of the land, but brought desperate poverty to its people.

In 1598, when the Mapuche communities of Carelmapu and Calbuco on the mainland rebelled against the Spanish invaders, the survivors retreated to Chiloé, where they established towns in 1602. The people of Chiloé twice joined forces with "pirates," destroying Castro with Baltasar de Cordes in 1600 and attacking Carelmapu and later Valdivia, across the channel, with Enrique Brouwer in 1643. In the centuries that followed, the Spanish and the Mapuche-Chonos of Chiloé lived in virtual isolation and extreme poverty, with occasional visits from Spanish ships sent from Lima, Peru, sometimes as many as three years apart. Despite this neglect, Chiloé became a royalist stronghold during the wars of independence in the early 19th century. The Governor of Chile fled to Chiloé, and despairingly offered the island to Britain. The offer was declined, and Chiloé surrendered to the mainland republic in 1826.

Over the centuries the two races, Spanish and Mapuche-Chono, fused, preserving much of the native languages and customs. The Chilotes all wore the same clothes and suffered the same hardships, creating a sense of social equality unusual in the Spanish Empire. Settlement continued along the coast until the early 1900s, when lands were given to German, English, French and Spanish "colonists" and the building of a railway in 1912 between Ancud and Castro finally opened internal communication between Chiloé's two main cities.

Map on page 262

LEFT: sheep shearing contest.
BELOW: a llama looking his best.

A distinct culture

There are more than 150 churches and chapels in Chiloé. The oldest churches were built entirely of wood, using wooden plugs instead of nails, and provide some of the world's few remaining examples of 18th-century wood architecture.

Today the Chilotes continue to be a proud, independent people, clearly distinguishable from their fellow Chileans, with their own dialect mixing influences from 16th-century Spanish with many indigenous words, and a rich tradition of music and dance beloved throughout Chile. However, the tragic poverty of early colonization continues to dominate the Chilote lifestyle, forcing most of the young men to migrate to other regions despite the introduction of salmon-farming.

The one great weakness of the Chilotes is the game of *truco*, which is played with the Spanish 40-card deck. *Truco*, which roughly translated means "trickery," is an extraordinary gambling game divided into two parts, the *envío* and the *truco* itself. The cards are half the game; the other half is the skill and imagination of the players who bluff and jest, using rhyming couplets laden with double meanings. Today, you are as likely to see a lively game of *truco* on a ship at Punta Arenas as in a Chilote bar. And the Chilotes who've gambled away a season's earnings on the sheep ranches and are unable to return home are legendary. This forced migration of working men has also given rise to the image of the Chilote family as a virtual matriarchy of distant, sometimes almost mythical men, and strong women raising their children, their livestock and tending their crops, keeping the island alive.

A land crowded with chapels

BELOW: Chilote man wearing one of Chiloé's rainproof woolen ponchos.

It was during the 200-year period when the Spanish were barred from the Mapuche lands in mainland Chile that the Jesuits began the evangelizing activities which left an enduring mark on the islands' legends and villages. Some of the most strikingly beautiful characteristics of Chilote architecture are the

wooden chapels built during the Jesuits' stay, many of which survive to this day. Between 2000 and 2001, UNESCO's World Heritage Committee declared 16 of these chapels sites of universal value on the grounds that they represent the only Latin American example of a rare form of ecclesiastical wooden architecture. In 2002, the tower of the chapel in Chonchi was toppled by a storm and others are in poor shape but, in early 2004, the InterAmerican Development Bank authorized a grant of US$2.8 million for their repair.

The chapels, which often stood completely alone on the coast unaccompanied by human habitation, were built as part of the Jesuits' "Circulating Mission." This consisted of a boat manned by two missionaries who started their annual rounds from Castro with religious ornaments and three portable altars, complete with a "Holy Christ" to be carried during ceremonies by the *caciqus* (chiefs); a "Holy Heart" to be carried by children; a "Saint John" to be carried by bachelors; a "Saint Isidro" for married men; "Our Lady of Suffering (Dolores)" for single women and "Saint Notburga" for married women.

To this day, a *fiscal*, a sort of native priest, has the custody of chapel keys, and in August people from nearby islands gather on Isla Caguache to celebrate their religion with ceremonies similar to those initiated by the Jesuits and modified by later Roman Catholic missions. The chapel of Vilupulli, near Chonchi, con-

Map
on page
262

tinues to stand alone, with no human settlement around it, exactly as the chapels did in the 1700s. These chapels are an interesting example of the Chilotes' outstanding ability to absorb foreign cultures without losing their own identity. Their design is strongly influenced by German architecture of the period, because several of the Jesuits were from Bavaria.

The *tejuelas* or wooden shingles commonly used to roof buildings throughout southern Chile, and which are one of the most striking characteristics of homes in Chiloé, were also a German idea, brought by the colonists who originally settled in Llanquihue and Puerto Montt on the mainland. The visible part of the *tejuela* is approximately a third of the total length, as they overlap so well that these buildings are extremely resistant to the heavy rains of the region. Before the *tejuelas* were introduced, Chilote homes usually had roofs of straw, similar to those of the Mapuches' *rucas*, and also extremely resistant to rain.

Colorful residence, Chonchi.

A tradition of handicrafts

For centuries, the women of Chiloé have spent the harsh winters producing clothing and household items. Different parts of the islands are associated with different crafts. The small town of **Chonchi** (south of Castro) is known for its woven wool products, especially blankets and ponchos, as well as *licor de oro,* a liquer made with saffron. **Quellón ❶** is famous for its ponchos, which are resistant to rain because the wool used for making them is raw and full of natural oils. On **Isla Lingue**, across from Achao, baskets are woven from local fibers, although some have fallen into disuse owing to the difficulty of working with them. Many of the islands' legends have been woven into decorative objects from all areas of Chiloé.

The largest market for Chilote handicrafts is actually on the mainland in

BELOW: chapel at Aldachildo.

Angelmó, in Puerto Montt, although they are mixed with items imported from other South American countries, principally Peru and Ecuador. However, early on Sunday mornings, there is a traditional market by the dock in **Dalcahue ❷**, where hundreds of craftspeople from all over the archipelago still gather to sell their wares. They also prepare traditional Chilote meals, particularly the *curanto*, a concoction prepared over a fire built in a hole scooped out of the earth, containing a variety of shellfish and meat and served with *milcao*, a traditional flatbread made with grated potatoes. The traditional woven fences of the Mapuche-Chonos can still be seen separating livestock from planted areas in some parts of the islands, and the *birloche* or *trineo*, a sled-like vehicle towed by oxen, continues to be used on several of the smaller islands.

Keep your eye out in markets and fairs for the *almudes*, wooden boxes of a fixed size, still used to display a seller's wares. The *almud* is also a unit of measurement, and the boxes have the peculiarity of measuring one *almud* on one end and half an *almud* on the other. Their origin is Spanish. Stone mills introduced by the Jesuits can be seen in several Chilote museums, and they are still in use in some areas between Castro and Dalcahue. In February, wooden *chicha* (cider) presses are still very much in evidence, pressing the sweet juices out of apples piled in traditional baskets. Hanging in the windows of many houses you'll see woolen socks or ponchos, or other handmade items for sale. If you're lucky you may also get a glimpse of a Chilote loom, which is horizontal and nailed to the floor. It is still used by the artisans, who must kneel to work it.

Chilote sweaters are made from sheep rather than llama wool. The women shear the sheep, clean and wash the wool by hand, dye it with colors prepared from local herbs, and spin it using a simple spindle which twirls on the floor.

BELOW: young farmer at work.

Holding on to the past

Chiloé is in many ways as mysterious, as long-suffering, and as contradictory as it has been for most of its history. Modern fish-processing plants and salmon-farming have begun to provide more employment. At the same time, pollution and over-fishing of coastal waters are now problems. Already the *loco*, a tasty shellfish marketed abroad as abalone, is virtually extinct, and attempts to protect it have created only a thriving underground of unscrupulous entrepreneurs.

Other Chilotes have tried to eke out a living from fishing, with mixed results, and developmental agencies have created programs for improving Chilote agriculture, marketing and handicraft techniques. Even as modern factory ships sail under foreign flags, just outside Chile's 322-km (200-mile) limit, the Chilotes themselves continue to live – and die – by traditional rowboats and small motor launches. Chilote culture itself – the music, poetry and stories – is increasingly packaged for a burgeoning tourist industry, a process which tends to create and preserve caricatures devoid of their original meaning. Like similar attempts in other parts of the world, this has harmed as well as helped the local economy.

Chilote cultural activity is on view during the *Festival Costumbrista*, held in the second or third week of February in Castro, and during local summer events.

Jumping-off points

Ancud and Castro, the main island's two cities, provide good bases for exploring the archipelago. Until 1982, **Ancud ❸**, which has a population of 27,000, was the capital of Chiloé. The city was an international port until the beginning of the 20th century, and it retains a peculiar mixture of traditional Chilote buildings, docks and plazas combined with more modern signs and structures.

Map on page 262

BELOW: splash of color on a gray day.

Ancud's central plaza is flanked by the **cathedral**, government buildings and the **Museo Azul de las Islas de Chiloé** (open Jan–Feb daily, Mar–Dec Tues–Fri 10am–5.30pm, Sat and Sun 10am–2pm; entrance fee), which contains exhibits about Chilote culture and mythology.

If you have a vehicle, you can enjoy a lovely drive along the **Costanera** (coast road), with a view of the Gulf of Quetalmahue. Lining the shore are the older, often impressive houses of Ancud's wealthier citizens. By following the Costanera, then Bellavista and San Antonio northward, you'll quickly reach **Fuerte San Antonio**, which was built in 1770. On January 19 1826, it became the last Spanish garrison to surrender to the wave of independence which had swept South America. Ancud then became the focus for colonizing expeditions aimed at southern Chile, including one that settled the Strait of Magellan in 1843. A replica of the tiny boat that took the first settlers to claim the far south is on show at the Museo Azul. In the late 19th century, Ancud boomed with the whale and wood industries and newly arrived settlers from Europe, primarily of German origin. However, when the railway extended to Puerto Montt in 1912, Ancud lost its importance, and in 1982 the trade and shipping center Castro became the capital of Chiloé.

There are good cheap places to eat seafood in Ancud's market, and craftspeople usually have booths both in the market and along the sea-side of the plaza. The **Mirador Cerro Huaihuén** (a lookout point) affords breathtaking views of the city and across the Chacao Channel toward the mainland.

An interesting side trip from Ancud is a visit to the oyster beds at **Caulín**. To get there you must travel back along the highway toward the ferry's arrival point at Chacao, and then turn left toward Caulín at Km 24. Occasionally, upon reaching the channel, you must wait until the tide has gone out before you can continue

In Curaco de Vélez, take a look at the stone mills which are still installed on the Los Molinos brook.

BELOW: fishing boats in Ancud.

along the beach to the oyster beds, where you can enjoy fresh oysters at reasonable prices, before spending an afternoon on the beach or heading back to Ancud.

If you drive south from Ancud and then west you'll find good fishing at the *refugio* (refuge) at **Puerto Anguay**, as well as several good places to picnic. Along the way, look out for the **Butalcura River** valley with great patches of dead trees in the water where the 1960 earthquake caused the earth to collapse.

Map on page 262

Settlement on stilts

Castro ❹, the main island's other city and its capital since 1982, has a population of about 29,000, and is located about 90 km (56 miles) to the south of Ancud. Although it is technically one of Chile's oldest cities, having been founded in 1567, Castro suffered so many attacks and privations that there are few signs of its antiquity within the city itself. On the highway just to the south of Castro are *palafitos*, Chiloé's distinctive wooden homes on stilts.

It's best to see Castro on foot, strolling from the **Plaza de Armas** with its painted **cathedral** shoreward to enjoy the market area with its lively crafts fair, then back up the hill toward the **Mirador** (lookout) with its Statue of the Virgin and its bird's-eye view of the city's cemetery, piled high with conventional gravestones and small structures resembling houses that shelter the city's dead.

Castro's **Museo Regional** (open Jan–Feb daily, closed Sun pm; Mar–Dec Mon–Fri 9.30am–1pm and 3–6.30pm; Sat 9.30am–1pm; voluntary contribution), is located near the central plaza, but due to move to a new building near the port in 2005. The plaza is also the focal point for the *Festival Costumbrista*, a celebration of Chilote customs, food and crafts, which traditionally takes place in February. The **Museo de Arte Moderno**, has an excellent collection of contemporary Chilean work (open Nov–Feb Tues–Sun; free). Set on a hill just outside the town, it also provides a spectacular view of the interior sea and of the snow-capped mountains across on the mainland. The building, built of Chiloé's traditional wood, has won architectural prizes.

One of the oldest shingle churches in Chiloé.

BELOW: an Achao elder on the steps of a typical wood-shingle house.

Exploring the islands

From Castro you can travel up the shore of Chiloé's interior sea to visit **Dalcahue**, **Llaullao** and, on **Isla Quinchao** (accessible by ferry), the small towns of **Curaco de Vélez** and **Achao ❺**. Achao's 18th-century church of **Santa María** is built entirely of cypress and *alerce*. Farther along the island highway is Chiloé's largest church, **Quinchao**, which was built in the 18th century and refashioned according to neoclassical ideas at the end of the 19th century. While driving around the area, keep an eye out for the traditional woven fences.

Chonchi ❻, about half an hour south of Castro, is a small town built on such a steep incline that it is also known as the *Ciudad de los Tres Pisos* (three-story city). Local handicrafts abound, and cardboard signs advertise the famous *licor de oro*. Near Chonchi it's possible to catch a ferry to **Isla Lemuy ❼** or head farther south to **Queilen ❽**, where the ferries to Aisén dock. **Parque Nacional Chiloé** can be reached by traveling across the island toward **Cucao**, one of only two towns on the Pacific side of Isla de Chiloé. It's a good place to hike or camp, with a long and wave-pounded beach. ❏

CHILOTE MAGIC

The island of Chiloé has a rich storytelling tradition with a tale or mythical anecdote to explain almost every traumatic occurrence and ancient beliefs that pre-date the arrival of Christianity

Map on page 262

Santiago

By any standards, the archipelago of Chiloé is a magical place. Gods and goddesses, ghost ships and the lost city of the Caesars (visible at dawn as the sun reflects gold off volcano cliffs and, some believe, the city's crystal skyscrapers) are as much a part of the archipelago as the people themselves.

Expressed in music, dance and popular beliefs, the *Trauco*, the *Pincoya*, the *Caleuche* and other mythical creatures haunt the forests and fields of Chiloé. Alongside them are the *brujos* or wizards, their human counterparts who have tried to harness the uncontrollable natural forces that still wield huge power over many of those who live on the islands.

Undoubtedly. many of the mythical characters of Chiloé also serve a social purpose: the *Trauco*, for example, is a creature that is able to seduce young women by hypnotizing them with his magical gaze. Accepting the existence of the *Trauco* provides an explanation for teenage pregnancies, and the mythical creature has even been used to cover up incest. Today, when so much of Chiloé's maritime wealth is threatened by over-exploitation, these people-sized gods also serve as symbols of an ecological balance that was achieved by Chiloé's earlier peoples, with warnings and messages of how that balance must again be achieved if the islanders' livelihood is to be preserved.

LEFT: cooking in a country house.
BELOW: "La Pincoya".

Seducer of virgins

As you walk through the forests of Chiloé, keep an eye out for the **Trauco**. No taller than a meter, this deformed, man-like creature may make his home in the fork of a tree or a small cave. He wears clothes made of vegetable fibers and always carries a staff which he knocks on the ground and against trees. His legs end in stumps and just one look from him can kill the beholder or leave him or her mute or stupid, or with a twisted neck or a hump.

Yet in spite of his limited physical charms, the *Trauco* enjoys considerable success with young women, whom he seduces with the hypnotic effect of his blazing eyes. To defend yourself from the *Trauco*, throw a handful of sand at him. While he's busy counting the grains, make your escape.

Another creature, the **Pincoya**, slips out of the surf at sunrise and dances on the shore. When her face is turned toward the ocean, it means that abundant shellfish will soon cover the beach. If she looks inland, this means she has taken the fish elsewhere, to where there is more need for them. If you fish or extract shellfish too long from one site, she gets angry and abandons it, leaving the place barren.

The ecologically aware *Pincoya* is blonde and beautiful and values good cheer. Her name comes from the languages of the Quechua or Aymara peo-

ples (native peoples of northern Chile's Andes). Legend also has it that the *Pincoya* will sometimes rescue drowning sailors and leave them on the beach.

Chiloé's ghost ship

It is difficult to imagine any seagoing culture without its ghost ship, and Chiloé is no exception. The **Caleuche** with its unlikely cargo of tragic guests, caught in an eternal party, sends haunting strains of accordion music across the waves and recovers the bodies of those who have died at sea. Its crew are *brujos*, Chilote wizards with enormous powers, and it travels in a constant cloud produced by the boat itself, always at night. The *Caleuche* also advances under the water, disappearing suddenly if someone goes too close. Or it turns into a floating trunk or a rock to put off pursuers. If caught looking at the *Caleuche*, your mouth will become twisted, your head crooked or you'll suddenly die.

The ship is said to put in at the ports of Llicaldac, Tren-Tren and Quicaví, where the *brujos'* most important cave is located. The writer Oreste Plath tells the story of a trim sloop piloted by a young man from Chonchi which disappeared on its maiden voyage. Although it never returned, the man's father did not mourn, and everyone realized the son was safe and sound aboard the *Caleuche*. Soon after, the father began to grow rich very quickly, from the invaluable merchandise delivered by the *Caleuche*.

A magical city

No traveler ever sets eyes on the lost city of the Caesars, even when walking through it. A thick mist always hides it from sight and the rivers carry approaching boats away. The lost city, with its gold- and silver-paved streets and its

The typical Chilote boats use a cross-shaped anchor, made with a stone and two planks of wood.

BELOW: mythological mural.

ability to make all who go there lose their memory, will appear only once, at the end of the world, to prove its existence to non-believers.

The city, with its enormous riches and infinite pleasures, where no one is born or dies, inspired centuries of expeditions by explorers, beginning in 1528. That was when 14 men led by Captain Francisco César, member of an advance group in Sebastian Cabot's party, ventured into the southern jungles for two months. Upon returning, they told tales of fabulous treasures, which may have belonged to the Inca Empire. The next expedition to search for the lost city started out from Castro on October 6 1620, led by Juan Tao. This and following trips were led primarily by the Spanish and their descendants, and included the Jesuit priests José García, Juan Vicuña and Juan Francisco Menéndez. Both the Spanish Council of the Indies and the Real Audiencia (Royal Audience) in Santiago officially authorized the search for the mystery city. Chile's southern mountain range is so rugged and impenetrable that there may well be a lost city of the Incas, hidden among the clouds and volcano peaks.

The brotherhood of warlocks

The **brujería** is a secret brotherhood of male witches organized into an underground of councils, which meets in cleverly disguised caves, the biggest of which is in Quicaví. The members arrive disguised as birds or as themselves, wearing the luminous *macuñ*, which gives them the power to flight. The *macuñ* is made of skin taken from the breast of a virgin's corpse and its light is fueled by oil taken from the bodies of dead Christians.

The apprenticeship to become a *brujo* begins at an early age, and consists of a series of increasingly cruel trials. One of the more bearable is a shower in a

Map
on page
262

BELOW: musical duo, Castro.

Centolla *(king crab)*
and fish for sale in
Chonchi market.

mountain waterfall, a ritual which is repeated for 40 nights, to cleanse away all trace of baptism. Then, the novice must cleanly catch a skull which is thrown by the instructor from the crown of a tricorn hat. To prove that he is not weakened by sentiment, the apprentice must murder his best friend. Finally, he should dig up the corpse of a recently buried virgin and remove the skin from the breast. Once it has dried, this can be sewn onto the *brujo*'s waistcoat – at night, the skin gives off a glow that can guide him on his missions. Anyone who reveals he is a *brujo* will be sentenced to death within a year. *Brujos* are not allowed to rob or rape, nor can they eat salt.

Other trials include races, leaps from cliffs at night, the use of the *macuñ*, corporal metamorphosis into animals or birds, wearing a lizard bound to the forehead (to transmit wisdom), and spending nights sleeping on a tomb in the cemetery. *Brujos* have the power to make people sleepy, to open doors, to cause illness, hair loss or deep cuts, and to throw *llancazos* (similar to the evil eye) or to conjure up bad spells cast at a distance. *Brujos* have a crystal stone called the *Challanco*, through which they can view every detail of peoples' lives. The *Challanco* looks like a glass bowl or a large round mirror.

Guarding the brujos

The **invunche** guards the *brujos*' cave and is the product of a long and painful process: to obtain an *invunche* the wizards rob a firstborn son from his parents, within the first nine days after his birth. They take the child to the cave: if he has been baptized they use black magic to annul it; then they break and twist his right leg, until it rides up the back. At three months old they split his tongue and rub his skin daily with a special infusion. In the early months the *invunche* lives on milk from a black cat and later on human flesh obtained from cemeteries.

BELOW: Chilote
woodcarver.

The origins of this macabre myth may be based in historical fact: the writer Narciso García Barría, considered an authority on Chiloé, relates the *invunche*'s deformities to the Inca culture. They often preferred men with some physical disability to be the guards of their temples.

Women's participation in the *brujería* is usually as a *voladora* (flying woman), for whom many of the secret practices of the brotherhood are forbidden knowledge. The *voladora* often transforms herself into a bird (the *bauda*), with a loud, raucous cry, and serves as a messenger for the *brujos*. In order to become the bird, the woman vomits up her intestines, which she leaves in a tree. If for some reason they're lost then she quickly dies.

The *camahueto* is a huge one- or two-horned cowlike creature that is born from the earth with such force that it leaves a small crater behind it. This creature is essential to the magic of the **machi**, the *brujos*' herbal doctor. The *machi* must grab the *camahueto*'s horn as it leaps from the earth and before it races to a cliff, from which it plunges into the ocean, where it completes its life-cycle. Usually, the *machi* plants pieces of horn in the ground, so that in 30 years' time, more *camahuetos* will grow. He then prepares powders from the rest of the horn, thoroughly boiling it first, so that the users won't end up with a *camahueto* growing inside them. These powders are believed to impart tremendous strength to anyone who takes them. *Camahuetos* are also effective in treating a variety of illnesses.

Map on page 262

Protective charms

The "clean," as non-*brujos* are called, can detect a *brujo* by throwing bran on a fire, a procedure which inevitably makes the *brujo* sneeze; or by placing two needles in the form of a cross over the door, making it impossible for the *brujo* to leave. Tuesdays and Fridays are the *brujos'* nights for roaming, and there is a chant commonly used to scare them away.

According to Narciso García Barría, *brujos* are almost always descended from native people and it is extremely difficult for whites to be admitted. He believes their origins may lie in an underground organization of native resistance to the Spaniards, a thesis which is supported by native Chilotes' eager participation in the attacks led by the corsairs.

García Barría harshly criticizes a series of well-publicized trials of *brujos*, which took place several decades ago, dismissing them as a "massive crusade against the descendants of indigenous people, especially. It was enough to mention that a person practised witchcraft for him to be dragged off to the prisons of Achao or Ancud."

In Chiloé, as in other cultures with communities of witches, the *brujería* is also the major source of a wealth of information on native herbs and medicines which are still commonly used on the islands. Scholars believe the tradition stems from the combination of European concepts of witchcraft brought by the Spanish with the beliefs of Chiloé's original inhabitants. ❏

BELOW: cottage industry.

AISEN

The gateway to Chile's far south, this beautiful region of lakes, forests and glaciers still has a certain wilderness quality, despite the recent construction of the Carretera Austral highway

Map on page 282

Santiago

Aisén is the hispanicized version, local folklore has it, of an English name for the area: "ice end" – the region of glaciers. English, Germans, Swedes, Spaniards, Argentines and Chileans all did their bit to explore and sparsely colonize this spectacularly beautiful and particularly inhospitable region of fiords, glaciers and, in parts, dense forest. The early settlers at the beginning of the 20th century cleared the land they needed by burning down the woods, and several times the fires got out of control and ravaged great areas. Now, the gray, petrified remains of huge trees stick up into the sky – from the air, it looks as if a giant box of matches has been scattered over the ground.

Inhospitable frontier

The first inhabitants were the Tehuelches and the Alacalufes. The Tehuelches were nomads who lived by hunting guanacos, *ñandus* (rheas), pumas and *huemules* (deer), and the Alacalufes navigated the coastal channels in their light canoes. The Spanish invaders sent down a couple of expeditions in the mid-1550s to explore, to make sure that English marauders were not establishing a presence there, and – incidentally – to convert the natives to Christianity; no-one bothered to try to find out how many of them there were. The Spanish were more interested, in fact, in the legendary "city of the Caesars" *(see pages 274–5),* said to be hidden in the forests, with fabulous treasures of gold and jewels.

The southern coastline was not properly mapped until 1831, when Charles Darwin and Captain Robert Fitzroy navigated the area in their famous voyage on the *Beagle,* and the region's interior remained unknown for most of the 19th century.

The Chilean government only began to pay attention to Aisén when border disputes began to arise with Argentina in the late 19th century. The first attempts to settle these were unsuccessful. Between 1859 and 1896 four colonies were founded, two of them at Melinka and Río Alvarez, as simple trading posts for collecting and distributing seal, otter skins and cypress wood from the area.

At the beginning of the 20th century, the first settlers made their way across the frontier at Balmaceda from Argentina. By 1907 there were thought to be 197 permanent colonizers, with their families; plus another 500-odd employees of the English-owned sheep-farming companies which had begun to exploit the region. The pioneers were naturally a hardy bunch. One government official in the 1920s tried to describe their indomitable spirit. "No incompetent or coward or milksop gives up his home and his fatherland to settle lands uncultivated before in Patagonia, isolated in these solitudes, far from the principles of all authority

PRECEDING PAGES: Lago Vichuquen. **LEFT:** a window onto the wilderness. **BELOW:** local deer.

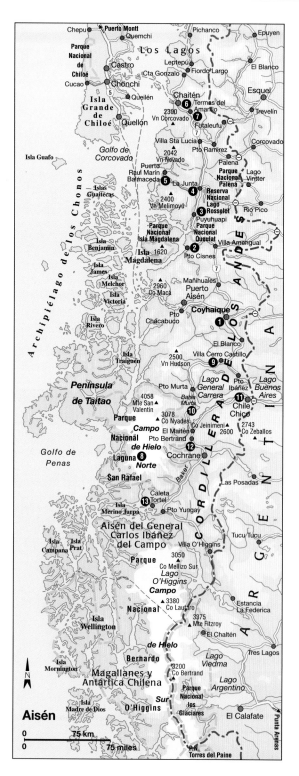

and justice, suffering hunger often and battling constantly against nature."

Hospitality, he noted, was one of the most developed virtues of the people of the region. "Dismount, unsaddle," the most common greeting to the stranger, was understood as an invitation to eat and stay the night. The guest's best way to repay such hospitality was "to present the most complete account possible of all events, human and divine, in the rest of the world," since other means of receiving news were non-existent.

Highway to the south

Today, the population of Aisén is just over 90,000, but many aspects of life there have not changed very dramatically from the way they were 50 years ago. The kinds of facilities that urban-dwellers take for granted – doctors, clinics, schools – are still scarce in the remoter parts of the region. There are cars and trucks and the occasional bus, but transport for some is still the traditional wooden-wheeled cart drawn by oxen. In the coastal regions the waterways are still important for communications and travel. In recent years, salmon farming has increased in importance, providing a new source of jobs, while in Puerto Chacabuco, Canada's Noranda has controversial plans for a vast aluminum smelter, which would use the hydroelectric generating capacity of the region's fast-flowing rivers.

One fairly recent improvement has been the completion of the **Carretera Austral Longitudinal** (to give it its official title). This is a mostly unpaved road, which runs the length of the region from Puerto Montt to Cochrane, (880 km/547 miles) and on to Villa O'Higgins.

Roads already existed from Puyuhuapi to Chaitén, between Puerto Aisén, Coyhaique and Balmaceda, and to Puerto Ibáñez, Chile Chico and Cochrane. But the Carretera scheme, started in 1976, has successfully linked the whole region with a single north-south route to which a network of east-west roads has been added. At various points the "road" becomes a ferry from one

Map on page 282

side of a river to another. Former President Augusto Pinochet claimed much of the credit for the project, and wanted it to carry his name. Apparently he did indeed support the project against the opposition of his finance ministers, and insisted that enough money be found to keep it going. The project was directed and partly built by army engineers. For the military, the road is considered a strategic necessity; the first ever route going from north to south through Aisén reinforces Chile's control of the territory.

For the inhabitants of Aisén, the highway has meant a real link-up with the rest of the region. What used to be an arduous boat trip from, for example, the scattered homes in the area around Puerto Cisnes to the nearest doctor, is now just a couple of hours' journey by road.

The road has also become a major tourist attraction for the more adventurous. The Chilean tourist office, Sernatur, distributes brochures with a description of the route, and the main stops along the way. It gives brief notes on the natural and man-made attractions, and also has a map giving details of facilities such as lodgings, telephones, first-aid posts and police. Information and organization is important – this is not really a suitable area to wander through without your own means of transport or a tour, unless you have all the time in the world.

It may be ever so humble, but there's no place like home.

Hub of the wilderness

The most central point for exploring Aisén is the region's largest town, **Coyhaique ❶**. It has a population of 50,000, and, while pleasant enough, travelers generally use it as a jumping-off point for trips to remoter parts. Coyhaique can be reached by plane from Santiago or Puerto Montt, or by following the Carretera Austral south, but there are sections of the road which have no bus services. The most popular route is by ferry from Puerto Montt to Puerto Chacabuco and then on by bus.

BELOW: fishing village.

Once in Coyhaique, take a casual stroll along Calle Prat. That's where most of the restaurants (specializing in seafood) and travel agents are found. You can book a tour here, or go by public transport to most parts of the recently opened South. The **Museo Regional de la Patagonia** has a fine collection of photographs depicting the region's history, including the construction of the Carretera Austral, although has irregular opening hours. Many different types of outdoor activity are available in the region, and Coyhaique is a good place to arrange them.

Fish – mostly salmon and rainbow trout – are plentiful in all of Aisén's rivers and lakes. Boats for lake expeditions can be organized from Coyhaique, either for the day or for a few days' stay in one of the area's fishing lodges. Skiing is available too, at **El Fraile**, 30 km (19 miles) south east of Coyhaique, and 1,000 meters (3,281 ft) above sea level. The resort has five slopes suitable for skiers of all skill levels, although facilities at the ski center are rather basic.

Traveling north from Coyhaique, the road runs through bright green woods of *mañío* and *coigüe*. A side road takes you to **Puerto Cisnes ❷**, a remarkably well-established little settlement whose mayoress for years was a formidable Italian lady who ruled the place with

Punctures are a frequent occurrence on the stony Carretera Austral, so it's wise to carry more than one spare wheel.

BELOW: waterfall near Puyuhuapi.

a very firm hand. She was a friend and admirer, initially of General Carlos Ibáñez del Campo, and then of General Pinochet (whose horoscope she used to tell). With the ear of both presidents she managed to get facilities in her village that many locals grumble would be better located farther up the main road, at Puyuhuapi.

On the main road just past the junction with Puerto Cisnes on the way to Puyuhuapi is Piedra El Gato, a massive boulder which had to be partly blasted away to build the road. Continuing north to Puyuhuapi, the road passes **Parque Nacional Queulat**, one of the supposed locations for the legendary city of the Caesars. Fishing, camping and hiking are possible amid lakes and glaciers.

Puyuhuapi ❸ is situated near Lago Risopatrón and has thermal springs, a luxury hotel, a garage and a carpet factory, which turns out sturdy hand-made woolen rugs to mostly old-fashioned Belgian designs. The settlement was started by four Sudeten Germans who emigrated from Czechoslovakia at the time of the Nazi invasion shortly before World War II, and made their way to this remote spot on the other side of the world, which they are said to have read about in a Baedecker guide. In the carpet factory you can see faded photographs of how they lived when they first arrived, in reed and wattle huts.

From **La Junta** ❹, the junction of the Palena and Rosselot rivers, it is possible for experienced sailors to navigate the Palena River to the wide beaches at its estuary, at **Puerto Raúl Marín Balmaceda** ❺, a six-hour journey. Beyond La Junta the road leads to Chaitén, 150 km (93 miles) to the north. There are some interesting sights along the way, such as the magnificent Cavi hanging glacier, which requires a short detour and a hike. **Chaitén** ❻ marks the northern boundary of the region of Aisén, as Cochrane marks the south – two dull little towns that are nevertheless the gateways to some of the most beautiful scenery on earth. Situated just north of Chaitén is the highly controversial, privately owned **Parque Natural Pumalín**, one of the world's largest private parks. Its owner, Douglas Tompkins, the North American conservationist businessman who founded the Esprit clothing chain, established the park in a bid to protect Chile's indigenous forest. Restaurant and camping facilities are available at Caleta Gonzalo.

Some 25 km (15½ miles) south of Chaitén, via the village of Amarillo, are the **Termas El Amarillo** ❼ thermal springs, where you can take a warm dip.

Whisky on the rocks

Aisén's most popular attraction is without doubt **Parque Nacional Laguna San Rafael** ❽, with its magnificent glacier. The sight provoked awe and gloom in Charles Darwin when he visited it in 1831. He described the place as "sad solitudes, where death more than life seems to rule supreme." He must have seen the glacier on one of the many days of low cloud. When the sun is shining, it is an awesome spectacle, with light glinting off the aquamarine ice and the landscape alive with black-necked swans and distinctive furry beavers. Passengers are taken by rowboat or motor launch to the very base of the glacier where it meets the sea. Icebergs float by so close you can reach out with your hand and touch them. The climax of any visit is to have a whisky on the rocks, using pieces of ice chipped straight from the glacier. The glacier can also be visited without going to Coyhaique. Several of the ferry companies in Puerto Montt run services to Chacabuco which detour via Laguna San Rafael. For those who wish to travel in comfort, cruisers such as the *Skorpios* operate from Puerto Montt. Their five-day trip is relatively expensive but provides international-level facilities.

Map on page 282

Traveling south

The route south from Coyhaique to Cochrane can be done in a day through hilly country, and then past the beautiful Laguna General Carrera. At **Villa Cerro Castillo ❾**, near Puerto Ibáñez, 100 km (60 miles) from Coyhaique, are two famous stone-age paintings, of which there are several in the area. A detour to **Bahía Murta ❿**, and from there a horse or boat ride, takes you to **Puerto Sánchez**, a former mining village of 200 people, where you can see the wave-sculpted "chapel of marble" and the underground caves of the Panichine islands.

A ferry to the other side of the lake takes you to **Chile Chico ⓫**, one of the region's earliest settlements. The area here enjoys a dry, warm microclimate, which gives the people who live here the opportunity to cultivate a much wider range of fruit and vegetables than in the rest of the region, although they have problems selling them. The place has a quiet, rustic charm that can be quite beguiling. Many travelers who had planned to pass straight through to Argentina find themselves staying for several days in Chile Chico, enjoying the sunshine and taking the occasional dip in the icy waters of the lake.

A six-day boat ride down Baker River, from **Puerto Bertrand ⓬** to **Caleta Tortel ⓭** the River, offers thrills and spills. The River Cisnes is another favorite trip. All of these can be organized from Coyhaique. ❑

A 1937 colonization law, which allowed only cleared land to be claimed, was responsible for many of Aisén's forest fires.

BELOW: warped house, Puerto Aisén.

CRUISING CHILE'S SOUTHERN SEAS

Beyond the Lake District, Chile breaks up into a mass of islands. Boats can take you to the most beautiful, unspoilt parts that roads cannot reach

Boats reign supreme in southern Chile's inhospitable but stunningly beautiful fiord region. They are the life-support system of the area's isolated fishing villages during the harsh winters, and in summer they ply a bustling tourist trade. The main attraction is the majestic San Rafael glacier, two days by boat out of Puerto Montt. This spectacular ice wall is the destination of the luxury Skorpios cruise boats, as well as several more modest services.

Another popular trip takes passengers from Puerto Montt down to Puerto Natales, gateway to the beautiful Parque Nacional Torres del Paine. Tourist cabins are modest, but the views and the atmosphere on board more than compensate. Puerto Montt is the starting point for any journey into the fiords, including Isla de Chiloé. But if you suffer from seasickness, beware. The narrow inland waterways are glassily calm, but the Gulf of Corcovado or, farther south, the Gulf of Penas, can test even the best sailor.

Several services run from Punta Arenas to the southern tip of Tierra del Fuego. The best – and most expensive – is the luxurious seven-day *Terra Australis* cruise.

There are also many enjoyable boat trips in the Lake District. One of the best starts from Petrohué on Lago Todos Los Santos and ends 12 stunning hours later in San Carlos de Bariloche in Argentina.

◁ **FISHERMAN'S FRIEND**
Pelicans are the constant companions of Chile's fishermen, picking up any scraps they leave behind.

▽ **MOAI MAGIC**
Few cruise boats go to Easter Island due to its extreme isolation, but yachts occasionally make the journey.

◁ **ANGELMO MARKET**
The restaurants are rough and ready but you can be sure of the freshness of the fish here.

◁ **CHEERS!**
What better way to celebrate the surreal, otherworldly atmosphere of Laguna San Rafael than with whisky on ice freshly chipped from the 30,000-year old glacier?

△ **SOUTHERN SPLENDOR**
The luxurious week-long *Terra Australis* cruise travels down the Magellan Strait from Punta Arenas to Puerto Williams, the world's southernmost port.

WILDLIFE OF THE FIORDS

Sea mammals such as seals and sea lions are a common sight in southern Chile's remote fiords. Like the Alacalufe Amerindians who once fished these waters, the modern inhabitants of the isolated villages dotted around the fiords still hunt and eat baby seals. In the most remote areas, you may also be lucky enough to see a blue whale. This huge animal migrates to the fiords in summer.

A sure companion for any boat trip south of Puerto Montt is the *tonina*, or Chilean dolphin. These fast-moving, playful animals usually swim in small groups and delight in chasing a boat, darting from side to side.

The steep sides of the fiords are covered with many native trees, including a type of cypress, and ferns, some of them almost tree-size. The dense vegetation is also home to an enormous variety of birds, including a colorful woodpecker and a tiny hummingbird.

Land animals are more difficult to see from the shore, but include foxes, weasels, small wildcats and the elusive puma.

△ **AQUATIC JEWEL**
Lago Todos Los Santos, also known as the Emerald Lake, can be visited just as a day trip or en route to Argentina.

▷ **PENGUIN PARADISE**
Each spring, several thousand penguins return to their breeding grounds on the Otway Sound, near Punta Arenas.

MAGALLANES

A harsh, inhospitable territory of bleak plains, fierce winds and wilderness areas of extraordinary beauty crowned by the rocky peaks of Torres del Paine

Map on page 292

Santiago

tretching toward the windswept southern tip of South America, the province of Magallanes exists quite apart from the rest of Chile. The hardy people who live here consider themselves first as Magallánicos, second as Chileans – hardly surprising, considering that they cannot reach Santiago by road without crossing the border into neighboring Argentina. In order to come and go from this stormy corner of the world, you have to either travel for days by bus across the endless stretches of Argentine Patagonia, fly direct, or take a lengthy, rocky cruise through the icy southern seas.

The terrain of Magallanes is formidably harsh. The region is split between impenetrable mountain ranges and bleak, barren Patagonian plains. Yet these harsh physical conditions have helped form a distinct local character. "The sheer difficulty of living here brings people together," says writer Francisco Coloane, the most famous chronicler of Magellanic life. "It creates a human solidarity and sense of honor that people from the rest of Chile don't always share."

Growing in isolation

History has conspired with the tyranny of distance to keep Magallanes apart from centralized rule in Chile. The region was first developed by foreign sheep companies – mostly British-owned – who had interests on both the Argentine and Chilean side of the border. Magallanes soon had more in common with Argentine Patagonia than the distant world of Santiago. English was spoken more often than Spanish – followed by a chorus of Serbo-Croat, Russian and Italian as workers arrived from all parts of the globe.

This cosmopolitan tradition can still be felt in the towns and old *estancias* (farm estates) of Magallanes, where the surnames are as likely to be MacMillan or Covacevic as anything of Spanish origin. The isolation of the south also developed its own political traditions: like the remote mining towns of the north, Magallanes has a long history of left-wing activism. Some of the bitterest strikes in Chilean history occurred in the province, and it was from Magallanes that the socialist leader Salvador Allende was first elected to Congress. Regional independence still marks its politics today, fed by a resentful belief that central government ignores the far south. Today, one of the region's complaints is that it lacks a broadband telecommunications connection to the rest of the country, making Internet access noticeably slower.

What today lures most travelers to this far end of the globe is the province's unspoiled wilderness. Much of Magallanes is made up of a jigsaw of tiny islands and channels without any permanent habitation or regular passenger services. These are the tips

PRECEDING PAGES: view over the Grey Glacier.
LEFT: the Torres (Towers) del Paine.
BELOW: bowsprit of the *Lonsdale*, wrecked near Punta Arenas.

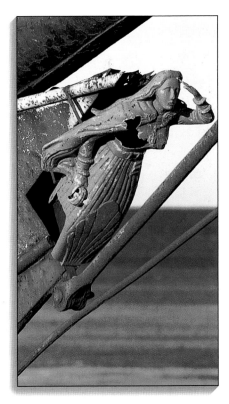

Port, Punta Arenas.

of underwater mountains – the continuation of the Andes range that has sunk into the icy sea – and they can only be glimpsed on rare boat journeys or from the air. Down towards the battered coastline of the Straits of Magellan are colonies of penguins, crystal lakes, trees gnarled by the ever-present Patagonian wind and some of the most spectacular mountain scenery anywhere in South America.

Horrifying sights

Magallanes takes its name from the Portuguese explorer Ferdinand Magellan who, while working for the Spanish Crown, became the first European to set eyes upon its shores in 1520. A gale blew his fragile sailing ships through what is now the Straits of Magellan toward the ocean he baptized the Pacific. On the way a landing party stopped off near modern-day Punta Arenas, to find a beached whale and 200 corpses raised on stilts. Shuddering at the gruesome sight, the navigator hurried toward the west.

Further Spanish contact with the area was hardly more encouraging. A group of 300 *conquistadores* under Pedro de Gamboa tried to set up a settlement on the straits, but the savage winter drove them all to starvation. A lone survivor was found three years later by the English pirate Thomas Cavendish, who had managed to survive by living among the local people.

For the next 250 years the region was visited by explorers, cartographers and naturalists, but few saw any reason to linger. Only in the 1830s did the Chilean government, spurred on by a wave of optimism and economic expansion, cast possessive glances toward the remote south. Prompting action was the occupation of the Falkland Islands by Britain in 1833 and the lengthy explorations made in the region by the British naturalist Charles Darwin in the *Beagle*.

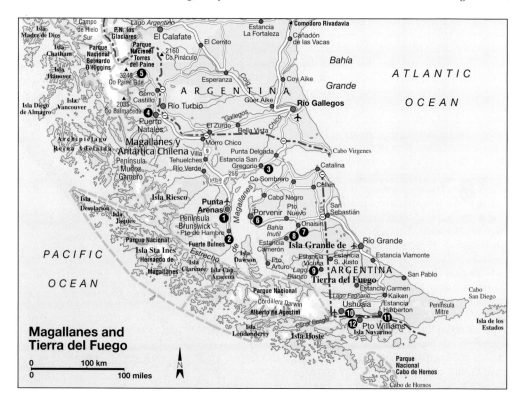

Magallanes and Tierra del Fuego

In 1843, President Manuel Bulnes claimed the land around the Straits of Magellan, Tierra del Fuego and southern Patagonia. A boatload of 21 motley soldiers was sent down to found Fuerte Bulnes on the straits, but the location proved to be so inhospitable that the outpost was abandoned and Punta Arenas was founded in its place five years later. This new settlement grew slowly into a town, with raids by native peoples and a bloody mutiny punctuating its early days. But Chile was forced to abandon its claim to much of Patagonia: Argentina took advantage of Chile's preoccupation with Peru and the north to take the lion's share of the south, leaving Magallanes with the border it has today.

Maps:
Area 292
City 294

The city at the end of the world

Today **Punta Arenas ❶** is a city of some 120,000 people, the hub of Magallanes and the first port of call for most foreign travelers. Facing out across the straits, it has an almost Dickensian flavor, full of rusting corrugated iron buildings and grandiose mansions from the late 19th century. The class divisions of old are still echoed in the streets: here you can find elegant, if rundown, parlors where apéritifs are sipped with an aristocratic flourish. Sitting adjacent are seedy bars full of sailors, naval recruits and a ubiquitous collection of weary old men – usually wearing woolen caps and tightly buttoned overcoats, huddled over their glasses of *pisco* and whisky, taking refuge from the biting wind.

The hard water of Punta Arenas produces some of Chile's best beer.

Weather dominates the city's mood. Despite its latitude, Punta Arenas never experiences the extremes of cold found in equally remote places in the Northern Hemisphere. Nevertheless, the skies bring few comforts. Even in summer, when the sun shines for up to 20 hours a day and temperatures are moderate, the wind and rain can often make Punta Arenas seem a gloomy frontier town. But

BELOW: Punta Arenas in winter.

when the sun breaks through the billowing clouds, its cool air is bracing and a stroll through the quiet streets can be pleasant as well as fascinating.

Memories of a golden age

Scattered around Punta Arenas are opulent monuments to a golden age when it was one of the busiest ports on earth. Its history is in many ways that of the whole far south. A series of unexpected events in the mid-19th century helped lift the town out of obscurity. The industrial age in Europe and North America was creating a boom in sea trade. The Panama Canal had not yet been thought of. Sea clippers and the new steamships making their journeys around the world – carrying anything from European machinery to Texan petroleum and Australian wheat – all had to stop in at Punta Arenas, the town at the end of the world.

The boom soon made Punta Arenas the logical center for Patagonian sheep farming. In 1877, an English trader brought a flock of stock from the Falkland Islands to Elizabeth Island in the Magellan Straits. The experiment was a success and soon other entrepreneurs were following suit. A Machiavellian Spaniard named José Menéndez and the Russian-born immigrant Mauricio Braun became leading figures: starting off as rivals, they were soon linked by marriage to form a Patagonian dynasty that would dominate the south for decades.

Farm administrators were brought in from Scotland, England, Australia and New Zealand, making Magallanes, as writer Bruce Chatwin noted in his classic *In Patagonia*, look like an outpost of the British Empire. But the *peons*, farm hands who worked the land in generally dismal conditions, almost all came from the overcrowded farmyards of Chile's own Chiloé.

Punta Arenas' golden age ended abruptly when the Panama Canal was opened

BELOW: Balmaceda Glacier.

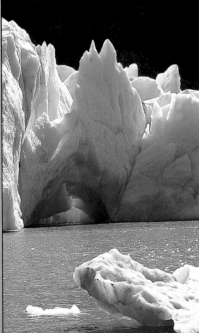

and boats no longer needed to travel round Cabo de Hornos (Cape Horn). Magallanes continued to be a profitable sheep region until towards the Great Depression, when a long decline began. Competition from Australia, New Zealand and Canada squeezed Chile and Argentina from the major world markets. Many of the English managers left for their homeland as land reform carved up the largest *estancias* of the south. Even Don José Menéndez decided to move to Buenos Aires. Today many of the farms are nearly bankrupt.

This downward economic spiral was only halted with the discovery of petroleum and natural gas in 1945. Oil companies stepped up exploration in the straits over the following decades and Magallanes again prospered. Workers looking for high wages flocked from the north, while fishing also boomed and Punta Arenas became a duty-free port. During this period, Magallanes achieved one of the highest per capita incomes in Chile. But now the oil wells have virtually dried up, although there is still natural gas and a Canadian company has built one of the world's largest methanol plants in Punta Arenas. But over the past few years, Magallanes has stagnated economically while the rest of the country has expanded quickly, leaving this most remote province lagging sadly behind.

Map on page 294

A tour of past glories

The modern center of Punta Arenas is, as it always has been, the **Plaza Muñoz Gamero Ⓐ**. Surrounded by trees and neat gardens, the plaza (currently being re-modeled) is dominated by a bronze statue of Magellan, looking proudly over the heroic figures of various local Amerindians, who were idealized by a sculptor after they had been largely wiped out by marauding European settlers, keen to ensure that no native would interfere with the

BELOW: tree bent in submission to the Patagonian wind.

profitable grazing of sheep. These days children pose for photographs while touching an Amerindian's foot for luck.

The plaza is a community meeting place in summer, when the trees are full and flowers bloom. Every Sunday morning in the warmer months a military brass band plays. Flanking the plaza are the box-like **Hotel Cabo de Hornos**, the **cathedral** and impressive **Social Club**. The latter was the first brick building to have been built in Punta Arenas, by the matriarch Sara Braun. Now a club for the old wealth and naval officers of the town, it offers guided tours to non-members (open Mon–Fri 10am–1pm and 5–8.30pm, Sat 10am–1pm and 8–10pm; open occasionally on Sun in summer; entrance fee). The interior is sumptuous, with extravagant Art Deco lampshades, giant Chinese vases and mahogany furniture imported from Europe. Lunch is served in a vine-covered glass annex.

Even more extravagant is the **Centro Cultural Braun-Menéndez** , opposite the Cabo de Hornos on Calle H. de Magallanes. Built by the Patagonian pioneer don Mauricio Braun in 1905, it is rightly referred to by locals as "El Palacio" (The Palace). The mansion was designed by a French architect to outstrip the finest houses of Santiago. Marble was imported from Italy, wood from Belgium, wallpaper from France and furniture from England.

Upon entering the mansion, visitors pass through the airy hall with classical frescos painted on its ceiling. Everything in the adjoining rooms is done on a grand scale: the main bedroom contains a massive Louis XV four-poster bed, while the games room has a gigantic billiard table and furniture in Art Nouveau style. The salon – the most important room in the house – is crowded with gilded tables and chairs under a glittering crystal chandelier and stern portraits of long-dead family members. The walls of the dining room are covered with pressed Italian leather, while the *escritorio* (office) still contains the mahogany desk from which the fate of the south was directed.

The rest of the house's ground floor has been converted into the **Museo Regional de Magallanes** (open Nov–Apr Mon–Sat 10.30am–5pm, Sun 10.30am–2pm; May–Oct: daily 10.30am–2pm; entrance fee, except Sun), with exhibits from the time of the foundation of Punta Arenas to the 1920s. Upstairs is the library, a picture gallery, and important historical archives. The mansion was shared by the Brauns and Menéndezes after constant inter-marriage linked the clans. But as land reform took its toll on their *estancias* and profits, the families handed over the building to the government. It became a national monument in 1974.

BELOW: a cargo boat plies the Southern Ocean.

The old port

Some of the oldest streets in Punta Arenas stretch down from Calle H. de Magallanes to the straits. A walk along Calle Roca takes you to the old port area, with its range of seedy flop houses, cafés and bars. Many of the old houses made of tin and corrugated iron seem to be on the point of collapse, but these vestiges of the late 19th century give a glimpse of the bustling days of the past.

Another walk out along Calle Bories leads to the fascinating **Museo Regional Salesiano** (open Oct–Mar Tues–Sun 10am–6pm, Apr–Sept Tues–Sun 10am–1pm and 2.30–6pm; entrance fee), one of the most unusual museums in South America. The Salesians are a religious order that once tried to "save" the native people of the region by creating missionary refuges, only to find that European clothes gave them influenza and killed the tribes as surely as the white settlers' bullets. The museum reflects the belief that the Salesians' paternalistic "civilizing" efforts were morally correct. But despite this self-congratulation, the museum's disordered exhibits provide a fascinating insight into the lives of several groups of people whose way of life and very existence has been largely destroyed.

A room full of prehispanic artifacts gives a good introduction to the four tribal groups that once lived in Magallanes. Inhabiting the barren plains east of the Andes were the fierce Tehuelches (or Aónikenk) peoples. Their impressive stature and enormous moccasins are traditionally believed to have inspired Ferdinand Magellan to exclaim "Ha! Patagon!" (big foot), giving Patagonia its name. The writer Bruce Chatwin has offered a more plausible explanation, suggesting that the name came from an early 16th-century romantic story where a monster called the Grand Patagon appears. Magellan was likely to have been familiar with the tale, where the man-like creature roars like a bull, just as Magellan noted that the Tehuelches did.

Canoeing around the rough islands of the southeastern Pacific were the maritime nomad tribe the Alacalufes (Kawéskar), who hunted sea lions and dived for shellfish. Today the last survivors of this race live in the remote fishing village of Puerto Edén. The Onas (Selk'nam) hunted guanacos on the northern plains of Tierra del Fuego, while the Yaghanes (Yamanas) navigated the icy forested islands south of the Beagle Channel. The Onas were wiped out in the early 20th century, and only a handful of mixed-blood Yaghanes are still alive.

Keep an eye out in the museum for a piece of skin and some 10,000-year-old

Map on page 294

Cemetery, Punta Arenas.

BELOW: a summer Santa, Punta Arenas.

droppings from the giant ground-sloth found in the Cueva del Milodón (Milodón Cave) near Puerto Natales *(see page 301)*. Also of interest are a *conquistador's* helmet found in Magallanes and a replica of the cross set up by Charles Darwin's crew on the straits over the grave of one of their members, who apparently died from the stress of navigating these treacherous waters.

Farther out along Calle Bories is the **Cementerio Municipal** ❺, comparable in splendor only to the famous Recoleta necropolis in Buenos Aires. Settlers from every part of the world are buried here, as well as the victims of the many shipwrecks that occurred on this savage coast. One site worth visiting is the monument to the local *Ameri*ndians, a belated memorial to the massacres of the 19th century. Just off the opposite side of the road, a small shop sells Punta Arenas artisan chocolate. It's tucked away in a side street, but the friendly local people will be happy to point you in the right direction.

Bories leads to the outskirts of town, where the **Instituto de la Patagonia** has its grounds. A collection of farming machinery, wagons and steam tractors from the region's past are littered about an open field, with a reconstructed settlers' house from 1880. There is a library here with a fine collection of old maps. Across the road from the Institute is the **Zona Franca**, where duty-free goods can be bought although prices are not that cheap and there's nothing you won't see elsewhere.

Excursions from Punta Arenas

A three-hour drive from Punta Arenas are the famous **pingüineros** (penguin colonies) of the south. Hundreds of these comical creatures live in burrows dug into the sandy southern shoreline. It is possible that this was where the Italian Antonio Pigafetta, a member of Magellan's crew in 1520, recorded the first

BELOW: Fuerte Bulnes.

European sighting of the penguin. The species seen here is the *Spheniscus magellanicus*, named for the straits on which it lives rather than the explorer himself. It is known as the jackass penguin for the odd braying sound it makes.

Try to visit the *pingüineros* in a small group, since large numbers of people send the penguins scurrying away on their flippers, which they use as front legs to run on all fours. The penguins spend most of April to August at sea, heading north to warmer climates before returning from September through March to their breeding grounds here.

Some 54 km (34 miles) south of Punta Arenas along the inky Straits of Magellan is the reconstructed **Fuerte Bulnes ❷** fortress on the site of the original 1843 settlement. The highway passes the skeleton of the wrecked ship *Lonsdale* on the outskirts of town, and some classic Patagonian scenery, but the fort itself has a disappointing Disneyland look. On the way back most tours stop at **Punta Hambre**, where the unfortunate Pedro de Gamboa tried to set up his settlement 300 years ago (*see page 292*). More exciting is a visit to the **centolla fishermen** nearby. The *centolla*, a bright orange king crab, is one of the great delicacies of the south. Caught in large wicker crab pots, they can be bought directly from the fishermen or ordered in any good restaurant in the south. They look huge and vicious but are actually rather timid creatures, whose claws are next to useless.

Maps:
Area 292
City 294

Contented penguin, Seno de Otway.

The road to Argentina

Along the highway 150 km (93 miles) north of Punta Arenas is the first sheep farm of the south, **Estancia San Gregorio ❸**. Built in 1878, it was taken over by José Menéndez four years later and extended to 90,000 hectares (222,400 acres). It can only be visited with the permission of the current owner (tel: 61-233-175), although a good deal can be seen from the road.

San Gregorio remains the classic example of many *estancias* that, in the 19th century, were like small, self-contained towns. The company's own launch, the *Amadeo*, lies rusting by the shore at the *estancia's* entrance, where the captain decided to leave it after 50 years of service. In the grounds are large wooden shearing sheds, still hanging the faded stock awards of decades past, as well as shops, a chapel, a theater for the landowners and bars for the workers. The house itself is a huge and lavish building, although now sparsely furnished: it still has hand-operated gramophones and a few relics of the past, but the land reforms of the early 1970s and the fall in international wool prices have shorn it of its former glory.

After decades of grinding oppression, the *peons* became drunk on freedom. In scenes reminiscent of the French Revolution they camped out in the mansion, put the bust of Don José in the out-house and went through the family cellar. Prize sheep munched freely at the garden before finally being slaughtered for mutton soup. The *estancia* was returned to private hands after the brutal 1973 military coup.

Farther along the road to Argentina is **Fell's Cave**, where some of the oldest prehistoric human remains in the Americas have been found. It can only be visited with the help of scientists at the Instituto de la Patagonia in Punta Arenas.

BELOW: guanacos, Parque Nacional Torres del Paine.

Gateway to the southern Andes

Puerto Natales ❹, 242 km (150 miles) north of Punta Arenas, is set prettily on the shores of the Ultima Esperanza Sound. Family hotels abound, and surprisingly, in view of Puerto Natales' small size, there are plenty of places to eat, drink and even to dance. This is the place that the inhabitants of Punta Arenas come to when they want a change of scene.

The waterfront, where black-necked swans bob on the cold waves, is a lovely place to walk, while the climb up the **Cerro Dorotea** hill gives fine views of the whole Ultima Esperanza area. Just outside town there is an old meat-packing plant bought by the British after World War I. In its heyday, thousands of sheep were slaughtered here weekly for the dinner tables of Europe, and many of the steam-driven engines used then are still lying about. One sits in the main plaza.

The meatworks ensured that Puerto Natales would be a leftist town. A riot began here in 1919 when Chilote workers killed an English assistant manager, lynched three policemen and looted the stores. But before long the government sent in the army, and 28 ringleaders were taken away, among them some Maximilianist Russians who were blamed as foreign agitators.

Puerto Natales is the gateway to some of the most spectacular sights in Magallanes. Most easily reached is the **Balmaceda Glacier** to the northwest. Boatloads of tourists leave most mornings to see this aquamarine river of ice that inches its way down from the Andes to the sea. Gigantic ice blocks crash regularly from the glacier, sending shock waves across to the boat, while powerful winds whistle through the narrow channel. Most boats pull up at a small jetty and passengers can safely walk along paths near the side of the glacier. On the way, the jagged Torres del Paine mountain peaks can be seen on the horizon, while the channel shore is

TIP

The road north from Puerto Natales crosses the border into Argentina to the popular El Calafate tourist center on Lago Argentina.

BELOW: the Grey Glacier.

lined with waterfalls. Groups of seals and sea lions sit on rocky outcrops, while porpoises, steamer ducks and black-necked swans can be spotted in the icy waters.

A quite different day trip can be made to the enormous **Cueva del Milodón** *(see box below)*, focus of a scientific furore nearly a century ago and a key element in Bruce Chatwin's classic travel book *In Patagonia*. Today, the Cueva del Milodón is a popular picnic spot outside Puerto Natales. A life-size model of the milodón, rearing back on its hind legs, has been placed at the cave mouth, but nothing else remains to suggest its past. A piece of the milodón skin and its dung can be seen in the Museo Regional Salesiano in Punta Arenas *(see page 296)*, and there are more milodón remnants in the British Museum in London.

From Puerto Natales, the road north continues to **Cerro Castillo** on the border with Argentina and, from there, to **El Calafate**, a touristy town that is the gateway to Argentina's **Los Glaciares National Park**. Inexpensive bus services run regularly from Puerto Natales to El Calafate (around a five-hour trip) in summer, when there is also a daily 40-minute flight (weekdays only). Rental cars are also allowed to cross the border but, unless you plan to return to Chile, beware of a hefty drop-off charge.

Map on page 292

The enormous milodón was a herbivore.

The untouched wilderness

By far the most impressive sight in the Chilean south is **Parque Nacional Torres del Paine ⑤** (pronounced pie-nee). Lying at the far south of the Andes mountain chain, it is one of the newest nature reserves in South America, having been formed in 1959 and only reaching its present size in the early 1970s (UNESCO made it a Biosphere reserve in 1978). The uninhabited park is crowded with glaciers, lakes and gnarled Magellanic trees, and provides some of the

BELOW: the Milodón Cave, near Puerto Natales.

THE GIANT SLOTH HUNT

In 1896, German-born landowner Herman Eberhard found a strange 1.2-meter (4-ft) long stretch of hairy skin on the floor of a cave. The following year, part of the skull of a huge mammal, a claw and a large human thighbone were found. Before long, a scientist in Argentina had announced that the skin was from a Milodón Listai (named after himself), a prehistoric giant ground sloth endemic to South America. The bones of several milodons had been found during the 19th century, but Listai asserted that this piece of skin was so fresh, the beast had only recently died – and a living example could not be far away.

"Positive sightings" of huge hairy beasts became the norm in the region. Excitement was sufficient in Britain for the *Daily Express* newspaper to finance a scientific expedition to search for a living milodón. Despite hearing many ghostly tales, they found no live example (although expedition leader Hesketh Prichard's book *Through the Heart of Patagonia* became an inspiration for Arthur Conan Doyle's *Lost World* tale). Meanwhile, a team of archeologists dug away in the cave, but they found little more than huge amounts of sloth dung. Radio-carbon dating has since shown that the skin is about 10,000 years old but was perfectly preserved in the dark, damp cave.

most magnificent walking in the world. The dramatic mountain formations are a sight that few people will forget, while the park itself is full of animals, including guanacos, flamingos and condors.

Every morning in summer and several times a week at other times of the year, vans and buses make the three-hour drive from Puerto Natales to the park along a rough dirt road. The trail winds through mountain passes before descending to the foot of the Andes, providing the first view of the **Cuernos del Paine** (Paine Horns), twisted pillars of gray granite, dusted with snow and rising from the flat Patagonian plains into a sky full of billowing gray clouds.

Like everywhere else this far south, weather in the park can be unpredictable, to say the least. The best times to visit are January to April, but even then clear skies are rare and can disappear within minutes. The famous Torres (Towers) del Paine are even more spectacular than the Cuernos, but often difficult to see because of cloud cover. The one thing that never seems to change is the gusting Patagonian wind that drives from the plains to the west.

All visitors to the park must sign on at the administration building, where the wardens *(guardaparques)* will give advice on the condition of the trails. The classic views of the park can be easily reached by road and on day trips operating from Puerto Natales. If you want to stay in the park, advance booking is essential. There are several small hotels, including the **Hostería Pehoé** on one of the lakes and the **Posada Río Serrano**, a converted *estancia* (farm estate) house. Its restaurant has the obligatory log fire and stuffed animal heads, as well as sculptures made from the park's bulbous wooden tree roots. A luxury hotel, the **Explora**, is beautifully designed and set on the shore of one of the lakes. It runs some of the best guided tours around the park but is very pricey. Five explorations are offered each day and are limited to ten guests, plus a guide.

The ñandú, Chile's ostrich, is quite commonly seen in and around Torres del Paine.

BELOW: waterfall, Parque Nacional Torres del Paine.

Roaming in the wilderness

Several day trips, as well as more ambitious walks, can be made from these bases. The park has more than 250 km (155 miles) of walking tracks, including the classic seven-day circuit. Along the way are *refugios* or shelters, often primitive wood and corrugated iron edifices that barely keep out the wind and rain – good sleeping bags, as well as cooking gear, are essential. If you plan to do the seven-day circuit you should bring a tent as well, since the *refugios* can get full.

This hike starts at the administration building at the southern end of **Lago Pehoé** and gives ever-changing views of the Cuernos. The walking can be strenuous – the longest stretch in one day is 30 km (19 miles). Many people make two- or three-day walks rather than the full circuit. A good compromise is to walk to the first *refugio* next to Lago Grey, camp overnight, take a day trip to **Grey Glacier** and then walk back to the administration center the next day. Or walk to the **Ventisquero del Francés** glacier or Lago Pingo, where a less-frequently used *refugio* can be found.

Those who make the effort are rewarded with superb views of snow-covered peaks, turquoise lakes and lush valleys. The walking trails are lined with flowers, sometimes crossing wide pasture and at other times hugging mountainsides or passing through verdant forests. The Grey and Dickson glaciers, when discovered in the wild, are somehow more impressive than others more easily reached.

Most routes in the park allow walkers to see plenty of animals, most commonly guanacos: unlike in other parts of South America, they appear unafraid of people and can be easily photographed from up close. Condors cruise between mountain peaks, hares and foxes dash about in the scrub and swans and flamingos can be seen on many of the lakes. Although the weather can turn from fair to foul and back again within minutes, the memories of the park will last well after your clothes have dried. Many people who go for a few days stay a week: the liberating sensation of being in one of the most remote and untouched wilderness areas on earth is worth savoring for as long as possible.

The remote archipelago

The map of Magallanes shows hundreds of scattered islands stretching to the Pacific. Very few are visited and fewer still are inhabited. A large area of the south has been incorporated into **Parque Nacional Bernardo O'Higgins** and into forestry reserves. There is little chance of visiting these wilderness areas without hiring your own boat in Punta Arenas or Puerto Natales.

For most travelers, the way of seeing these islands is to take the pricey week-long Skorpios cruise from Puerto Natales or to travel on the Navimag passenger boats between Puerto Natales and Puerto Montt. This three-day journey goes through the Estrecho Smith and Estrecho Estebán. It is not particularly comfortable unless you hire a cabin – in which case the sea journey costs more than the air ticket. But some travelers are captivated by the romance of a sea voyage and the chance to watch the remote islands drift by. ❑

Map on page 292

Punta Arenas statue of Chile's El Libertador, Bernardo O'Higgins.

BELOW: bird's-eye view of Punta Arenas.

THE PICK OF THE NATIONAL PARKS

With most of the population concentrated around Santiago and Concepción, the rest of Chile has some beautiful wilderness areas to explore

Almost one-fifth of Chile is protected to varying degrees in national parks and reserves. The national forestry commission, CONAF, administers 31 national parks, 48 national reserves and 15 natural monuments. The first national park in Chile, Vicente Pérez Rosales *(see page 251)*, in the southern Lake District, was founded in 1926. Entrance fees contribute to maintenance and conservation work.

Chile's long, narrow geography means that its national parks are very varied. Not many people want to trek in the hot, dry desert north – the main attractions of parks like Lauca and Volcán Isluga are the wildlife and the superb scenery. These parks are best tackled in a four-wheel-drive vehicle, preferably with a driver who knows the area well. Farther south, coastal parks like the popular Pan de Azúcar give protection to sea life.

Many national parks such as Nahuelbuta, Alerce Andino and Conguillío have been created to protect Chile's native forest. Unfortunately, the popularity of Parque Nacional Conguillío, in the northern Lake District, has brought with it serious erosion.

In the far south, parks like Laguna San Rafael and Bernardo O'Higgins protect Chile's southern lakes and glaciers, while prime trekking territory is found in the magnificent Parque Nacional Torres del Paine, in Magallanes *(see far right)*.

Finally, the archeological monuments of Easter Island are protected by Parque Nacional Rapa Nui. For more information, contact CONAF's central office, at Av. Gral Bulnes 285, Santiago; tel: 02 390 0000.

△ **FOREST SANCTUARY**
Parque Nacional Nahuelbuta was named after the puma, but was founded in 1939 to protect Chile's endangered *araucaria* trees.

▷ **VALUABLE WOOD**
This reserve was created in 1982 to protect the valuable *alerce* wood, used to make the famous tiles of Chiloé.

◁ **FLORAL FANFARE**
The *copihue*, Chile's national flower, grows on a tree ivy in the Central Valley and farther south.

△ **WILD HUNTERS**
Parque Nacional Torres del Paine is a sanctuary for rare birds of prey such as the black-breasted hawk, or gray eagle.

THE PLEASURE OF THE PAINE

Parque Nacional Torres del Paine, 112 km (70 miles) north of Puerto Natales in Magallanes, covers a wilderness area of 181,400 hectares (450,000 acres). Created in 1959, the park achieved World Heritage status from UNESCO in 1978, and is today one of Chile's most popular tourist attractions, despite frequent bad weather. The park's crowning glories are the spectacular Torres (towers) and Cuernos (horns, *pictured above*), stark granite peaks that form part of the Paine Massif. The range continues into Argentina's Parque Nacional Los Glaciares, with the Fitzroy Range, attracting climbers from all over the world.

P N. Torres del Paine is a haven for the *ñandú* (rhea) and the guanaco, which European settlers slaughtered to near-extinction to make room for cattle. You might also see flamingos, condors and, if you're really lucky, a puma.

△ **FABULOUS FALLS**
Trails go to Petrohué Falls in P.N. Vicente Pérez Rosales. White-water rafting is done on the Petrohué River.

◁ **WINTER WONDERLAND**
The active Volcán Laima crowns the devastatingly popular P.N. Conguillio in the Lake District.

▷ **CHILE'S ÑANDÚ**
Unusual for the bird world, it is male *ñandues*, or rheas, which incubate the female's eggs and raise the chicks. When scared, they run away fast, constantly changing direction.

REPUBLICA DE CHILE
BIENVENIDO
PARQUE NACIONAL
ALERCE ANDINO
...ONAL FORESTAL X REGION

TIERRA DEL FUEGO

The land at the southernmost tip of South America is the bleakest,
stormiest part of the continent, yet it exerts a constant fascination
for travelers who want to visit the last stop before Antarctica

Map on page 292

Santiago

Lashed by wind and wild seas at the southern tip of South America, **Tierra del Fuego** exerts a perverse fascination. Despite – or because of – its desolate image, few who travel to the far south of Chile can resist paying a visit to the literal end of the earth, the last fragment of land before the treacherous, forbidding territory of Antarctica.

The archipelago's name, which means "land of fire," came from the explorer Ferdinand Magellan, who in 1520 saw smoke rising from campfires on its shores (Magellan originally called it "land of smoke" but the Spanish King Charles 1 thought "land of fire" might be more poetic). It took the navigator no less than 38 days to force a passage through the strait that now bears his name. Fear of returning through these waters drove Magellan's men ever westward after their captain's death in the Philippines, eventually making the few survivors of the expedition the first to circumnavigate the globe.

For centuries afterwards, Tierra del Fuego was dreaded by sailors for its frequent storms and freezing rains. Rounding Cape Horn between the Atlantic and Pacific oceans became a nautical vision of hell, as can be seen in the works of Herman Melville, Samuel Taylor Coleridge, Jules Verne and Edgar Allen Poe. Today Tierra del Fuego maintains its sense of being a Klondike-style frontier. Despite the grisly past, the people of its remote, windswept towns have a rawness and surprising warmth towards strangers. And, most importantly for many travelers, the islands of Tierra del Fuego contain some of the last great wilderness areas on earth.

Darwin among the savages

The British naturalist Charles Darwin added a new dimension to the image when he visited Tierra del Fuego on the *Beagle* in the 1830s. He pronounced the native people, who had been living in the far south for tens of thousands of years, to be the lowest on the human evolutionary scale:

"I never saw such miserable creatures," Darwin wrote in his classic *Voyage of the Beagle*; "stunted in their growth, their hideous faces bedaubed with white paint and quite naked... Their red skins filthy and greasy, their voices discordant, their gesticulation violent and without any dignity. Viewing such men, one can hardly make oneself believe that they are fellow creatures placed in the same world... What a scale of improvements is comprehended between the faculties of a Fuegian savage and a Sir Isaac Newton!"

Darwin's verdict was to be shared by the first settlers of Tierra del Fuego. By the end of the 19th century the Fuegian Amreindians would be exterminated in one of the most extraordinary cases of genocide in history (*see page 308*).

LEFT: the Straits of Magellan.
BELOW: car ferry from Tierra del Fuego to Punta Arenas.

The Lost Tribes

In the mid-19th century, Tierra del Fuego was home to four native groups. The most numerous were the Onas, or Selk'nam, a nomadic race that hunted guanacos over the open plains with bows and arrows. The Haush people occupied the eastern tip of the Isla Grande, living in huts of branches and skins. Roaming the southern islands with bark canoes and in seal hides were the Yaghans. The men hunted otters with spears and Yaghan women would sometimes dive into the icy waters to pluck *centollas* (king crabs) from the ocean floor. Finally, living in the fiords of southern Chile, were the Alacalufes.

Missionary Thomas Bridges compiled a dictionary of the Yaghan language that shows how they ordered their harsh world with metaphors. Bruce Chatwin lists a few phrases in his book, *In Patagonia*: "mussels out of season" was a synonym for shrivelled skin and old age; "Jackass penguin" meant lazy; "sleet" was the same word as "fish scales."

Traditionally roaming the pampas to hunt guanaco, the Onas naturally found sheep an easy and satisfying prey. For the farm owners, stealing their property was the ultimate crime: they killed the Onas in retribution. But the Onas could not accept that the fences across their traditional lands were meant as boundaries, and continued to hunt the "white guanaco." The *estancia* owners hired gunmen to protect their lands – although the gruesome rumor began that they were paid one pound sterling bounty for each Amerindian they shot dead (ears were supposedly demanded as proof).

Salesian missionaries argued that the Amerindians could only be saved if they were removed *en masse* to nearby Isla Dawson, and the *estancia* owners agreed to this method of removing the "pest" *(see page 297)*.

Official records show that most of the indigenous people died of disease in the Dawson mission, but the folk memory persists of active resistance, battles and massacres. Old-timers still tell of such gruesome characters as the Scotsman Alex McLennan, nicknamed the "Red Pig" by the Amerindians for his face made ruddy by constant boozing. He is said to have lured native families into traps by offering food, only to have his men open fire from their position in hiding. The Englishman Sam Hyslop, who boasted of gunning down 80 Onas, was finally caught by Indians and flung to his death from a cliff.

Argentines were well schooled in eradicating Amerindians and hunts went on unrestricted on that side of the border, but the Chilean population had moments of conscience-stricken doubt. The ugly rumors, coupled with the fact that mostly women and children were being brought back from raids, caused a public outcry. The Chilean police found a mass grave and were going to prosecute the *estancia* owners. But by this stage some Amerindians were fighting back – a handful of white deaths (a total of seven in 10 years) were registered and few people raised their voices against clearing the island any longer. In the Isla Dawson mission, epidemic followed epidemic. By 1925 no Ona was alive. A similar fate awaited other native groups. Today only a handful of *mestizo* Yaghans survive. ❑

LEFT: the last of the Onas.

Map on page 292

A fitful invasion

Although a constant stream of explorers and later whalers followed Magellan's path, European settlement of Tierra del Fuego was generally slow in coming. The Spanish had constant plans to outwit the English and Dutch pirates by setting up a naval base on the island, but the dismal conditions prevented settlement. It was not until the 1840s that Chile and Argentina both laid claim to the area, and several decades later before anybody could be convinced to actually live there. A border was drawn up; some missionaries made tentative landings; and in the 1880s the first miners arrived in search of gold.

While there were some clashes between these fortune seekers and the indigenous peoples, the real problems between newcomers and natives did not begin until entrepreneurs realized that the Northern Plains were possibly the best sheep country in South America *(see page 308)*. On the Chilean side of the border, the first *estancia* or ranch was set up in 1893 by the Sociedad Explotadora de Tierra del Fuego, with the Russian-born Don Mauricio Braun as director general. He named it Josefina after his wife and appointed a New Zealand-born sheep farmer as manager.

The elimination of the Amerindians allowed sheep farming to reach new heights. Some of the largest farms ever built were opened up on Tierra del Fuego and became enormously profitable for the mostly British-owned companies. As in the rest of Patagonia, immigrants drifted in from around the world, including a large number of exiles and eccentrics. Chilean Tierra del Fuego received an unusual number of arrivals from what was then Yugoslavia.

In modern times, the discovery of oil gave the island's economy a temporary boost. But the population remains thin. Argentina has tried to settle its part of

Burnt tree trunks are a familiar sight in the far south.

BELOW: the elimination of Amerindians left more room for sheep.

Tierra del Fuego by making Ushuaia a duty-free zone and holiday resort, but the Chilean section remains a sleepy and undeveloped part of the country, where little seems to have changed since the late 19th century.

Exploring the "large island"

The term "Tierra del Fuego" properly includes the whole archipelago at the southern tip of South America, although the Isla Grande de Tierra del Fuego is the largest island and is usually the one referred to. It is divided between Chile (70 percent) and Argentina (30 percent), with its northern and western sections a treeless Patagonian plain and the southeastern part a lush, mountainous land full of forests and sodden swamps. The Chilean section is physically the less dramatic of the two, and travelers to the island crossing over from Punta Arenas will normally want to visit both sides.

Thanks to relatively warm ocean currents, the island's weather is not as harsh as parts of Alaska, Norway and Canada which lie at an equivalent latitude in the northern hemisphere. Even so, it lives up to its stormy reputation. A recommended time to visit is during the summer months, from November to March, when daylight lasts for up to 20 hours and the sun is relatively warm. The weather shifts erratically from cloudless sky to drizzle or a deluge and back again within minutes, with the only constant being a gusty wind. It is worthwhile preparing for a range of weather conditions to pass by every day.

Travelers coming from Chile usually cross the dark Straits of Magellan from Punta Arenas on the ferry that leaves at 9am daily except Monday (prior booking required for vehicles; tel: 61-218-100). As tradition suggests, the crossing is usually a rough one, but the water is also on occasion as smooth as glass. The

Beavers, brought from Canada, have become a pest on Tierra del Fuego, damming rivers and destroying woods.

BELOW: the southern outpost of Porvenir.

optimistically named port of **Porvenir** (Future) is the landing point on Tierra del Fuego, heralded by a cluster of battered fishing boats on shore and a sign that gives the distances to every point in Chile. Arica, Chile's northernmost town, is 5,299 km/3,249 miles away.

Descendants of Yugoslavs still make up the bulk of Porvenir's 4,700 inhabitants, few of whom seem to take to the streets. At weekends, it is like a ghost town. The buildings are corrugated iron constructs mostly dating from before World War I. A wooden church steeple dominates the skyline, adding to the haunting impression. The **Museo de Tierra del Fuego** (open Mon–Thur 9am–5pm, Fri 9am–4pm, Sat and Sun 10am–1.30pm and 3–5pm; free) is connected to the municipal buildings on the main plaza, with historical photographs and a Fuegian mummy discovered in the nearby countryside. A waterfront stroll brings you to a lookout on the south side of Bahía Porvenir.

Porvenir started out as a police post during the 1880s gold rush. Today, pink flamingos and black-necked swans swim along the waterfront.

Into the plains

Most travelers spend one night at the most in Porvenir before heading for the open countryside. A dirt highway runs along the barren slopes of **Bahía Inútil** (Useless Bay) for 90 km (56 miles) to **Onaisin** ❼, the original home of the Caleta Josefina *estancia*. Keep an eye out for the **Cementerio de los Gigantes**, (Cemetery of the Giants), a set of huge, regularly shaped stones scattered in the pampa. Just a couple of minutes farther south is the historic **Cementerio Inglés** (English Cemetery), where the British-born *estancia* workers were buried. In this windswept, forsaken spot are the graves of the few whites who fell to Amerindian arrows at the end of the 19th century.

Along the bay 50 km (31 miles) farther south is **Estancia Cameron** ❽,

BELOW: Porvenir, a long way from home.

founded in 1904. Nestled in a picturesque gully by the choppy gray sea, the farm's blue wooden buildings have not been altered for a century. Nor, it seems, have the methods of work: itinerant sheep shearers still crowd into a wooden shed during the December season and carry on their back-breaking trade as they did 100 years ago. In January and February, traditional sheep-shearing methods are also demonstrated here as part of rural tourism programs (more information from the Sernatur office in Punta Arenas).

Travelers with their own vehicles can continue along the road into the more remote, mountainous and rainy area of the island, taking their own fuel, food and camping gear, although lodging is available on some of the *estancias*. **Lago Blanco**, surrounded by Fuegian peaks, is considered the most beautiful in the far south of Chile. The highway then leads south, to the doorway of Chile's last *estancia*, **Vicuña** ❾. From here the road returns north along the frontier. A road from Vicuña to Yendegaia, 140 km (87 miles) south on the Beagle Channel, is being built and, by early 2004, approximately a third had been completed.

Across the border

Most travelers who come this far south will want to continue into the Argentine side of Tierra del Fuego. The easiest way is to head directly from Porvenir to the frontier at **San Sebastián**, then continue onward to **Río Grande**. This rough-and-ready oil town on the island's east coast is little more than a place to pass the night before continuing south.

On the southern coast of Tierra del Fuego, squeezed between dramatic mountain peaks and the blue Beagle Channel, is the island's largest and most attractively placed town, **Ushuaia** ❿. Its setting is majestic, with the wicked-looking granite peak of Mount Olivia dominating the skyline. Despite the often bitter weather, this is a popular resort town and base for exploring the area. Its energy and faith in progress sets it apart from other towns of the south, with new buildings being flung up everywhere amongst mud and twisted trees. As a result, there is little historical charm left in Ushuaia: the main street is like an open-air department store, with duty-free electronic goods on display from the new Japanese factories set up nearby.

Boat trips on the Beagle Channel pass islands crowded with sea lions and penguins, or scattered with the rotting remains of shipwrecked boats. And only an hour outside of Ushuaia is **Parque Nacional Tierra del Fuego**, which preserves the sense of being at the end of the world: paths wind over spongy moss oozing cold water, past tough shrubs, thorny bushes and trees that have grown bent 45 degrees with the prevailing wind.

A pleasant drive eastward along the Beagle Channel leads to **Estancia Harberton** ⓫, the first farm on the Argentine side of Tierra del Fuego set up by the missionary, the Reverend Thomas Bridges, in 1886. On a narrow peninsula surrounded by green meadows of bright flowers, the *estancia* is worth visiting as much for its serene beauty as its history. Guided tours are now offered in both English and Spanish. Across the

Ramshackle house, Porvenir.

BELOW: *centolla* (king crab) is a Fuegian specialty.

water are three obscure islands over which Chile and Argentina nearly went to war in 1978, until Pope John Paul II intervened and drew up a settlement.

Map on page 292

The most southerly settlement

While Ushuaia is the southernmost town of its size in the world, the title of southernmost permanent human settlement outside of Antarctica goes to Chile's **Puerto Williams ⑫** on Isla Navarino. Established in 1953 as a naval base, it can be reached by plane or ferry from Punta Arenas. The setting is, once again, magnificent and there are many walks in the unspoiled countryside nearby.

Isla Navarino was home to the native Yaghan people and was first visited by the *Beagle* on its maiden journey. The captain, Robert Fitzroy, took four young Yaghans back to England for education, and returned with them on the famous journey with Charles Darwin. The friendliest Yaghan was named Jimmy Button by the crew. He had learned some of the manners of an English gent, but on his return to Tierra del Fuego he quickly returned to his former Yaghan lifestyle. Fitzroy had hoped that Button would be a force for "civilizing" the Amerindians and converting them to Christianity, but the reverse proved true: two decades after his return, Button was to command attacks on the first European settlements in the area; he led the slaughter of several missionaries on Isla Picton and Isla Navarino.

Today, there are no full-blooded Yaghans, though a few *mestizos* live near Puerto Williams in a settlement called **Ukika**. The **Museo Martín Gusinde** (open Oct–Mar Mon–Thur 9am–7.15pm, Sat and Sun 2.30–6.30pm; Apr–Sept, Mon–Thur 9am–1pm and 2.30–6pm, Sat 2.30–6.30pm; free) in the naval township is considered one of the best in the south; it chronicles the sad tale of European settlement and the utter devastation of a unique culture. ❑

Some estancias *have been converted into fishing lodges in an attempt to develop a new tourist trade.*

BELOW: derelict boat on the Beagle Channel.

EASTER ISLAND

Chile's Polynesian possession, nearly 4,000 km west of the mainland, is one of the world's most intriguing islands, dominated by more than 600 giant stone statues of unknown origin

Map on page 318

The first inhabitants of Easter Island called their home Te Pito o Te Henua – the Navel of the World. Gazing down from one of the island's two volcanic crater rims, it is easy to see why. This tiny volcanic island, only 117 sq. km (45 sq. miles) in area, is almost lost in the endless blue of the Pacific Ocean. The nearest Polynesian island, Pitcairn, is 2,000 km (1,240 miles) to the west; the coast of South America is some 3,800 km (2,360 miles) to the east. The island has a maximum length of 24 km (15 miles) and width of 12 km (8 miles). Volcanic in origin, it has several dead craters dotted over its sparsely covered surface, two of which now contain freshwater lakes. The terrain on the treeless volcanic slopes is fairly grassy, but most of the island is covered in rugged lava fields. Dotted around the coast are hundreds of caves, which were once used as refuges (in times of war) or secret burial places.

Until 30 years ago, Easter Island was visited only once a year by a Chilean warship bringing supplies. But even though few people before the 1960s could make a personal visit, Easter Island has gripped the world's imagination for centuries. One baffling image made it famous: littering the island are hundreds of giant, tight-lipped basalt statues, unique in the whole of Oceania. The tiny island and its mysterious statues have presented us with one of the most fascinating archeological riddles of all time.

How did an early seafaring people find this remote speck in the Pacific Ocean? Where did they come from? How did they transport their enormous statues, carved from a quarry in the side of a volcano, to the coast and erect them on giant stone altars? And above all – *why* did they do so?

Today, regular flights from Santiago have broken the island's isolation. People visiting Chile have the chance to see this legendary site, marvel at the remains of an enigmatic Pacific culture and make up their own minds on the origin of the statues.

PRECEDING PAGES: mysterious *moai* at Rano Raraku. **LEFT:** *moai* Ko Te Riku, Ahu Tahai. **BELOW:** an actor depicts how an Easter Islander may have looked in prehispanic times.

Polynesian or American?

The long-standing assumption that the first Easter Islanders were Polynesians was thrown into doubt in 1947 when the Norwegian explorer Thor Heyerdahl sailed a balsa raft, *Kon-Tiki*, from Peru to Tahiti. The highly publicized journey showed that it was theoretically possible for a pre-Inca South American culture to have colonized the Pacific.

Heyerdahl went on to spend a year digging on Easter Island, and concluded in his best-selling book *Aku-Aku* that the first islanders actually came from the Peruvian coast, fleeing the destruction of the ancient South American empire of Tiahuanacu around Lake Titicaca in Bolivia. According to this theory, the seafarers brought with them a number of American

plants that are still found on the island (including the sweet potato and totora reeds) as well as their sun-worshipping religion and famous skills as stonemasons. Heyerdahl argued that they were eventually joined by a group of Polynesian settlers. The two groups lived in harmony until an eventual war finally destroyed the islanders of South American origin.

Most archeologists now discount the bulk of Heyerdahl's findings, although his groundwork is still valuable and makes stimulating reading. Nor do his theories seem so outlandish compared to an extraordinary rash of more recent claims. Crackpot visionaries have announced that the Easter Islanders were descendants of ancient Egyptians, interplanetary travelers, red-haired North Africans or even survivors of the lost continent of Atlantis.

The Long Ears and the Short Ears

The speculation has been fueled by the absence of historical records on the island. Almost all of the original islanders were wiped out by slave raids during the 19th century, so that by the time serious archeological work began in the 1980s the old culture was virtually dead.

According to those few surviving inhabitants who were first interviewed in the late 19th century, Easter Island was discovered by King Hotu Matua – a name meaning "prolific father" in Polynesian – who arrived on Anakena beach on the island's northern coast from a scorched land to the east. Tradition holds that 57 generations of kings succeeded Hotu Matua until the 1680s, during which time another set of ancestors arrived under a chief called Tuu-ko-ihu.

The legend goes that the two groups were divided between so-called "Long-Ears," who carved the *moai*, and the newcoming "Short Ears," who were kept

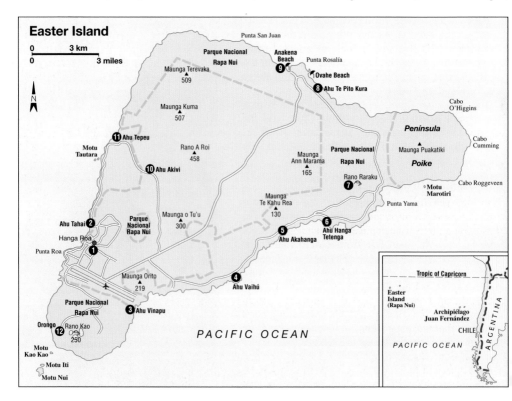

in an inferior class and helped in manual labor. Eventually the Short Ears rebelled and slaughtered all of the Long Ears bar one. Unfortunately, so many different versions of this story soon cropped up – mostly completely contradictory – that they only added confusion to research. Most investigators are now finding it safer to believe that none of the versions is authentic.

Orthodox opinion now holds that Easter Island was first populated before AD 500 by Polynesians coming from the Marquesas Islands, remaining in isolation until the arrival of Europeans. The bizarre culture was developed by the islanders themselves, who lived in a fairly egalitarian society dominated by small independent warring tribes. According to this view, 1,200 years of total isolation allowed the creation of a new language, of the famous statues that still preside over the island and of the only writing system known in all Polynesia and the Americas – the *rongo rongo* script. This conclusion is far from watertight and most visitors to Easter Island will want to decide the truth for themselves.

The first European contact

The first European to stumble across this speck in the Pacific Ocean was the Dutch Admiral Jacob Roggeveen. He and his crew landed and spent a day ashore on Easter Sunday, 1722 – and christened the island for the occasion. Roggeveen's log book tells how the party anchored off the mysterious island at dusk and were greeted by fair-skinned Polynesians, similar to those in Tahiti and Hawaii. Some had darker skins, the Dutchman wrote, while others were "quite white" like Europeans, with reddish hair.

Roggeveen records with awe that the *moai* were still standing, many up to 9 meters (30ft) tall, and with great cylinders on their heads. The inhabitants of

Map on page 318

Foundations of a hare paenga boat-shaped house at Ahu Tahai.

BELOW: the *moai* in this 18th-century European engraving look like European aristocrats.

the island, he wrote, "kindle fires in front of certain remarkably tall figures they set up; and, thereafter squatting on their heels with heads bowed down, they bring the palms of their hands together and alternately raise and lower them." The islanders kept up the ritual until dawn, when they praised the sunrise. Many of the worshippers wore long wooden plugs in their ear-lobes, lengthening them to their shoulders – a practice found in much of Polynesia and also among nobles of Peru, whom the *conquistadores* called *orejones* or "Long Ears."

The islanders lived in long, low huts of reed, that looked strangely like boat hulls turned upwards. Their lands were neatly cultivated, Roggeveen noted, and "whole tracts of woodland" were visible in the distance. Examining the *moai* closely, the Dutchmen decided that they were not of stone but were modeled from a strange clay stuffed with small stones. With that curious decision, the crew rowed back to their ships and weighed anchor.

After less than 24 hours on shore, they had decided that the islanders were friendly but expert thieves, pinching a few hats and tablecloths. A misunderstanding led to one Easter Islander being shot on board their boat, followed by another dozen being gunned down on shore, giving islanders an ominous taste of what European contact would bring.

Easter Island was given the name Rapa Nui *(Great Rapa) by Tahitian sailors in the early 1860s, as it reminded them of an island called Rapa near their home. That island is now known as Rapa Iti, or Small Rapa.*

The Spaniards, English and French

The island was left in peace for another 50 years before the arrival of a Spanish captain named Don Felipe González. In typical colonial Spanish fashion, he marched with two priests and a squadron of soldiers to a high point on the east coast, planted the cross and claimed the island for his king. The men of the island, he noted later, were naked except for feather headdresses, while women wore short cloaks around their breasts and hips. Don Felipe also observed with some interest that the islanders looked nothing like the Amerindians of South America, then recorded how he taught some to recite in Spanish, "Ave Maria, long live Charles III, King of Spain" before disappearing over the horizon.

BELOW: archeologists have always been part of the landscape.

Next came the renowned English navigator Captain James Cook, landing in 1774 after a journey through the Society Islands, Tonga and New Zealand. Cook had no doubt that the islanders were of Polynesian descent, although they seemed to be few in number and living in a miserable state. Little land was in cultivation. Meanwhile, dozens of the stone statues had been overturned, Cook found, and those that remained were no longer worshipped but used as burial sites. The scurvy-ridden Englishmen were forced to leave with nothing but a few baskets of sweet potatoes – although even then they were cheated, since islanders had weighed down the baskets with stones and laid only a few potatoes over the very top.

What had happened since the days of the Dutchmen's visit? Modern evidence confirms that serious environmental degradation was already well underway on Easter Island by the time of the Dutch visit in 1722: pollen samples show that the island was heavily forested when man first arrived in AD 500, yet there were no trees left by the beginning of the 19th century. Most writers now believe that the population of Easter Island had simply outgrown its resources. The food supply began to fail, the island's forests were felled and the soil began to erode. Without wood for canoes to escape the island, the tribes turned on one another in destructive wars: the giant statues were toppled and broken, while cannibalism became common. The resulting ruin is seen by many today as a taste in miniature of the Earth's own future, as the human race consumes the planet's limited resources with increasing voracity.

Map on page 318

The slave traders arrive

Easter Island's internal destruction pales into insignificance compared with the devastation finally wreaked by contact with the outside world during the 19th century. Whalers and slave traders put the island on their itineraries, bringing a series of tragedies to this hitherto isolated outpost.

Easter Island's Polynesian heritage is celebrated in the Tapati festival, held from late January to early February.

The most dramatic blow was the Peruvian slave raid of 1862. Early on Christmas Eve, strangers rowed ashore with brightly colored clothes and presents that enticed the islanders out to greet them. On a given signal, the slave-hunters attacked, tying up those who surrendered and shooting any who resisted. One thousand islanders were kidnapped, including the king and most of the learned men, to be taken to work on the guano islands off the coast of Peru – but not before the slavers celebrated Christmas on board with rum and salt pork.

Brutal conditions at the guano mine, starvation and epidemics had killed off 900 islanders before the Bishop of Tahiti was finally able to intervene on their behalf. Of the remaining hundred who set sail for their homeland, 85 died en route from smallpox. The handful who returned brought the plague with them: by the 1870s only 110 men, women and children were alive on Easter Island.

BELOW: the almost treeless landscape of the island.

Following this devastation came the first missionary to the island, Eugene Eyraud. Unsurprisingly, he met a hostile reception and was forced to flee – only to return two years later with reinforcements. Many of the islanders were converted to Christianity, however superficially, over the next few years.

Chile takes over

Spain may have claimed Easter Island for itself in 1770, but the Crown hardly bothered to maintain its claim. No other expeditions were sent to the island, and with the collapse of Spanish control of Latin America in the early 1800s, the way was left open for another colonial power to walk in and take over.

As part of its 19th century burst of expansionism, Chile annexed Easter Island in 1888. The republic wanted to show off its powerful naval force and show itself the equal of major European powers by grabbing a piece of South Pacific territory. Apart from the perceived prestige of such an acquisition, Chile saw the island as having valuable agricultural potential, and a gateway to Asian trade.

Few Chileans showed much interest in colonizing this new jewel in the nation's crown. The government found itself handing over control of the island to sheep-grazing companies – first a Chilean concern run by a Valparaíso businessman, then in the early 1900s to the British company Williamson and Balfour. The Liverpool-based company used the Compañía Explotadora de la Isla de Pascua (CEDIP), leased from the Chilean government, to manage the island, and made handsome profits until their license was revoked in 1953.

BELOW: island elder relates legends using string.

Islanders recall the company's rule as a time of dismal subjugation. They were effectively restricted to living in Hanga Roa, the island's only town, so that the rest of the island would be free for sheep to roam. Generally they were

Map on page 318

forced to work for little or no wages. It was during this period that immigrants interbred with the remaining few Easter Islanders, leaving little trace of the original inhabitants. Three-quarters of the population in the 1930s was of mixed descent, with everyone from North Americans to Germans and Tahitians living in Hanga Roa. Many years later, when news arrived that Thor Heyerdahl had floated a raft from Peru to Tahiti, several islanders made boats to stage their own escape. Some succeeded, and guards were posted to stop the exodus.

After 1953, the island's government was given to another authoritarian hand: the Chilean navy. The islanders suffered the same humiliations as in the days of the sheep company: the inability to vote, their local language suppressed and having to endure the navy's arbitrary and often absurd decisions.

The biggest change came in 1967, when the completion of the airport finally allowed flights from Tahiti and Santiago. The sudden possibility of large-scale tourism helped focus international attention on the island and the Chilean government was forced to make some improvements. During the 1970s and 1980s, better water supplies, electricity, a hospital and a school were installed. The most astonishing change to the island was the extension of its airport as an emergency landing site for the US space shuttle. Completed in 1988, the airstrip (considerably longer than Santiago's) has completed the Easter Islanders' transition from the Stone Age to the Space Age.

Native Easter Islander in festive costume.

If you walk around the outskirts of Hanga Roa you may encounter some unusual *moai* which bear a striking resemblance to some of the ancient megaliths found in Latin America. According to National Park staff, these *moai* were produced by the fertile imaginations of a Hollywood film crew, who designed them as props for the film *Rapa Nui*, which was shot on Easter Island in 1993. Produced by Kevin Costner, the film caused much controversy among archeologists and historians, who asserted that it presented a distortion of the facts and a crass ignorance of Polynesian ritual. On the other hand, one of the archeologists at the National Park praised the project for bringing economic wealth to the island, which has allowed many islanders to make improvements to their homes and hotels or to purchase vehicles.

BELOW: film extra takes a break.

Downtown Hanga Roa

Almost all visitors now arrive at the airport, on one of the two weekly (more in summer) Lan flights, and are greeted by their first glimpse of Easter Island's famous *moai* (statues). Rather small affairs compared to others on the island, the airport *moai* still provide a taste of the mysteries to come.

About fifteen minutes walk from the airstrip is the tiny township where Easter Island's 3,800 people all live, **Hanga Roa ❶**. Built around a few wide dirt roads, with thick, heavy palm trees hanging at regular intervals, the village looks like a classic South Pacific hideaway. The pace of life is relaxed, and a speed limit of 20kph (12mph) is imposed on the town.

There are a handful of large hotels on Easter Island, but many visitors prefer to stay in one of the small *residenciales* scattered about Hanga Roa. Reservations are not necessary – the owners crowd

around the airport gates after every arrival offering their prices. There are also some small restaurants, several bars, and no less than three discotheques.

It's impossible to get lost in Hanga Roa. Most of the amenities are near the harbor, and if you can't find something there's usually someone around to point you in the right direction.

Tourism is Easter Island's biggest industry, and many of Hanga Roa's inhabitants now make a living from selling wood carvings to travelers, endlessly repeating the same basic forms. The best known piece is also the ugliest: the *moai kavakava* or "statue of ribs." This human figure with a huge nose, ears and starved physique is said to have been first carved by King Tuu-ko-ihu. Apparently, the king was sleeping at the foot of a cliff when he awoke to find two ghosts staring down at him. He ran home and immediately carved their image, and islanders have followed the pattern ever since.

In search of *moai* and *ahus*

Each of the brooding *moai* was carved from the island's soft volcanic rock to the same general pattern (there are over 600 on the island: all with the distinctive heavy foreheads, pointed chins and (in all but a couple of cases) elongated ears. The hand position is typical of Polynesian carving, but the form of the figures is clearly unique. Their average height is around six meters (20 ft).

It is worth noting that while the *moai* are of the same standardized form, they all have slight differences. Most are male, but some are women with breasts and vulvas. While archeologists originally thought they were carved eyeless, it has been recently shown that the *moai* had eyes: the whites were made of coral and the pupils from the glistening black obsidian that can be found everywhere on

TIP

Food on Easter Island is moderately expensive and not particularly interesting, except for the fish and fruit juices, which tend to be excellent.

BELOW: painting event at the Tapati festival.

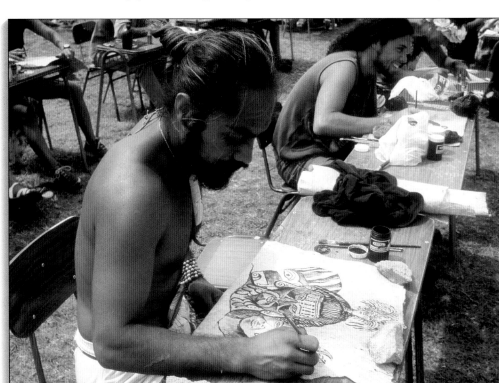

the island. Many *moai* also have "hats"– the red stone cylinders balanced on their heads that represent either hair or headdresses.

The island has 300 or so stone *ahus* or *moai* platforms (the name derives from a Polynesian root for "to pile up"). Many represent several stages of rebuilding to accommodate *moai,* while other *ahus* were buried and apparently never associated with statues at all. Bodies were buried in and around the *ahus.*

Exploring the island

While one or two archeological sites can be reached on foot, the best way to explore the island is on an organized tour or by jeep (the island has a couple of car rental outlets). Motorbikes can be hired by the hardy (anyone who doesn't mind bouncing over volcanic rock for several hours), as can horses (although these are often in poor shape) and bicycles.

Most hotel or *residencial* owners will provide information about island tours. Some of these tours are great value for money, with university-trained guides who will explain the orthodox history as well as discussing some of the wackier theories. The most important *ahus* can be covered in one day, and the rest are accessible on foot if you're fit, or in another day's tour. Certainly, if you want to visit all the sites on foot, you'd better bring a tent! Whichever mode of transport you choose, take plenty of sunblock, especially in summer, a good sun hat and a large supply of water – the tropical sun on Easter Island is notoriously fierce, yet the sea breeze can make the temperature seem deceptively cool.

One short stroll from Hanga Roa allows a pleasant introduction to what Easter Island has to offer. Starting from the small fishing port, follow the coast road north, away from the shops. On the outskirts of the village, a cemetery appears.

Map on page 318

BELOW: fierce "statue of ribs."

THE RONGO RONGO SCRIPT

As if enigmatic megaliths and intriguing legends were not enough, there is yet another Easter Island mystery that may never be solved: the strange inscriptions known as *rongo rongo* writing. Found on small wooden boards, this script contains 120 different figures based on bird man or human forms and is read alternatively from left to right then right to left. When outsiders first glimpsed the boards in 1865, none of the surviving islanders knew how to read them, the priests who understood them having perished after the Peruvian slave raids. Attempts by Russian and German experts to decipher the strange script have so far borne little fruit.

Nor do scholars agree on where the writing first came from. Guesses range from the Indus valley of Pakistan to the Andes. But other archeologists have begun to doubt whether *rongo rongo* is in fact prehistoric at all: since no similar pictographs are carved in stone elsewhere on the island, it is possible that the script is an emulation of European writing. *Rongo rongo* may have developed from observation of the Spanish treaty of annexation in 1770, possibly fixing chants into some concrete form – only to be forgotten as the island priests died in droves on Peru's guano islands.

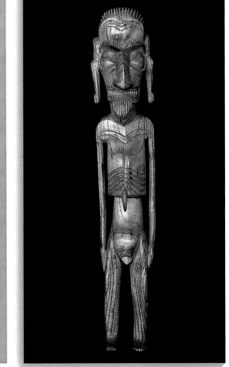

The missionary presence has ensured that the population is at least nominally Catholic, and one of the less well-known pleasures of Easter Island is visiting a mass service on Sunday and listening to the singing.

Just past the cemetery stands one of the most photographed archeological sites, **Ahu Tahai ❷**. Here, five statues stand in a row on their *ahu* with their backs to the sea. Like other *ahu moai*, they were knocked down, probably some time in the 18th century *(see page 319)*. The archeologist William Mulloy restored them to their rightful position in the 1960s; his grave is only meters from the site. You can also see the remains of ancient boat-shaped houses. This is a favorite spot at sunset, when the *moai* are silhouetted against a scarlet sky.

Just north of Ahu Tahai is the small **Museo Antropológico** (open Tues–Fri 9.30am–12.30pm, 2–5.30pm, Sat–Sun 9.30am–12.30pm, closed Mon; entrance fee). Exhibits include the *rongo rongo* tablets, *moai kavakava* figures and some wonderful late 19th/early 20th century photographs of Easter Island's original inhabitants.

The purpose of the moai

Archeologists generally agree that the *moai* were figures of deceased chiefs or gods. (A key piece of information recorded by George Foster on Captain Cook's 1774 visit was that the *moai* were often named after these dead heroes.) It has been suggested that, as the living conditions on tiny Easter Island became increasingly crowded and difficult, the island's inhabitants turned to carving these abstract cultural forms as a way to direct community energy and labor.

BELOW: the crater of Rano Kao.

Mounted on an *ahu*, the *moai* are believed to have transmitted *mana* or power to the living family chief. Sent through the statue's eyes, *mana* meant prosper-

ity in peacetime and success in war. At one point there were as many as 15 *moai* set up on any particular *ahu*, all glaring down from on high and sending *mana*, or power, to the family head. From this viewpoint, it is not difficult to imagine what effect a fully constructed *ahu* must have had on its family – as well as the utter devastation of morale when the family *ahu* was pulled down.

Map on page 318

An island circuit

Having had a taste of the most accessible *moai*, your appetite will be whetted for a day tour of the island. By heading east from Hanga Roa you can follow the general chronology of the island and gain an insight into how archeologists and historians have pieced together their theories on where the Easter Islanders came from, as well as how, why and when they carved their statues. In the process, you will probably see enough *moai* in one day to last a lifetime.

From the airport, follow the airstrip southeast, then turn right past an oil depot to reach **Ahu Vinapu** ❸ – probably the most important site in establishing the chronology of Easter Island. There are two *ahus* here, both of which once supported *moai* before they were toppled and broken – *moai* parts are scattered all around the site. The most famous *ahu* – known as Vinapu No. 1 – contains a wall of perfectly carved and fitted stone blocks that is strikingly similar to the walls at Tiahuanaco near Lake Titicaca, Bolivia, and some of the Inca walls around Cuzco. Not surprisingly, it is a key element in Thor Heyerdahl's argument that the Easter Islanders themselves originally came from South America. Vinapu No. 2 is a much rougher version of the same model *ahu*.

Moai at Rano Raraku.

Thor Heyerdahl's Norwegian expedition used Carbon 14 dating of fire remains and other materials near here to divide the island's prehistory into the Early Period (AD 400–1100), Middle Period (1100–1680) and Late Period (1680–1868). It appears that some *ahus* – including Vinapu No. 2 – were constructed in the Early Period, in the earliest centuries of human colonization, although their exact purpose is a matter of conjecture. The erection of the majority of *ahus* and *moai* belongs to the Middle Period; while the Late Period belongs to the bloody cannibal wars that probably resulted in the end of *moai* production and the destruction of the statutes and their *ahus*.

BELOW: "Fancy a spin?"

Heyerdahl found that the finely worked *ahu* of Vinapu No. 1 actually predated the cruder No. 2, supporting his argument that the first inhabitants of the island were skilled South American carvers. But later archeologists have reinterpreted the Norwegian expedition's findings to show that No. 2 came first. It is now generally believed that the masonry skills of the islanders improved over many generations and that Vinapu No. 1 is the climax of their own achievement, independent of developments in Bolivia or Peru.

The south coast

Continuing along the southern coast of the island brings you to the most striking examples of the Late Period's *moai*-toppling wars.

Ahu Vaihú ❹ is probably the most extraordinary sight along this stretch. Eight large statues have been pulled in a row from their *ahu*, looking rather forlorn

with their noses in the dirt and top-knots scattered. One of the *moai* has been completely shattered. Farther along, **Ahu Akahanga ❺** has four similarly humiliated statues, with another bunch scattered from a second *ahu* across a nearby estuary. The remains of a village have been found on the hill slopes opposite – the foundations of several boat-shaped houses can be seen as well as some round houses. Another site, **Ahu Hanga Tetenga ❻**, has been almost completely devastated and its two *moai* shattered.

The moai mine

From here, a dirt road runs inland toward the huge volcanic crater of **Rano Raraku ❼**. This so-called **Road of the Moai** is littered with more and more fallen giants before reaching the most impressive site on the island.

By far the most famous of the *moai* are the 70 standing sentinels embedded up to their shoulders in grass on the south slope of the volcanic crater. They lead the way to the quarry or "nursery" cut into the side of the impressive crater rim. This was where the *moai* were cut from volcanic tufa. Some 150 figures have been left there in all stages of completion, paying mute testimony to the unknown disaster that stopped all work dead in its tracks.

A trail leads straight up from the car park to the largest *moai* ever built – a 21-meter (69-ft) monolith. Leading off to the right, the trail comes to two other huge statues still part of the rock, while 20 or so more stand on the inside of the crater. A total of over 300 statues can be found around the area, apparently in the process of being cut or moved to *ahus* when work ceased.

Many obscure differences have been found in the *moai* of Rano Raraku. There are several female statues among the crowd of males, while others have

BELOW: *moai* at Tongariki beach.

unusual carvings on their flanks or backs. One figure displays a rough three-mast sailing ship on its chest. A line hangs from its bow to a round figure that may be an anchor or turtle caught on a fishing line. With a little imagination, the boat has been explained as either a European ship or a large totora reed vessel.

Also found buried at Rano Raraku by the Norwegian expedition was the unique kneeling statue, now found on the right slope of the crater, which looks like no other *moai*. Somewhat less than four meters (13 ft) high, it has a rounded head and face, as well as a beard and short ears.

Map on page 318

Carving from the rock

The remains in the quarry give very clear evidence on how the *moai* were originally modeled from the rock. Trenches were cut for the easy access of carvers, who chipped away until only the spine was left down the *moai*'s back. Eventually, the spine was severed and the statue was lowered by ropes to a temporary upright position on the slopes below, where it was finished off. The sheer fact that these figures up to 21 meters (69 ft) tall were cut from vertical as well as horizontal rock-faces testifies to the skill of the workers, while the number of broken statues on the slopes reveal the work's danger. The tools used to carve the *moai* were small basalt picks called *toki* – thousands of them have been found at the quarry.

Thor Heyerdahl's Norwegian expedition decided to find out how long it might take to carve a *moai* by commissioning a team of islanders to work on a statue at Rano Raraku. The incident is recounted in Heyerdahl's *Aku-Aku*: the then mayor of the island brought a family team to work non-stop for three days before giving up with fingers twisted from the work. But they had begun to

BELOW: crater of Rano Raraku.

make an impression and the experience suggested that it would take a skilled team between 12 and 15 months to carve a *moai* about four meters long (13 ft), using two teams constantly in shifts. But how did the islanders move the other *moai* to different parts of the island?

Making the statues walk

Following the coast road on to the north of the island gives you an idea of the enormous scale of the problem. Here is located **Ahu Te Pito Kura ❽** – at some 9.8 meters (32 ft) in length, it is the largest *moai* ever transported. The name means "navel of light" and the rock from which it was hewn is said to have been brought by Hotu Matua himself.

Heyerdahl was able to convince some 180 merry dinner guests to pull one 4-meter (13-ft) long *moai* across a field with ropes made from tree bark, showing that it was easier to move the statues than had first been expected. In *Aku-Aku* he suggested that a much larger statue could be pulled using more people and wooden rollers. Others suggested that small rocks could be used like marbles to move the statues. But these theories still seem unconvincing when faced with the size of Ahu Te Pito Kura and the ruggedness of the volcanic terrain around Rano Raraku.

The archeologist William Mulloy came up with a theory that has won widespread support. First a huge forked sled (made from the large trees that tests have shown once covered the island) would be attached to the front of each statue, tied into place over the protruding belly and stuck beneath the chin. This sled protected the statue from the ground and allowed it to be moved by leverage using a bipod. The statue's own weight could then be used to help move it along

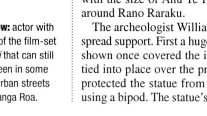

The moais' *"top-knots" were made from volcanic scoria quarried at the small volcanic crater of Puna Pau, a couple of kilometers east of Hanga Roa.*

BELOW: actor with one of the film-set *moai* that can still be seen in some suburban streets of Hanga Roa.

in a repetitive series of upward and forward movements. While hardly fool-proof (and there are numerous broken *moai* around the island), the method is at least possible. Curiously, the theory of short jerking movements recalls the islanders' own belief that the *moai* "walked" to their *ahu*.

Map on page 318

An experiment in ancient engineering

One more baffling mystery remains: once the statues had been moved by this painstaking method, how did the islanders then erect them – along with top-knots – onto their stone altars?

When the Norwegian expedition arrived in the mid-1950s, not one *moai* was at its post on an *ahu*. All lay where they had fallen centuries before, and nobody had even attempted to move them. Heyerdahl resolved to raise a *moai* using only the materials that would have been available to the original islanders. The lone statue now standing at **Ahu Ature Huki** on **Anakena Beach ❾** was the result of the experiment that put the first *moai* upright since they were toppled.

Having dragged the *moai* to the *ahu*, Heyerdahl's team carefully worked a series of long poles underneath the statue's stomach. Three or four men heaved at the end of each pole as another man, lying on his belly, slipped small stones underneath the giant's face. Slowly the statue began to rise from the ground, supported on this mattress of tightly packed pebbles. It took a dozen men working for nine days to get the statue on a 45-degree angle. Another nine days and it was almost upright. Finally, it slid with the guidance of ropes to a standing position. Raising a *moai* with a top-knot would have been done in the same fashion, Thor Heyerdahl argued, strapping the stone "hat" to the statue's head with ropes and poles.

BELOW: stone sentinels at Anakena Beach.

Wooden Christ figure, Hanga Roa Church.

Since that date many other *moai* have been restored to their *ahus*, as can be seen today. But it is still astounding to consider raising a statue on Ahu Te Pito Kura – with its top-knot it would have been a massive 11.5 meters (38 ft) tall. William Mulloy estimated that it would have taken 30 men one year to carve this *moai*, 90 men two months to move it 6 km (4 miles) from the quarry to the *ahu* and 90 men three months to erect it. Yet this pales in comparison with the 21-meter (69-ft) monolith still being cut in the quarry when work was abandoned.

These theories of how the *moai* were moved and raised also suggest why carving suddenly ceased at the Rano Raraku quarry: the Easter Island workers simply ran out of trees. Eighteenth-century explorers had reported the island's lack of timber. It seems likely that work was abandoned when there was no wood left to take the statues from their nursery to the coast.

Golden beaches

Only 100 meters away on the headland at Anakena is **Ahu Nau Nau** and seven more *moai*. But having viewed statues all day, it probably comes as a welcome relief to find that these last *moai* look over the white sands of **Anakena Beach**. This was the legendary landing place of Hotu Matua, the founder of the island. Many of the caves nearby are said to have been his refuge while waiting for a boat-shaped house to be built nearby.

BELOW: *moai restored to their positions at Ahu Tahai.*

But if you are in the mood for a swim after a hard day of *moai*-spotting, one small bay is even more appealing than the wider expanses of Anakena: nestled beneath a cliff of volcanic rock, **Ovahe Beach** must be one of the most beautiful on earth. Its sands are pure and golden, a match for any South Pacific paradise, and the water is so clear that you can count your toe hairs while swimming.

From here you also have a view of the **Poike Peninsula**. This area has a major place in local legend. When the "Short Ears" tired of working for their "Long Ear" rulers and rebelled, the Long Ears were said to have gathered on this peninsula behind the Poike trench. Filled with branches and tree trunks, the ditch was intended as a fiery defense rampart. But a traitor who was married to a Short Ear woman alerted the Short Ears, who slipped into the peninsula and surrounded the Long Ears, driving them into their own flaming ditch – where all but the traitor died.

Interestingly, while this had been considered a fable by most researchers, the Norwegian expedition found thick layers of charcoal and ash here. They were able to show that a great fire had occurred in the trench some 350 years before, suggesting that there may be some truth in the islanders' tales.

From here, the road through the center of the island leads past the old sheep *estancia* back to Hanga Roa. From the town you can make another excursion along the island's northern roads to sites like **Ahu Akivi ⑩** and **Ahu Tepeu ⑪**. These are interesting enough sites, but they offer few surprises to those who know the rest of the island.

Center of the "Bird Man" cult

A quite different excursion from Hanga Roa can be made directly south to the volcanic crater of **Rano Kau**. Instead of *moai*, its interest centers on a bizarre "bird man" ritual that flourished here among the original inhabitants. It is also without doubt the most visually spectacular spot on Easter Island.

A road and path run steeply upward from Hanga Roa through typical scrubby terrain. Without warning, the enormous crater of Rano Kau appears below. It's not hard to see why Heyerdahl described it as a "giant witch's cauldron." Filled with black water and floating green fields of totora reeds, its steep, 200-meter (656-ft) high wall is gently eroded on the seaward side to include a view of the Pacific. The ruined village of **Orongo** ⓬ is perched atop this breathtaking location, with the volcano on one side and sheer cliffs on the other, dropping some 400 meters (1,300 ft) down to the crashing sea. Scattered in the briny void are three tiny, craggy islands – Motu Kau Kau, Motu Iti and Motu Nui.

Orongo is now restored and part of a specially created national reserve. Entry costs US$11 at the ranger's office. The ancient village contains a range of 53 oval buildings, constructed in the 16th century, with their floors cut into the side of the slope. Walls were made from overlapping slabs of stone, with other large slabs meeting horizontally to make an arch. The entrances are small tunnels big enough for only one person to enter at a time. But the main attraction is a string of 150 "Bird Man" carvings on rocks on the edge of the cliffs: a man's body is drawn with a bird's head, often holding an egg in one hand.

Archeologists know a considerable amount about the Bird Man cult as its ritual was performed up until 1862, and survivors were able to describe it in detail to later investigators. The strange ceremony is linked to the supreme deity

Map on page 318

BELOW: the crater of Rano Kao.

Makemake, who is said to have created the earth, sun, moon and stars. Make-make rewarded good and punished evil, and for centuries was considered responsible for bringing the only visitors to the island from the outside world: an annual migration of sooty tern birds.

Begun in the warring period of the 18th century, the bird man cult may have been an esoteric attempt to direct tribal competition toward a peaceful course. It may also have symbolized a wish to escape from the increasing horror of confinement of the island.

The quest for the first egg

The basis of the bird man cult was finding the first egg of spring laid by the sacred *Manu Tara* bird, or sooty tern. The chief of each tribe on the island sent one chosen servant to Moto Nui, the largest of the islets below Orongo. Swimming across the dangerous waters, the unfortunate servants or *hopus* each spent about a month looking for the first egg while islanders gathered on the Orongo cliffs making offerings and prayers to Makemake. When the egg had been found, the successful *hopu* plunged into the swirling waters (with the egg apparently strapped to his forehead), swam to the mainland and climbed back up the cliffs to present the prize to his master.

The successful master would then be named the "bird man" for that year, an important status position. Strangely, the advantages which this office conferred are far from clear. The chief would have his head, eyebrows and eyelashes shaved, then his head painted red and black. His standing in the community would be increased, but for the whole of the following year he would remain in seclusion in a special house, presumably having gained the favor of Makemake.

BELOW: memories of the "birdman" cult" at Orongo.

A final verdict?

After visiting all the major sites and immersing one-self in the mystery of Easter Island, few visitors can resist making some sort of decision for themselves on the most debated question of all: did the first islanders travel from Polynesia or were they South American refugees as Thor Heyerdahl suggests, escaping in fleets of reed boats from the collapse of a magnificent Andean empire?

It is fair to say that modern archeological opinion weighs heavily against Thor Heyerdahl's dramatic interpretation. Peter Bellwood in his work *Man's Conquest of the Pacific* provides a fairly balanced summary of the latest research, arguing that while nobody can prove Heyerdahl 100 percent wrong, the chances of him being right are quite remote.

Firstly, the language of Easter Island – which is believed to have been spoken since before AD 500 – is completely Polynesian. Secondly, the skeletons found on the island are Polynesian – although they are all from the Late Period. Thirdly, there is no evidence that any portable artifacts dug up on the island came from South America, while many items are certainly Polynesian in style. Finally, the posture of the *moai* can be found in the art of Polynesia as well as in Tiahuanaco-style carving from South America, and may be a common inheritance from past millennia.

Map
on page
318

But there are some points on which Heyerdahl apparently has a case. The sweet potato and totora reed are South American plants and may have been introduced at a late date; and the stone house designs found on the island recall those of Peru. However, the most surprising piece of evidence for anyone who has visited Peru and Bolivia must be the close-fitting stonework of Ahu Vinapu 1, so strikingly reminiscent of Tiahuanaco and Inca work. Its date is set at around AD 600, within the classic period of Tiahuanaco culture.

Yet of the 300-plus *ahus* on the island, this is the only piece of stonework on the island that is uniquely reminiscent of a South American culture. So while a case for major South American migration cannot be made, it is not impossible that at some point people from Tiahuanaco visited Easter Island in the remote past.

The orthodox view of Easter Island's past can be summed up simply: Polynesian seafarers arrived between AD 400 and 500, slowly increasing in numbers and building their statues. As the centuries passed, the island's environment could no longer sustain them. They fought amongst themselves, destroyed their own achievement and left the rest of the world to puzzle over the ruins.

To some this may seem a little dull without the grand arrival of Incas or survivors of an unknown Atlantis carrying on their lost civilization. But, to quote Bellwood: "Is it not even more exciting that a group of isolated Polynesians could have evolved such a magnificent prehistoric record by using their own ideas, brawn and procreative ability rather than someone else's? Too many anthropologists in the past have held the view that all good things come from a very few areas, and that most of these areas were inhabited by Caucasoids... The peoples of Oceania deserve the credit for their achievements, not the peoples of some imaginary Mediterranean colonial enterprise". ❑

Dwarfed by a giant.

BELOW: "te pito o te henua" – the navel of the world.
OVERLEAF: sunset at Ahu Tahai.

INSIGHT GUIDES
Travel Tips

CONTENTS

Getting Acquainted

Total area: 756,626 sq. km (292,134 sq. miles)
Coastline length: 4,300 km (2,700 miles)
Capital: Santiago (population 5 million)
Population: 15.1 million, mostly *mestizo*; 690,000 of indigenous descent.
Language: Spanish
Religion: Roman Catholic
Currency: Peso ($)
Electricity: 220 volts
Weights and measures: Metric
International dialing code: 56 + 2 (Santiago)

Climate

As a general rule, Chile's climate makes a steady transition from the extreme arid heat of the desert north to the bitterly cold and wet conditions of the far south.

THE NORTH

Rainfall is virtually non-existent in the Atacama Desert. Typical desert conditions prevail all year round, with searingly hot days and chilly nights. High winds shift the desert sands and make northern highways more dangerous for motoring. The northern skies are generally very clear, although on the far northern coast, at Arica, there is higher humidity and frequent cloud cover. Temperatures here are less extreme, ranging from 15°C (59°F) to 22°C (72°F). At the same latitudes, towards the Bolivian border, snow often covers the high mountain passes.

CENTRAL VALLEY

The area known as the transitional zone, between Copiapó and Illapel, only receives light winter rainfall, and agriculture is therefore dependent on artificial irrigation.

Immediately south, the lush central region continues through to Concepción with higher inland temperatures and ever-increasing rainfall from north to south. The climate is idyllically Mediterranean, mild and temperate, the warmest months being November to February when the temperatures can reach 34°C (93°F). July and August are the coolest months, with temperatures as low as 10°C (50°F) during the day. Nights are rather cool, even in summer.

The best months in Santiago are between October and April when the days are nearly always fine – although December and January can be uncomfortably hot in the congested city center.

The summer heat is more tolerable on the coast at the famous seaside resorts, with fresh cooling breezes. The weather is excellent for skiing during the winter months at the resorts of Portillo, Farellones and Valle Nevado, east of Santiago.

LAKE DISTRICT

As far south as Puerto Montt, the Lake District has a temperate climate, although heavy rain falls throughout much of the year. The temperature is cooler than in the central region, and icy winds originate from the lakes and mountains. Winter brings snow to the chalet-style resorts in the higher regions of Petrohué, Puella and Lago Todos los Santos, and some Andean highways between Chile and Argentina can become snowbound or otherwise impassable due to fog and storms.

CHILOÉ

The islands of Chiloé are cold and foggy for most of the year, but for about 60 days, usually from December to March, when the sun shines, the countryside is especially picturesque. Chiloé is a particularly rainy place, especially along its western, Pacific coast.

AISÉN

South of Puerto Montt, the region of Aisén has a steppe climate with fairly low temperatures all year round. Abundant snow falls from early autumn to late spring, so the best months to visit are November to March. Summer brings beautifully crisp, clear days to the region, although cold winds and torrential rainstorms can also occur unpredictably. Worth noting is the agreeable microclimate found around the village of Chile Chico, which is suitable for growing fine fruit and vegetables.

MAGALLANES

In this region of glaciers and wilderness, snow covers the land in winter (except along the coastline), while rain is frequent in summer, and freezing winds of up to 80 kph (50 mph) are common in spring. The climate and scenery have been likened to that of Norway. It is best to visit the far south in December, January or February, when the sun is higher in the sky and the summer average temperature climbs to 11°C (52°F).

EASTER ISLAND

This isolated Pacific Island has a semi-tropical climate throughout the year, with a particularly fierce sun that is not to be underestimated. July and August are the coolest months for wandering among the *moai*.

Chile's economy is one of the most stable in South America, and living standards are among the highest in the region. The economy has benefited from mineral wealth since the mid-19th century. Chile was the first Latin American country to adopt a free-market economy, and from the mid-1980s to the mid-1990s GDP almost doubled. A policy of export-led growth, begun under Pinochet, has continued under subsequent democratically elected governments, which have signed important free-trade treaties with most other Latin American countries, Canada, the United States, the European Union, and South Korea. Chile's position on the Pacific coast means that trade with Japan, China, and the Pacific Rim is particularly important.

The rush for growth pursued by Pinochet has now been consolidated into a more balanced approach to the economy, in which housing, healthcare and education are given more attention. Increasing prosperity has reduced the number of poor, but not the gap between rich and poor.

Minerals, timber, fruit, farmed salmon and wine have been the major growth industries, with foreign investors encouraged in each sector.

Government

In the 1990s Chile returned to democratic rule after 16 years of military dictatorship under General Augusto Pinochet.

Democratic government was re-established after Pinochet lost a national referendum in 1988. Christian Democrat Patricio Aylwin succeeded the dictator as president in 1990, heading a center-left coalition that remains in power. Another Christian Democrat, Eduardo Frei, succeeded Aylwin in 1994.

Ricardo Lagos, a member of the Socialist Party, was elected president in 2000.

The full exercise of democracy is, however, still limited by a constitution that was drawn up by the dictatorship. This gives each branch of the Armed Forces a non-elected Senate seat, as well as depriving the Government of the power to remove military officials from their posts.

The changeover of power ending military rule was held on March 11, 1990. The event was marked by a large celebration in Santiago's Estadio Nacional (National Stadium), the same place that was used as a detention center for political prisoners by the military forces in 1973. The Congreso Nacional (National Congress) is located in the port city of Valparaíso.

Pinochet insisted on staying on as head of the army until 1998 when he took up the life Senate seat to which his regime's constitution entitled him. However, after he returned from arrest in London and the Chilean courts declared him unfit to stand trial on human-rights charges, he resigned from the Senate. In 2004 the Supreme Court stripped him of immunity to prosecution, opening the way for a trial.

Until 1998, the economy boomed, helping to ease the transition to democracy. Civilian rule is now firmly established, with its legitimacy boosted by an efficient bureaucracy and welcome social reforms.

Culture and Customs

Chilean literature is well represented on the world stage, with the successes of novelist Isabel Allende and playwright Ariel Dorfman following on the achievements of Nobel Prize-winning poets Gabriela Mistral and Pablo Neruda. Musicians such as the late celebrated pianist Claudio Arrau have also made their mark internationally, as have some film directors, such as Raúl Ruiz.

SANTIAGO

Urbanized Chileans enjoy shopping, dining, dancing and socializing.

Santiaguinos are justly proud of their fine arts and opera season, and they welcome international performers. The Teatro Municipal is the symbol of their artistic life.

Each Santiago barrio, or neighborhood, has its own flavor. For example, Bellavista holds the reputation as most bohemian, and the El Golf office area is considered one of the most exclusive.

Life in the city center can be decidedly hectic during the working week but, in the barrios, outdoor cafés are busy at all hours of the day. Promenading is popular: on weekends, if they're not strolling around the shops or lining up for the cinema, santiaguinos will be meandering through the parks. The Plaza de Armas is a popular venue for resting, strolling and watching open-air theater – especially at dusk, when the best amateur comedians, musicians and dancers perform. On any night, ice-cream vendors and pizza-sellers do a roaring trade, while portrait painters have more spectators than customers.

Metropolitan Life

About 40 percent of Chile's total population lives in Santiago's metropolitan region, the hub of the nation's commercial activity and a conglomeration of cultures.

INDIGENOUS CULTURE

After the Spanish conquest, many of the indigenous peoples of Northern Chile accepted the European Christian culture, but the Araucanians or Mapuches put up a strong resistance until the mid-19th century. Tourists may see the traditional dress, silver jewelry and straw huts of these people as they continue their rural existence in parts of the Lake District.

In the northern regions of Chile, descendants of the pre-Hispanic peoples of the Andes still play traditional instruments and celebrate religious dates with folkloric festivals. A religious figure is considered a protector of the village and is venerated with colorful masquerade dances.

Evidence of earlier cultures can be seen in the geoglyphs of Tiliviche, near Pisagua in the far north, and there are excellent collections of ancient artifacts in the Le Paige museum at San Pedro de Atacama *(see page 203)*.

Cowboy Culture

The **huaso**, or Chilean cowboy, still carries on traditions in distinctive dress on the farms and rural lanes of the south central valley. The guitar and harp provide lively accompaniment for the *cueca*, Chile's national dance, traditionally performed at the Media Luna rodeo. Traditional food and drinks, such as *empanadas* (savory turnovers filled with meat or cheese) and *chicha* (fermented grape juice) are served following the dancing.

Island Traditions

The inhabitants of **Isla de Chiloé** have a distinct local culture woven around an elaborate and beguiling mythology *(see page 273)*.

The Polynesian inhabitants of **Easter Island** in the Pacific are proud of their ancestry and culture, although much of the population is of Chilean descent, and their influence is increasingly strong.

Social Behavior

Chileans are nearly always interested and happy to welcome foreign tourists, especially in rural areas, where life is led at a more relaxed pace. Chileans have many idiosyncrasies. They have a passion for discussing politics. They are not as unpunctual as other Latin Americans, but are still likely to be half an hour late for social appointments. They are often concerned to show themselves as either "feminine" or "macho" and can seem painfully obedient to their children's whims.

Young men attract women's attention by hissing through their teeth – an irritating feature of daily life for young women walking alone (strangely, a hiss is not considered impolite when attracting a waiter's attention).

Youth

The majority of young people in Santiago meet at bars and cafés, and smoking is still very fashionable. Rock bands and Latin pop are heard almost everywhere. Nightlife starts very late; most discotheques don't open until 11pm and don't fill up until around 1am. Stifled sexuality is let loose by some in the darkened corners of the city parks, while many special hotels rent rooms by the hour.

Etiquette

Chileans have a warm but clearly defined way of greeting. Men and women meeting, or women greeting women, will kiss one another once on the cheek. Men greeting men will always shake hands. When dealing with officials, you'll find the response more agreeable if you say "*Buenos Días*" (Good Day), and wait for the reply before you continue speaking.

Planning the Trip

What To Bring

Chile is probably the most materially modern country in South America, with exhaustive shopping potential in Santiago, so if you forget to pack something, you'll probably be able to purchase it there.
• Beware: foreign books, including travel guide books in English, can be surprisingly expensive due to the sales tax, so take them with you.
• Clothing for all weathers is necessary if you plan to tour the whole country.
• Take a first-aid kit for travel to remote areas.
• Good camping and hiking equipment is available, but the range is limited and prices are high.
• A pocket knife or Swiss Army knife might come in handy, since fruit should be peeled, or at least washed, before eating.
• Take your driver's license if you plan to hire a road vehicle.
Other useful items: a small sewing kit, a water container for walking trips, sunglasses, aspirin (often desirable in areas of high altitude), swimming costume, and protective clothing for sports and boat trips.

Maps

Maps are available at the Santiago office of Sernatur, the national tourist board (Providencia 1550).
• The *Plano del Gran Santiago* (city map), which can be purchased at most newsstands, shows the city center and inner suburbs, and metro lines. Outside Santiago, Sernatur branch offices can supply free city maps.

• Addresses in Santiago can readily be found using www.mapcity.cl, a free website, from which maps can also be printed.
• The *Gran Mapa Caminero de Chile* is the most practical map of Chile – also available at newsstands.
• Excellent road maps are available from the Automóvil Club de Chile, Av. Andrés Bello 1863, Santiago.
• Turistel is the name of a series of Chilean guidebooks (in Spanish) which contain maps, details of accommodations ranging from campsites to hotels, and other tourist information.
• Gas stations sell road maps.
• Topographical maps are sold by the Instituto Geográfico Militar in Santiago (sales office: Dieciocho 369, tel: 2-460 6863).

What To Wear

Most middle-class Latin Americans spend a great deal of their income on their appearance. Travelers aren't expected to appear as immaculately groomed as residents; however, it's sensible, especially in Santiago, to take a little extra care. You might receive better service in some establishments if you dress more formally, or if your casual wear is fairly smart. If in doubt about the dress requirements, err on the formal side. Chileans are naturally conservative dressers.

Women in business generally wear skirts and high heels or smart trouser suits. Older business men mostly wear the standard tie and two-piece suit in all seasons, but smart casual has gained ground.

On the Road

If you are traveling extensively through Chile, take clothing that is most useful for all extremes of climate. Remember that southern Chile is as cold as the northern deserts are hot, so take warm socks, gloves, headgear and a wind and waterproof jacket. The ozone layer is particularly thin in the southern regions, so bring sunglasses, sunscreen and headgear. Thermal underwear will

come in handy if you're heading for southern regions such as the Paine National Park, Punta Arenas or Tierra del Fuego. Travelers often prefer to buy their woolen sweaters or ponchos from *artesanías* in Santiago or en route, since they are very reasonably priced and of high quality.

If you're trying to cut down on shoe luggage, take some solid walking shoes that won't look too out of place in a casual restaurant. Synthetic fabrics won't crush in your suitcase but these don't breathe as well in the hot weather. It's a good idea to use your hotel's laundering service, as cleaners tend to be less reliable and just as expensive.

Visas and Passports

All foreigners require a valid identity document. While residents of neighboring countries can use their Identity Card in Chile, all other foreigners require passports and a few of these must obtain visas. Countries requiring visas to enter Chile include: Russia, China, India and some East European, Arab and African countries. It would be wise to check on the current situation before departing. All foreigners wishing to work in Chile need visas.

A tourist card is issued to all foreigners on arrival. Visitors from some countries are charged an administration fee (United States, US$100; Canada, US$55; Australia, US$34 and Mexico, US$100), which must be paid in cash. The tourist card contains your identification data and is generally valid for 90 days. It is renewable for a further 90 days, though if you wish to stay longer than six months, it's simplest to take a short trip to an adjoining country and you will be issued with a new tourist card on your return. Renewal applications must be submitted personally at the Passport Office (Moneda 1342, Santiago, 2-tel: 697 0403), open Monday through Friday 8.30am–2pm. The card must be surrendered when leaving the country. Don't lose it.

Customs Regulations

During your flight you will fill out a customs declaration form and supply identity details on your tourist card. The allowed quota of duty-free goods extends to 400 cigarettes, 50 cigars, 2.5 liters of liquor, and all items for personal use.

It is prohibited to import meat products, flowers, fruit, vegetables and seeds. Most overseas visitors with "nothing to declare" find no delays in passing through customs. Chilean wine and finely crafted stones such as lapis lazuli are popular souvenirs.

Health

Chile is one of the safest countries in South America as regards health concerns. There is no malaria or yellow fever, the tap water in most cities is chlorinated, and the general standard of hygiene is high. The country is fortunate in producing an abundance of fresh fruit and vegetables in its Central Valley region while meat products are also plentiful, thus ensuring quality foods for most people.

Precautions

Most travelers go without vaccinations. Some people have hepatitis and typhoid shots, although the possibility of encountering these diseases is remote, as long as you avoid unwashed salads. The tap water in Santiago is safe to drink, although sensitive systems should use bottled mineral water and avoid the adjustment period.

Sudden changes in diet and lifestyle often cause temporary **bowel disorders**, which are rarely anything to worry about and just a typical part of travel. The best remedy is to eat very little and drink plenty of liquid in small sips for a day or so. Tea without milk or flat lemonade is ideal. Symptoms should improve within 48 hours. If the problem lasts longer than a week, antibiotics or a visit to the doctor may be necessary.

Pharmacies in Chile are usually well stocked with the latest medical supplies, and most products are available without a prescription. There are also increasingly popular homeopathic outlets in most cities.

Hot and Cold

The only other problems come from Chile's extreme climate and geography. In the Atacama Desert and on Easter Island, the heat can cause serious **exhaustion** and **sunburn**. Don't over estimate your skin's resistance. Bring sufficient water, sunscreen, a hat and preferably sunglasses, too. Even thus prepared, the sun and heat can be trying to the mildest of temperaments. Take things slowly and don't expect to achieve as much as usual.

In the far south, from Puerto Montt to Tierra del Fuego, the bitter cold in mountain areas and at all altitudes in winter can cause **hypothermia** to those who are unprotected: symptoms include exhaustion, numbness, slurred speech and shivering. High winds are notorious in Patagonia, often carrying icy rain and sleet, so bring protective clothing to cover your head and body. Again it's best to move more slowly, staying aware of your energy level. Mountain climbers should take the usual precautions.

Altitude

Though not as severe as the altitudes of Bolivia or Peru, some popular sightseeing spots in the north, and some Andean passes between Chile and Argentina, are high enough to cause slight **altitude sickness** in some people. The symptoms can become noticeable from around 900 meters (3,000 feet), and include shortness of breath, headache, weakness and mild nausea. Aspirin is one of the best remedies for mild altitude sickness. In rare cases, severe altitude sickness is indicated by dizziness and intensity of the other

Insurance

All travelers should invest in comprehensive travel insurance, which is available through travel agents. Check that this will cover the cost of your return flight if you're flown home in an emergency, as well as covering stolen or damaged valuables.

symptoms. The immediate treatment for this condition is to move to a lower altitude.

Money Matters

Money can be exchanged in hotels, exchange bureaux (casas de cambio) and banks. The rate varies little between establishments, although it might not be quite as good at hotels. Banks are open to the public Monday through Friday 9am–2pm. If you have a credit card, cash can be withdrawn from ubiquitous automatic cash machines, which also take most bank cash cards.

Casas de Cambio

If you don't have a credit card, exchange bureaux are probably the best choice. They are usually found within travel agencies and are open Monday through Friday 9.30am–2pm and 3.30–5.30pm. In Santiago, exchange offices and banks are located mostly in the central business district and Providencia, but there are also exchange offices in the main shopping malls. Banks, exchange offices and hotels will change dollar travelers' checks, and some shops and restaurants also accept them. Money can be sent to major banks from other parts of the world with minimum delays.

US dollars are the most easily exchanged unit of currency throughout Chile. In Santiago, it's possible to exchange pounds sterling, Australian dollars, yen and other currencies at banks, but elsewhere you'll need either US dollars cash or travelers' checks from a major company like American Express or Thomas Cook.

Public Holidays and Festivals

Chile's annual calendar of national holidays consists mainly of religious and folkloric festivals.

January

Año Nuevo en el Mar (1st)
Outdoor new year celebrations, Valparaíso.
Fiesta de San Sebastián
Catholic festivity in Yumbel, south of Chillán.
Semanas Musicales de Frutillar
Classical music festival on the shores of Lago Llanquihue.
Festival Folklórico de San Bernardo
Folkloric music festival, Santiago.
Open-air Theater Season
Different parks in Santiago.

February

Muestra Cultural Mapuche
Traditional music and dancing of the Mapuches, Lago Villarrica.
International Song Festival
Viña del Mar.
Semana Valdiviana
A week-long festival on Valdivia's Calle-Calle River.
Regata de las Mil Millas
Thousand mile-long nautical race starting from Viña del Mar.

April

Campeonato Nacional de Rodeo
Chilean rodeo championships, Rancagua.
Fiesta de Cuasimodo (Easter)
Religious and folkloric festival, Santiago.

May

Labor Day (1st)
National Holiday (21st)
Commemoration of the Iquique naval battle during the War of the Pacific.

June

Inauguration ceremony for Central Chile's ski season. Locations vary.

July

La Tirana (16th)
Native and religious festivity east of Iquique.

Festival Folklórico de la Patagonia
Folklore festival, Punta Arenas.
Industrial and craft fair
Punta Arenas.

August
Ascension of the Virgin Mary
(15th) National holiday.
Santa Rosa de Lima Celebration
Pelequén, near San Fernando.

September
Independence Day (18th)
National holiday.
Armed Forces Day (19th)
National holiday, military parade.

October
Columbus Day (12th)
National holiday.

November
All Saints Day (1st)
National holiday.
**Latin American Craft and
Artisan Exhibition**
Parque Bustamante, Santiago.
National Book Fair
Estación Mapocho Cultural Center,
Santiago.

December
**Feast of the Immaculate
Conception** (8th)
National holiday
Fiesta de la Virgén de Andacollo
(23rd–27th)
Religious festivity near La Serena.
Christmas Day (25th)
National Holiday.

Getting There

BY AIR

It's possible to fly direct to Santiago
from the United States and Canada.
Alternatively, many travelers going
to Chile take the opportunity to fly
via one or more South American
country. US airlines fly from New
York, Miami, Dallas, Atlanta and Los
Angeles. Air Canada flies from
Montreal, Toronto and Vancouver.
Chile's excellent airline, Lan, has
several flights nightly to major US
cities, as well as to Spain and
Germany and operates reciprocal
arrangements with many leading

international airlines. European
airlines serving Chile include Air
France, Iberia and Lufthansa, each
offering several flights per week,
while other European airlines have
connections via Buenos Aires.
   Other South American airlines ,
including Varig, and Avianca, also fly
to Chile from Europe with
connections in Rio de Janeiro,

Buenos Aires, Caracas and Bogotá.
From Santiago, there are regular
Lan flights to most major Latin
American destinations and the
airline also has a service to Tahiti
via Easter Island.

UK Travel Agents
In the UK, tickets can also be
obtained through specialist travel

Lan International Offices

ARGENTINA
Buenos Aires: Cerrito 866
Tel: (54-11) 4378 2200.
Córdoba: Cólon 564
Tel: (54-11) 425 3030.
Mendoza: Rivadia 135
Tel: (54-11) 425 7900.
AUSTRALIA
64 York Street, Sydney.
Tel: (61-2) 9244 2333.
BOLIVIA
La Paz: Edificio 16 de Julio,
Of. 104, El Prado
Tel: (591-2) 235 8377.
Santa Cruz: Libertad 144,
Tel: (591-3) 334 1010.
BRAZIL
Sao Paulo: Rua da Consolaçao
247, 12º andar, Conj. B
Tel: (55-11) 2121 9000.
Río Janeiro: Rua da Assembléia 92
Tel: (55-21) 2220 9722.
COLOMBIA
Calle 100 No. 8 A-49, Torre B,
piso 7, Of. 708, Bogotá.
Tel: (57-1) 611 1533.
DOMINICAN REPUBLIC
Av. George Washington 353, Edificio
ET Heinsen, Santo Domingo.
Tel: (1809) 689 2221.
ECUADOR
Quito: Av. Amazonas y Psj. Guayas
E3-131.
Tel: (593-2) 299 2300.
Guayaquil: Galerías Hotel Hilton
Colón, Corner of Malecón 1400
and Illingworth.
Tel: (593-4) 269 2850
GERMANY
Liebfrauenstrasse 1-3+60313,
Frankfurt.
Tel: (49-69) 298 00133.
MEXICO
Mexico City: Ignacio Ramírez 20,
Of. 302.

Tel: (52-55) 5566 5211.
Cancún: International Airport.
Tel: (52-98) 848 236.
NEW ZEALAND
Level 16, Price Waterhouse Crt.,
66 Wyndham St, Auckland.
Tel: (64-9) 309 8673.
PARAGUAY
15 de Agosto 588-602,
Asunción.
Tel: (595-21) 491 784.
PERU
Av. José Pardo 805, piso 5,
Miraflores, Lima.
Tel: (51-1) 213 8200.
SPAIN
Madrid: Leganitos 47, Edificio
Compostella, piso 1,
Plaza España, Madrid.
Tel: (34-91) 902 112424.
Barcelona: tel: (34-93) 902
194694.
Bilbao: tel: (34-94) 464-0922.
TAHITI
Centro Comercial Vaima,
piso 2, BP 1350, Papeete
Tel: (689) 426 455.
UNITED STATES
Miami: 9700 South Dixie Hwy.
11th floor, Miami, Florida 33156.
Tel: (1-305) 670 9999.
New York: 630 5th Avenue,
Suite 809, NY 10111.
Tel: (1-718) 751 4580.
Los Angeles: 1960 East Grand Av.
St 520, El Segundo CA 90245.
Tel: (1-310) 416 9061.
URUGUAY
Colonia 993, piso 3,
Montevideo.
Tel: (598-2) 902 3881.
VENEZUELA
Av. Francisco de Miranda, Edificio
Parque Cristal, Caracas.
Tel: (58-212) 284 1211.

firms such as Journey Latin America (tel: 020-8747 3108), Cox & Kings (tel: 020-7873 5000) and South American Experience (tel: 020-7976 5511).

From Australia
The most direct route from Australia or New Zealand is the Lan flight from Sydney with a stopover in Auckland – three flights weekly. It is also possible to combine this route with a stop at Easter Island en route to Santiago. Qantas also flies to Santiago via Auckland.

Vegetarians

Non-meat eaters may face some problems when traveling with Latin American airlines. Lan provides attractive vegetarian meals – options excluding dairy products are also available – on 48-hour request. Other major airlines provide similar facilities, but smaller operators are less reliable, even if you make arrangements in advance.

BY RAIL

International rail travel is infrequent and sparse. The Ferrocarril de Antofagasta a Bolivia (www.fcab.cl) is primarily a freight carrier, but runs a weekly passenger service from Calama in northern Chile to Oruro in Bolivia.

Practical Tips

Telecommunications

International Calls
Calls overseas can be made direct from public telephones and from call centers. You must prefix the code of the carrier you want to handle your call – there are 18, but the largest – although not necessarily the cheapest – are Entel (its code is 123) and CTC (181). It is possible to call collect and the quality of the lines is excellent. Off-peak rates apply after 9pm on weekdays, after 2pm on Saturday and all day on Sunday.

Faxes
Faxes are easy to send, although there is an added charge on most public fax services, which can make it quite expensive. Available at Entel and CTC call centers, in most large supermarkets, some service stations and at photocopy shops.

Telegrams
These can be sent through a private company, Chilexpress (tel: 800-200 102). A telegram to the UK takes three to four days.

E-mail
Chilean cities and towns of any size have cybercafés and other places that provide public access to e-mail. Shopping malls and some cinemas in Santiago have Internet centers and most hotels from the medium-price range upwards have connections for guests. WiFi is also available at some large hotels, restaurants, shopping malls, and in Santiago's airport.

Cybercafés come and go. Check the latest venues, either by asking at the local tourist office, or by referring to the up-to-the-minute information posted on www.netcafeguide.com

Media

Broadcast
There are many AM and FM radio stations and seven television stations currently broadcasting in the country. The radio stations play mostly rock and pop music. As you would expect, the popular stations, such as Pudahuel, concentrate on Spanish-speaking singers and groups, while their up-market competitors offer a more international variety. Only three stations – Radios Beethoven, Universidad de Chile and Universidad de Santiago – regularly broadcast classical music. For news bulletins, try either the popular Cooperativa, a stalwart that goes back to the dictatorship days when it dared say things that other stations didn't, or Radio Chilena.

If you're out in the country, listen to the local radio stations. In remote areas, people use them to keep in touch and you'll get an interesting insight into local life.

Opening Times

- **Banks** are open to the public Monday through Friday 9am–2pm. Exchange bureaux are open Monday through Friday 9.30am–2pm and 3.30–5.30pm, except in the main shopping malls where they open until 9pm and at weekends.
- **Government offices** are usually open to the public only in the mornings (8.30am–1.30pm). Other businesses are open 8.30am–1.30pm and then 3–6pm, Monday to Friday.
- **Most shops** in Santiago are open 10.30am–7.30pm Monday to Friday and 9.30am–1.30pm on Saturday. In the major shopping centers, such as Parque Arauco and Alto Las Condes, shops are open throughout the week, including on Sunday, until 9pm.

Tourist Offices (Sernatur)

Ancud: Libertad 665, tel: (065) 622 665.
Antofagasta: Prat 384, piso 1 tel: (055) 451 818.
Arica: Prat 375, piso 2, tel: (058) 232 101.
Chillán: 18 de Septiembre 455, tel: (042) 223 272.
Concepción: Bdo. O'Higgins 650, Of. 603, tel: (041) 741 416; Aníbal Pinto 460, tel: 741 337.
Copiapó: Los Carrera 691, tel: (052) 212 838.
Coyhaique: Bulnes 35, tel: (067) 231 752.
Iquique: Serrano 145, piso 3, Of. 303, tel: (057) 427 686.
Isla de Pascua (Easter Island): Tu'u Maheke, esq. Apina, tel: (032) 100 255.

La Serena: Prat, esq. Matta, piso 1, tel: (051) 225 138.
Osorno: Edificio Gobernación piso 1, tel: (064) 234 104.
Puerto Montt: Av. X Región 480, piso 2, tel: (065) 259 615.
Punta Arenas: Waldo Seguel 689, tel: (061) 248 790.
Rancagua: Germán Riesco 277, Of. 11 & 12, tel: (072) 230 413.
Santiago: Av. Providencia 1550, tel: (02) 731 8331.
Talca: Uno Poniente 128 1, tel: (071)233 669.
Temuco: Bulnes 586, tel: (045) 211 969.
Valdivia: Prat 555, tel: (063) 342 300.
Viña Del Mar: Av. Valparaíso 507, Of. 303, tel: (032) 882285.

Print

Chile has eight main national newspapers, as well as around 50 provincial dailies. One of the most widely read is the conservative morning daily *El Mercurio*, which first appeared in 1827. Every Thursday it publishes a supplement called *Wikén* (weekend), which provides information about events in Santiago.

Other newspapers include *La Tercera* and *La Nación*, as well as two business newspapers, *Estrategia* and *El Diario Financiero*. An afternoon paper, *La Segunda,* circulates in Santiago.

Weekly magazines include *Qué Pasa* and *Ercilla*, while *Newsweek* and *Time* are readily available in Spanish and English. In central Santiago's Paseo Ahumada, newsstands offer a wide variety of slightly out-of-date international newspapers.

Postal Services

The Chilean postal service is more reliable than that of most South American countries. Mail sent by air *(por aéreo)* takes around four days to the US and United Kingdom or 10 days to Australia. Sea mail takes about 10 weeks. There is a daily air mail service to Europe with connections to the United Kingdom.

The general delivery service, or poste restante *(Lista de Correos),* is located in the Correo Central (central post office) on the Plaza de Armas, in Santiago. The system is fairly well organized, although they will hold your mail no longer than 30 days before returning to sender. Opening times vary, but most are open Monday to Friday, 9am to 6pm and on Saturday morning. No offices are open on Sunday.

Embassies and Consulates

The following addresses are all in Santiago:

Argentina
Miraflores 285
Tel: 582 2500.
Australia
Isidora Goyenechea 3621, pisos 12 y 13
Tel: 550 3500.
Bolivia (Consulate only)
Av. Santa María 2796
Tel: 232 8180.
Brazil
Alonso Ovalle 1665
Tel: 698 2486.
Canada
Nueva Tajamar 481
Torre Norte, piso 12
Tel: 362 9660.
New Zealand
El Golf 99, Office 703
Tel: 290 9802.
Peru
Av. Andrés Bello 1751
Tel: 235 6451.
South Africa
Av. 11 de Septiembre 2353 piso 16
Tel: 231 2862.
United Kingdom
El Bosque Norte 0125
Tel: 370 4100.
United States
Av. Andrés Bello 2800
Tel: 232 2600.

Medical Treatment

The Chilean national health service is generally of a reasonable standard. Hospitals have out-patient departments, which will treat visitors' accidents and emergencies, but are likely to be much busier than private clinics. Ask your embassy or hotel to recommend doctors who speak English.

Many pharmacies remain open until midnight and some operate round-the-clock. Ask your hotel for a list of addresses.

Clinics in Santiago

For a private clinic contact:
• Clínica Las Condes, Lo Fontecilla 441, tel: 210 4000
• Clínica Santa María, Av. Santa María 0410, tel: 461 2000
• Clínica Alemana, Av. Vitacura 5951, tel: 210 1111.

Emergencies

For any emergency services, call the following numbers:
Ambulance Service: 131
Fire Brigade: 132
Police: 133/134
Police Information: 139
Tourist Card Extension: Passport Office, Moneda 1342, tel: (02) 96 0403. Hours: 8:30am–3pm, Monday to Friday.

Getting Around

From the Airport

Arturo Merino Benítez International Airport (tel: (02) 690 1752) is 26 km (16 miles) west of central Santiago.

Porters are available to assist you with your luggage. A respectable tip for this service would be about US$0.50.

If you're traveling by taxi, fix the fare with the driver before starting out. Alternatively, you can use the regular airport shuttle service, which will take you to most destinations within the city.

The major car rental firms all have offices in the airport terminal.

Domestic Travel

Domestic travel in Chile is surprisingly comfortable considering the country's difficult topography. The easiest, most convenient mode of transport is the airplane. The popularity of flying has kept services growing and prices competitive.

The quality of the main highways enables fast and comfortable long-distance bus services as well as problem-free private transport. In the far south, where the roads end, ferry services cover most of the important tourist destinations. The long thin shape of the country makes planning an itinerary quite straightforward.

Domestic Airlines

Flying long distances in Chile can be no more expensive than the sum cost of coach travel and accommodations, and very cheap if you take advantage of last-minute offers. **Lan** and its subsidiary **LanExpress**, as well as **Sky Airline**, operate domestic flights.

Lan has a **national booking service** on 600 526 2000 (from anywhere in the country). For Sky Airline, call 600 600 2828 (also from anywhere in the country). Lan has offices in most large towns, but attends telephone enquiries or bookings only through its national number. It also has a reliable Internet booking service (www.lan.com), with tickets for pick-up at the airport on presentation of identification.

To Juan Fernández Islands

Two airlines offer flights to Isla Robinson Crusoe:
• Transportes Aéreos Isla Robinson Crusoe, Av. Los Pajaritos 3030,

In Santiago

Santiago's city center, especially between the Plaza de Armas and the Alameda, is incredibly hectic and congested during the working week – you'll find yourself tiring very quickly. The most pleasant time to stroll around Santiago is in January and February, when the city empties for the summer holidays, although it gets hot at this time, so don't plan to do too much.

office 604, Santiago, tel: (02) 531 4343.
• Lassa, Av. Larraín 7941, Santiago, tel: (02) 273 5209.

To and Within Aisén

Lan flies from Santiago to **Coyhaique** and **Balmaceda**, generally with a stop-over in Puerto Montt. In addition, shorter routes within the region are covered by a number of smaller companies, including Aeromet, Aeropuelche, and Don Carlos:
Coyhaique:
Don Carlos, tel: (067) 231 981.
Chaitén:
Aerosur, tel: (065) 731 228.
Aeropuelche, tel: (065) 253 219.
Puerto Montt:
Aerosur, tel: 252 523.
Aeropuelche, tel: (065) 731 800.
Don Carlos, tel: (065) 252 523.

Airline Reservations in Santiago

• **Aerolíneas Argentinas**, Moneda 765. Tel: (02) 639 5001.
• **Air France**, Alcántara 44, piso 6 Tel: (02) 290 9300.
• **Air New Zealand**, Av. 11 de Septiembre 1881, Of. 713. Tel: (02) 376 9039.
• **Alitalia**, Av. El Bosque Norte 0107, Of. 21. Tel: (02) 378 8230.
• **American Airlines**, Huérfanos 1199. Tel: (02) 679 0000.
• **Avianca**, Isidora Goyenechea 3365, Of. 1201. Tel: (02) 270 6600.

• **British Airways**, Ebro 2743, Of. 1. Tel: (02) 330 8600.
• **Air Canada**, Av. Andrés Bello 2687, piso 16. Tel: 337 0022.
• **Iberia**, Bandera 206, piso 8. Tel: (02) 870 1070.
• **Japan Airlines**: Av. Isidora Goyenechea 2934, Of. 301. Tel: (02) 232 9561.
• KLM, San Sebastián 2839, Of. 202. Tel: (02) 233 0991.
• TACA, Dr. Barros Borgoño 105, piso 2. Tel. (02) 235 5500.
• **Lan**, Av. Américo Vespucio 901. Tel: (02) 526 2000.

• **Lloyd Aéreo Boliviano**, Moneda 1170. Tel: (02) 688 8680.
• **Lufthansa**, Moneda 970, piso 16. Tel: (02) 630 1655.
• **Qantas**, Isidora Goyenechea 2934, Of. 301. Tel: (02) 232 9562.
• **Swissair**, Barros Errázuriz 1954, Of. 810. Tel: (02) 940 2910.
• **Delta Air Lines**, Isidora Goyenechea 2939, Of. 601. Tel: 800 202 020.
• **Varig**, Av. El Bosque Norte 0177, piso 9. Tel: (02) 707 8000.

In Magallanes

The airline DAP connects Punta Arenas to destinations on Isla Tierra del Fuego and in the Argentine Patagonia.
- Punta Arenas:
tel: (061) 223 340.
- Puerto Williams:
tel: (061) 621 051.
- Porvenir: tel: (061) 580 089.

By Bus

Chilean bus companies provide comfortable conditions for long-distance travel. The routes are well-served, so you rarely need to book more than a few hours in advance, and the cost is low. There is no shortage of international services, and the journeys, especially through the Lake District, are scenically spectacular. From Argentina, there are quite a number of overland routes – the popular journey from Buenos Aires to Santiago takes about 24 hours. The crossing from Peru goes from Tacna to Arica in the far north of Chile. From Bolivia, buses take the road from La Paz to Arica.

Chile is probably the easiest and most comfortable place in South America for bus travel. The vehicles are well maintained, clean – except for the rest rooms – and comfortable. They always depart on schedule, refreshments are provided on board and smoking is prohibited.

For long trips, you have the luxurious option of traveling on a bus cama (sleeper bus), with first class seating arrangements – reclining seats with lots of leg-room. These buses are very comfortable and include meals and wine, color TV, stereo headphones and hostess service.

Make sure that you do not lose your token for any baggage placed under the bus.

Santiago Bus Stations

There are four main bus terminals in Santiago managing nearly all international and domestic traffic. Most international bus companies depart from the Terminal de Buses Santiago, Av. B. O'Higgins 3848.

However, buses bound for Mendoza in Argentina depart from the Terminal de Buses Norte, San Borja 184, commonly referred to as the Terminal San Borja.

International bus companies include Tas Choapa, Cata and Tur-Bus. Some make the epic three-day journey to Río de Janeiro via Mendoza and Sao Paulo.

There are also colectivos (communal taxis) to Mendoza, departing from the Terminal de Buses Santiago.

The main bus companies, which cover most domestic destinations, are:

Tur-Bus: Bookings can be made to all destinations on (02) 270 7400 or at offices around the city (including the Universidad de Chile and Tobalaba metro stations). When booking, make sure to ask from which station your bus leaves.

Pullman Bus: tel: 800 320 320. This company also has offices in the Universidad de Chile, Pedro de Valdivia, Los Leones, and Tobalaba metro stations. Again, ask from which station your bus will depart.

By Rail

Sadly, rail travel in Chile is a shadow of its past glories. The remaining services cover only destinations between Santiago and Temuco in the south. There are no services to the north or the coast. All trains leave from Santiago's Estación Central.

However, the state railway company, Empresa de Ferrocarriles

Night Buses

Nearly all long-distance buses in Chile are equipped with TV/video screens, so unless you really enjoy watching beauty contests and violent films, remember to bring a good pair of earplugs. An even more unfortunate fact for travelers who enjoy watching the scenery, and who prefer a bed to the most luxurious reclining seat, is that nearly all long-distance buses in Chile travel during the night.

del Estado (EFE), has recently made considerable improvements to these remaining services, which are an option worth considering when traveling south. The dormitorios (sleeping cars), available on some night services, are wood-paneled jewels from the past, as are the dining cars, which serve pricey, but reasonably good meals. In non-peak periods, the train is even cheaper than the bus if you choose the salon, which has coach-style reclining seats. Económico is the cheapest class and not so comfortable, especially in winter.

Train timetables can be obtained and bookings made by phoning: tel: (02) 376 8500 or calling at Estación Central, Av. B. O'Higgins 3170, daily 7am–10.30pm or at the railway office in the Universidad de Chile metro station (tel: (02) 688 3284), Monday through Friday 9am–8pm and Saturday 9am–2pm.

Illegal Products

It is illegal to transport any type of seafood on buses. The officials of SAG (the Ministry of Agriculture) conduct rigorous searches at all international borders and several regional borders and, depending on the area of the country, may confiscate fresh fruit, vegetables and artisan dairy products. SAG checkpoints are clearly marked on road maps.

By Boat

Puerto Montt to Puerto Chacabuco

- Navimag operates a regular roll on–roll off ship, which, once a week in summer, makes a detour to the San Rafael glacier. Its offices are located in the following towns:
Santiago: Av. El Bosque Norte 0440, tel: (02) 442 3120; fax: (02) 203 5025.
Puerto Montt: Angelmó 2187, tel: (065) 432 300; fax: (065) 276 611.

Coyhaique: Pdte. Ibáñez 347, tel: (067) 233 306; fax: (067) 233 386.
Puerto Natales: Manuel Bulnes 533, tel: (061) 414 300; fax: (061) 414 361.
Punta Arenas: Magallanes 990, tel: (061) 200 200; fax: (061) 225 804.

Puerto Montt to San Rafael

• Skorpios operate two boats, each with weekly departures from September to May.
Santiago: Augusto Leguía Norte 118, Las Condes, tel: (02) 231 1030;
fax: (02) 232 2269.
Puerto Montt: Angelmó 1660, tel/fax: (065) 275 613.
• Navimag operate a weekly service from September through March (twice monthly during the rest of the year; see above).

Termas de Puyuhuapi to San Rafael

• Catamaran Patagonia Express offers a day trip for guests at the Hostería Termas de Puyuhuapi (see page 359).

Puerto Montt to Puerto Natales

• Navimag operates a weekly service (see above).

The Southern Channels

Other charter boats operate from Puerto Montt, Puerto Chacabuco, Puerto Natales and Punta Arenas, but run subject to demand.

From the beginning of March, the ferry service from Hornopirén on the Carretera Austral is suspended for the winter. Alternative services run from Chiloé to.lén.

The Lake District offers dozens of spectacular boating options. The trip from Petrohué to Puella across Lago Todos los Santos is the first leg of the "Journey of the Seven Lakes," a magnificent route to Bariloche in Argentina.

By Car

Car hire in Chile is relatively expensive, especially in the provinces. However, in some places, it is well worth the cost, particularly if you share expenses with other travelers. For example, in the Lake District and the Central Valley, having one's own transport opens up many more opportunities.

Car drivers should make sure they have the original registration document of their vehicle. There are plenty of modern service stations on the tourist routes and fuel is about US$0.80 per liter, but varies in line with international oil prices.
• Hertz has one of the largest car rental networks, with branch offices in most major cities. Their main office is in Santiago: Av. Costanera 1469, tel: (02) 496 1000; and at the airport, tel: (02) 601 0477. Other major companies are:
• Budget (tel: (02) 362 3200).
• Avis (tel: (02) 601 9747).
• The Automóvil Club de Chile also rents cars and has offices throughout Chile.

Car hire rates start at around US$50. Some companies offer weekly rates with unlimited mileage. It's worth shopping around. A substantial deposit or credit-card voucher may also be required.

See the Maps section (page 342) for locating detailed road maps if you're planning to drive in Chile.

Public Transport in Santiago

Subway: Santiago's metro is comfortable and efficient. There are three lines: one runs east-west beneath Av. B. O'Higgins and on through Providencia, while the other two link residential suburbs in the south of the city to this line. Buy tickets at the various stations – currently US$0.40 per ticket.
Buses: The bus system is basically unfathomable and the interval between buses unpredictable. No city bus maps are available, but on main arteries most bus-stop signs now show the principal destinations of the bus numbers that stop there. All types of buses have signs in their windscreens displaying the destination and fare (around US$0.40). Watch for pickpockets.
Taxis: Taxis are black with yellow roofs. They each display on the windshield their minimum fare and the rate per 200 meters. These fares depend on the condition of the car or the nature of the driver. It's a free market. Fares are likely to double at night, after 9pm. All taxis have meters that should be turned on when you enter the car, although some drivers conveniently forget. Most city taxi drivers, however, are trustworthy, and this is a very economical means of transport. Nevertheless, women on their own at night are best advised to call a radio taxi rather than to flag one down in the street.
Colectivos: These are simply taxis that take up to four passengers for a flat rate on a fixed route. Colectivos are even cheaper than taxis, but the routes they take are limited. The price is usually US$0.40 and $0.50, and the routes are similar to those of the buses. Colectivos are readily available, and particularly useful, at the metro terminal stations.

Orientation in Santiago

Santiago is a sprawling city, but the city center is relatively small and easy to explore. "El centro" is roughly triangular-shaped, bounded on one side by the enormous Avenida del Libertador General Bernardo O'Higgins, more conveniently known as the Alameda; on another side by the muddy Río Mapocho; and on the third by the North–South Highway.

In the center is the Plaza de Armas, a city square common to most Spanish-founded cities in South America. Another typical feature is the grid pattern of city streets, which couldn't be simpler for your orientation – although keep in mind that the street names change on either side of the plaza.

Here, you'll find the Correo Central, the cathedral and a string of outdoor cafés and restaurants.

Between the plaza and the Alameda is where the traditional hive of business activity can be found, with wall-to-wall office blocks, shops, hotels and cinemas. Two main streets, Paseo Huérfanos and Paseo Ahumada, have been turned into pedestrian precincts to accommodate the crowds, but are still almost always highly congested. The Alameda continues eastwards into Avenida Providencia and the suburb of the same name.

Tourist Information

The Sernatur Tourist Office is located at Av. Providencia 1550 (tel: 600 7376 2887), between metros Manuel Montt and Pedro de Valdivia. The office opens Monday through Friday 8.45am–6.30pm, Saturday 9am–2pm.

A Sernatur information desk in the Santiago airport is open daily 8.30am–5.30pm.

Outdoor Excursions

Chile, with its fabulous scenery, is a paradise for hikers, with an excellent national park system, offering everything from easy day-treks to challenging professional expeditions. The Corporación Nacional Forestal (CONAF) runs the national parks, to which it publishes a guide, available from its offices, Bulnes 285, Santiago, tel: (02) 390 0125.

The hot, dry desert north is definitely not ideal hiking territory. If you do take any walks here, pack a hat and lots of water.

Parque Nacional Torres del Paine is the country's most famous trekking destination, but there are countless beautiful locations to explore in Chile's south. If you plan to get out and about in the Lake District or Chiloé, you will need a good raincoat, and in the far south you should take precautions against exposure, as the weather can – and regularly does – turn in an instant.

Here is a selection of the country's outdoor highlights, and details of specialist tour operators.

ARICA

Taxis or guided tours can easily be arranged to make the 32-km (20-mile) round trip up the Azapa Valley to see the hillside geoglyphs, visit pre-Inca *pukaras* (fortresses) and see the Chinchorro mummies in the archeological museum.

A trip to Parque Nacional Lauca, 260 km (160 miles) east of Arica, is highly recommended, and easily arranged. It's a good idea to spend a night in Putre and make a detour to the ritual villages of Socoroma and Parinacota. This region is rich in birdlife and wild camelid (members of the camel family). If you have a sleeping bag, it is possible to spend the night at the CONAF ranger station by Lago Chungará, but make a prior booking at CONAF's office in Arica, Vicuña Mackenna 820, tel: (058) 250 739.

Expedition Advice

A useful source of advice if you are planning an Andean trek is: **La Federación de Andinismo**, Almirante Simpson 77 Santiago. Tel: 220 0888; Fax: 635 9089 Their members often organize expeditions for both amateurs and professional climbers.

There's a very good website – www.tricuspide.cl – that has lots of useful information, including contacts with groups that are planning climbs, but it's only in Spanish.

Tour Operators
• Aacción Tours, Bolognesi 301, tel: (058) 257 216.
• Agencia de Viajes Turismo Tacora, 21 de Mayo 171, tel: (058) 232 786.
• Aricadena Tour, Rafael Sotomayor 199, tel: (058) 233 189.

Check Your Itinerary

Before you embark on a tour, check with the organizer that you will get to see everything described on the list. Plans are liable to change more frequently than printed schedules.

• Geotour, Bolognesi 421, tel: (058) 253 927.
• Globotour, 21 de Mayo 260, tel: (058) 232 909.

IQUIQUE

Tours are available to the oasis villages of Pica and Matilla, famous for their citrus fruits and date palms. Other attractions include the July festival of the Virgin at La Tirana, the mining "ghost town" of Humberstone, and its surrounding hills with enormous ancient geoglyphs. Tours to the "ghost towns" can also be combined with a trip to the hot springs at Mamiña.

Tour Operators
• Agencia de Turismo Mané, Baquedano 1067, tel: (057) 473032.
• Agencia de Viajes Iquitour, Patricio Lynch 563, tel: (057) 412415.
• Agencia de Viajes Turismo Mamiña, Latorre 769, tel: (057) 412305.
• Civet Adventure, Bolívar 684, tel: (057) 428483.
• Coki Tour, Baquedano 982, tel: (057) 428984.

CALAMA

There is a half-day free tour of the Chuquicamata copper mine with breathtaking views of one of the largest open-cast pits in the world. *Colectivos* run regular services from the center of town to the mine.

Hotels and tour operators can arrange trips to the most interesting villages in the area – Chiu Chiu,

Aiquina and Caspana – with their famous churches, thatched buildings and a lifestyle which has changed little since Inca times.

Tour Operators
• Agencia de Viajes Chuqui Tour, Latorre 1512, tel: (056) 340 190.
• Tour Aventura Valle de la Luna, Abaroa, tel: (056) 310 720.

SAN PEDRO DE ATACAMA

Surrounded by historical sites, which can be visited on foot, this attractive village makes an ideal base for longer excursions. The village's *hosterías* (hostels) and tour agencies all run dawn trips to the geysers at El Tatio, as well as guided tours to the Atacama salt flats and lakes, to ancient pre-Hispanic forts and to the Valle de la Luna (Valley of the Moon).

Tour Operators
There is a multitude of tour operators in San Pedro, most of whom offer very similar services. They include:
• Atacama Desert Expedition, Tocopilla 411, tel: (055) 851 045.
• Cosmo Andino Expediciones, Calle Caracoles s/n, tel: (055) 851 069.
• Southern Cross Adventure, Caracoles 119, tel: (055) 851 416.

ANTOFAGASTA

Excursions can be made by bus, taxi or with tour groups to the derelict nitrate *oficinas* (mining towns) as well as to María Elena and Pedro de Valdivia, the last two left in production. There is some dramatic coastal scenery north of the town including La Portada, a giant rock with a natural archway in it, rising out of the sea.

Tour Operators
• Agencia de Turismo Astro Tour, Achao 5733, tel: (055) 773749.
• Nortour, Baquedano 474, tel: (055) 227171.

CHAÑARAL

This is an ideal base from which to visit Parque Nacional Pan de Azúcar, which has an unusual ecosystem caused by the *camanchaca*, a dense sea mist that drifts across the hills. Boat trips can also be made to Isla Pan de Azúcar, which has colonies of Humboldt penguins, sea lions and abundant bird life.

Tour Operator
• Chango Turismo, Panamericana Norte s/n, tel: (052) 80484.

COPIAPÓ

The Andes are at their most magnificent in this region, and several agencies organize excursions to visit Ojos de Salado (Chile's highest peak at 6,893 metres/22,625 ft) and the awe-inspiring Laguna Verde. This region is known for its variety of cacti.

Tour Operators
• Agencia de Viajes Turismo Atacama, Los Carrera 716, tel: (052) 214 767.
• Desertur Ltda., Jotabeche 214, tel: (052) 241 365.
• Maricunga Expediciones, Maipú 580, tel: (052) 211 191.
• Peruvian Tours, O'Higgins 12, tel: (052) 249 995.

LA SERENA

Famous for its beaches, this is also one of the most important centers for astronomers, and visits can be arranged to the observatories of Tololo, Gemini South, Las Campanas and La Silla. An interesting day trip can be made along the Elqui valley, renowned for its *pisco* (a grape-based liquor), and the birthplace of the famous poet Gabriela Mistral.

Tour Operators
• Agencia de Viajes San Bartolomé, M. Aguirre Perry 1920, tel: (051) 221992.

• Agencia de Viajes Giratour, Arturo Prat 689, tel: (051) 218 209.
• Elqui Valley Tour, Balmaceda 551-B, tel: (051) 214 846.

SANTIAGO

You could be blinded by the choice of tour services in Santiago. Actually, many of them are affiliated in some way, and the tours offered will be basically the same at each office. All seem to offer a city tour, which starts from your hotel and visits many of the landmarks listed in the Places section of this book. The cost is around US$30. Night tours include a view from the top of Cerro San Cristóbal and a restaurant meal with floorshow for US$60.

There are various day excursions to Viña del Mar and Valparaíso, visiting the lush Chilean vineyards en route, which include lunch at an elegant restaurant for around US$90. More specific tours to certain vineyards to purchase and sample the wines are popular. These tours offer a narrated journey through colonial cellars such as at the Concha y Toro Vineyard and a scenic drive through the Cajón del Maipo. At weekends a number of buses make the day trip to the open-air hot mineral water baths of Termas de Colina, in the mountains.

Day trips are also available to visit Portillo or Farellones for a taste of pure mountain air and some excellent ski-slopes.

The tourist office will give you a long list of travel agencies; some have offices in the main hotels.

Tour Operators
• Andina del Sud, Av. El Golf 99, piso 2, tel: (02) 388 0101; fax: (02) 388 0102.
• Sportstour, Moneda 970, piso 14, tel: (02) 549 5200; fax: (02) 698 2981.
• Turismo Cocha, Av. El Bosque Norte, 0430, tel: (02) 464 1000; fax: (02) 464 1010.
• Turismo Mostrando Chile, Antonio Varas 175, Of. 205, tel: (02) 235 0625.

• Latitud 90, Av. Kennedy 7268, tel: (02) 247 9100; fax: (02) 954 2019. Well-organized tours, with English-speaking guides, but significantly more expensive than other options.

TEMUCO

This was previously the heartland of the indigenous Mapuche people, unconquered until the late 19th century, and trips can be made which pass through the communities in which they live. A 92-km (58-mile) round trip through Cholchol and Nueva Imperial can be made by local bus or by arrangement with a taxi driver. A longer trip of 400 km (250 miles) to the source of the Bíobío River at Liucura offers the added opportunity to visit Parque Nacional Conguillío, dominated by Volcán Llaima and containing forests and *araucaria* (monkey puzzle) trees. Accommodations are available at Curacautín and Melipeuco where the owner of Hostería Hue-Telén (tel: (045) 581 005) organizes tours into the park. However, this trip is best done with the freedom offered by your own vehicle, and Temuco is a good place from which to rent a car.

Tour Operators
• Caminos del Sur, Gerona 670, tel: (045) 321 857.
• Viajes Trébol, Antonio Varas 854, tel: (045) 747 474.

PUCÓN

Pucón is a resort town that comes alive during the holiday season. In summer, the tour operators run groups to the various *termas*

Rafting

For white-water rafting:
• Altué Expediciones, Encomenderos 83, Santiago, tel: (02) 232 1103, fax: (02) 233 6799.

(thermal springs), or to participate in adventure sports like white-water rafting and volcano climbing.

The Tourist Office can arrange trips for five people or more to the Termas de Palguín, or to the 12-km (8-mile) mark on the slopes of Volcán Villarrica.

Tour Operators
• Andean Sport Tours, O'Higgins 535-A, tel: 441 048.
• Turismo Sol y Nieve, Fresia 415, Local 6, tel: (045) 444 098.
• Politur, O'Higgins 635, tel: (045) 441 373.

VALDIVIA

Half-day boat tours are made to the mouth of the Calle-Calle River at Corral, Niebla and Isla Mancera, to see 17th-century Spanish fortress ruins. All leave from the quayside in the center of Valdivia; prices vary, according to the length of the trip and whether a meal (lunch or dinner) is included.

Tour Operators
• Anticura Expediciones, Anfión Muñoz 327, tel: (063) 212 630.
• Turismo Coch (063) 292 858.
• Turismo Patagonia Sur, Picarte 957, tel: (063) 291 977.

The boat companies include Bahia, Calle-Calle, Neptuno and Reina Sofía and they have their offices on Av. Arturo Prat.

PETROHUE

From Petrohué there are boats that make regular one-day trips across Lago Todos los Santos, some of which include lunch at Hotel Peulla on the far side. These tours begin in Puerto Varas or Puerto Montt.

PUERTO MONTT

This is the gateway to the Lake District, Isla de Chiloé and southern Patagonia, with excellent bus services to other regions as well. Ancud, on Isla de Chiloé, can be

visited in a day. Several regular buses leave from the bus terminal on the seafront. A visit to Castro, farther south on the island, really requires an overnight stay.

In Puerto Varas, a number of companies organize white-water rafting trips down the Río Petrohué, as well as excursions to the summit of Volcán Osorno.

Andean Crossing

The most interesting way of traveling to Argentina is by a combination of buses and boats, which start by crossing Lago Todos Los Santos. This journey is operated by Andina del Sud *(see left)* and can be made in either one or two days, finishing in Bariloche.

Tour Operators in Puerto Montt
• Ace Lagos Andinos, Varas 445, tel: (065) 254 998.
• Agencia de Viajes Andina del Sud, Antonio Varas 437, tel/fax: (065) 257 797.
• Agencia de Viajes Petrel Tours, Benavente 327-A, tel/fax: (065) 251 780.
• Travellers, Angelmó 2456, tel: (065) 262 099.

Tour Operators In Puerto Varas
• CTS Turismo, San Francisco 333, tel: (065) 237 328.
• Agencia de Viajes Andina del Sud, Del Salvador 72, tel: (065) 232 811.
• Agencia de Viajes Aqua Motion, San Francisco 238, tel: (065) 801 8259.

CASTRO-CHILOÉ

The most interesting excursions involve short boat trips to the smaller islands of the archipelago. Pehuén Expediciones have different trips each day of the week. Achao on the island of Quinchao can be visited using the regular bus service that also visits Dalcahue. One of the most beautiful beaches in Chile is at Cucao on the Pacific coast, where horseback excursions and treks into the Parque Nacional Chiloé can be made. Basic accommodations are available in Cucao.

Tour Operator
• Agencia de Viajes Pehuén Expediciones, Blanco 299, tel/fax: (065) 635 254.

COYHAIQUE

Numerous trips are possible in this area of lakes and mountains. From December to April the area is a center for trout and salmon fishing.

Tour Operators
• Andes Patagónicos, Horn 40, tel/fax: (067) 216 711.
• Aventura Turismo, 21 de Mayo 477, tel/fax: (067) 234 748.

PUERTO NATALES

This is the starting point for excursions to Parque Nacional Torres del Paine and farther north to El Calafate in Argentina, where the southern ice field forms the Moreno glacier. From Puerto Natales, regular boat trips operate to the Balmaceda and Serrano glaciers.

Tour Operators
• Agencia de Viajes Tour Express, Bulnes 769, tel: (061) 411 639.
• Big Foot Expediciones, Bories 206, tel: (061) 414 611.

PUNTA ARENAS

A number of boat excursions depart from Punta Arenas. One of the shortest goes to the penguin colony on Isla Magdalena. A longer land trip of 265 km (165 miles) is worth making to see the virgin forests and abundant wildlife near Lago Blanco.

Tour Operators
• Turismo Aventour, España 872, tel: (061) 241 197.
• Turismo Pehoé, José Menéndez 918, tel: (061) 241 373.
• Turismo Viento del Sur, Fagnano 585, tel: (061) 226 930.

Where to Stay

Choosing a Hotel

Take Chilean hotel star ratings with a pinch of salt. In Santiago, they're generally reliable, but in the rest of the country, they can be a bit haphazard. However, standards are mostly high and are improving all the time, with international chains now expanding down into the three- and even two-star market. As a general guide, three-star and up is almost always comfortable and certainly clean.

Unfortunately, for budget travelers and vegetarians who might prefer to cook for themselves, Chile has limited self-catering accommodations. Hostels with public kitchens are most common in southern Chile.

The busy seasons are the summer months (December–March) and the week around the Independence Day holiday, on September 18. Even during these periods, however, it is not really necessary to book in most places. The exceptions are the Torres del Paine National Park, where there's a serious shortage of hotel accommodation, and a few provincial cities, such as Antofagasta and Concepción, which can suddenly get swamped by a business conference or some other special event.

Booking Ahead

It's a good idea to have accommodations reserved for your first night in Santiago, although a booking service is available in the airport. Contact **Sernatur** (the national tourist office). *See page 347 for details.*

Hotel Listings

SANTIAGO

Hyatt Regency Santiago
Av. Kennedy 4601
Tel: (02) 218 1234
Fax: (02) 218 2513
www.santiago.regency.hyatt.com
Rather out of the way, especially by public transport, but has a very attractive garden and swimming pool. **$$$$**

Crowne Plaza Holiday Inn
Av. Libertador B. O'Higgins 136 Tel: (02) 638 1042
Fax: (02) 633 6015
Situated close to city center. Facilities include swimming pool, tennis courts, gymnasium and conference rooms. **$$$$**

Hotel Plaza San Francisco Kempinski
Av. Libertador B. O'Higgins 816
Tel: (02) 639 3832
Fax: (02) 639 7826
Situated in the heart of downtown Santiago. Very high standard of accommodation, meeting rooms and excellent restaurant. **$$$$**

Sheraton San Cristóbal
Av. Santa María 1742
Tel: (02) 233 5000
Fax: (02) 234 1729
www.sheraton.cl
Lovely setting at the base of Cerro San Cristóbal, but out of the way for sightseeing. Swimming pool. **$$$$**

Apart Hotel Santa Magdalena
Santa Magdalena 104, Providencia
Tel: (02) 374 6875
Fax: (02) 374 6876
www.santamagdalena.cl
Self-service flats in the heart of the Providencia district, near to the main metro line. **$$$**

Hotel Foresta
Victoria Subercaseaux 353
Tel: (02) 639 6261
Fax: (02) 632 2996
Located directly opposite Cerro Santa Lucía: idyllic views from front rooms. **$$$**

Hotel Gran Palace
Huérfanos 1178, piso 10
Tel: (02) 671 2551
Fax: (02) 695 1095
www.hotelgranpalace.cl

Rooms away from the street are less noisy. **$$**

Hotel Montecarlo
Victoria Subercaseaux 209
Tel: (02) 638 1176
Fax: (02) 633 5577
Three-star hotel, great location with view of Cerro Santa Lucia. **$$**

Residencial Londres
Londres 54
Tel/fax: (02) 633 2215
Ramshackle antique interiors. Good-value accommodation. **$$**

Youth Hostel/Albergue Juvenil
Cienfuegos 151
Tel: (02) 671 8532
Fax: (02) 672 8880
A friendly institution. **$**

THE NORTH

Arica
Azapa Inn
G. Sánchez 660, Azapa
Tel: (058) 244 537
Fax: (058) 225 191
www.azapainn.cl
Located in pleasant grounds although some distance from beach. Facilities include a swimming pool. **$$$**

Hotel Arica
Av. San Martin 599, Playa El Laucho
Tel: (058) 254 540
Fax: (058) 231 133
Four-star hotel, swimming pool, easy access to the best beaches in Arica. **$$$**

Hotel Savona
Yungay 380
Tel: (058) 231 000
Fax: (058) 231 606
Small, basic hotel near the main square. **$$**

Price Categories

All prices are for double occupancy per night with breakfast unless otherwise stated. Non nationals paying in dollars avoid the 19 percent IVA (sales tax).

$	less than US$25
$$	US$25–60
$$$	US$60–120
$$$$	more than US$120

Hosterías, hospedajes and residenciales

There's not much difference between *hosterías* and hotels, but *residenciales* are more basic affairs, with none of the hotel frills – usually no meals apart from breakfast and, possibly, shared bathrooms. At an *hospedaje*, you'll get a room in a private house, but standards vary a lot (they are particularly good value for money in the Lake District.) Ultimately, the best guide as to what sort of stay you'll have at an *hospedaje* is the friendliness of the owner, so it is worthwhile having a chat with him or her before making your choice.

Iquique
Hotel Arturo Prat
A. Pinto 695
Tel: (057) 427 000
Fax: (057) 429 088
Four-star hotel which faces onto Plaza Prat. **$$$**

Hostería Terrado Suites
Los Rieles 126
Tel/fax: (057) 488 000
Situated by Cavancha Beach, with swimming pool. **$$$**

Hotel Barros Arana
Barros Arana 1302
Tel/fax: (057) 412 840
www.hotelbarrosarana.cl
Close to the beach, with pool. **$$**

Antofagasta
Hotel Antofagasta
Balmaceda 2575
Tel: (055) 228 811
Fax: (055) 268 415
www.hotelantofagasta.cl
Four-star hotel, with swimming pool, and excellent views of the port and city. **$$$**

Holiday Inn Express
Av. Grecia 1490
Tel: (055) 228 888
Fax: (055) 285 457
Slightly out of the way, but very pleasant. **$$$**

Hotel Diego De Almagro
Condell 2624
Tel: (055) 268 331
Fax: (055) 251 721
www.diegodealmagrohoteles.cl
A comfortable and centrally located hotel. **$$**

Calama
Park Hotel Calama
Camino Aeropuerto 1392
Tel: (055) 319 900
Fax: (055) 319 901
www.parkplaza.cl

Comfortable four-star hotel near the airport. Has an excellent restaurant, bar, gym and games room. **$$$**

Hostería Calama
Latorre 1521
Tel: (055) 310 306
Fax: (055) 342 033
Comfortable and quiet hotel, with good restaurant **$$$**

Hotel Universo
Sotomayor 2064
Tel/fax: (055) 361 640
Well located. **$$**

San Pedro de Atacama
Explora Hotel
Domingo Atienza s/n
Tel: (055) 851 110
Fax: (055) 851 115
www.explora.com
This hotel's all-inclusive 3-, 4- and 7-day deals include excellent excursions to nearby Atacama Desert archeological sites and salt-flats (no overnight stays allowed at these attractions). **$$$$**

Hostería de San Pedro
Toconoa 460
Tel: (055) 851 011
Fax: (055) 851 048
www.diegodealmagrohoteles.cl
Has 54 beds, 5 cabins (6 persons), swimming pool. **$$$**

Hostería Casa de Don Tomás
Tocopilla n/n
Tel: (055) 851 055
Fax: (055) 851 175
www.dontomas.cl
New, well-equipped hotel. **$$$**

Hostería/Camping Takha-Takha
Caracoles 101
Tel: (055) 851 038
A pleasant and comfortable place for budget travelers, with quaint cabins and serviced camping ground. **$**

Copiapó
Hostería La Casona
O'Higgins 150
Tel: (052) 217 728
Fax: (052) 211 633
www.lacasonahotel.cl
A small hotel in a converted old
house; close to the center. **$$**

La Serena
Jardín Del Mar
Av. Costanera 5425
Tel: (051) 242 835
Fax: (051) 242 991
www.hoteljardindelmar.cl
A tourist complex with 164 beds,
divided between apartments and
cabins (5 persons). **$$$**

Hotel Francisco De Aguirre
Cordovez 210
Tel: (051) 222 991
Fax: (051) 210 992
A very pleasant old hotel with a
swimming pool. **$$$**

Hostal Croata
Cienfuegos 248
Tel/fax: (051) 224 997
Centrally located. **$$**

CENTRAL CHILE

Valparaíso
Hotel Casa Thomas Somerscales
San Enrique 446
Tel: (032) 331 006
Fax: (032) 331 379
www.hotelsomerscales.cl
A new hotel in the restored home of
an English-born 19th-century
painter. **$$$**

Hotel Brighton
Pasaje Atkinson 151
Tel: (032) 223 513
Fax: (032) 598 802
www.brighton.cl

Certified B&Bs

Casa Latina (see Valparaíso) is
one of several bed and
breakfasts that have recently
qualified under the certification
program of a private development
foundation. Others include **The
Grand House**, tel: (032) 212
376, and **Bed & Breakfast
Patricia**, tel: (032) 220 290.

Hostels

There are 14 youth hostels in
Chile, mostly in the south, with
accommodations costing around
US$6–8 per person. The IYHA
(International Youth Hostel
Association) card is widely
accepted. Hostels fill up quickly
in the summer months, when
they can be very noisy, with only
floor space available in the most
popular places. The Chilean
YHA's handy guidebook, which
lists all the hostels in the
country, may be purchased at
their Santiago headquarters:
**Asociación Chilena de Albergues
Turísticos Juveniles**, Av.
Hernando de Aguirre 201,
Of. 602. Tel: (02) 233 3220.
www.hostelling.cl (includes an
English version).

A marvelous view, especially from
the terrace, but could do with better
maintenance. **$$**

A number of bed & breakfasts in
Valparaíso, as well as in other
leading tourist centers, have
received training and certification
under a program developed by
Corfo, the government's economic
development agency, and Fundación
Chile, a technology transfer
institute. A full list of this
accommodation is available on
www.ecoredlatina.com.
    In Valparaíso, where the program
started, they include:
Casa Latina, Papudo 463, tel:
(032) 494 622
The Grand House, Federico Varela
27, tel: (032) 212 376
Bed & Breakfast Patricia, 12 de
Febrero 315, tel: (032) 220 290.
All prices: **$–$$**

Viña del Mar
Hotel Cap Ducal
Av. Marina 51
Tel: (032) 626 655
Fax: (032) 655 471
Built jutting out into the sea with
breathtaking views of the Pacific;
some people love it, others aren't
impressed. **$$$**

Hotel O'Higgins
Plaza Vergara s/n
Tel: (032) 882 016
Fax: (032) 883 537
www.panamericanahoteles.cl
Centrally located traditional hotel.
$$$

Residencial Victoria
Av. Valparaíso 40
Tel/fax: (032) 977 370
Large and characterful place,
opposite the railway station; shared
bathrooms. **$**

Concepción
Hotel El Araucano
Caupolicán 521
Tel: (041) 740 606
Fax: (041) 740 690
Situated just on the main square,
with above-average facilities,
function/conference rooms. **$$**

Hotel Alborada
Barros Arana 457
Tel/fax: (041) 911 121
www.hotelalborada.cl
A comfortable, unpretentious hotel,
located just off the main square.
Recommended. **$$**

Hotel Alonso de Ercilla
Colo Colo 334
Tel: (041) 227 984
Fax: (041) 230 053
www.hotelalonsodeercilla.co.cl
One block from the main square;
modern with average facilities – no
restaurant, but a snack service. **$$**

Hotel Ritz
Barros Arana 721
Tel: (041) 226 696
Fax: (041) 243 249
Centrally located and cheaper than
the other alternatives. **$$**

LAKE DISTRICT

Chillán
Gran Hotel Isabel Riquelme
Arauco 600
Tel: (042) 213 663
Fax: (042) 211 541
Facing one of the most attractive
main squares, above-average
facilities, 87 rooms and three
suites. Function/conference
rooms. **$$**

Hotel Rukalaf
Arauco 740

Tel: (042) 230 393
Fax: (042) 233 366
www.rukalaf.cl
A slightly cheaper but comfortable alternative, very central and a good choice for an overnight stay. **$$**

Los Angeles
Mariscal Alcázar
Lautaro 385
Tel/fax: (043) 311 725
www.hotelalcazar.cl
On the main square, 60 rooms and suites. Function/conference rooms. **$$**

Temuco
Hotel de La Frontera
Av. Bulnes 733
Tel: (045) 200 400
Fax: (045) 200 402
www.hotelfrontera.cl
Just off the main square, modern with above average facilities, pool, sauna, function/conference rooms. **$$$**
Apart Hotel Tierra de Sur
Av. Bulnes 1196
Tel/fax: (045) 232 439
www.tierradelsur.cl
A modern hotel, with indoor and outdoor swimming pools, but no restaurant. **$$**
Hotel Continental
Antonio Varas 708
Tel: (045) 238 973
Fax: (045) 233 830
Located one block from the main square; famous past guests include Pablo Neruda and Salvador Allende; the bar is worth a visit. **$**

Pucón
Hotel Antumalal
1 km outside Pucón
Tel: (045) 441 011
Fax: (045) 441 013
www.antumalal.com
Small, luxury hotel where Queen Elizabeth II once stayed. Two "royal" chalets and 15 rooms, set

Hotel Addresses

s/n = *s in número*, no number, for places, usually in smaller towns, where there is no street number in the address.

Price Categories

All prices are for double occupancy per night with breakfast unless otherwise stated. Non nationals paying in dollars avoid the 19 percent IVA (sales tax).
$ less than US$25
$$ US$25–60
$$$ US$60–120
$$$$ more than US$120

in 4 hectares (10 acres) of quiet woodland on a peninsula overlooking Lake Villarrica. Heated swimming pool. **$$$$**
Termas de Huife
Situated 36 km (20 miles) east of Pucón.
Tel/fax: (045) 441 222
Open-air thermal swimming pools in an idyllic natural setting. The luxury cabins all have private thermal baths. **$$$$**
Gran Hotel Pucón
Clemente Holzapfel 190
Tel/fax: (045) 441 001
www.granhotelpucon.com
Large luxury lakeside hotel with 550 beds. Its extensive facilities include a casino. **$$$**
Hostería "Ecole"
General Urrutia 592
Tel: (045) 441 675
Fax: (045) 441 949
www.ecole.cl
Hostelling International affiliate. American-owned, centrally located *hostería* with private rooms and dorms; excellent vegetarian restaurant open to non-guests; "gringo" meeting place and a source of honest advice about local activities and operators. **$–$$**
La Tetera
Urrutia 580
Tel/fax: (045) 441 462
www.tetera.cl
Guesthouse run by Swiss/Chilean couple. **$$**

Villarrica
El Ciervo
General Koerner 241
Tel: (045) 411 215
Fax: (045) 4109 25
www.hotelelciervo.cl

A 12-room centrally located hotel with swimming pool. It also has a cabin for five people. **$$**

Lican-Ray
Nearly everything in this holiday settlement is closed outside the tourist high season, which is from mid-December to mid-March.
Hostería Inaltulafquén
Cacique Punulef 510
Tel/fax: (045) 431 115
Homey guest house; one of the few places open all year round. **$$**

Choshuenco
Hotel Rucapillán
San Martín 85
Tel/fax: (063) 318 220
www.rucapillan.cl
Traditional lakeside hotel and cabins. **$$**
Hostería Pulmahue
Casilla 545, Panguipulli
Tel: (063) 318 224
Fax: (063) 201 616
Small, well-situated hotel with cabins overlooking the lake. **$$**

Panguipulli
Hostal España
B. O'Higgins 790
Tel: (063) 311 166
Fax: (063) 311 327
Small, centrally located hotel. **$$**

Valdivia
Hotel Villa Del Río
Av. España 1025
Tel: (063) 216 292
Fax: (063) 217 851
www.hotelvilladelrio.com
On the river across from the center of Valdivia, with 100 rooms, cabins, swimming pool, sauna and tennis court. Conference rooms. **$$$**
Hostal Torreón
Pérez Rosales 783
Tel: (063) 212 622
Fax: (063) 203 217
In an old German-style house, down a long driveway away from street noise. Very friendly owners. **$$**
Airesbuenos
General Lagos 1036
Tel/fax: (063) 206 304
www.airesbuenos.cl
Hostelling International affiliate. Dorms as well as rooms with

shared and private bathrooms.
$–$$

Futrono
Hostería Rosengarten
Two minutes' drive out of Futrono
on the road to Llifén
Tel/fax: (063) 481 044
Attractive family home owned by a
pleasant German/Chilean couple.
Double and single rooms and
cabins that sleep 6–7 people.
Board includes abundant "famous"
German-style breakfasts. **$$**

Llifén
Hostería Chollinco
Km 3 Camino Llifén–Maihue
Tel/fax: (063) 197 1979
www.hosteriachollinco.cl
Gorgeous cabins, extensive
gardens, pool and a spectacular
view of mountain scenery and river.
Full board provided. Horseback
riding and fishing excursions
available. **$$**

Lago Ranco
Casona Italiana
Viña del Mar 367
Tel/fax: (063) 491 225
Small lakeside hotel with five rooms
and four cabins. Shared bathrooms.
$–$$

Puerto Octay
Hotel Centinela
On the Centinela Peninsula
Tel/fax: (064) 391 326
www.hotelcentinela.cl
A peaceful setting on the shore of
Lake Llanquihue. **$$$**

Frutillar
Hotel Ayacara
Av. Philippi 1215
Tel: (065) 421 550
Fax: (065) 421 831
www.hotelayacara.com
Attractive rooms with spectacular
views. **$$$**
Hotel Klein Salzburg
Av. Philippi 663
Tel: (065) 421 589
Fax: (065) 421 599
www.salzburg.cl
Impeccable rooms. The restaurant
is one of the town's favorites.
$$$

Puerto Varas
Hotel Colonos del Sur
Del Salvador 24
Tel: (065) 233 369
Fax: (065) 233 394
www.colonosdelsur.cl
Well-equipped modern hotel facing
lake, with pool. **$$$**
Casa Azul
Manzanal 66
Tel: (065) 232 904
www.casaazul.net
Quaint and comfortable hostel;
shared and private bathrooms.
$–$$

Puyehue
Hotel Termas de Puyehue
Located close to Lago Puyehue,
76 km (47 miles) east of Osorno.
Tel: (064) 371 272
Fax: (064) 232 157
Famous "spa" facilities include
indoor and open-air thermal
swimming pools, sauna, mud and
sulfur baths, tennis courts and
gymnasium, with mountain bikes,
horse trekking, fishing and boat
tours available. **$$$$**
Hotel Antillanca
Km 98, Ruta 215, Osorno
Tel/fax: (064) 235 114
www.skiantillanca.com
Modern hotel situated in the center
of Parque Nacional Puyehue.
Provides an ideal base for trekking
and mountain climbing in the
summer and skiing in the winter.
Facilities include a swimming pool,
sauna, gym and conference center.
$$$

Petrohué
Hostería Petrohué
Tel/fax: (065) 258 042
Attractive hotel by Lago Todos los
Santos and Petrohué River in
Parque Nacional Pérez Rosales.
Handy for lake excursions, white-
water rafting, fishing and walking.
$$$

Osorno
Gran Hotel Osorno
O'Higgins 615
Tel: (064) 232 171
Fax: (064) 239 311
Situated on the main square, with
70 rooms. **$$**

Hotel Rayantú
Patricio Lynch 1462
Tel: (064) 238 114
Fax: (064) 238 116
A modern hotel five blocks from
main square, with swimming pool
and conference facilities. **$$**
Residencial Alemana
Colón 666
Tel/fax: (064) 250 588
Rooms with/without bathroom. **$**

Price Categories

All the prices are for double
occupancy per night with
breakfast unless otherwise
stated. Non nationals paying in
dollars avoid the 19 percent IVA
(sales tax).
$ less than US$25
$$ US$25–60
$$$ US$60–120
$$$$ more than US$120

Puerto Montt
Puerto Montt doesn't live up to the
south's reputation for generous
hospitality. In the middle and low
price range, lodgings here tend to
be dowdy; Puerto Varas, 21 km
(13 miles) north, offers much better
choice.
Hotel Viento del Sur
Ejército 200
Tel: (065) 258 701
Fax: (065) 314 732
www.hotelvientosur.cl
Perched above the center of the city
with great views. **$$$**
Don Luis Gran Hotel
Quillota 146
Tel: (065) 259 001
Fax: (065) 259 005
This modern, centrally located hotel
has standard facilities but only
offers a snack service. **$$$**
Residencial Urmeneta
Urmeneta 290
Tel/fax: (065) 253 262
One of the better choices at the
cheaper end of the range. **$$**

Chiloé

For budget accommodation in
Chiloé, the *residenciales* or
hospedajes (see page 355) are

the best value, and also provide a friendly atmosphere and a place to meet local people.

Ancud
Hostería Ancud
San Antonio 30
Tel: (065) 622 340
Fax: (065) 622 350
www.hosteriancud.com
Beautiful interior of wooden pillars supporting an impressive cane ceiling, but the rooms are very small. Set on a hillside overlooking the water. **$$$**
Hotel Madryn
Bellavista 491
Tel/fax: (065) 622 128
www.hotelmadryn.co.cl
Close to Plaza de Armas. **$**

Castro
Hotel Unicornio Azul
Pedro Montt 228
Tel: (065) 632 359
Fax: (065) 632 808
Lovely hotel with a good view over the harbor. **$$$**

The sea-end of Calle Sotomayor in Castro is full of guest houses and family homes that offer lodging at very reasonable prices, usually around US$10/person. The best plan is to walk around, talk to the owners and ask to see the rooms, before making a choice.

Achao, Isla Quinchao
Hostería La Nave
Prat s/n
Tel: (065) 661 219
Clean hotel with a good restaurant built on stilts over the sea in an attractive fishing harbor. **$**

Chonchi
Esmeralda By The Sea
Irarrázaval 8
Tel: (065) 671 328
Canadian-owned hostel, with dorms and private rooms with/without private bathroom; special attraction is dinner with shellfish raised on the hostel's own farm. **$–$$**

Cucao
This is a tiny village in a beautiful setting on the Pacific coast near the Chiloé National Park. There are three *residenciales*: the **Posada**, **El Arrayán** and **El Paraíso**. All prices: **$** The National Park also has four cabins, each for six people, but it is wise to book ahead (tel: (02) 390 0125).

AISEN

Coyhaique
Hostería Coyhaique
Magallanes 131
Tel: (067) 231 137
Fax: (067) 233 274
Relatively new guest house in a beautiful park setting with large well-kept gardens. **$$$**

Puyuhuapi
Hostería Termas de Puyuhuapi
Bahia Dorita s/n, Canal Puyuhuapi
Tel: (067) 325 103.
A luxury hotel in countryside of unrivaled beauty, but difficult to get into, except as part of a four-day package deal. Most people come here to relax in the thermal waters, but the hotel also organizes walks and horseback-riding excursions for its more energetic guests. **$$$$**

MAGALLANES & TIERRA DEL FUEGO

Torres del Paine
Very early booking is essential for hotels in Parque Nacional Torres del Paine. The season is short and demand far exceeds supply.
Hotel Explora Patagonia
Tel: (02) 395 2533 in Santiago
Fax: (02) 228 4655 in Santiago
www.explora.com
This is a beautifully designed hotel, offering all-inclusive 3-, 4- and 7-day deals with excellent guided excursions around the park. Minimum stay: three nights. **$$$$**
Hostería Lago Grey
Tel: (061) 410 172
Fax: (061) 225 986
www.austrohoteles.cl
Pleasant hotel overlooking the spectacular Grey glacier. **$$$$**

Hostería Pehoé
Tel: (061) 244 506
Fax: (061) 248 052
www.pehoe.com
A small, comfortable hotel on the shores of the turquoise Lago Pehoé. **$$$$**
Posada Río Serrano
Km 339 Ruta 9 Norte
Tel: (061) 412 911
A restored *estancia* (estate) and one of the few cheaper alternatives in this area. **$$$**

Puerto Natales
Puerto Natales has plenty of budget accommodation – most of it clean, friendly and family-run – that is used by hikers making for Torres del Paine.
Hotel Costaustralis
Pedro Montt 262
Tel: (061) 412 000
Fax: (061) 411 881
www.costaustralis.com
A luxury hotel on the waterfront. **$$$$**
Hotel Juan Ladrilleros
Pedro Montt 161
Tel: (061) 415 798
Fax: (061) 415 983
Friendly with good views. **$$$**
Concepto Indigo
Ladrillero 105 (on the outskirts of the town)
Tel/fax: (061) 413 609
www.conceptoindigo.com
Eight rooms with/without bathroom; vegetarian restaurant. **$$**

Punta Arenas
Cabo de Hornos
Plaza Muñoz Gamero 1025
Tel: (061) 242 134
Fax: (061) 229 473
www.hotelcabodehornos.cl
Grandiose block adjacent to the main plaza. **$$$$**
Hotel Plaza
José Nogueira 1116
Tel: (061) 241 300
Fax: (061) 248 613
www.chileaustral.com/hplaza
Centrally located and comfortable. **$$$**
Hostal O'Higgins
O'Higgins 1205
Tel/fax: (061) 227 999
Rooms with/without bathroom. **$–$$**

Price Categories

All the prices are for double occupancy per night with breakfast unless otherwise stated. Non nationals paying in dollars avoid the 19 percent IVA (sales tax).

$ less than US$25
$$ US$25–60
$$$ US$60–120
$$$$ more than US$120

PACIFIC ISLANDS

Easter Island
Hotel Hanga Roa
Av. Pont s/n
Tel/fax: (032) 100 299
Expensive hotel, as are most on the island. This one is considered the most luxurious. **$$$$**
Hotel Iorana
Policarpo s/n
Tel/fax: (032) 100 312
www.hoteliorana.cl
The island's other top-range hotel; lovely views, but rather out of the way – near the airport. **$$$**

There are also plenty of inexpensive *residenciales*, some of which offer evening meals, and many restaurants on the island.

Juan Fernández Islands
All accommodations on Isla Robinson Crusoe are agreeable, if not delightful. Bookings can be made through the airlines that fly to the island, some of which own hotels there.

There are a handful of other hotels, mostly in the moderate price range. Cheaper accommodations are provided by island families, usually in cabins.
Hostería Aldea Daniel Defoe
Larraín Alcalde 449
Tel/fax: (032) 751 075
Cabins in the town of San Juan Bautista. **$$**

Where to Eat

Eating Out

The number – and quality – of Santiago's restaurants has increased dramatically in recent years. A small drawback to eating here is that not all places display their menus but, as a general guide, prices tend to vary according to neighborhood. Restaurants in the center of town, Baquedano and Bellavista are usually cheaper, while Las Condes is definitely the pricey end of town.

Most restaurants, including the more expensive ones, offer a reasonable set lunch *(menú fijo)*, which is better value than individual dishes on the menu and is a good way of sampling restaurants that would be out of your price range in the evening.

Hotels
The five-star hotels in the city all have their own high-class restaurants. The **Bristol** in Plaza San Francisco in the center of town (tel: 639 3832) is a regular award winner for its modern version of traditional Chilean cuisine. In summer, the **Hyatt Regency** (tel: 02 218 1234) and the **Sheraton** (tel: 02 233 5000) both offer pool-side dining with excellent food.

Snacks and Cafés
For a relaxed atmosphere and a budget meal, there are numerous cafés and restaurants bordering the Plaza de Armas and along Huérfanos.

When you just want a good coffee in Las Condes, wander along Isidora Goyenechea Avenue, where you'll find not only Starbucks, but also many other home-grown coffee shops. In the downtown area,

coffee bars also abound, but many, especially on side streets, correspond to an odd Chilean phenomenon, known as *café con piernas* – which literally means "coffee with legs". Here, your coffee will be served by a very skimpily clad waitress. The traditional Café Haití (of which there are several branches in the downtown area, the largest on Paseo Ahumada) have always been known for their mini-skirted waitresses and are totally respectable. However, the *café con piernas* bars have taken this several steps further and, although perfectly safe, some have a sideline in prostitution.

Breakfasts are not easy to find except in the Providencia and Las Condes coffee shops. One of the best places for a leisurely breakfast is the Café Melba *(see page 362)*.

Santiago Restaurant Listings

There are five main restaurant centers in Santiago. Each district has many restaurants well worth recommending as well as its own distinctive character. The telephone code for Santiago is 02.

EL CENTRO

El Centro is at its liveliest Monday through Friday from 1 to 4pm, during business lunchtimes. Whether it's in a bustling hamburger joint, or a formal Italian buffet, lunch is an important meal in Chile. For great value, *el menú fijo* – sometimes referred to as *la colación* – is highly recommended. Here's a variety of reliable choices:

Price Guide

$ under US$15
$$ US$15–25
$$$ US$25–40
Prices are per person for a three-course à la carte meal, not including drinks.

Prego Tenderini
Tenderini 171, piso 2
Tel: (02) 639 5612
Italian food. Only open for lunch. **$$**
Le Due Torri
San Antonio 258, Local 9
Tel: (02) 633 3799
Serves varied Italian food and is
popular at lunch-time; buffet entrée
table. **$$**
El Naturista
Moneda 846
Tel: (02) 672 7627
Chile's oldest vegetarian
restaurant. Fast, but slightly
unimaginative food. **$**
Donde Augusto
Mercado Central
Tel: (02) 698 1366
Excellent fish and shellfish in
Santiago's historic fruit and
vegetable market; open until 5pm. **$**

For a cheap meal right in the center
of town, it's also worth trying the
small Peruvian restaurants near the
cathedral, where the local Peruvian
community tends to gather. The
furnishings are sparse, but the food
is usually first-rate.

BAQUEDANO

The tiny district of Baquedano is a
picturesque niche of cultural
activity and intimate restaurants.
Not far from the center of town,
the Plaza Mulato Gil de Castro
provides a showcase for the
artists and intellectuals who live
in the area. To get there, just ask
the taxi driver for the Plaza Mulato
Gil, or walk along Merced and turn
right into Lastarría. The exact
address is José Victorino Lastarría
305–7.

The **Pérgola de la Plaza** in the
square is a very attractive escape
from the city chaos. There are
tables in the courtyard and lunches
are reasonably priced. **$**

Other restaurants to try include:
Restaurante Japonés Izakaya Yoko
Merced 456
Tel:(02) 632 1954
Excellent, authentic Japanese food.
Don't be put off by the seedy
exterior. **$$**

Squadritto
Rosal 332
Tel: (02) 632 2121
A successful Italian restaurant,
pleasantly decorated. Not cheap,
but reliable. **$$**

BELLAVISTA

Bellavista holds the reputation for
being Santiago's most bohemian
neighborhood. Within easy striking
distance of the center (a US$2 taxi
ride – ask for Calle Pío Nono – or a
half-hour walk), restaurants line
Bellavista's main street, as well as
the more charming backstreets.
The emphasis here is on having
a relaxed night out – which might
include an after-dinner drink or
listening to salsa at a local
salsoteca – but watch your
belongings. Drugs are sold in
Bellavista, which has meant an
increase in crime in recent years.
El Otro Sitio
Antonia López de Bello 53
Tel: (02) 777 3059
Some of the best Peruvian food
available in Santiago. **$$**
San Fruttuoso
Mallinkrodt 180
Tel: (02) 777 1476
Excellent Italian food in a trattoria-
style setting. **$$**
Sarita Colonia
Dardignac 50
Tel: (02) 737 0242
Bar, as well as a restaurant serving
Peruvian food; favorite gay meeting
place. **$$**
La Tasca Mediterránea
Purísima 161
Tel: (02) 735 3901, and
Domínica 35
Tel: (02) 737 1542
Reasonably priced Spanish seafood

Feeding the Children

If you're traveling with children,
relax about eating out. Most
restaurants are child-friendly and
although most don't provide child-
sized dishes, will readily split up
a normal portion into two, or
provide a plate of French fries.

Service Charge

Service charge is not included
on menu prices and it's usual to
leave a 10 percent tip. If you're
paying with a credit card, you can
add it to the total.

served in an appealing
Mediterranean atmosphere. **$**
El Caramaño
Purísima 257
Tel: 737 7043
Traditional Chilean dishes at very
reasonable prices. **$**

PROVIDENCIA

In Providencia, you'll find very good
food, usually at reasonable prices.
Some places not to miss are:
Aquí Está Coco
La Concepción 236
Tel: (02) 235 8649
Not cheap, but one of the best
places in Santiago to sample
Chile's wonderful fish. **$$$**
Osadía
Av. Tobalaba 477
Tel: (02) 232 2732
Imaginative food by one of Chile's
top young chefs; the menu includes
dishes using traditional Mapuche
ingredients. **$$$**
El Parrón
Providencia 1184
Tel: (02) 251 8911
One of Santiago's most traditional
places to eat barbecued meat. **$$**
Rivoli
Nueva de Lyon 77
Tel: (02) 231 7969
Good, well-priced Italian food.
Outdoor seating in summer. **$**
El Huerto
Orrego Luco 054
Tel: (02) 233 2690
Excellent vegetarian food, prepared
with care and imagination. **$**
Café del Patio
Av. Providencia 1670-A, Local 8
Tel: (02) 236 1251
Another good vegetarian café that
also serves drinks until 2am. **$**
Le Flaubert
Orrego Luco 0125
Tel:(02) 231 9424

A pleasant place for a light lunch or tea; nice garden. One of the few places to provide a British-style pot of tea. **$$**

Phone Box Pub
Av. Providencia 1670, Local 1
Tel: (02) 235 1652
Traditional British fare, including steak and kidney pie. **$**

LAS CONDES AND VITACURA

The Las Condes and Vitacura districts are home to Santiago's most fashionable restaurants. Many cluster along the connecting streets of Isidora Goyenechea and El Bosque Norte, and along the even more exclusive Alonso de Córdova. We suggest:

Europeo
Alonso de Córdova 2417
Tel: (02) 208 3603
Perhaps Santiago's best restaurant and one of its most expensive; the right place for a real splurge. **$$$**

Akarana
Reyes Lavalle 3310
Tel: (02) 231 9667
Imaginative food in pleasant surroundings; same owner as Café Melba *(see below)*. **$$**

Isla Negra
El Bosque Norte 0325
Tel: (02) 231 3118
Traditional Chilean food. **$$**

Pinpilinpausha
Isidora Goyenechea 2900
Tel: (02) 233 6507
Excellent Spanish food is served at this traditional restaurant. **$$**

Sakura
Av. Vitacura 4111
Tel: (02) 206 7600
One of Santiago's most popular sushi bars. **$$**

Le Fournil
Av. Vitacura 3841
Tel: (02) 228 0219
A French bread shop that also serves light meals. The meals are good, but the bread is even better, and there's a supermarket opposite to buy the filling for your sandwich. **$**

Café Melba
Don Carlos 2898
Tel: (02) 232 4546
This place offers excellent service and is a good place for breakfast, lunch or just a coffee. **$**

Drinking Notes

Nothing brings out the flavor of local dishes better than one of Chile's famous wines – possibly the best-value wine in the world *(see features on page 106)*. A citrusy, ice-cold *pisco sour* serves as a popular *aperitif*, as does *vaina*, a light blend of brandy or sherry with egg, vanilla and cinnamon. Chilean *chicha* is freshly fermented grape juice, and *borgoña* is a concoction of red wine, ice and fresh strawberries. It is generally bought by the jug.

Culture

Art Galleries

Santiago has an abundance of art galleries. The largest – and most expensive – are in the up-market Vitacura neighborhood. These include **Galería Animal**, **Galería ArtEspacio** and **Galería Isabel Aninat**, not far from each other on Alonso de Córdova, and **Galería Tomás Andreu** and **AMS Marlborough**, both on Nueva Costanera.

In the Baquedano neighborhood, the Telefónica telecommunications company puts on interesting shows in the ground-floor gallery of its corporate building on Plaza Italia.

Many smaller and often more experimental art galleries can be found in the Baquedano and Bellavista neighborhoods. In Baquedano, take time to visit the **Museo de Artes Visuales** in Plaza Mulato Gil and perhaps to look at the art shops on Merced, across from Lastarría.

In Bellavista, by strolling around, you'll find many galleries – often shoestring ones – showing the work of younger artists.

Classical Music and Ballet

For classical music, the **Teatro Municipal**, on the corner of San Antonio and Agustinas, offers a complete season between April and December, as well as a ballet and opera season. Tel: (02) 463 1000 for further information and tickets. Tickets are also available at the theater and in the Parque Arauco shopping mall.

The **Teatro Oriente**, Av. Pedro de Valdivia, between Avenidas Providencia and Costanera, presents overseas artists during the season of May through October. Information and tickets from Av. 11 de Septiembre 2214, Of. 66, tel: (02) 251 5321.

Quality recordings of international music are available at the various branches of **Feria del Disco**, Chile's main music-store chain.

Theater

There are over 100 theaters in Santiago, putting on classical, modern or avant-garde plays by Chilean and foreign playwrights, as well as outdoor performances in several city parks during January (take a cushion and warm clothing).

Theater in Santiago has traditionally been excellent and Chileans are very proud of it. However, the number of theaters has mushroomed over recent years, and quality now varies.

If you don't have a great command of Spanish, there are plenty of lively, comical or expressive performances to choose from. Have a look at the busking comedians in the Plaza de Armas on weekends, an interesting place for talent-spotting.

Tickets can usually be booked by phone without payment and are held for collection until half an hour before the performance starts.

Some of the best-equipped and most reliable theaters are:
Centro Cultural Matucana 100
Av. Matucana 100
Tel: (02) 682 4502
Teatro La Comedia
Merced 349
Tel: (02) 639 1523
Teatro Antonio Varas
Morandé 25
Tel: (02) 698 1200
Used by the University of Chile theater group.
Teatro de la Universidad Católica
Jorge Washington 26
Tel: (02) 205 5652

Exhibition Listings

Most of the newspapers have listings of art exhibitions. The "Artes y Letras" section of Sunday's *El Mercurio* has the most extensive.

This theater is run by the Catholic University and stages some of the country's best productions.
Multisala Arena
Jaime Guzmán Errázuriz 3283
Tel: (02) 225 2896
Usually puts on commercial, but high-quality plays, although it's a little out of the way.

There are also a large number of theaters in Bellavista that usually present new or modern pieces.

Cinema

Santiago's traditional neighborhood cinemas have mostly been replaced by multi-screen complexes, usually in shopping malls. These new cinemas, introduced by overseas chains, have better seats and sound than their older equivalents, but the fare they show stems mainly from Hollywood; for independent films, you'll need to go to the smaller "art cinemas".

The daily papers carry complete film listings and the *Wikén* supplement of Thursday's *El Mercurio* reviews each week's new arrivals. Its critics tend to be on the conservative side. Most cinemas charge around US$4.50. Tickets are half-price on Wednesday.

In the center of town, the **Hoyts Paseo Huérfanos** and the **Hoyts San Agustín** carry most of the current films. Other cinemas in the center, especially the smaller ones, tend to show soft porn.

The best of the multi-screen complexes, **Cinemark 12**, is in the Alto Las Condes shopping mall, while the nearby Parque Arauco mall houses another complex, **Showcase Cinemas Parque Arauco**. Both of these malls are a distance from the center, in Las Condes' Av. Kennedy.

The main "art cinemas" are **El Biógrafo**, Lastarría 81 (tel: (02) 633 4435), **Alameda**, Alameda 139 (tel: (02) 664 8890) and **Tobalaba**, Providencia 2563 (tel: (02) 231 6630). In the center of town, the **Normandie**, Tarapacá 1181 (tel: (697 2979) is a bit run-down, but shows films that aren't often available elsewhere. Cinemas do not usually accept phone bookings.

Nightlife

Santiago

Santiago nightlife might range from backgammon in Bellavista to a concert at the Teatro Municipal or a vanguard performance at the theater. Chileans also love to dance and many do so very well, though typically as a couple performing well-known steps.

The night starts late in Santiago. Restaurants open at eight, but don't start to fill up until ten o'clock. For the young, that's still early.

Outside Santiago

Entertainment beyond the capital is very limited, except in the summer months, when the main beach and lake resorts get into gear. But even then, don't expect live theater or good cinema. Most of the activity centers around temporary discotheques and live productions of popular television music shows. One honorable exception is the music festival that the town of Frutillar on Lake Llanquihue puts on in late January, which is of a very high standard.

Dancing

Don't even consider going to a discotheque before midnight or 1 o'clock in the morning, and be prepared to dance until dawn. Those looking for a night's dancing

Casinos

If you're in Arica, Pucón or Puerto Varas, you might want to try the casino, which besides the usual gaming activities, also provides the center of local nightlife.

can try any one of a vast number of discotheques that spring up and often disappear just as quickly. Trends change rapidly, so ask around for advice on the best, newest, and the age group targeted.

Floorshows

In Bellavista, bars with live music begin when the restaurants finish. **La Casa en el Aire Arte**, Antonia López de Bello 0125, has live music most nights of the week, except Wednesday, which is reserved for the bar's collective story-telling tradition. For salsa, also try **La Havana Salsa**, Dominica 142. There is an abundance of other bars in Bellavista, where many new groups and bands give their first performances.

In Ñuñoa, you'll find the **Batuta**, Jorge Washington 52, which is one of Santiago's best places for live music (10.30pm onwards, most nights except Monday; for the current program, see www.batuta.cl) as well as the **House of Rock** (Irarrázaval 5032) and the **Club de Jazz** (Av. José Pedro Alessandri 85).

Santiago takes folklore from the provinces and turns it into live shows at a number of popular, but touristy restaurants.

Los Buenos Muchachos
Ricardo Cumming 1031
Tel: (02) 698 0112
Typical Chilean food and floorshow.
Los Adobes de Argomedo
Argomedo 411
Tel: (02) 222 2104
Set in a huge barn-like hall, three orchestras and a dozen dancers perform on an extendable hydraulic stage, everything from Polynesian *hulas* to Chilean *cuecas*.
La Querencia
Av. Las Condes 14980
Tel: (02) 321 5522
Good food and live music for dancing.
El Refrán
Av. Larraín 5961
Tel: (02) 226 8603
Typical Chilean food. A bit cramped, but the show, which usually includes at least one comedian and a magician, is one of the best.

Pubs

The Chilean version of a pub has mushroomed in recent years, encouraged by the greater availability of imported beers and increasing prosperity. The bars on Suecia, in Providencia, are often recommended to visitors; discard that advice – the area used to be fashionable, but has degenerated into a center for drug dealing and prostitution and, at night, is potentially dangerous. Instead, go further up Providencia where, a few steps down Luis Thayer Ojeda, towards the canal, you'll find a newly opened branch of the traditional **Liguria** bar. Or walk down Providencia to the junction with Manual Montt. There you'll find another Liguria and plenty of other good bars nearby, such as the **Barcelona** and the **Ozono** on Santa Beatriz.

Another alternative is Plaza Ñuñoa. This is a US$5 taxi ride from Providencia, but you'll save that on the price of your drinks. This lovely square is surrounded by lively bars, catering for different age groups. Nearby is the **Batuta** *(see above)*.

The Las Condes pubs are more exclusive and expensive than their Providencia or Ñuñoa equivalents, but there's more space between tables, the food is better and the waiters are professionals, rather than students. Try **Pub-Licity** on El Bosque Norte or **Play Back Studio**, Isidora Goyenechea 2901. Alternatively, move up to the Vitacura area, where you'll find pubs such as the Dublin Irish Pub, Vitacura 9191.

Gay Scene

In Santiago, apart from the **Sarita Colonia** *(see page 361)*, another gay-friendly bar and restaurant is **Santo Remedio** on Román Díaz, two blocks in from Av. Providencia (tel: 235 0984). This bar also has the advantage that it is one of the few in Santiago that opens on Sunday. Gay discotheques include **Fausto** (Av. Santa María 0832) and **Bunker** (Bombero Nuñez 159) in Bellavista. A favorite lesbian discotheque is **Mascara** (Purísima 129), also in Bellavista.

Shopping

What To Buy

Chile's rich geology provides a wide diversity of minerals for handicrafts. Most outstanding are lapis lazuli, (found only in Chile and Afghanistan), silver, bronze and wrought copper.

Other popular souvenirs include:
• Pottery from Arica.
• The unique black pottery of Pomaire, near Santiago.
• The colorful attire of the *huaso* (Chilean cowboy) from the south central valley, some of which can be bought in local *talabarterías* (saddlers' shops).
• Leather goods, boots and handbags, available in the high-street stores of Santiago.
• The beautifully worked silver jewelry of the Mapuches.
• Chilean wine and *pisco*, the local grape liquor.

Where to Shop

Crafts
On Santiago's Avenida Apoquindo 9085, next to the Church of San Vincente Ferrer, **El Pueblito de los Dominicos** is a collection of old-style buildings, comprising about 200 shops where more than 300 craftsmen and women work before the public. Handicrafts, antiques and plants are for sale. At weekends there is music and dancing, and *empanadas* (savory turnovers) for sale. Open daily.

By far the best place to buy handicrafts in Santiago, both as regards to quality and price, is:
Artesanías de Chile
Av. Bellavista 0357
Tel: (02) 777 9427
www.artesaniasdechile.cl
This shop is run by a foundation, presided over by the wife of Chile's

president, that not only markets handicrafts, but also advises artisans on how to improve their work and obtain a fair price. There is another outlet in Pueblito de los Dominicos.

Artesanía is also available at a variety of markets around the city, including one on Av. Manquehue, near the Apumpanque shopping center, and another on Av. Vitacura, near the Cobres de Vitacura shopping center.

Antiques

Antique shops are plentiful in Santiago, usually grouped in specific neighborhoods. Try Avenida Brasil or in and around the Galpones Balmaceda (Balmaceda 2500), in the western part of Santiago. **Centro Lo Castillo**, Candelaría Goyenechea esq. Vitacura, is a good hunting-ground, if you prefer to go up-market.

Shopping Malls

For clothing and more general shopping, there are several modern shopping centers, incorporating a huge number of stores.

Parque Arauco
Av. Presidente Kennedy 5413
Tel: (02) 299 0500.
A shopping mall, containing three department stores and more than 200 specialty stores/boutiques. Take Metro Line 1 to Escuela Militar Station and then the Red Bus service which runs from there.

Alto Las Condes
Av. Kennedy 9001
Tel: (02) 959 0001.
The same stores as Parque Arauco, but in a more spacious setting and sometimes slightly higher prices. Take a *colectivo* from the Escuela Militar metro station.

Lapis Lazuli

Lapis lazuli is crafted in the workshops of Bellavista into many things, not only jewelry. The quality and value of the stone depends on the intensity or depth of the color, i.e. a very dark stone is more valuable than a stone that has a paler color.

Vitacura Neighborhood

The city's most prestigious shops are located on Nueva Costanera and Alonso de Córdova in the Vitacura neighborhood, alongside art galleries, smart coffee shops and bars. The majority of stores are open Monday through Friday 10am–1pm and 4–8.30pm, Saturday 9.30am–2pm. The city center and Providencia are also important shopping areas.

Bookshops

A good range of English books is hard to find but there are a few interesting outlets.

The English Reader, Av. Los Leones 116, offers a wide range of second-hand English books; coffee is served.

Librería Books, Av. Providencia 1652, Local 5, also offers second-hand English books.

Librería Inglesa, Pedro de Valdivia 47, for classical literature and best-sellers.

Librairie Française, Estado 337, Local 22 for books in French.

Photography

There are many one-hour or one-day photo processors along Huérfanos and Ahumada, in the shopping malls and most large supermarkets. Camera supplies are available along McIver and Merced. **Harry Muller**, Ahumada 312, Of. 402, provides a camera-repair service and speaks English and German.

Jewelry and Stonecraft

For lapis lazuli in Santiago:
The main shopping area for lapis lazuli is along Bellavista between Del Arzobispo and Pío Nono, but for more up-market products, try the Parque Arauco and Alto Las Condes shopping malls.

For copper handicrafts:
• **Bozzo** Av. Providencia 2231
Tel: (02) 233 2393. Also in the Parque Arauco shopping mall.
• **H. Stern** jewelry is available at the large hotels, as well as the International Airport.

For silver Mapuche jewelry:
• **Crowne Plaza** shopping gallery.

Sport

Spectator

Certain spectator sports are overwhelmingly popular in Chile. Consider a visit to the Club Hípico, the top-class horse-racing circuit in the capital; experience the enthusiasm of 70,000 football fans at Santiago's main stadium; or enjoy the spectacle of a colorful rodeo on your travels through the Central Valley. It would be difficult to exaggerate the pride Chileans have for these sports in particular.

Horse-racing

There are races at the Club Hípico, Av. Blanco Encalada 2540 (tel: (02) 693 9600), every Sunday and every second Wednesday afternoon from January to March in Viña del Mar. The less-exclusive **Hipódromo Chile**, Av. Vivaceta 2753 (tel: (02) 270 9200) has racing every Saturday afternoon.

The quality of horse breeding in Chile is world famous. A special tour is possible to **Los Lingues**, a private *hacienda* (ranch) 120 km (75 miles) south of Santiago, where it is said the best horses in Chile are bred. Arrangements can be made in Santiago (Av. Providencia 1100, Torre C., Of. 205, tel: (02) 235 2458) for a one-day excursion, which includes lunch, transport and a horse show for around US$55 per person, but don't let them persuade you to stay overnight at the hotel; it's expensive and very sub-standard.

Soccer

Soccer is easily the most popular sport in Chile, attracting vast crowds, who wear their team colors, carry flags and signs and chant all day and late into the evening.

Processions of enthusiasts will come storming into the Plaza Baquedano sounding like a political rally.

Participant

Chile's long sea coast and its lakes and rivers are conducive to watersports, such as water-skiing, windsurfing, rowing, white-water rafting, canoeing, skin diving, fishing and swimming.

There are numerous quality ski resorts in the Andes mountains. From June to October they are popular worldwide. Facilities include ski lifts and luxury lodges, and many are also blessed with outstanding scenery. The same mountains challenge hikers and climbers with a choice of gentle trails or some of the most rugged peaks in the world (see page 123–9).

Facilities exist for many other sports, such as golf, tennis, swimming, cycling, car-racing and horsemanship. For more information contact the National Sports Office: DIGEDER, Direccion General de Deportes, Fidel Oteíza 1956, piso 3; tel: (02) 274 3701.

Language

Of the many versions of Latin-American Spanish in South America, the Chilean version is one of the hardest to understand. Chileans neglect to pronounce consonants clearly, if at all. Television newsreaders are the only exception.

So Chile is not the ideal place to learn Spanish. (Best value for classes as well as best for understanding is probably Quito, Ecuador, if you are considering further travel in South America.) At any rate, it is much better to know a little Spanish when you arrive. English is spoken at major hotels and by quite a few Chileans, but don't count on it with taxi drivers, waiters or porters.

Language schools, apart from advertised private tuition, include the Chilean-British Institute and the Chilean North-American Cultural Institute. The main private language schools, including Berlitz, offer tailor-made individual courses, but these tend to be expensive. Most reputable language schools ask for at least US$1,300 a week for full-day courses. Berlitz also offers a cassette that is worthwhile for beginners:

Berlitz Language Centers
Moneda 1160, piso 7, Santiago
Tel: (02) 672 7639.

It may not always be essential for foreign speakers to have the correct form of address, i.e. formal or informal, or even the correct masculine or feminine conjugations, as long as you can make yourself understood. Many travelers learn Spanish to the present tense stage and manage very well on this alone. However, in order to be well received in Chile, there are a few things worth remembering. Upon meeting someone, whether they be a taxi driver or a long-lost uncle, you should always use the greeting, "Good morning" or "Good afternoon/evening." It is then appropriate to wait for the response before continuing your conversation. A woman is addressed as *Señora*, a girl or young woman as *Señorita* (unless she's wearing a wedding ring), and a man as *Señor*, although *chica* (for a young woman) or *chico* (for a young man) may be more common in certain situations.

Basic Communication

Yes *Sí*
No *No*
Thank you *Gracias*
You're welcome *No hay de que/ Por nada*
Alright/Okay/That's fine *Está bien*
Please *Por favor*
Excuse me (to get attention) *¡Permiso!/¡Por favor!*
Excuse me to get through a crowd) *¡Permiso!*
Excuse me (sorry) *Perdóneme, Discúlpeme*
Wait a minute! *¡Un momento!*
Please help me (formal) *Por favor, ayúdeme*
Certainly *¡Claro!/¡Claro que sí!/ ¡Por cierto!*
Can I help you? (formal) *¿Puedo ayudarle?*
Can you show me...? *¿Puede mostrarme...?*
I need... *Necesito....*
I'm lost *Estoy perdido(a)*
I'm sorry *Lo siento*
I don't know *No sé*
I don't understand *No entiendo*
Do you speak English/French/ German? (formal) *¿Habla inglés/ francés/alemán?*
Could you speak more slowly, please? *¿Puede hablar más despacio, por favor?*
Could you repeat that, please? *¿Puede repetirlo, por favor?*
Slowly *despacio/lentamente*
here/there *aquí* (place where), *acá* (motion to)/*allí, allá, ahí* (near you)
What? *¿Qué?/¿Cómo?*
When? *¿Cuándo?*
Why? *¿Por qué?*
Where? *¿Dónde?*

Greetings

Hello! ¡Hola!
Hello (Good day) Buenos días
Good afternoon/night Buenas tardes/noches
Goodbye Ciao/¡Adios!
My name is... Me llamo...
What is your name? (formal) ¿Cómo se llama usted?
Mr/Miss/Mrs Señor/Señorita/Señora
Pleased to meet you ¡Encantado!
I am English/American/Canadian/Irish/Scottish/Australian Soy inglés(a)/ norteamericano(a)/ canadiense/irlandés(a)/ escocés(a)/australiano(a)
Do you speak English? (formal) ¿Habla inglés?
How are you? (formal/informal) ¿Cómo está? ¿Qué tal?
Fine, thanks Muy bien, gracias
See you later Hasta luego
Take care (informal) ¡Cuídate!

Who? ¿Quién(es)?
How? ¿Cómo?
Which? ¿Cuál?
How much/how many? ¿Cuánto?/ ¿Cuántos?
Do you have...? ¿Hay...?
How long? ¿Cuánto tiempo?
Big, bigger Grande, más grande
Small, smaller Pequeño, mas pequeño/chico, más chico
I want.../I would like.../I need... Quiero.../Quisiera.../Necesito...
Where is the lavatory (men's/women's)? ¿Dónde se encuentra el baño (de caballeros/de damas)?
Which way is it to ...? ¿Cómo se va a ...?

Telephone Calls

The area code El código de área
Where can I buy/do you sell telephone cards? ¿Dónde puedo comprar tarjetas telefónicas?/¿Se venden aquí tarjetas telefónicas?
May I use your phone to make a local call? ¿Puedo usar su teléfono para hacer una llamada local?
Of course you may ¡Por supuesto que sí!/¡Como no!/¡Claro!

Hello (on the phone) ¡Aló!
May I speak to...? ¿Puedo hablar con... (name), por favor?
Sorry, he/she isn't in Lo siento, no se encuentra
Can he/she call you back? ¿Puede devolver la llamada?
Yes, he/she can reach me at... Sí, él/ella puede llamarme en (number)
I'll try again later Voy a intentar más tarde
Can I leave a message? ¿Puedo dejar un mensaje?
Please tell him/her I called Favor avísele que llamé
Hold on Un momento, por favor
Can you speak up, please? ¿Puede hablar más fuerte, por favor?

In the Hotel

Do you have a vacant room? ¿Tiene una habitación disponible?
I have a reservation Tengo una reservación
I'd like... Quisiera...
a single/double (with double bed)/ a room with twin beds una habitación individual/ una habitación matrimonial/una habitación doble
for one night/two nights por una noche/dos noches
on the ground floor/first floor/top floor/with sea view en el primer piso/en el segundo piso/en el último piso/con vista al mar
Does the room have a private bathroom or shared bathroom? ¿Tiene la habitación baño privado o baño compartido?
Does it have hot water? ¿Tiene agua caliente?
Could you show me another room, please? ¿Puede mostrarme otra habitación, por favor?
Is it a quiet room? ¿Es una habitación tranquila?
What time do you close (lock) the doors? ¿A qué hora se cierran las puertas?
I would like to change rooms Quisiera cambiar de habitación
This room is too noisy/hot/cold/small Esta habitación es demasiado ruidosa/calorosa/ fría/pequeña
How much is it? ¿Cuánto cuesta?

Does the price include tax/breakfast/meals/drinks? ¿El precio incluye el impuesto/ desayuno/ comidas/ bebidas?
Do you accept credit cards/travelers' checks/dollars? ¿Se aceptan tarjetas de crédito/ cheques de viajeros/dólares?
What time is breakfast/lunch/dinner? ¿A qué hora está servido el desayuno/almuerzo/la cena?
Please wake me at... Favor despert arme a...
Come in! ¡Pase!, ¡Adelante!
I'd like to pay the bill now, please Quisiera cancelar la cuenta ahora, por favor

USEFUL WORDS

Bath el baño
Dining room el comedor
Elevator/lift el ascensor
Key la llave
Push/pull empuje/tire
Safety deposit box la caja de seguridad
Soap el jabón
Shampoo el champú
Shower la ducha
Toilet paper el papel higiénico
Towel la toalla

Drinks

What would you like to drink? ¿Qué quiere tomar?
coffee... un café...
with milk cortado
milky coffee café con leche
strong fuerte
small/large pequeño/grande
with sugar con azúcar
tea... té...
with lemon/milk con limón/ cortado
herbal tea té de hierbas
hot chocolate chocolate caliente
fresh orange juice jugo de naranja natural
orangeade naranjada
soft drink bebida/refresco
mineral water still/carbonated agua mineral sin gas/con gas
with/without ice con/sin hielo
cover charge entrada
minimum consumption consumo mínimo

beer hall/pub *pub*
discotheque *disco/discoteca*
nightclub *club nocturno*
a bottle/half a bottle *una botella/media botella*
a glass of red/white/rosé wine *una copa de vino tinto/blanco/rosado*
beer *una cerveza*
Is service included? *¿Incluye el servicio?*
I need a receipt, please *Necesito un recibo, por favor*
Keep the change *Está bien, gracias*
Cheers! *¡Salud!*
ice cream *helado*
sandwich *sandwich*
turnover (filled with meat, cheese, etc.) *una empanada*

IN A RESTAURANT

I'd like to book a table *Quisiera reservar una mesa, por favor*
Do you have a table for...? *¿Tiene una mesa para...?*
I have a reservation *Tengo una reservación*
breakfast/lunch/dinner *desayuno/almuerzo/cena*
I'm a vegetarian *Soy vegetariano(a)*
Is there a vegetarian dish? *¿Hay un plato vegetariano?*
May we have the menu? *¿Puede traernos la carta (or el menú)?*
wine list *la carta de vinos*
What would you recommend? *¿Qué recomendaría?*
home-made *casero(a)*
fixed-price menu *menú fijo*
special of the day *plato del día/sugerencia del chef*
The meal was very good *La comida fue muy buena*
Waiter *Garzón/mozo*

Menu Decoder

ENTRADA (FIRST COURSE)

sopa/crema **soup/cream soup**
sopa de ajo **garlic soup**
sopa de cebolla **onion soup**
ensalada... **salad...**
  mixta **mixed**

ensalada de palta con tomate **avocado pear and tomato salad**
pan de ajo **garlic bread**

PLATO PRINCIPAL/DE FONDO (MAIN COURSE)

crudo **raw**
vuelta y vuelta **rare**
término medio **medium rare**
tres cuartos **medium**
bien cocido(a) **well done**

La Carne (Meat)
a las brasas/a la parrilla **charcoal grilled**
a la plancha **grilled**
ahumado(a) **smoked**
albóndigas **meat balls**
asado(a) **roasted**
cerdo/chancho **pork**
chorizos **Spanish-style sausage**
chuleta **chop**
conejo **rabbit**
cordero **lamb**
costillas **ribs**
apanado(a) **breaded**
frito(a) **fried/batter fried**
guisado(a) **stewed**
hamburguesa **hamburger**
higado de res **beef liver**
jamón **ham**
lomito **tenderloin**
milanesa **breaded and fried thin cut of meat**
pernil **leg of pork**
riñones **kidneys**
salchichas/vienesas **sausage or hot dogs**
ternera **veal**

Ave (Fowl)
alas **wings**
chicharrón de pollo **chicken cut up in small pieces and deep fried**
truto **thigh**
pato **duck**
pavo **turkey**
pechuga **breast**
truto chico **leg**
pollo **chicken**

Mariscos/Pescado (Fish/Seafood)
almejas **clams**
anchoa **anchovy**
atún **tuna**
bacalao **cod**

calamares **squid**
camarones **prawns**
centolla **king-crab**
cholgas **mussels**
congrio **kingclip**
corvina **sea bass**
jaiba **crab**
langosta **lobster**
lenguado **sole or flounder**
mariscos **shellfish**
mero **grouper**
ostiones **scallops**
ostras **oysters**
pulpo **octopus**
salmón **salmon**
sardinas **sardines**
trucha **trout**

Verduras (Vegetables)
ajo **garlic**
alcachofa **artichoke**
arvejas **peas**
berenjena **eggplant (aubergine)**
betarraga **beets/beetroot**
brócoli **broccoli**
camote **sweet potato**
cebolla **onion**
champiñones **mushrooms**
choclo corn **corn on the cob**
coliflor **cauliflower**
espárrago **asparagus**
espinaca **spinach**
lechuga **lettuce**
pepino **cucumber**
pimentón **green (bell) pepper**
porotos verdes **green beans**
puerro **leek**
repollo **cabbage**
zanahorias **carrots**
zapallo **pumpkin or yellow squash**
zapallito italiano **zucchini (courgette)**

FRUTAS (FRUIT)

cereza **cherry**
ciruela **plum**
dátil **date**
durazno **peach**
frambuesa **raspberry**
frutilla **strawberry**
guayaba **guava**
higo **fig**
limón **lemon**
mandarina **mandarin**
manzana **apple**
melón **cantaloupe/melon**
mora **blackberry**

naranja **orange**
palta **avocado pear**
papaya **mountain papaya**
plátano **banana**
pera **pear**
piña **pineapple**
pomelo **grapefruit**
sandía **watermelon**
uvas **grapes**

MISCELLANEOUS

arróz **rice**
azúcar **sugar**
empanada **savory turnover**
huevos (revueltos/fritos/ a la copa) **eggs (scrambled/fried/boiled)**
mantequilla **butter**
mermelada **jam**
mostaza **mustard**
pan **bread**
pan integral **wholewheat bread**
pan tostado **toast**
pimienta negra **black pepper**
queso **cheese**
sal **salt**
salsa de tomate/ketchup **ketchup**
salsa picante **hot sauce**
tallarines **spaghetti**
tocino **bacon**
tortilla **omelette**

Tourist Attractions/ Terms

aguas termales **hot springs**
artesanía **handicrafts**
campamento **camp**
capilla **chapel**
castillo/fuerte **fort**
catedral **cathedral**
cerro **hill**
comunidad indígena **(indigenous) community**
convento **convent**
cumbre **(mountain) peak**
galería **gallery**
iglesia **church**
isla **island**
jardín botánico **botanical garden**
laguna **lagoon**
lago **lake**
mar **sea**
mercado **market**
mirador **viewpoint**
montaña **mountain**
monumento **monument**

Oceano Pacífico **Pacific Ocean**
oficina de turismo **tourist information office**
parque infantil **playground**
parque **park**
piscina **swimming pool**
playa **beach**
plaza **town square**
postal **postcard**
puente **bridge**
quebrada **gorge**
río **river**
ruinas **ruins**
sanctuario **sanctuary**
teleférico **cable car**
torre **tower**
zona colonial **colonial zone**
zoológico **zoo**

Road Signs

autopista **freeway**
bajada/subida peligrosa **dangerous downgrade/incline**
calle ciega **dead-end street**
calle de un sentido **one-way street**
carretera **highway, road**
cede el paso **yield/give way**
circunvalación **loop road (ring road)**
con precaución **caution**
conserve su derecha **keep to the right**
conserve su pista **do not change lanes**
cruce **crossroads**
cruce de ferrocarril (sin señal) **railway crossing (without signal)**
despacio **slow**
desvío **detour**
doble vía **two-way traffic**
Enciende luces en el túnel **Turn on lights in the tunnel**
entrada prohibida **entrance prohibited**
estacionamiento **parking**
fuera de servicio **not in service**
hundimiento **sunken road**
no estacionar/prohibido estacionarse aquí **no parking**
no gire en U **no U-turn**
no hay paso, vía cerrado **road blocked**
no hay salida **no exit**
no pare **no stopping here**
no toque la bocina **no horn honking**
¡ojo! **watch out!**
pare **stop**
paso de ganado **cattle crossing**

paso de peatones **pedestrian crossing**
peaje **toll booth**
peligro **danger**
pendiente fuerte, curva fuerte **steep hill, sharp curve**
pista derecha **right lane**
pista izquierda **left lane**
reductor de velocidad **speed bump**
resbaladizo al humedecerse **slippery when wet**
rotonda **traffic circle (roundabout)**
salida **exit**
semáforo **traffic light**
sólo tránsito local **local traffic only**
trabajos en la vía **roadworks**
una sola pista **single lane**
velocidad controlada **speed controlled or restricted**
vía en reparación **road under repair**
zona de derrumbes **zone of landslides**
zona de niebla (neblina) **fog zone**
zona de remolque **tow zone**
zona escolar **school zone**
zona militar **military zone**
vulcanización **tire repair shop**

Traveling

airline *línea áerea*
airport *aeropuerto*
arrivals/departures *llegadas/salidas*
bus stop *parada (de bus)*
dock for small boats/large boats *embarcadero/muelle*
bus terminal *terminal de buses*
bus *bus/micro*
car *auto*
car rental *arriendo de autos*
connection *conexión*
ferry *transbordador*
first class/second class *primera clase/segunda clase, clase de turista*
flight *vuelo*
luggage, bag(s) *equipaje, maleta(s)*
Next stop please (for buses) *En la próxima parada, por favor*
one-way ticket *pasaje de ida*
platform *el andén*
round-trip, return ticket *boleto de ida y vuelta*
sailboat *velero*
ship *barco*
subway *Metro*
taxi *taxi*
yacht *yate*

Terms for Addresses/ Directions

a la derecha **on the right**
a la izquierda **on the left**
al lado de **beside**
alrededor de **around**
arriba/abajo **above/below**
avenida (Av) **avenue**
calle **street**
cerca de **near**
cruce **crossroad(s)**
cruce con/con **at the junction of (two streets)**
doble hacia la izquierda/la derecha **turn to the left/right**
debajo de **under**
delante de **in front of**
derecho **straight ahead**
detrás de **behind**
edificio (Edif) **highrise building**
en frente de/frente de/frente a **in front of**
en **in, on, at**
en la parte de atrás **in the rear area (as behind a building)**
encima de **on top of**
entre **between**
esquina (Esq) **corner**
penthouse/primer piso/ segundo piso/entrepiso/ subterráneo **penthouse/ ground floor/second floor/ mezzanine/basement**
residencial (Res) **small pension**
torre **tower**
una cuadra **a block**

Airport, or Travel Agency

customs and immigration *aduana e inmigración*
travel/tour agency *agencia de viajes/de turismo*
ticket *pasaje/boleto*
I would like to purchase a ticket for... *Quisiera comprar un pasaje (boleto) para...*
When is the next/last flight/ departure for ...? *¿Cuándo es el próximo/último vuelo para ...?*
What time does the plane/bus/ boat/ferry leave/return? *¿A qué hora sale/regresa el avión/el bus/ la lancha/el transbordador?*
What time do I have to be at the airport? *¿A qué hora tengo que estar en el aeropuerto?*

Is the tax included? *¿Está incluido el impuesto?*
What is included in the price? *¿Qué está incluido en el precio?*
departure tax? *¿el impuesto de aeropuerto?*
I would like a seat in first class/ business class/tourist class *Quisiera un asiento en primera clase/ejecutivo/clase de turista*
lost luggage office *oficina de reclamos de equipaje*
on time *a tiempo*
late *atrasado*
I need to change my ticket *Necesito cambiar mi pasaje*
How long is the flight? *¿Cuánto dura el vuelo?*
Is this seat taken? *¿Está ocupado este asiento?*
Which is the stop closest to ...? *¿Cuál es la parada más cerca a ...?*
Could you please advise me when we reach/the stop for ...? *¿Por favor, puede avisarme cuando llegamos a/a la parada para ...?*
Is this the stop for ...? *¿Es ésta la parada para ...?*

Driving

Where can I rent a car? *¿Dónde puedo arrendar un auto?*
Is mileage included? *¿Está incluido el kilometraje?*
comprehensive insurance *seguro completo*
spare tire/jack/emergency triangle *rueda de repuesto/*

Colors

light/dark *claro/oscuro*
red *rojo*
yellow *amarillo*
blue *azul*
brown *café*
black *negro*
white *blanco*
beige *beige*
green *verde*
wine *burdeo*
gray *gris*
orange *color naranjo*
pink *rosado*
purple *púrpuro*
silver *plateado*
gold *dorado*

gato/triángulo de emergencia
Where is the registration document? *¿Dónde se encuentra(n) el padrón/los documentos del auto?*
Does the car have an alarm? *¿El auto tiene alarma?*
a road map/a city map *un mapa carretero/plano de la ciudad*
How do I get to ...? *¿Cómo se llega a ...?*
Turn right/left *Doble a la derecha/izquierda*
at the next corner/street *en la próxima esquina/calle*
Go straight ahead *Siga derecho*
You are on the wrong road *No está en el camino correcto*
Please show me where am I on the map *Por favor, indíqueme dónde estoy en el mapa*
Where is...? *¿Dónde se encuentra...?*
Where is the nearest...? *¿Dónde se encuentra el/la ... más cercano(a)?*
How long does it take to get there? *¿Cuánto tiempo se requiere para llegar?*
driver's license *licencia de conducir*
service station, gasoline station *estación de servicio, bomba de bencina*
My car won't start *Mi auto no parte*
My car is overheating *Mi auto se está recalentando*
My car has broken down *Mi auto está en pana*
tow truck *una grúa*
Where can I find a car repair shop? *¿Dónde se encuentra un taller mecánico?*
Can you check the...? *¿Puede revisar/chequear...?*
There's something wrong with the... *Hay un problema con...*
oil/water/air/brake fluid/ light bulb *aceite/agua/aire/ líquido de frenos/ampolleta*
trunk/hood/door/window *maleta/capó/puerta/ventana*

Emergencies

Help! *¡Socorro! ¡Auxilio!*
Stop! *¡Párate!*
Watch out! *¡Cuidado! ¡Ojo!*

Numbers

1 uno	**18** dieciocho	**500** quinientos
2 dos	**19** diecinueve	**600** seiscientos
3 tres	**20** veinte	**700** setecientos
4 cuatro	**21** veintiuno	**800** ochocientos
5 cinco	**25** veinticinco	**900** novecientos
6 seis	**30** treinta	**1,000** mil
7 siete	**40** cuarenta	**2,000** dos mil
8 ocho	**50** cincuenta	**10,000** diez mil
9 nueve	**60** sesenta	**100,000** cien mil
10 diez	**70** setenta	**1,000,000** un millón
11 once	**80** ochenta	
12 doce	**90** noventa	
13 trece	**100** cien	
14 catorce	**101** ciento uno	
15 quince	**200** doscientos	
16 dieciséis	**300** trescientos	
17 diecisiete	**400** cuatrocientos	

NOTE: In Spanish, in numbers, commas are used where decimal points are used in English and vice versa. For example, in English: $19.30 = in Spanish: $19,30; 1,000 m = 1.000 m; 9.5 percent = 9,5 percent.

I've had an accident He tenido un accidente
Call a doctor Llame a un médico
Call an ambulance Llame una ambulancia
Call the... Llame a...
...police la policía/los carabineros
...the fire brigade los bomberos
This is an emergency, where is there a telephone, please? Es una emergencia. ¿Dónde hay un teléfono, por favor?
Where is the nearest hospital? ¿Dónde se encuentra el hospital más cercano?
I want to report a robbery Quisiera denunciar un robo
Thank you very much for your help Muchísimas gracias por su ayuda

Health

shift-duty pharmacy farmacía de turno
hospital/clinic hospital/clínica
I need a doctor/dentist Necesito un médico/dentista (odontólogo)
I don't feel well Me siento mal
I am sick Estoy enfermo(a)
It hurts here Duele aquí
I have a headache/stomach ache/cramps Tengo un dolor de la cabeza/del estómago/retorcijones
I feel dizzy Me siento mareado(a)
Do you have (something for)...? ¿Tiene (algo para)...?
a cold/flu resfrío/gripe
diarrhea diarrea
constipation estreñimiento
fever fiebre
aspirin aspirina
heartburn ácidez
insect/mosquito bites picadas de insectos/zancudos

Shopping

antique shop antigüedades
bakery panadería
bank banco
barber shop/hairdresser peluquería
beauty shop peluquería, salón de belleza
bookstore librería
butcher shop carnicería
currency exchange bureau casa de cambio
delicatessen delicatessen
department store tienda por departamentos
florist florería
gift shop (tienda de) regalos
greengrocer's verdulería
hardware store ferretería
shopping center centro comercial, mall
jewelry shop joyería
laundry lavandería
library biblioteca
liquor store botellería
market mercado
newsstand kiosco
pastry shop pastelería
post office oficina de correos
shoe repair shop/shoe store zapatería
small grocery store almacén
small shop tienda
supermarket supermercado
toy store juguetería

Useful Phrases

What time do you open/close? ¿A qué hora abren/cierran?
Open/closed Abierto/cerrado
I'd like... Quisiera...
I'm just looking Estoy sólo mirando, gracias
How much does it cost? ¿Cuánto cuesta?
It doesn't fit No queda bien
Do you have it in another color? ¿Tiene en otro color?
Do you have it in another size? ¿Tiene en otra talla (clothing), tamaño (objects)
smaller/larger más pequeño/más grande
It's too expensive Es demasiado caro
Do you have something less expensive? ¿Tiene algo más económico?
Where do I pay for it? ¿Dónde está la caja?
Anything else? ¿Quiere algo más?
a little more/less un poco más/menos
That's enough/no more Está bien/no más

Days and Dates

morning *la mañana*
afternoon *la tarde*
late afternoon, dusk *el atardecer*
evening *la noche*
early morning *la madrugada*
sunrise *el amanecer*
sunset *la puesta del sol*
last night *anoche*
yesterday *ayer*
today *hoy*
tomorrow *mañana*
the day after tomorrow *pasado mañana*
now *ahora*
early *temprano*
late *tarde*
a minute *un minuto*
an hour *una hora*
half an hour *media hora*
a day *un día*
a week *una semana*
a year *un año*
weekday *día laboral/hábil*
weekend *fin de semana*
holiday *día feriado*

Months

January *enero*
February *febrero*
March *marzo*
April *abril*
May *mayo*
June *junio*
July *julio*
August *agosto*
September *septiembre*
October *octubre*
November *noviembre*
December *diciembre*

Days of the Week

Monday *lunes*
Tuesday *martes*
Wednesday *miércoles*
Thursday *jueves*
Friday *viernes*
Saturday *sábado*
Sunday *domingo*

Further Reading

Travel In Chile

In Patagonia by Bruce Chatwin (Pan Books, London).
Aku-Aku – The Secret of Easter Island by Thor Heyerdahl (Unwin, London).
Tierra del Fuego by Rae Natalie Prosser Goodall.
The Old Patagonian Express by Paul Theroux (Penguin, 1980).

Fiction

House of the Spirits by Isabel Allende (Black Swan).
Burning Patience by Antonio Skármeta (Plaza y Janes, Mexico). The book that inspired the film *Il Postino (The Postman)* weaves a story around Pablo Neruda's life and death after the military coup.
Robinson Crusoe by Daniel Defoe. Based on Alexander Selkirk's time on the Juan Fernández islands.
The Last Song of Manuel Sendero by Ariel Dorfman (Viking Penguin).
Pablo Neruda – Selected Poems. Bilingual edition, Penguin, International Poets Series.

Political & Historical Insights

Chile: The Pinochet Decade by Brian Lovemen. Latin American Bureau.
Chile – The Legacy of Hispanic Capitalism. Oxford University Press.
Allende's Chile by Edward Boorstein (International Publishers, 1977).

Chilote Mythology

Tesoro mitológico del archipiélago de Chiloé by Narciso García Berrío (Editorial Andrés Bello, Santiago, 1989).
Geografía del mito y la leyenda chileno by Oreste Plath (Nascimento, Santiago, 1983).
Cuentos araucanos la gente de la tierra, by Alicia Morel (Editorial Andrés Bello, Santiago, 1982).
Casos de brujos de Chiloé, by Umiliana Cárdenas Saldivia (Santiago, 1989).

The New Song Movement

Books about pre- and post-coup music include Osvaldo Rodriguez's *Cantores que reflexionan*, published by LAR; Joan Jara's *Victor, An Unfinished Song*, published by Jonathan Cape (London, 1983); Patricio Mann's *Violeta Parra*, Ediciones Jucar (Madrid 1984), and Luis Cifuentes' *Fragmentos de un Sueño*, about the group Inti Illimani (Ediciones Logos, Santiago, Chile).

Mapuche History

Los Primeros Americanos. Editorial Antártica, SA.
Brevisima Relación de la Destrucción de las Indias, by Fray Bartolomé de las Casas. Editorial Nascimento.
Mapuches, Pueblo de la Tierra, Inter-Church Committee on Human Rights in Latin America. Canada.
Rasgos de la Sociedad Mapuche Contemporánea, by Milán Stuchlik. Ediciones Nueva Universidad.
Arauco Domado, by Lope de Vega. Zig Zag.
Historia del Pueblo Mapuche, by José Bengoa.
La Araucaria, by Alonso de Ercilla. A 16th-century epic poem.

Other Insight Guides

Over 200 *Insight Guides* have been joined by more than 100 *Insight Pocket Guides*, *Insight Compact Guides*, and a series of laminated *Insight Guides Fleximaps*.

Insight Guide: South America is a broad introduction to the continent. Other titles focus on specific countries and cities, including **Argentina**, **Rio de Janeiro**, **Ecuador**, **Brazil**, **Peru**, **Venezuela**, and **Buenos Aires**. Insight Guide: **Amazon Wildlife** is one of the series' nature guides.

ART & PHOTO CREDITS

Picture Spreads

INSIGHT GUIDE
CHILE

Cartographic Editor **Zoë Goodwin**
Production **Linton Donaldson**
Design Consultants
Carlotta Junger, Graham Mitchener
Picture Research **Hilary Genin**
Monica Allende

Map Production
Polyglott Kartographie
© 2005 Apa Publications GmbH & Co.
Verlag KG (Singapore branch)

Index

Numbers in italics refer to photographs

A
B
C
D

F
G
H
I
J
a
b
c
d
e
f
g
h
i

k
l